Cuban Privilege

For over half a century, the United States granted Cubans, one of the largest immigrant groups in the country, unique entitlements. While other unauthorized immigrants faced detention, deportation, and no legal rights, Cuban immigrants were able to enter the country without authorization, and have access to welfare benefits and citizenship status. This book is the first to reveal the full range of entitlements granted to Cubans. Initially privileged to undermine the Castro-led revolution in the throes of the Cold War, one US President after another extended new entitlements to Cubans, even in the post-Cold War era. Drawing on archival, interview, and survey data, *Cuban Privilege* highlights how Washington, in the process of privileging Cubans, transformed them from agents of US Cold War foreign policy into a politically powerful force influencing national policy. By comparing with the exclusionary treatment of neighboring Haitians, the book discloses the racial and political biases embedded in US immigration policy.

SUSAN EVA ECKSTEIN is Professor in the Pardee School of Global Studies and the Sociology Department at Boston University. Specializing in Latin American social movements, rights, justice, and immigration, she has single-authored, edited, and co-edited nine books. This is her third book that focuses specifically on Cuba and Cuban immigrants. She is the recipient of many fellowships, including from the John Simon Guggenheim Memorial Foundation, the John D. and Catherine T. MacArthur Foundation, and the Radcliffe Institute.

Cuban Privilege

The Making of Immigrant Inequality in America

SUSAN EVA ECKSTEIN
Boston University

University Printing House, Cambridge CB2 8BS, United Kingdom

One Liberty Plaza, 20th Floor, New York, NY 10006, USA

477 Williamstown Road, Port Melbourne, VIC 3207, Australia

314–321, 3rd Floor, Plot 3, Splendor Forum, Jasola District Centre, New Delhi – 110025, India

103 Penang Road, #05–06/07, Visioncrest Commercial, Singapore 238467

Cambridge University Press is part of the University of Cambridge.

It furthers the University's mission by disseminating knowledge in the pursuit of education, learning, and research at the highest international levels of excellence.

www.cambridge.org
Information on this title: www.cambridge.org/9781108830614
DOI: 10.1017/9781108902465

© Susan Eva Eckstein 2022, 2025

This publication is in copyright. Subject to statutory exception and to the provisions of relevant collective licensing agreements, no reproduction of any part may take place without the written permission of Cambridge University Press.

First published 2022
First paperback edition 2025

A catalogue record for this publication is available from the British Library.

ISBN 978-1-108-83061-4 Hardback
ISBN 978-1-108-82239-8 Paperback

Cambridge University Press has no responsibility for the persistence or accuracy of URLs for external or third-party internet websites referred to in this publication and does not guarantee that any content on such websites is, or will remain, accurate or appropriate.

For EU product safety concerns, contact us at Calle de José Abascal, 56, 1°, 28003 Madrid, Spain, or email eugpsr@cambridge.org.

To Meera, Reena, Deven, Ellis, and Aubrey
With love for the joy you provide and in anticipation
of the world you will improve

Contents

List of Figures		page ix
Foreword to the Paperback Edition by William M. LeoGrande		xi
Preface: Privileged Cubans		xv
List of Acronyms		xxix
1	The Making of Cuban Immigration Exceptionalism, 1959–1979	1
2	The Privileging of Cuban Immigrants in the United States, 1959–1979	43
3	The Immigration Crisis of 1980: Carter Administration Privileging of Cubans Anew, Spillover Benefits for Haitians	74
4	Delinking Cubans from Haitians: The Deepening of Cuban Privileging and the Turn against Haitians under the Reagan and Bush I Administrations	127
5	Taking with One Hand, Giving with the Other: Clinton Administration Retraction and Expansion of Cuban Immigrant Entitlements	182
6	From Further Expansion to the Unraveling of Cuban Privileging amid Mainly Exclusion of Haitians: The George W. Bush and Barack Obama Administrations	241
7	From Heaven to Hell under the Trump Administration: Walls for Cubans After All	287
8	Exceptionalism in Practice? Actual Immigration, Lessons Learned	317
Index		343

Figures

8.1 Persons obtaining LPR status by country of last residence: Cuba, Dominican Republic, and Haiti, FY1950–2019 *page* 322
8.2 Percentage of persons born in Cuba, the Dominican Republic, and Haiti granted LPR status as refugee and asylee adjustments, 2000–2019 326
8.3 Refugee admissions from Cuba and Haiti, 1984–2019 329

Foreword to the Paperback Edition

William M. LeoGrande

The story of how Cuban migrants came to the United States and established a politically and economically powerful diaspora community in South Florida is inseparable from the history of the Cold War and Cuba's unique role in it. Shortly after Fidel Castro's revolution triumphed in 1959, Cuba became a focal point of the global rivalry between the United States and the Soviet Union, and that shaped Washington's migration policy toward Cubans. From the beginning, political refugees fleeing Cuban socialism were welcomed "with open arms," as President Jimmy Carter put it during the 1980 migration crisis known as the Mariel Freedom Flotilla. They received exceptional privileges to enter and remain in the United States – privileges enjoyed by no other nationality. Many of these privileges remain in place today, even though most of the people fleeing Cuba in recent decades have been economic migrants rather than political refugees.

In this book, Susan Eckstein provides a deep dive into the history of how the US government structured its immigration policy to the advantage of Cuban migrants in order to further its attempts to destabilize Cuba's revolutionary government. The book caused quite a stir among some Cuban Americans, who were insulted that someone pointed out policies that helped make the Cuban American community a success story.

Cuban Privilege is not Eckstein's first book on the Cuban diaspora. She has written extensively on the threads that connect Cubans abroad with their family still on the island. In *The Immigrant Divide: How Cuban Americans Changed the U.S. and Their Homeland*, she authored one of the first in-depth studies of how the Cuban American community began reconnecting to the island in the 1980s and 1990s, building bridges based mainly on family ties. In the 1960s and 1970s, both the Cuban and US governments erected a "sugar cane curtain" that made it almost impossible for families to stay connected across the Florida Strait. There was no travel allowed, no direct mail service, and connecting by phone was nearly impossible and prohibitively expensive. But in the 1980s, travel opened up and remittances began to flow. Ever since the Special Period, Cuba's economic crisis in the 1990s, Cuban American remittances have made an essential contribution to the standard of living of millions of Cuban families.

Cuban Privilege reverses the lens to look not at Cuban immigrants but at the US immigration policies that brought them here. It is the definitive account of how Washington, motivated by the Cold War, gave Cuban immigrants unprecedented, privileged access to the United States and unprecedented support once they got here. Key elements of that privilege persist to this day, defended by powerful Cuban American legislators. Among the most important is the Cuban Adjustment Act, which allows most Cuban arrivals, who have made their way to the United States without official immigration visas, to apply for permanent residence after being in the United States for just a year.

Most of the time academics toil in relative obscurity, writing for one another in hopes of contributing new knowledge to their chosen field. On occasion, they write for a broader audience, hoping that their expertise might have some positive impact on public policy. And most of the time, when they speak truth to power, power is not listening. Rarely do academic contributions to the public debate attract much attention or make much difference.

Susan Eckstein's *Cuban Privilege* is a cautionary tale of what can happen when the public *does* take notice. When she was invited by Florida International University (FIU) to give a talk on the book in December 2022, a political furor erupted. Miami-Dade County Commissioner Kevin Cabrera called the book "hate-filled" and "anti-Cuban," even though he admitted he had not read it. Other politicians and influencers jumped on the bandwagon. Eckstein was denounced as a Cuban government agent, and both she and the event's organizers were threatened with violence. The event, held in an FIU auditorium packed with hundreds of mostly hostile people, amounted to an Orwellian 60 minutes of hate. A commentator, added at the last minute to mollify critics, said almost nothing about the subject of the book – US migration policy – but instead accused Eckstein of "deficient" scholarship because she did not chronicle the pain endured by Cuban migrants.

Eckstein hit an emotional nerve by pointing out that Cuban migrants have received extraordinary privileges enjoyed by no other nationality – a simple fact starkly demonstrated by comparing migration policy toward Cubans with migration policy toward Haitians, as Eckstein does throughout the book. Some Cuban Americans seem to think that the impressive success of their community is entirely of their own making, and they resented Eckstein for pointing out that they received – and are still receiving – a major assist from Washington.

Ironically, the policy of privileged immigration for Cubans, which was intended to weaken and embarrass the Cuban government, has instead embarrassed the US government, producing a series of migration crises: the Camarioca crisis in 1965; the Mariel Freedom Flotilla in 1980; the rafters crisis in 1994; and the post-COVID crisis that is ongoing today. The privileges Cuban migrants receive have also distorted US domestic politics by creating one of the most powerful foreign policy lobbies in history. Since the 1980s, Cuban Americans in South Florida have exercised a disproportionate influence over US policy toward Cuba.

For thirty years, successive presidents – with the sole exception of Barack Obama – have been afraid to stand up to the Miami lobby. As President George H. W. Bush's National Security Adviser Brent Scowcroft put it, "Cuba is not a foreign policy question. Cuba is a domestic issue." The result is a US policy that has focused for sixty-five years on regime change, even though it has done nothing to advance the cause of democracy or human rights in Cuba, and has alienated Washington from allies in Latin America and Europe. Its only "success" has been to cripple the Cuban economy, lowering the living standard of the Cuban people, and setting the stage for future migration. That is the legacy of the immigration policies that Susan Eckstein so expertly chronicles in *Cuban Privilege*.

William M. LeoGrande is Professor of Government at American University in Washington, DC, and co-author with Peter Kornbluh of *Back Channel to Cuba: The Hidden History of Negotiations between Washington and Havana* (University of North Carolina Press, 2015).

Preface

Privileged Cubans

In 1991, during George H. W. Bush's presidency, the US Coast Guard stopped a leaky Haitian fishing boat carrying 161 Haitians and 2 Cubans who the Haitians had picked up in a gesture of brotherhood.[1] Two years later, when Bill Clinton was president, a boat carrying seven Cubans and ten Haitians landed in Florida. All those aboard the boats wanted to come to the land of opportunity. They arrived, however, without US-granted immigration visas. The Immigration and Naturalization Service, nonetheless, admitted the Cubans. In contrast, the Haitians were whisked off to detention facilities. Almost all were repatriated. The Clinton administration refused to admit the Haitians even though Clinton had promised during his campaign that, if elected, he would end the George H. W. Bush administration's cruel practice of sending unauthorized Haitians back to a brutal dictatorship. With the support of Haitian voters, Clinton hoped to make President Bush, running for reelection, a one-term president. Clinton succeeded in winning the election, but even before taking office he announced that he would continue to enforce Bush's Haitian repatriation policy. How could the presidents treat Cubans and Haitians so differently?

Fast forward to May 1, 2006. On that international day honoring workers, approximately three-fourths of a million unauthorized immigrants across America courageously absented themselves from their jobs to participate in what organizers of the work stoppage called the "Day Without Immigrants." They wanted to convince owners of businesses and

---

[1] Anthony Depalma, "For Haitians, Voyage to a Land of Inequality," *New York Times* (July 16, 1991), sec. A, p. 1.

the American people, and members of Congress in turn, how important immigrants were to the economy. At the time, Congress was deliberating legislation that would determine whether to legalize or continue to criminalize the eight million undocumented workers then in the country.[2] Most of the immigrants who participated in the nationwide demonstrations that May Day came from Latin America. They wanted legal rights to stay and work. Some of them had been in the United States for as long as a quarter of a century without labor rights and other protections.

Even though Cubans constituted the second-largest Hispanic immigrant group in the country, they were noticeably absent from the demonstrations. Were Cubans treated so differently that they saw no reason to join? The United States, indeed, treated them differently, as the book reveals. Despite most Cubans coming to the country without visas issued in conformity with immigration regulations set by Congress, they were admitted and, since 1966, permitted to become lawful permanent residents offering a path to citizenship. The Cubans on the boats with Haitians in 1991 and 1993 were among the hundreds of thousands of Cubans who, by the Day Without Immigrants, were legal residents, even if they had arrived without US-authorized immigration visas. By 2006, many of them also were citizens who enjoyed voting rights.

Fast forward again to 2016. That year as many as 56,000 Cubans came to the United States without authorization,[3] at a time when the United States capped annual lawful immigration from any single country at 20,000 a year. After brief detention, these Cubans were admitted into the country, granted a range of immediate and long-term entitlements, and spared the risk of deportation. That same year the Obama administration deported over 1,500 Haitians[4] and nearly half a million unauthorized immigrants from other countries.[5]

---

[2] Michael Hoefer, Nancy Rytina, and Christopher Campbell, "Estimates of the Unauthorized Immigrant Population Residing in the United States: January 2007," Department of Homeland Security, Office of Immigration Statistics, August 2007, p. 2 (www.dhs.gov/xlibrary/assets/statistics/publications/ois_ill_pe_2007.pdf).

[3] Jens Krogstad, "Surge in Cuban Immigration to U.S. Continued through 2016," *Facttank* (January 13, 2017) (www.pewresearch.org/fact-tank/2017/01/13/cuban-immigration-to-u-s-surges-as-relations-warm/).

[4] Data for October 2016 to January 2017. Makini Brice, "After Daring Voyage to U.S., Haitians' Dreams End in Deportation," *Reuters* (February 10, 2017) (www.reuters.com/article/us-haiti-usa/after-daring-voyage-to-u-s-haitians-dreams-end-in-deportation-idUSKBN15P2RM).

[5] Data for 2016. Muzaffar Chishti, Sarah Pierce, and Jessica Bolter, "The Obama Record on Deportations: Deporter in Chief or Not?," *Migration Information Source* (January 26,

WHY CUBAN PRIVILEGING?

Why were Cubans exempt from the fate of other "illegals"? This book explains why and describes the range of unique entitlements they have received since January 1959, when Fidel Castro came to power. The United States extended unique entitlements to Cubans even after Castro died and even after his brother Raúl's tenure as head of state.

January 12, 2017, however, marks a turning point in US Cuban immigration policy. On that day, President Barack Obama ended special entitlements that a succession of eleven presidents, across the partisan divide, had granted Cuban immigrants. One president after another will be shown to have honored entitlements their predecessors granted and, typically, to have extended additional entitlements to Cubans. At times, Cubans even were privileged *at the expense* of both other foreigners and native-born Americans. In some years, for example, Cubans enjoyed preferential access to limited immigration slots allotted by the United States, and labor market advantage owing to special job training, special job placement services, and special funding for university studies. Cubans who arrived without authorization even enjoyed certain entitlements that were denied authorized immigrants, such as immediate rights to welfare.

Sometimes Congress was the enabler by authorizing funding for special resettlement benefits and granting Cubans unique entitlements. At other times, however, presidents circumvented Congress' official authority over immigration to privilege Cubans. If interested in immigrating to the United States, it was good to be Cuban. However committed presidents and legislators were to equality and equity, they made exception for Cubans.

Yet, the reasons for privileging Cubans changed over time. Republican Dwight Eisenhower, who was president when Castro assumed power with widespread – though not unanimous – support from his country's people, immediately welcomed opponents of Castro and the revolutionary remaking of Cuba that he oversaw. President Eisenhower singled them out for special entitlements. His successor, President John F. Kennedy, a Democrat, singled out more Cubans for special entitlements and expanded entitlements for them. Both presidents hoped that, in reaching out to Cubans, they would convince those who remained on the island of the superiority of capitalist democracy over Castro's nationalist,

2017) (www.migrationpolicy.org/article/obama-record-deportations-deporter-chief-or-not).

populist, and increasingly state-dominated Marxist-Leninist Soviet-allied regime. They also hoped to induce a "brain drain" that would debilitate the Cuban economy to the point of collapse. Meanwhile, they turned to incoming Cubans to assist covert efforts to oust Castro and contain his influence over other Third World countries, especially in America's "backyard." They even invested in training Cuban arrivals for leadership positions in a US-friendly post-Castro government.

Both presidents envisioned their immigration policy to serve their Cold War concern with defeating global communism. Paradoxically, though, their outreach to Cubans helped Castro solidify his base of power and the island's political-economic makeover by ridding the country of opponents to the revolution and by rallying Cubans against US meddling in their national affairs.

Despite the unique welcoming of Cuban immigrants leaving Castro entrenched in power, subsequent presidents granted yet more Cubans unique immigration rights and unique resettlement benefits. They did so to address problems that earlier entitlements generated or left unresolved, and to address new problems that arose. By the time the United States "won" the Cold War, with the Soviet Union's collapse, Cuban immigrants who had been beneficiaries of earlier entitlements had become so politically influential that they pressed for continued privileging of "their people." Domestic politics replaced foreign policy as the driver of privileging Cubans. Even presidents who tried to end special entitlements for Cubans reversed their stance in response to pressure from Cuban immigrants who, in increased numbers, made use of their unique path to citizenship, with accompanying voting rights, for ethnic gain. The Reagan administration even facilitated Cuban immigrant transformation into savvy lobbyists for their own concerns, including under subsequent administrations. Presidents, and their administrations, found themselves "locked in" to continued privileging of Cubans. Earlier privileging contributed to continued privileging. Presidents perceived the domestic political costs of ending entitlements for Cubans antithetical to their own interest in reelection.

President Obama finally revoked key entitlements during his last full week in office. He did so against the backdrop of a surge in unauthorized Cuban immigration that undermined US control over its borders, as well as a growing socioeconomic and political divide among Cuban Americans that eroded support for continued Cuban immigrant privileging. He did so when he committed to a new Cuba foreign policy, premised on cross-border bridge building, not continued Cold War hostility. Because he was completing his second term of office, he was also not personally constrained by possibly alienating Cuban American voters. He took advantage of the new domestic political and foreign policy juncture to make immigration policy more equitable by retracting rights for Cubans, rather than by extending rights Cubans enjoyed to other immigrants.

Campaigning on an anti-immigrant platform, Donald Trump made no effort to reopen Cubans' path of privilege when winning the presidency and succeeding Obama in office. Rather, he further shuttered the path, and aggressively so. He outsourced and offshored immigration control, including of Cubans. He thus opened a new chapter in Cuban immigration history involving privilege and justice for few.

REASONS FOR WRITING THIS BOOK

I wrote this book for several reasons. Most importantly, Cuban privileging for over half a century, and its basis, are not well known. The book is the first to describe and explain US Cuban immigration policy, and its unintended as well as intended consequences, from the time Castro assumed power in 1959 through the first non-Castro to become head of state in October 2019.

I wrote the book also because there are lessons to be learned from the Cuban experience about how policy can be improved so that the United States benefits from immigrants while treating them more equitably. Washington's immigration system is widely believed to be broken and in need of reform. In comparing the Cuban with the Haitian, and in the final chapter, also with the Dominican, immigrant experiences, I highlight how differently the United States has treated immigrants depending on their country of origin, and how differently immigrants have experienced America as a result.

I consider myself particularly qualified to write the book. It draws on my expertise. I have studied Cuba and Cuban immigrants for decades. It builds on my earlier books, *Back from the Future: Cuba under Castro* and *The Immigrant Divide: How Cuban Americans Changed the U.S. and Their Homeland*. The earlier works inform my understanding of Cuba and Cuban immigrants in transnational and historical context, and of US Cuban immigration policies over the years and their unintended as well as intended consequences.

OVERVIEW OF THE BOOK

During the period on which the book focuses, beginning with the Eisenhower and ending with the Trump administration, the world changed considerably, including Cuba.

Assuming power in the throes of the Cold War, Castro challenged US hegemony over Latin America, a region Washington had claimed as its sphere of influence. Eisenhower, president at the time, believed that he could leverage immigration to debilitate and delegitimize the Castro-led government to the point of collapse. He accordingly offered Cubans special immigration privileges. With rare exceptions, subsequent presidents not only honored but expanded entitlements for Cuban immigrants. By the time Trump assumed the presidency nearly sixty years later the Soviet Union was history and Cuba struggled to adapt to the market-dominated world order. Despite efforts by Obama to improve bilateral relations, Trump both revitalized efforts to strangulate the Cuban economy and imposed new barriers on Cuban immigration, both authorized and unauthorized.

Because Cuban immigration policy is best understood in the context of Washington's general immigration as well as refugee policies, the next chapter begins with a brief overview of those policies, insofar as they are relevant to Cubans. I then address Cuban immigration policy during the first two decades of Castro's rule, which provide backdrop for understanding Cuban immigration policy since 1980, the main focus of the book

I proceed in the chapter to describe how both the Eisenhower and Kennedy administrations turned to Cuban émigrés to help topple the Castro-led government. They trained émigrés to carry out the famed failed Central Intelligence Agency (CIA) orchestrated invasion of Cuba. The CIA relied on Cuban émigrés to conceal US violation of international law protecting countries' rights to self-determination. The Eisenhower, and especially the Kennedy, administrations also funneled funds to Cuban immigrant groups ostensibly to empower them but in fact to try to control them and involve them as co-conspirators in other plots as well to overthrow Castro. Yet, I describe how the groups, in turn, used US resources to advance their own agendas.

In this and subsequent chapters, Cuban immigrants, and aspiring Cuban immigrants, will be shown to pursue their own interests within constraints imposed by the United States. Cuban immigration history needs to be understood from the vantage point not merely of state institutions with formal power but also of ordinary Cubans, including in transnational context. On several occasions, changes in US–Cuban immigration policy resulted from pressure from ordinary Cubans with no formal power, who defied official policy at the time.

Chapter 1 highlights how Vice President Lyndon Johnson, on assuming the Presidency in 1963 after Kennedy's assassination, built on precedents set both by Eisenhower and Kennedy, and privileged yet more Cubans. To gain the upper hand over mounting unauthorized Cuban arrivals he extended a welcome mat to all Cubans who wished to come – at US taxpayers' expense. He announced the welcoming on the very occasion that he signed a new omnibus immigration reform into law that ended the national origin basis of US admission and capped yearly admission from any single country at twenty thousand. His welcome mat authorized the immigration of more than a quarter million new Cubans before President Nixon withdrew it in 1973. The welcoming brought, on average, nearly twice as many Cubans yearly as the new immigration reform permitted from any single country.

The chapter then proceeds to reveal that in the course of the 1970s Cuban privileging appeared to run its course. After 1973, the Republican administrations of Richard Nixon and Gerald Ford, and the administration of Democrat Jimmy Carter during its first three years, admitted few Cubans and reined in resettlement benefits for the Cubans who came. Even fervently anti-Communist Nixon slashed funds for Cubans who sought refuge in America.

Meanwhile, Chapter 2 focuses on the Cuban immigrant experience *in* the United States in the 1960s and 1970s. I describe the unique entitlements Cubans received on arrival and the impact entitlements had on their adaptation to the United States.

Chapters 3–5 focus, in turn, on President Carter's last year in office and the Ronald Reagan, George H. W. Bush, and Bill Clinton administrations. They show the contraction of Cuban immigrant privileging to have been short-lived. Cuban privileging resumed in 1980, during President Carter's last year in office: initially less by design than in response to Castro giving Cubans a green light to immigrate without US entry permission. After initially opposing the onslaught of unauthorized Cuban boatpeople, Carter welcomed approximately 125,000 of them. He built on past privileging of Cubans.

President Carter, together with President Clinton, both Democrats, admitted over 150,000 new Cubans who had not been screened abroad in compliance with Congressionally mandated regulations. President Carter, in addition, extended exceptionally generous entitlements to the arrivals under his watch. Although both presidents initially had tried to block entry of the unauthorized Cubans, they quickly reversed their stance and followed the precedent of previous presidents. They welcomed the new Cubans. President Clinton even privileged Cubans against the backdrop of a nationwide surge in nativist, anti-immigrant sentiment. He did retract one prerogative Cubans had enjoyed for decades, but concomitantly piled new unique entitlements for Cubans onto old. While calling for the repatriation of Cubans picked up at sea, he guaranteed Cubans a minimum number of immigration visas yearly, a guarantee offered no other nationals; he approved of unique welfare rights for Cubans; and he exempted Cubans from new restrictions imposed on unauthorized immigrants from all other countries.

In the years between the Carter and Clinton presidencies, the Reagan and Bush Republican administrations admitted fewer Cubans. Yet, they permitted a Cuban immigrant group to admit new Cubans on their own. President Reagan, with the assistance of Bush when his Vice President, also will be shown to have turned, anew, to Cuban émigrés to assist covert efforts to rein in Left-leaning movements – this time in Central America, not Cuba. At the same time, President Reagan reimagined the 1980 unauthorized Cuban arrivals as refugees, after President Carter very explicitly had deemed them not to be. The Cubans thereby were able to become lawful permanent residents and enjoy citizenship and voting rights. President Reagan also helped transform Cuban Americans into a political force in their own right, able to independently influence US Cuba policy. Cuban immigration policy, as a result, subsequently became rooted in domestic politics, including after the Cold War's end when foreign policy toward Cuba ceased to be a primary concern of Washington.

Then, Chapter 6 focuses on US Cuban immigration policy after the turn of the century. Republican George W. Bush (Bush II) was the last President to grant Cubans new, unique entitlements, and also honor earlier entitlements. He went international in extending new entitlements to Cubans, circumventing official Congressional control over immigration. He initiated a program to welcome Cuban medics working for their government overseas. As if the Cold War had not ended, he hoped "defecting" Cubans would discredit their government and deprive it of earnings aid workers generated overseas. President Bush also arranged for Cuban families to reunify in the United States before officially cleared for immigration visas. President Obama continued the policies of President Bush as well as of earlier presidents – until his last days in office, when he reined in Cuban privileging "as we knew it" for over half a century. The chapter details the entitlements he retracted, how, and why.

Chapter 7 focuses on how the Trump Administration took advantage of the Obama policy shift to make Cuban immigration more difficult. It retracted entitlements, de facto if not de jure, such that authorized as well as unauthorized Cuban immigration became near-impossible, and unauthorized immigration became costly and exceedingly dangerous. At the same time, in further strangulating the Cuban economy, President Trump gave Cubans all the more reason to want to leave. He reversed President Obama's efforts to improve bilateral relations.

The final chapter of this book addresses the impact that more than half a century of privileging had on inducing Cubans to move to America, and how immigration rates from Cuba compare to rates from other Caribbean countries, namely from the Dominican Republic and Haiti. Remarkably, the number of Cubans who immigrated proves to be less exceptional than the formal privileging would suggest. Although US Dominican policy is not a central concern of the book, comparisons with Dominican immigration are noteworthy. Despite the United States offering Dominicans few special entitlements, in the 1980s Dominicans' informal diasporic ties fueled more immigration than Cubans' formal entitlements. The Dominican–Cuban immigration gap did close significantly after the turn of this century, through Obama's presidency, though not because Cubans received new entitlement incentives. Rather, three decades of strained ties between Cuban immigrants in the United States and family they left behind, rooted in their opposing views toward the revolution, broke down when Cubans suffered from the economic crisis caused by the Soviet Union's collapse. Under the circumstances, Cubans turned to family in the United States to help them immigrate, as had Dominicans for decades – with the help of human smugglers who capitalized on an opportunity to profit.

In contrast, far fewer Haitians will be shown to have settled in the United States: the result of decades of US discrimination and exclusion that I detail throughout the book. During the Cold War, Haitians had the misfortune of coming from a country allied with the United States. Consequently, their admission did not serve US foreign policy interests at the time. Haitians also had the political misfortune of being dark-skinned, unlike most Cuban immigrants. As a result, Haitians were victims of racial biases in US immigration policy, before, during, and after the Cold War. The racial biases against Haitians continued even after the 1965 omnibus immigration reform officially ended earlier racial biases in Washington's admissions. Haitians gained special immigration entitlements only when they had the good fortune of arriving without authorization alongside Cubans, when discrimination against them became blatantly transparent, and when immigration rights lawyers and activists fought on Haitians' behalf.

The final chapter also addresses "lessons learned" from the Cuban experience, including when viewed from a cross-national perspective. In a partial preview of what is to come, the book reveals:

1. An initial privileging of Cuban immigrants set in motion a chain of privileging across presidential administrations, Republican and Democratic alike, in what sociologists and political scientists would call a "locked in" path-dependent manner:[6] namely, one set of entitlements spurred implementation of other entitlements, to address problems earlier entitlements generated or left unresolved and new problems that arose, as well as emergent interests in continued Cuban privileging. By the same token, presidents found it difficult to retract entitlements, even after their initial rationale no longer justified their continuation. Only when Cuban privileging worked both against new US foreign policy interests and against interests of influential Cuban Americans did the United States revoke key entitlements. The changed context did not make termination of Cuban exceptionalism inevitable, but made it possible with little political pushback. Even then, Congress did not sunset entitlements it had legislated, reflecting a "stickiness" to its legislation.

2. The Eisenhower, Kennedy, and Johnson Administrations extended immigration entitlements partly as a "soft power" strategy to convince Cubans of the virtues of capitalist democracy.[7] They

---

[6] On path dependence, see Jack Goldstone, "Initial Conditions, General Laws, Path Dependence, and Explanation in Historical Sociology," *American Journal of Sociology* vol. 104, no. 3 (November 1998): 829–45; Paul Pierson, "Increasing Returns, Path Dependence, and the Study of Politics," *American Political Science Review* vol. 94, no. 2 (June 2000): 251–67; Paul David, "Path Dependence: A Foundational Concept for Historical Social Science," *Cliometrica* vol. 1 (2007): 91–114; James Mahoney, "Path Dependence in Historical Sociology," *Theory and Society* vol. 29 (2000): 507–48; Ruth Collier and David Collier, *Shaping the Political Arena: Critical Junctures and the Labor Movement, and Regime Dynamics in Latin America* (Princeton, NJ: Princeton University Press, 1991); Anik Leithner and Kyle Libby, "Path Dependency in Foreign Policy," *Oxford Research Encyclopedia of Politics* (July 2017) (oxfordre.com/politics).

[7] On soft power, see Joseph Nye, Jr., *Soft Power: The Means to Success in World Politics* (New York: Public Affairs, 2004). "Soft power" entails influencing other countries without use of force or coercion; "hard power" rests on utilizing force and coercion. Nye argues that successful states need both hard and soft power: the ability to coerce others as well as the ability to shape their long-term attitudes and preferences. On use of "soft power" by global dominant countries vis a vis Third World countries, see Atul Kohli, *Imperialism and the Developing World: How Britain and the United States Shaped the Global Periphery* (New York: Oxford University Press, 2020).

promoted "soft power" initiatives amid mounting international pressure not to intervene in the internal affairs of other countries.

3. Under the Eisenhower administration, and even more so under the Kennedy administration, the CIA covertly embedded "hard power" in "soft power" strategies to topple the Castro-led regime. Even though neither the "hard" nor the "soft" power strategies accomplished their intended foreign policy purpose, subsequent administrations continued to privilege Cubans.

4. No single factor explains the ongoing privileging of Cubans for over half a century. The initial Cold War foreign policy rationale created vested domestic interests in the continued privileging of Cubans, such that Cuban privileging continued after the Cold War's end.

5. With and without Congressional backing, presidents and their administrations privileged Cubans by deliberately imagining them as refugees, by imagining them as if they were refugees when recognizing that they were not, and by introducing unique criteria for refugee status in order to enable Cubans to qualify for refugee entitlements for which they would not otherwise qualify. Social science "constructivists" would say that in conceiving Cubans as refugees, policy makers could and did privilege Cubans.[8] Accordingly, Presidents and their administrations, as well as Congress, have not subjected all nationals to the same entry requirements and the same entry queue. They even privileged Cubans on the basis of their nationality after the United States officially ended national origins-based admission. Nonetheless, Cuban exceptionalism ebbed and flowed over the years.

6. Washington has not set and implemented immigration policy entirely to its choosing. The Cuban experience demonstrates that even weak states within the international arena, such as Cuba, as well as ordinary people through their force of numbers, diasporic ties, and defiance of official regulations, may shape US immigration policy and determine who immigrates.

---

[8] "Constructivists" point to the role of ideas, norms, and culture. For an overview of "constructivism," see Martha Finnemore and Kathryn Sikkink, "Taking Stock: The Constructivist Research Program in International Relations and Comparative Politics," *Annual Review of Political Science* vol. 4 (2001): 391–416. In this book I demonstrate that by framing Cubans as refugees, successive administrations and Congress circumvented immigration regulations to privilege Cubans.

In disrespecting Cuba's right to self-determination, the US rationale for privileging Cubans was never noble. Yet, in due course, Cuban immigrants helped transform Miami into an economically and culturally dynamic city with hemispheric reach. So too did they become politically influential, not only in Florida where they mainly settled, but also nationally. They have made important contributions to America, from which the country at-large has benefited.

THE WRITING OF THIS BOOK

I used a range of sources in writing this book. I have drawn on archival materials from the official libraries of Presidents Kennedy, Johnson, Nixon, Carter, Reagan, Bush I, and Clinton. I am grateful for the assistance of their respective archivists. I have also made use of the *Congressional Record*, Congressional hearings, and other documents. As a sociologist, I draw on the primary sources in an interpretive, analytically grounded manner, to understand policies and their consequences.

Particularly concerned with policy ramifications, I have also drawn on materials compiled by US agencies; immigration statistics; survey and voting data; and news analyses. In addition, I have drawn on secondary sources on Cuba, Cuban immigrants, and US immigration policy.

In writing this book I also benefited from interviews and conversations I had with several members of Congress (and their staff), US diplomats who served in Cuba, officials of the Departments of State and Homeland Security and the former Immigration and Naturalization Service, and former mayors of Miami. I also benefited from interviews and conversations with Cuban American politicians and other Cuban American leaders in Miami, with Cuban American lobbyists and Cuban Americans involved in nongovernmental organizations, with scholars and others well-informed about Cuban immigration, and with ordinary Cubans both in the United States and their homeland. In Cuba, I also benefited from discussions with foreign service officials at the American Embassy and with Cuban scholars knowledgeable about Cuban immigration policy.

The interviews and conversations that I had were open-ended and focused on individuals' expertise. They were designed to deepen my knowledge about and understanding of Cuban immigration policy and Cuban immigrants. I am most appreciative of the insights I gained from these discussions, although, with rare exception, I respect the anonymity of the individuals with whom I spoke and do not refer to them by name.

My understanding of Cuba and Cuban immigrants also draws on decades of research related to my previously noted books, which I wrote while making use, in the main, of a similar mix of source materials. Taken together, my research over the years has helped me understand how and why Cubans benefited from special immigrant privileges for over half a century, and the impact their privileging has had (including in Cuba).

My understanding of Haitian and Dominican immigration, in contrast, derives almost entirely from secondary sources, plus Congressional hearings and immigration statistics, and discussions with Haitian and Dominican scholars. Unfortunately, I do not have the same depth of knowledge about Haitian and Dominican experiences. I compare immigration from the three countries primarily to highlight how differently and inequitably most presidents, along with Congress, have treated immigrants and aspiring immigrants from the three countries. If Cuban privileging merits close attention, so too does what I call the disprivileging of Haitians: a task I leave to others.

I am most appreciative of the grants, fellowships, and other support I have received over the years that released me from teaching obligations and helped fund the research on which this book is based. The John Simon Guggenheim Memorial Foundation and the Frederick S. Pardee School of Global Studies at Boston University very generously funded this book project. The Guggenheim Foundation fellowship, in addition, gave me confidence in the worth of the project when first conceiving it. The American Council of Learned Societies, the Radcliffe Institute, the John D. and Catherine T. MacArthur Foundation, the Christopher Reynolds Foundation, the Social Science Research Council, and the Mellon-MIT Inter-University Program on NGOs and Forced Migration, and, at Boston University, the Frederick S. Pardee Center for the Study of the Longer-Range Future, in turn, very kindly funded earlier work of mine on Cuba and Cuban immigrants, on which the book builds. The book is better thanks to these sources of generous support.

Since this book draws on decades of my research on Cuba and Cuban immigrants, I cannot begin to thank all the people who contributed indirectly to it. Specific to this book, I am grateful to very insightful comments on earlier drafts of the manuscript by Lars Schoultz, Jeffery Paige, Rachel Nolan, Alex Stepick, and Carl Lindskoog, and to very helpful comments on certain chapters by Holly Ackerman, Cybelle Fox, Wayne Cornelius, and Adam Isaacson. Also, Maria de los Angeles and Christopher Mitchell deepened my understanding of aspects of US Cuban and Dominican policy, and Douglas Massey my understanding of general US immigration. I am grateful also to Renata Keller who most helpfully introduced me to the world of archival research, and to comments by anonymous reviewers for Cambridge University Press. In addition, I am most appreciative of my husband, Paul Osterman, who tolerated living with me when I worked on the book, in his view, for too many years. He influenced ideas incorporated into the book.

Last but not least, my thanks to the team at Cambridge University Press (CUP), beginning with Deborah Gerschenowitz, who oversaw the press' acquisition of my manuscript. The CUP team included Cecilia Cancellaro, as well as Rachel Blaifeder, Victoria Inci Phillips, Lisa Carter, and Neena Maheen. I am indebted also to Kevin Hughes who very carefully copyedited my manuscript for CUP.

Acronyms

BTTR	Brothers to the Rescue
CAA	Cuban Adjustment Act
CBP	Customs and Border Protection
CDA	Cuban Democracy Act
CERF	Cuban Exodus Relief Fund
CFRPP	Cuban Family Reunification Parole Program
CHTF	Cuban-Haitian Task Force
CIA	Central Intelligence Agency
CMPPP	Cuban Medical Professional Parole Program
CRP	Cuban Refugee Program
DHS	Department of Homeland Security
FEMA	Federal Emergency Management Agency
HEW	Department of Health, Education, and Welfare
HHS	Department of Health and Human Services
HRIFA	Haitian Refugee Immigration Fairness Act
ICE	Immigration and Customs Enforcement
IIRIRA	Illegal Immigration Reform and Immigrant Responsibility Act
INA	Immigration and Nationality Act
INS	Immigration and Naturalization Service
IRCA	Immigration Reform and Control Act
LPR	Legal (Lawful) Permanent Residence
MPP	Migrant Protection Protocols
NACARA	Nicaraguan Adjustment and Central American Relief Act
NSC	National Security Council
PRWORA	Personal Responsibility and Work Opportunity Act

PSI	Private Sector Initiative
SCLC	Southern Christian Leadership Conference
SSI	Supplementary Security Income
USCIS	US Citizenship and Immigration Services

I

The Making of Cuban Immigration Exceptionalism, 1959–1979

On January 1, 1959, Cuban President Fulgencio Batista fled the country. His notoriously corrupt government, which tortured opponents, allied with Washington in its Cold War contest with the Soviet Union for global domination. Disrespecting the 1940 Constitution and the country's 1944 election, Batista mainly ruled in the interests of the upper and middle classes and of US business that invested in and traded with Cuba. Cubans born rich and poor, light- and dark-skinned, had very different lived experiences and opportunities.

Batista fled as Fidel Castro mobilized a movement that captured many Cubans' imagination. He rode to power as a nationalist who sought to end US domination of the country that dated back to when Cuba gained independence from Spain in 1898,[1] and as a populist committed to improving the well-being of the country's less privileged citizens. At the time he was not a communist. Yet, within a few years he oversaw a radical remaking of Cuba. In the throes of the Cold War he declared himself a Marxist-Leninist, allied with the Soviet Union, and established the Communist Party as the sole political party. The country's makeover included expropriation of most private businesses, both domestic and foreign-owned, and promotion of new egalitarian, collectivistic norms and values. The pre-revolution privileged classes lost their base of wealth and status, while the lower classes gained access to health care, schooling, jobs in the expanding state sector, and a new sense of dignity. The

---

[1] On US influence prior to 1959, see Louis Pérez, *Cuba under the Platt Amendment, 1902–1934* (Pittsburgh: University of Pittsburgh Press, 1986).

different social classes thus experienced the country's makeover very differently.

Washington resented and resisted Castro's rule because his revolution-in-the-making both undermined US business interests in Cuba and challenged US hegemony over Latin America and, to a lesser extent, other Third World countries. While global opinion by 1959 considered intervention in the internal affairs of another country unprincipled and illegal, that did not stop Republican Dwight Eisenhower, who was president at the time, from trying to oust Castro. It did, however, shape his strategies. Eisenhower turned to "soft power" means,[2] which included welcoming Cubans, among them Cubans who initially sided with Castro but who became disaffected with the radicalization of the revolution and who fled persecution in fear for their lives. Eisenhower hoped to convince the Cuban arrivals of the virtues of capitalist democracy. His presidential successors, John F. Kennedy (1961–1963) and Lyndon Johnson (1963–1969), both Democrats, did the same. They offered Cubans unique immigration rights and resettlement benefits to help them adapt well. In sapping Cuba of its human capital, immigration was intended to spur regime collapse.

This chapter summarizes general US immigration and refugee policies, backdrop for understanding Cuban immigration policies during the first two decades of Castro's rule that are then detailed in this chapter.[3] While the United States restricted admission of most foreigners, that was not the case with Cubans. Its welcoming of Cubans was a "soft power" Cold War–driven effort to contain Soviet influence and protect US interests ninety miles offshore. Successive presidents also offered Cubans new entitlements to address problems that earlier entitlements generated or left unresolved, and to address new problems that arose. The chapter proceeds to detail how first the Eisenhower and then the Kennedy administrations turned to Cubans they had admitted for one "hard power" effort to overthrow Castro, and how they tried to control anti-Castro undertakings of the Cubans they admitted without success. The Cubans

---

[2] See See Oscar Trelles, "Cuba and the United States: A Review of the Immigration Laws of the Two Countries before and during the Castro Government," *Immigration & Nationality Law Review* (1979–80): 26–48.

[3] For a summary of US immigration and refugee laws, see "The New Immigration," *The Annals of the American Academy of Political Science* (September 1966), especially pp. 1, 48. On US commitment to admit refugees only sparingly (Cubans aside), see David Scott FitzGerald, *Refuge beyond Reach: How Rich Democracies Repel Asylum Seekers* (New York: Oxford University Press, 2019).

to whom they turned had their own ambitions and own views about how to end Castro's rule. Cuban émigrés sought to use and not merely be used by the United States. Washington even had difficulty controlling which Cubans came. Who immigrated quickly came to hinge on Cuban government exit policies, on which Cubans wished to leave, and on the willingness of earlier immigrants to assist family they had left behind. Combined, the Cuban government, ordinary Cubans, and their family members who preceded them to the United States limited Washington's control over Cuban immigration: immigration that, in principle, Congress (and presidents under exceptional conditions) regulated.

SUMMARY OF IMMIGRATION AND REFUGEE POLICIES

Over the years, the United States selectively admitted foreign-born people. As is well known, historically, immigration policies favored White northern Europeans. However, as the country began to industrialize in the late 1880s, southern and eastern Europeans were welcomed to provide needed unskilled labor for factories. By the 1920s, mechanization of production reduced the demand for labor, especially for unskilled labor, such that native-born people resented immigrants who competed with them for jobs in the changed labor market. Racist nativist sentiment led Congress to limit immigration in a manner favoring light-skinned people from northern Europe (while barring certain Asians altogether). Fortunately for Western Hemisphere peoples at the time, including Cubans, they were exempt from newly instituted country admissions quotas.

The United States was more selective in the refugees it admitted.[4] Despite its European bias in refugee admissions, it welcomed few Jews and others seeking refuge from Nazism, which led millions of them to die in the Holocaust. As a result, after World War II, political pressure built up for the United States to admit its "fair share" of refugees from the war. In response, Congress passed a series of laws to admit refugees, independent of laws regulating general immigration. The laws, each with expiration dates, allowed for the admission of selective Europeans displaced by the war.[5] As Washington focused on the emergent Cold War and

---

[4] FitzGerald, *Refuge beyond Reach*. Refugees accounted for one-fifth of all immigrants admitted between 1945 and 1966. After Castro came to power in 1959, Cubans accounted for the vast majority of those the United States officially admitted as refugees.

[5] For example, Congress passed the Displaced Persons Act of 1948, the Refugee Relief Act of 1953, the Refugee-Escapee Act of 1957, and the Fair Share Refugee Act of 1960.

competition with the Soviet Union for global influence, Congress proceeded to pass legislation to also admit refugees from communist countries, on which it based special legislation for Cubans.[6] Several laws were passed under Eisenhower's presidency, but, relevant to Cubans, after Kennedy assumed the presidency and Castro officially allied with the Soviet Union, Congress enacted the Migration and Refugee Assistance Act of 1962. Cubans became the key beneficiaries of this new legislation.[7]

Amid post–World War II international concern about refugees, the United Nations issued the 1951 Convention Relating to the Status of Refugees. It defined refugees as persons who fled their homeland because of events that occurred before January 1951, owing to persecution based on their race, religion, nationality, membership in a particular social group, or political views. On the principle of non-*refoulement*, such persons were not to be forced to return to the lands from which they had fled. Seventeen years later, the United States ratified an extension of the Convention, the Protocol Relating to the Status of Refugees, which eliminated the 1951 cutoff date for qualification for refugee status, and extended the applicability of the Convention to non-European victims of persecution. The Convention, as modified by the Protocol, serves as the "Bill of Rights" for refugees. To date, it is considered the most important international refugee document. Building on the principles of this "Bill of Rights," Congress passed the Refugee Act of 1980, which officially eliminated previous political, racial, and country-of-origin biases in US refugee policy and committed the president, in consultation with Congress, to agree on the number of refugees to be admitted annually from different regions of the world, including from Latin America, and, accordingly, from Cuba. The legislation is described in detail in Chapter 3 as it applies to Cubans.

Paralleling its concern with refugees, after World War II, Congress passed legislation to correct earlier biases in general immigration policy. Immigrants are persons admitted for whatever reason, in contrast to refugees who fled actual or likely persecution. In 1952, Congress passed the Immigration and Nationality Act (INA), known commonly as the McCarran-Walter Act after its key sponsors, which slightly modified the national origins admissions policy that had been in effect since the 1920s. It also ended earlier exclusion of Asians. Relevant to Cubans, it exempted

---

[6] See Trelles, "Cuba and the United States."
[7] US Senate, "Assistance to Refugees, Migrants, and Escapees," 87th Congress, 1st session, Report 989 (September 12, 1961).

Western, but not Eastern, Hemisphere peoples from country quotas. So, too, did it codify Attorney General parole authority to admit persons temporarily for "urgent humanitarian reasons or significant public benefit" on a case-by-case basis, independent of Congress-controlled admissions. Persons paroled into the country were expected to return to their homeland after the purpose of their parole was served. Eisenhower, on assuming the presidency in 1953, immediately (re)interpreted Executive Branch parole authority. He did so, in the context of the emergent Cold War, first to admit Hungarians who fled a failed uprising against their Soviet-allied communist government, and then to admit Cubans after Castro assumed power in 1959. Subsequent presidents will be shown in this book to have followed Eisenhower's example and allowed their Attorneys General to parole Cubans into the United States on the basis of their national origins, though not on a case-by-case basis, as specified in the INA.[8] Parole became the main basis by which Cubans were admitted into the United States, both before and after passage of the Refugee Act of 1980.

In 1965, during Johnson's presidency, Congress amended the INA with Public Law (P.L.) 89-236, popularly known as the Hart–Celler Act, after the names of its key sponsors. This legislation capped Western Hemisphere yearly admissions for the first time, at 120,000, without assigning country quotas.[9] Most significantly, the 1965 reform replaced the much-criticized racist national origins quota system with a seven-category non-country-specific "preference system." The preference system prioritized admission of relatives of US citizens and lawful permanent residents, and, secondly, persons with skills who had secured certification from the Secretary of Labor that they addressed a labor shortage. The seventh category permitted conditional annual admission of 10,200 persons who either had fled persecution or were uprooted because of natural

---

[8] Subsequent presidents paroled Chinese and Vietnamese communist escapees into the United States, but only during limited, delineated periods of time. See Laura Murray-Tjan, "'Conditional Admission' and Other Mysteries: Setting the Record Straight on the 'Admission' Status of Refugees and Asylees," *N.Y.U. Journal of Public Policy* 37 (2013–2014), p.48.

[9] At the same time, P.L. 89-236 capped total annual immigration from Eastern Hemisphere countries at 170,000, and from individual countries in the region at 20,000. It also entitled Eastern Hemisphere entrants on non-immigration visas to apply for lawful permanent residence (LPR) without having to leave the country. In contrast, it specified that persons from the Western Hemisphere needed to apply from abroad for LPR rights.

disasters.[10] This marked the first time that the United States committed to admit refugees on a routine, annual basis.[11] The seventh category, however, was dropped in 1980 with passage of the Refugee Act.

President Johnson signed the new immigration bill when delivering a well-crafted speech against the backdrop of the Statue of Liberty. In his words, "We will never again shadow the gate to the American Nation with the twin barriers of prejudice and privilege.... [T]hose who do come will come because of what they are, and not because of the land from which they sprung."[12] President Johnson added that the national origins system had violated the basic principle of American democracy to value and reward "each man on the basis of his merit as a man." Officially, nation of birth remained important only in that the 1965 reform included an annual country admissions cap on people from the Eastern Hemisphere.

While the new legislation, in effect though not stated intent, continued the European bias in immigration of the past by prioritizing admission of persons with family already in the country, European interest in immigration to the United States tapered off around the time that the Hart–Celler Act was enacted. It tapered off as opportunities in Europe expanded first with recuperation from the devastation of World War II and then with the formation of the European Union. Also, the fertility rate in Europe declined, which reduced demographic pressures to emigrate. Consequently, the Hart–Celler Act facilitated family-based migration from non-European countries, potentially advantageous to Cubans. However, the signing ceremony took on particular significance for Cubans in that President Johnson used the occasion to extend an

---

[10] The first, second, fourth, and fifth preference categories apply to relatives of US citizens and legal permanent residents. The third and sixth categories are occupation related. The seventh category allowed for conditional entry of a select number of refugees that drew on the parole procedure incorporated into the Fair Share Refugee Act. On usage of parole, see the John Fitzgerald Kennedy Presidential Library (JFKPL), White House Central File (WHCF), 19-2, Folder: Displaced Persons-Refugees, "Caribbean Crisis: A Danger and an Opportunity," prepared by the Special Sub-committee on Caribbean Refugee Problem, the International Rescue Committee, New York City (January 30, 1961), p. 15, Box 636.

[11] Initially, persecuted peoples were admitted on only a provisional basis. After two years, they could apply for lawful permanent residence if they demonstrated that they did not subject the United States to outside pressure. Murray-Tjan, "'Conditional Admission' and Other Mysteries," p.51.

[12] Lyndon Baines Johnson Presidential Library (LBJPL), *Public Papers of the Presidents of the United States: Lyndon B. Johnson*, "Remarks" at the Signing of the Immigration Bill, Liberty Island, New York, October 3, 1965.

open-ended invitation to Cubans, described later in this chapter, independent of the preference system.

Amendments to the INA in 1976, under President Gerald Ford, removed differences in immigration entitlements for people from the Western and Eastern Hemispheres. They set a 20,000-person yearly country cap on Western as well as Eastern Hemisphere immigration, and specified that Western, along with Eastern, Hemisphere people in the United States on non-immigration visas could apply for lawful permanent residency without having to leave the country to apply from abroad. Specific to Cuba, the 1976 INA Amendments denoted that, when adjusting the status of Cubans to lawful permanent residence, the number of entry visas granted to non-Cubans would not be reduced. Accordingly, admissions of Cubans would not be at the expense of others from the hemisphere.

Subsequent legislation focused on strengthening immigration enforcement, exclusion, and border security while selectively expanding opportunities for immigration. This was true of the Immigration Reform and Control Act of 1986 (IRCA), the Immigration Act of 1990, and the Illegal Immigration Reform and Immigrant Responsibility Act of 1996 (IIRIRA). Their relevance for Cubans, and for Haitians with whom Cuban experiences are contrasted in this book, is detailed in the chapters that address the administrations under which each of these laws were enacted.

Thus, in the course of the twentieth century, Congress enacted legislation that typically favored immigrants and refugees from light-skinned northern European countries. Although people of the Western Hemisphere were initially exempt from regulations imposed on Eastern Hemisphere people, in the course of the twentieth century, legislation restricted their entry entitlements as well and subjected them to criminalization, detention, and deportation.[13] While Congress officially ended racially biased, country-based immigration admissions in 1965, and subsequently broadened eligibility for refugee admissions, after 1959 Congress as well as presidents implemented policies favoring Cubans over other foreign-born people, including over others from the Americas. Cubans, however, will be shown to have been favored more under certain administrations than others: including long after the Cold War's end ceased to justify privileging them as communist escapees.

---

[13] See Mae Ngai, *Impossible Subjects: Illegal Aliens and the Making of Modern America* (Princeton: Princeton University Press, 2004).

THE MAKING OF SPECIAL BASES TO ADMIT CUBANS, 1959 TO 1965

While Castro assumed power with widespread support, the United States welcomed opponents of the radical makeover of Cuba that he oversaw. First welcomed were those closely associated with the discredited Batista regime, followed by those who opposed the revolution's Marxist-Leninist turn. Some fled persecution and fear of persecution. However, increasing numbers of Cubans fled the nationalization of businesses, schools, country clubs, and the like, which deprived the upper and middle classes of their livelihood and lifestyle.

President Eisenhower, followed by Presidents Kennedy and Johnson, initiated ways to admit Cubans that circumvented congressional-set immigration restrictions. They implemented measures to admit Cubans expeditiously and imagined Cubans in ways that granted them special entry prerogatives. The three presidents also convinced Congress to finance assistance to Cubans on their arrival. They piled new entitlements onto old as conditions changed. How did they do so?

Imagined Tourists

With the State Department issuing only limited numbers of immigration visas, and with the visa application process time-consuming and cumbersome, the Eisenhower administration permitted Cubans to come with easier-to-obtain nonimmigration visas: mainly as tourists, but secondarily as students. Tourist visas were valid for four years for multiple entries, lasting a month per each visit. Already during the Batista era, the United States had issued tourist visas to upper- and middle-class Cubans who vacationed and shopped in the United States, infatuated with the American way of life.[14] However, toward the end of 1960, the Eisenhower administration issued an unprecedented 1,600 tourist visas to Cubans weekly,[15] and it did so in an expedited, pro-forma manner.[16]

---

[14] Louis Pérez, *On Becoming Cuban: Identity, Nationality, and Culture* (Chapel Hill: University of North Carolina Press, 1999).

[15] Eight to ten times that number applied for tourist visas. See JFKPL, WHCF, 19-2, "Caribbean Crisis."

[16] John Scanlan and Gilburt Loescher, "U.S. Foreign Policy, 1959–80: Impact on Refugee Flow from Cuba," *Annals of the American Academy of Political and Social Science* 467, special issue "The Global Refugee Problem: U.S. and World Response" (May 1983), p. 119.

The Eisenhower administration understood that the Cubans to whom it issued the visas were not typical tourists. Nonetheless, tourist visas provided a basis for admission. When the tourist visas expired, the Eisenhower administration granted the Cubans "involuntary indefinite departure" or "extended voluntary departure" status that spared them the risk of deportation. If deported, US law would have barred their reentry for ten years; at the time, it would also have likely subjected returnees to persecution in Cuba for having fled the revolution, in which case the United States would have violated the principle of non-*refoulement*.

Imagined Refugees

The Eisenhower administration also allowed Cubans to use tourist visas differently after Castro assumed power, and it allowed them to use visas differently than other nationals. It (re)imagined Cubans as "refugee-tourists,"[17] "tourists" transformed into "refugees" in the United States, where they were safe from persecution.[18] When visitor visas expired, Cubans could officially become refugees. As refugees, they would not be forced to return to Cuba.

If the United States only reluctantly and belatedly admitted Jewish refugees who fled persecution during World War II, the Eisenhower administration was quick to imagine Cubans as refugees, even when their lifestyle but not lives were at risk. Less than half of the Cubans that the United States admitted had fled persecution, the near-universally recognized criterion for refugee status, as previously noted.[19] As imagined, Cubans enjoyed rights to work, they were spared the risk of deportation, and they qualified for the most generous set of benefits the United States had ever offered immigrants or refugees.

However, a deterioration in relations between the United States and Cuba that led the two countries to sever diplomatic ties on January 3, 1961, weeks before Eisenhower left office, put a stop to "refugee tourism." With the shutdown of the US Embassy in Havana, the United States could no longer issue visas of any type. Cubans with still-valid nonimmigration visas could continue to come legally to the United States, but only until their visas expired. At the time, approximately 100,000 Cubans still

---

[17] JFKPL, WHCF 19-2, "Caribbean Crisis," p. 14.   [18] Ibid.
[19] Jorge Domínguez "Cooperating with the Enemy? U.S. Immigration Policies toward Cuba," in Christopher Mitchell (ed.), *Western Hemisphere Immigration and United States Foreign Policy* (University Park: Pennsylvania State Press, 1992), pp. 31–79.

had usable multiple-entry visas.[20] The embassy shutdown also meant that Cubans could not apply for the more difficult-to-attain immigration visas. For immigration visas, the United States required individuals to be screened abroad, a service it ceased to be able to offer in Cuba.

On assuming the presidency later in January, Kennedy continued to perceive Cubans as refugees. His administration admitted more Cubans as refugees, who it entitled to an expanded array of resettlement benefits.[21] During its first year it admitted 33,000 Cubans, more than the Eisenhower administration had admitted in 1959 and 1960 combined.[22] The benefits offered the new arrivals are described in Chapter 2.

Visa Regulation Bending: The Granting of Visa Waivers, Admission with Fraudulently Dated Visas, and Admission of Visaless Cubans

While the embassy shutdown might have put a halt to immigration, President Kennedy invented new ways to enable Cubans to come. Some bases were legally questionable.

The Kennedy administration, for one, granted Cubans unique visa waivers. It permitted commercial airlines to forward requests to the Attorney General and the Secretary of State to waive passport and visa requirements for Cubans. Cubans thereby could be processed for admission after arrival in the United States, while other nationals needed to be screened abroad. The Kennedy administration also authorized nongovernmental organizations, such as the Catholic Welfare Bureau and the International Rescue Committee, to issue visa waivers. In 1962, his administration granted as many as 1,800 visa waivers to Cubans in a week, more visa waivers than the number of tourist visas the Eisenhower administration had issued to Cubans as nontourists. US officials rejected only about 1 percent of all visa waiver requests.[23]

---

[20] JFKPL, National Security Files: Countries, Cuba, Cuba, Subjects Exiles, Folder: "Annex A: Control of Exile Movement," Box 48.

[21] Foreign Relations of the United States (FRUS), *Cuba 1961–1963*, National Security Action #2422, "U.S. Policy toward Cuba," memorandum for NSC Action, May 4, 1961, p. 482.

[22] Félix Masud-Piloto, *From Welcomed Exiles to Illegal Immigrants: Cuban Migration to the U.S., 1959–1995* (Lanham, MD: Rowman & Littlefield,1996), p. 52.

[23] Domínguez, "Cooperating with the Enemy?," p. 41; JFKPL, Abba Schwartz Papers, Folder: State Department Security 1963–1965, Testimony of Abba Schwartz August 15, 1964, Box 6.

The Making of Cuban Immigration Exceptionalism

The Kennedy administration even allowed Cubans to use backdated visas. If backdated, the visas appeared valid because the denoted date preceded the embassy shutdown, when the United States still issued visas. The Kennedy administration accordingly permitted immigration fraud to admit Cubans.

The United States Coast Guard and the Immigration and Naturalization Service (INS) further conspired to admit Cubans. They facilitated entry of Cubans who had not been pre-screened and pre-approved abroad for admission. Following orders, members of the Coast Guard helped unauthorized Cubans they picked up at sea come ashore, at the same time that they blocked other visa-less boatpeople from US entry. Once they were ashore, the INS admitted them.

The Financing of Cuban Immigration

The Kennedy administration also financed the transport of Cubans to the United States, at American taxpayers' expense. It did so when the Cuban government imposed financial obstacles to Cuban departures.

In order to make it more difficult for Cubans to leave, as well as to generate foreign exchange from those who did depart, in late 1961 the Cuban government began to require Cubans to pay their airfare in hard currency. As anticipated, many Cubans did not have the currency. However, the Kennedy administration came to their rescue. It set aside $350,000 for transporting Cubans to the United States,[24] and it sent a bill to Congress in order to create a $10 million annual fund to address an "unexpected refugee migration problem."[25] Cubans thereby immigrated who otherwise would have been unable to do so. As detailed later in the chapter, President Johnson expanded, on a grand scale, the number of Cubans whose airfares US taxpayers funded.

Unique Program for Unaccompanied Children

The Eisenhower, followed by the Kennedy administration, targeted children for special admission to the United States. They allowed unaccompanied minors entry, while their parents stayed behind in Cuba.

The Eisenhower administration initiated a unique immigration program for Cuban children shortly before leaving office that President

---

[24] Masud-Piloto, *From Welcomed Exiles to Illegal Immigrants*, p. 52.   [25] Ibid.

Kennedy continued and expanded on. Although little publicized at the time, the program came to be known as Operation Peter Pan.[26] Tracy Voorhees, Eisenhower's Personal Representative for Cuban Refugees, had recommended the program. Between December 1960 and October 1962 Operation Peter Pan brought some 14,000 unaccompanied children to the United States. Administered by the CIA, the program had an open-ended budget line. Before its termination, the program cost American taxpayers approximately $28,500,000.[27]

Allegedly, Operation Peter Pan was designed to spare Cuban children from being sent, without their parents, to the Soviet Union for schooling. However, President Eisenhower authorized the program before Castro officially declared the revolution to be Marxist-Leninist and before he allied with the Soviet Union,[28] despite no evidence that the children would be shipped to the Soviet Union if not admitted to the United States.

The program provided parents with a way that their children could escape repression for their anti-government involvements, as well as political indoctrination, and a way, they believed, for themselves also to flee, so as to reunite with their children in the United States.[29] Father Bryan Walsh, who directed the Catholic Welfare Bureau in Miami, administered the program, in coordination with the headmaster of Ruston Academy, an elite private American school in Havana that the Cuban government closed when it nationalized all education.

Out of commitment to the Eisenhower-initiated program, after the United States and Cuba severed diplomatic relations in 1961 and Cubans could no longer obtain visas in Cuba. President Kennedy gave Father Walsh, a private citizen, blanket authority to issue visa waivers for unaccompanied minors.[30] In October 1962, President Kennedy ended the program, though not voluntarily. It ended when US–Cuban relations

---

[26] Maria de los Torres very kindly contributed to my understanding of Operation Peter Pan.
[27] Masud-Piloto, *From Welcomed Exiles to Illegal Immigrants*, p. 40.
[28] Maria de los Torres, *The Lost Apple: Operation Pedro Pan, Cuban Children in the U.S., and the Promise of a Better Future* (Boston: Beacon Press, 2003); John Thomas, "Cuban Refugees in the United States," *International Migration Review* vol. 1, no. 2 (Spring 1967): 48. The program also spared boys from military conscription.
[29] While children suffered psychologically from the separation from their parents, many of them grew up to be prominent Cuban Americans. "Peter Panners" include Joe Carollo and Tomás Regalado, mayors of Miami, Senator Mel Martínez, the prominent real estate investor and developer Armando Codina, and the Latin Grammy Lifetime Achievement Award winner Willy Chirino.
[30] The Kennedy administration granted several organizations the authority to issue visa waivers.

further deteriorated with the so-called Missile Crisis, at which time the Cuban government halted commercial flights between Cuba and the United States, on which Operation Peter Pan depended (although versions of the program subsequently continued through Spain).

Half of the "Peter Panners" were fortunate to fairly quickly reunite with their parents in the United States, before the Missile Crisis. The others, however, could not reunite until President Johnson launched another extraordinary, to-be-described special immigration program for Cubans in December 1965. In the interim years, the children whose parents remained in Cuba were placed in foster care unless relatives in the United States agreed to sponsor them.

Use and Abuse of Parole Authority

In order to circumvent regulations set by Congress so as to admit Cubans, the Eisenhower administration also drew on the parole authority the 1952 INA granted to the Executive Branch for "urgent humanitarian reasons or sufficient public benefit." The Kennedy administration followed suit, and, indeed, paroled many more Cubans into the United States.

Parole became the main basis for admitting Cubans. By mid-1962, the Kennedy administration had paroled 59,000 Cubans into the country, up from 4,000 the preceding year.[31] Cubans thereby enjoyed work rights, although technically not indefinitely. Among those granted parole status were the Cubans who had been initially admitted with visa waivers. They were granted "indefinite parole" six months after their arrival. Their initial immigration entitlement proved a stepping stone for the new immigration entitlement.

The Kennedy administration then proceeded to extend an additional entitlement to Cubans. It waived their parole fees.[32]

Yet, in reaching out to Cubans, the Kennedy administration abused its parole authority. First, it knowingly paroled Cubans into the country with backdated visas: These people would have been accused of visa-fraud and been subject to deportation had they immigrated from any

---

[31] LBJPL, Collection: Administrative History, Department Justice, "Cuban Refugees," Folder: Administrative History, Department of Justice, vol. IX, INS, Part 13, Box 8.
[32] JFKPL, WHCF, "Caribbean Crisis," p. 14.

other country.³³ Also, the administration used its parole authority differently than Congress intended. It paroled Cubans on the basis of their nationality, rather than individually, case-by-case, as specified in the INA.

With parole status sparing Cubans the risk of forced removal, the number of "deportable Cuban aliens" dropped from 27,000 in 1962 to 4,800 the following year, as the number of Cubans who were paroled into the country soared. The remaining "deportable Cuban aliens" were mainly "tourists," but also students and other non-immigrants who stayed in the United States after their visas expired, and, as a result, were "out of status."³⁴ "Deportable Cuban aliens" also included "illegal entrants" who came visa-less without authorization: for example, Cubans who illicitly entered the United States on small boats. In granting these Cubans parole status the Kennedy administration enabled them to stay in the country legally without fear of deportation: although without permanent residency rights.

Thus, building on Eisenhower's initiatives, President Kennedy introduced new bases to admit Cubans. Both presidents worked around US immigration and refugee regulations, while circumventing the constraints that the deterioration of US–Cuban relations imposed. They introduced new entitlements to address new problems that arose.

IMMIGRATION CONSTRAINTS IMPOSED BY THE BREAKDOWN IN US–CUBAN RELATIONS

When the October 1962 Missile Crisis brought the United States to the brink of nuclear war, immigration became even more difficult than after the United States and Cuba severed diplomatic relations in January 1961 and the US embassy was closed. Following the discovery of Soviet missiles on the island, Washington ordered a naval quarantine of Cuba. It was against this backdrop that the Cuban government suspended commercial flights to the United States.³⁵ Because the Cuban government had

---

[33] JFKPL, National Security Files, Countries, Cuba, Folder: Cuba, Subject Exiles, Annex B: Revised Cuban Refugee Program, Department of Health, Education and Welfare, April 29, 1961, Box 48.

[34] JFKPL, Abba P. Schwartz Personal Papers, "Annual Report of the Immigration and Naturalization Service," 1963, p. 8.

[35] The Kennedy administration imposed a naval blockade around Cuba when it discovered the Soviets were constructing nuclear missile sites in Cuba. The Soviets agreed to dismantle the sites and remove the missiles in exchange for the United States pledging not to invade Cuba.

prohibited departure by sea (to maximize control over emigration), Cubans were left without a direct way to get to the United States.

As a result, the number of Cubans admitted to the United States dropped precipitously, from 215,000 between 1959 and 1962 to 74,000 during the next three years.[36] Following the Missile Crisis Cubans could only enter the United States via third countries. The only other option was to go to the United States in small, often unsafe, boats, without authorization. If they survived the voyage across the Florida Straits, the INS immediately granted them asylum and work permits. Thus, while the deterioration in US–Cuban relations dramatically constricted Cuban immigration options, Washington welcomed the Cubans who circumvented the obstacles.

Among the only Cubans the United States and Cuba permitted to immigrate directly from Cuba after the Missile Crisis came on planes with émigrés the Cuban government had taken hostage in the to-be-described CIA-orchestrated Bay of Pigs invasion. The Cuban government required that half the seats on the flights be reserved for Cubans who wished to join family in the United States (allotting, in fact, over 60 percent of the seats to such Cubans). Some 5,000 Cubans entered the United States in this manner.[37] In addition, the American Red Cross brought slightly less than one thousand Cubans to the United States as refugees.

Thus, although Cuban immigration did not come to a standstill, by the time of Kennedy's assassination in November 1963, it had tapered off substantially: not by US design but as a result of the deterioration in US–Cuban relations. On assuming the presidency, Lyndon Johnson, Kennedy's vice president, continued to bend the rules in Cubans' favor. However, during his first two years as president he granted Cubans no new immigration entitlements, and relatively few Cubans came to the United States.

In 1965, President Johnson did convince Congress to pass the previously noted Hart–Celler comprehensive immigration reform. In order to attain sufficient congressional support for the legislation he agreed to the deletion of a controversial provision in a draft bill that would have extended another entitlement to Cubans: It would have allowed

---

[36] Javier Arteaga, "The Cuban Adjustment Act of 1966: More Than Forty Years Later, A Proposal for the Future," *Florida International University Law Review* vol. 3 (2007–2008): 518.
[37] Domínguez, "Cooperating with the Enemy?, p. 60.

Cubans in the United States with only temporary entry rights to adjust their status and become lawful permanent residents. Members of Congress who claimed that granting Cubans lawful permanent residence implied both permanency of Castro's rule and a shift in the US stance toward the Cuban government withheld their support for the entire bill until the deletion of the Cuban status adjustment provision.[38] Michael Feighan, chairman of the House Judiciary Subcommittee on Immigration, noted an additional reason to omit the Cuban status adjustment provision: Status adjustment was a foreign policy matter, and thus the responsibility of the Department of State and the administration, not Congress.[39] Faced with the congressional resistance, President Johnson agreed to drop from the bill the status adjustment enabling provision. While deletion of the provision was a setback for Cubans who wanted permanent residency and associated rights. Johnson valued passage of the general immigration legislation over granting Cubans a new entitlement.

EXPANSION OF CUBAN IMMIGRATION ENTITLEMENTS UNDER THE JOHNSON ADMINISTRATION

Although President Johnson had sacrificed Cubans' ability to adjust their status in 1965, in order to convince Congress to pass the Hart–Celler Act, he soon thereafter extended new immigration rights to Cubans, including to Cubans residing in third countries.

The Cuban government was not entirely passive as the United States extended one immigration entitlement after another to Cubans. It had mixed and contradictory views toward Cubans who left the country. On the one hand, Castro welcomed the opportunity to rid the country of disaffected citizens. On the other hand, he was wary about losing skilled labor that was essential for the country's development; about enabling Cubans to organize opposition to the revolution from abroad; and about the political implications of Cubans "voting with their feet" in large numbers, which would reveal rejection of the revolution. To discourage departures, the Cuban government stigmatized those who left as "worms" and traitors, and unpatriotic. It also penalized them in prohibiting their return to Cuba. Also, it restricted the number of exit permits it issued.

---

[38] *Congressional Record* Volume 112, Part 14, U.S. Senate, August 10, 1966, p. 18930; *Congressional Record* House of Representatives September 19, 1966, p. 22913-21.

[39] Domínguez, "Cooperating with the Enemy?," p. 68.

The Making of Cuban Immigration Exceptionalism

Yet, with emigration pressures building up after the Missile Crisis-linked suspension of commercial air travel, Castro announced at a large gathering in Havana in late September 1965 that Cubans who wished to leave could have family in the United States pick them up by boat at the port of Camarioca, without US entry permission. While many Cubans enthusiastically supported the revolution, especially the young, the poor, and Afro-Cuban victims of discrimination, by 1965 disaffection with the revolution had built up among Cubans who resented the country's political-economic transformation, the institutionalization of Communist Party rule, demands for voluntary labor, new scarcities, and the construction of a new society premised on collective moral values, in place of individualistic and materialistic ones. As a result, when Castro lifted exit restrictions, some five thousand Cubans immediately took advantage of the opportunity to leave. Others contemplated doing the same.

Open-Ended Invitation to Cubans to Immigrate at US Taxpayers' Expense

Following the precedents set by the Eisenhower and Kennedy administrations, the Johnson administration paroled the unauthorized arrivals from Camarioca into the United States. It even ordered the Coast Guard to help bring them ashore and arranged for them to receive emergency assistance.[40] Unauthorized immigrants from other countries not only were offered no comparable entitlements; they were subject to deportation.

President Johnson then went a step further. So as to prevent more Cubans from coming without authorization, his administration negotiated an official airlift with Cuban authorities, in which Cubans could immigrate on what he dubbed, in Cold War parlance, Freedom Flights. He responded to the threat of greater unauthorized immigration, from Camarioca, by offering Cubans new unique lawful immigration rights. In having US taxpayers finance the flights, he followed Kennedy administration precedent.

The airlift addressed an open-ended immigration invitation extended to Cubans that President Johnson had announced at the Hart–Celler Act signing ceremony. Quite remarkably, at the signing ceremony he made it

---

[40] RNPL (Richard Nixon Presidential Library), White House Special Files, Staff Member and Office Files, Ronald Ziegler, Subject File, Foreign Affairs and Defense, Folder: Ronald Ziegler, "Cuba," Fact Sheet: Cuban Refugees, Box 28.

known that Cubans "who seek refuge here in America will find it,"[41] on the basis of their country of origin, despite the newly enacted legislation ending US admission on the basis of nationality. After noting that " ... from this day forth those wishing to emigrate to America shall be admitted on the basis of their skills and their close relationship to those already here," no longer on the basis of where they were born, he extended the invitation to Cubans. Furthermore, he set no limit to the number of Cubans that were to be permitted entry, even though the Hart–Celler legislation capped total yearly Western Hemisphere admissions at 120,000. In paroling the Freedom Flight entrants into the country, he circumvented the regional quota the legislation set, and spared them from having to compete with others from the Hemisphere for the admission slots set by Congress. Only when the Cubans applied for lawful permanent residence were they charged against the Hemisphere quota, at which point, though, they were granted admission at the expense of other nationals.[42] When President Johnson extended the entry invitation to Cubans, he also announced that he would immediately request $12,600,000 in supplementary funds from Congress to help incoming Cubans to adapt to America. Never before had a president extended such an explicit welcome mat to people from one nation: paradoxically, when signing legislation that officially ended country-based admissions.

The immigration invitation led to rare bilateral collaboration. The United States and Cuba arranged for two US-financed daily flights, five days a week, which began on December 1, 1965. The flights operated on the basis of a Memorandum of Understanding (MOU) which specified that the United States could only admit Cubans who were pre-approved by Cuban authorities.[43]

With the signing of the MOU, Castro closed Camarioca, from where unscreened Cubans had emigrated. Most importantly from the Johnson administration's vantage point, going forward Cubans would be admitted

---

[41] LBJPL, *Public Papers of the Presidents of the United States: Lyndon B. Johnson 1965*, Book II (Washington: GPO, 1966), p. 1039.

[42] RNPL, President Materials Staff, NSC Institutional Files, Meetings Files 1969–1974, Senior Review Group Meetings, Folder: Review Group NSSM, 32 Cuba, H-039, "Annex to National Security Study Memorandum 32-Cuba, Factors Bearing on U.S. Policies," Box H-039.

[43] In order to discourage departures when applying for exit permits, Havana authorities dismissed Cubans from their jobs and, if able-bodied, required them to undertake agricultural work until permitted to leave. George Volsky, "Cuba Reassessing Refugee Airlift," *New York Times* (December 6, 1970), p. 25.

in an orderly manner, subject to US approval. The MOU thereby nipped an incipient immigration crisis in the bud by granting unique entry rights to yet more Cubans, who, in turn, received unique resettlement assistance. Alternatively, his administration might have aggressively blocked Cuban immigration, as other administrations will be shown to have done over the years in the case of Haitians. In 1966, alone, the Johnson administration admitted some fifty-five thousand Cubans,[44] which was nearly half the yearly number of immigrants the Hart–Celler Act permitted from the entire Western Hemisphere. President Johnson justified the unique invitation to Cubans by claiming that "The dedication of America to our traditions as an asylum for the oppressed is going to be upheld." He added that "it stamps the mark of failure on a regime when many of its citizens voluntarily choose to leave the land of their birth."[45] Cuban arrivals, he added, would showcase Cubans' preference for democracy over dictatorship.

Nonetheless, the Johnson administration proved to be more restrictive regarding the Cubans it admitted than the president's open-ended welcoming of Cubans in front of the Statue of Liberty suggested. The welcoming was limited to relatives of Cubans who were already in the United States. In President Johnson's words, "Our first concern will be with those Cubans who have been separated from their children and their parents and their husbands and their wives ... now in this country." In agreeing to admit parents of the unaccompanied children sent to the United States in Operation Peter Pan, the Johnson administration resolved the problem of family separation that the child immigration program had caused. He resolved the problem by permitting more Cubans to immigrate.

President Johnson had intended also to admit political prisoners on the Freedom Flights.[46] However, the Cuban government used its discretionary power to restrict departures of political prisoners (as well as technicians essential to the economy, and fifteen to twenty-six-year-old military age men). Castro preferred to keep "counter-revolutionaries" under his government's control than allow them to leave and be free to subvert the revolution from abroad.

---

[44] Metro-Dade County Planning Department Research Division, "Background Paper on Cuban Immigration into Dade County," *Cuban Information Archives Document 0072* (http://cuban-exile.com/doc_051–075/doc0072.html).
[45] *Public Papers of the Presidents of the United States: Lyndon B. Johnson 1965*, p. 1040.
[46] Ibid., p. 1038.

In focusing on family reunification, Cuban admissions reinforced earlier racial biases in US immigration: despite the Hart–Celler reform having ended the racist national origins immigration policy. Because 97 percent of the first Cubans who fled the revolution were White (by self-definition),[47] their typically light-skinned relatives in Cuba went to the front of the immigration queue. President Johnson thereby added a Western Hemisphere racial bias to the earlier European racial bias in US immigrant admissions. Had kinship-based admissions not been prioritized, the Cubans who came on Freedom Flights would likely have been more racially diverse, as were the more than one hundred thousand unauthorized Cubans, described in Chapter 3, who immigrated in 1980.

The Cubans who arrived on the Freedom Flights were paroled into the United States officially as refugees, even though the Cuban government at the time prevented political prisoners, who were victims of persecution, from leaving, and even though the Cubans who the United States admitted never needed to demonstrate that they were fleeing persecution. When welcoming Cubans in front of the Statue of Liberty in 1965 President Johnson suggested that their stay might be temporary. In his words, "in another day" they could "return to their homeland," when Cuba was "cleansed of terror and free from fear."[48] He never, however, encouraged their return, and they stayed. And a year later he oversaw passage of legislation that entitled them to legal permanent residency.

While "a gift" to Cubans who wished to immigrate, the Freedom Flight program faced domestic opposition. In Miami, African Americans resented the preferential treatment that they felt incoming Cubans received for welfare, jobs, housing, and education. There were others who considered the program too costly, and felt that the funds could be better spent on more deserving minorities.[49] However, the State Department pressed for its continuation, including after President Johnson left office, on the grounds that the United States had a moral

---

[47] Susan Eckstein, *The Immigrant Divide: How Cuban Americans Changed the US and Their Homeland* (New York: Routledge, 2009), p. 19.

[48] LBJPL, *Public Papers of the Presidents of the United States: Lyndon B. Johnson,* "Remarks," at the Signing of the Immigration Bill," New York, October 3, 1965 (www.lbjlibrary.net/collections/selected-speeches/1965/10-03-1965.html), p. 1039.

[49] RNPL, President Materials Staff, NSC Institutional Files, Meetings Files 1969-1974, Senior Review Group Meetings, Folder: Review Group NSSM, 23 Cuba, H-039, "Annex to National Security Study Memorandum 32-Cuba, Factors Bearing on U.S. Policies," Box H-039.

commitment to continue honoring President Johnson's declaration at the Statue of Liberty that Cubans "who seek refuge in America will find it."[50] By the time the Nixon administration terminated the program in 1973, the United States had admitted some 270,000 new Cubans, roughly the same number of Cubans that the United States had admitted during the first few years of Castro's rule, before the Missile Crisis.

Extension of Immigration Entitlements to Cubans in Third Countries

The Johnson administration also granted Cubans in third countries unique immigration rights. It thereby, in effect, transnationalized Cuban immigration entitlements.

For one, the Johnson administration bent immigration regulations to expedite the entry of Cubans who were second category priority according to the Hart–Celler reform, namely distant relatives of American citizens, thus low in the queue of possible entrants on Freedom Flights. It allowed them to attain immigration visas in Mexico City and Madrid.[51] These Cubans were admitted with "green cards," as lawful permanent residents, LPRs, in contrast to the Cubans on the Freedom Flights who were paroled into the country. Moreover, the Cubans admitted via Mexico and Spain did not need to compete with nationals of those countries for US visa slots.

Then, in 1966 the Johnson administration granted special immigration privileges to relatives of Cubans in the United States who lived in third countries.[52] The relatives did not even need to have been born in Cuba. They needed only to be relatives of people who were born there. The Johnson administration thereby stretched the meaning of "being Cuban" for US entry, just as the Eisenhower and Kennedy administrations had stretched the meaning of "refugee" to Cubans' advantage. The United

---

[50] LBJPL, *Public Papers of the Presidents of the United States: Lyndon B. Johnson,* "Remarks at the Signing of the Immigration Bill."
[51] LBJPL, Letter from Robert Stevenson, Coordinator of Cuban Affairs, to Antonio Solar of Miami, February 11, 1966, ND, 19-2/co55 (December 11, 1965–March 11, 1966), Box 74.
[52] LBJPL, Collection: Administrative History of the Department of Justice Volumes 8 and 9, "Cuban Refugees," Folder: Administrative History, Department of Justice, Volume IX INS Part 13, DOT-p21/23, Box 8.

States also admitted these third country entrants independently of immigration regulations that it applied to nationals of those countries.[53]

The Departments of Labor, Justice, and State all supported the extension of parole entry privileges to the third country-based kin of Cubans in the United States.[54] For example, Undersecretary of State George Ball sent a letter in 1966 to then Attorney General Nicholas Katzenbach to request relaxation of the "self imposed limitation on parole of Cuban refugees" to persons immigrating directly from Cuba. He argued that Cubans who previously had been uniquely entitled to parole should have the same right extended to their relatives, wherever those relatives lived.[55] He expressed no concern about the INA specifying that parole only be granted for "urgent humanitarian reasons" or when there was a "significant public benefit," or about the United States thereby privileging Cubans over others who wished to move to America.

Ball argued for the new Cuban entitlement on the grounds that the third-country entrants would make the Cubans already in the United States "less dependent on welfare,"[56] a domestic, not foreign, policy matter. Yet, he offered no explanation of why their admission would reduce earlier Cuban immigrant dependence on welfare. Indeed, their admission could be expected to have the opposite effect. Arriving relatives might well seek welfare as they struggled to adapt to life in the United States.

In turn, the Secretary of State exempted the Cubans in third countries from the Hart–Celler legislation requirement that aspiring immigrants be admitted only if they attained certification that they would not displace US workers from jobs or adversely affect wages of US workers. Nationals of the countries from where the Cubans were immigrating, in contrast, needed the certification to be admitted. The labor certification exemption for Cubans in third countries was an extension of the exemption extended to Cubans who immigrated directly from Cuba.[57]

Thus, the Johnson administration extended unique entitlements to Cubans not only in Cuba but also in third countries. It admitted them irrespective of whether they jeopardized economic opportunities for native-born Americans, and it admitted them independent of immigration regulations applied to nationals of the countries from which they entered.

---

[53] Ibid. [54] Ibid.
[55] LBJPL, Collection: Legislative Background: Immigration Law 1965, Cuban Refugees, Folder: "After the Fact," Box 1.
[56] Ibid.
[57] *Congressional Quarterly Almanac*, "Major Legislation: Foreign Policy," *East-West Trade* 3 (1966): 440.

AN END TO CUBAN IMMIGRATION EXCEPTIONALISM?

Beginning in 1973, President Nixon, followed by President Ford, and President Carter during his first three years in office, appeared to put a stop to Cuban privileging. On taking office, President Nixon did continue the Freedom Flight program he had inherited from President Johnson, though he did so amid mounting congressional criticism of the program's cost. He finally ended the program in 1973, but at Castro's insistence, after over a quarter million Cubans had been airlifted to the United States.[58]

For the remainder of the 1970s, Cuban immigration was unexceptional. The United States admitted only 50,000 Cubans: less, on average, annually than the 20,000 country cap Congress had established for Western Hemisphere countries in the 1976 INA Amendments.

President Nixon did introduce one new entitlement for Cubans, which built on earlier entitlements for Cubans in Spain. In December 1973, he initiated a program to parole 25,000 Cubans who were at the time living in Spain into the United States. The Cubans were to be admitted as refugees, even though they suffered no persecution in Europe.[59] The initiative was reputed to be aimed at generating positive news coverage for the President—although it had no political payoff in that he resigned in disgrace over the Watergate scandal in 1974. It did, nonetheless, entitle yet more Cubans to immigrate.

Then, later in the 1970s, President Carter extended one new entitlement to Cubans, in this instance to Cubans who indeed had suffered persecution. He arranged with the Cuban government to admit over three thousand Cuban political prisoners. Castro agreed to their emigration, after having refused to allow them to leave on Freedom Flights.

USING EXILES, USED BY EXILES: THE "HARD POWER" BAY OF PIGS INVASION[60]

President Eisenhower did not envision that his exceptional welcoming of Cubans would, in itself, bring the Castro-led regime to heel. By 1960 he

---

[58] Volsky, "Cuba Reassessing Refugee Airlift."
[59] RNPL, WHCF, Subject: Co, Folder [Ex] Co 39, Cuba, Memorandum for Ken Clawson, from Anne Armstrong, Subject: Cuban Refugee Flights, December 6, 1973, Box 24.
[60] Because Cubans who fled to the United States after Castro took power refer to themselves as exiles, so do I, in deference to their self-identity. Some of them indeed fled because they felt that their lives were at risk. Many others, however, fled for economic reasons, to take

also turned to new Cuban arrivals to do covertly what he felt his administration could not do overtly on its own: invade Cuba to topple the Castro government by "hard power" means. The Charter of the Organization of American States specified that no state had the right to intervene in the affairs of another state. Cuban émigrés could provide a front.

Already, a few months after Castro took power, Nixon, then Eisenhower's vice president, proposed to train disaffected Cubans to form a guerrilla force for the first stage of a military occupation of Cuba,[61] which the Cuban government viewed as a US orchestrated counter-revolution.[62] Although Nixon failed to convince Eisenhower to pursue the plan, a strong, if not dominant, wing of the expanding Cuban community, who perceived themselves as exiles, solicited US support for every conceivable means to overthrow Castro, including arming and training an invasion force.[63]

A year into Castro's rule, the CIA proposed a secret masterplan, "A Program of Covert Action against the Castro Regime," to overthrow Castro.[64] Cuban exiles were essential to the plan, both to carry it out and to conceal US involvement. The Eisenhower White House approved the CIA's proposal, which was estimated to cost a modest $4.4 million.[65] Especially following widespread international condemnation of CIA involvement in the 1954 coup in Guatemala that ousted democratically elected Jacobo Arbenz,[66] President Eisenhower resisted direct, overt US intervention. The covert plan called for training exiles for guerrilla warfare, if needed; for directing anti-Castro activity on the island; for infiltration and exfiltration of Cubans on the island; for arranging defections; and for assisting in intelligence gathering.[67] A high-level Special Group, also known as the 5412 Committee, oversaw the program.[68] The Special

---

advantage of economic opportunities in the United States and to preserve a lifestyle that the revolution threatened.

[61] Theodore Draper, "Cuba and U.S. Policy," *The New Leader* (June 5, 1961), p. 8, filed in JFKPL, President's Office Files, Cuba-General June 1961–December 1961, Box 114A.

[62] Jesús Arboleya, *Havana Miami: The US-Cuba Migration Conflict* (Melbourne: Ocean Press, 1996).

[63] Draper, "Cuba and U.S. Policy," p. 11.

[64] JFKPL, National Security Files, Cuba-Subjects, Para-Military Study Group, Taylor Report Part III, Annex 1, "Paramilitary Study," March 17, 1960, Box 61A. The goal was to install a government devoted to Cubans more acceptable to the United States.

[65] Ibid. [66] Ibid.

[67] Ibid.; National Security Files: Cuba, Folder: Cuba Para-Military Study Group, Taylor Report Part 1, Memorandum No. 1 (June 13, 1961), Box 61.

[68] The Special Group included high-ranking members of the State and Defense Departments, Eisenhower's Special Assistant for National Security Affairs, and the

The Making of Cuban Immigration Exceptionalism

Group met weekly to review the CIA covert operations that were authorized by the National Security Council.[69]

The CIA proceeded to finance, equip, and train exiles as a paramilitary force. It recruited Cuban exiles who had settled in Florida. By the summer of 1960 the CIA, however, had lost confidence in how effective an exile guerrilla force would be, and thus arranged, in addition, for the Army Special Forces to train exiles as an assault force.[70] Because an armed attack by the United States would violate international law and outrage Latin Americans, no US military personnel were to be used in combat;[71] instead, exiles trained in Guatemala by US Special Forces were to seize a limited land area in Cuba, from where they would trigger an uprising on the island to topple Castro's government.[72] The Guatemalan government provided cover, payback for US support for the 1954 coup that brought it to power.[73] The world was to believe that only disaffected Cubans were involved in the operation.

When assuming the presidency in January 1961, Kennedy not only continued but expanded on Eisenhower's commitment to the CIA-orchestrated plot involving exiles. His administration nearly tripled the number of exiles trained as an invasion force.[74] Although Kennedy had taken an extreme anti-Castro position during his campaign,[75] as president he felt boxed into policies that the Eisenhower Administration had put in place.[76]

There was disagreement within the Kennedy administration about the likely success and legality, as well as the ethics, of an invasion, and concern about the reaction of foreign allies. In the main, the Department of Defense supported the CIA plan,[77] with Secretary of

   Director of the CIA. JFKPL, National Security Files, Cuba-Subjects, Para-Military Study Group, Taylor Report, Part 1, Memorandum No. 1, June 13 1961, Box 61A.
[69] JFKPL, National Security Files, Cuba, Folder: Cuba: Para-Military Study Group, Taylor Report, Part 1, Memorandum No. 1, "Narrative of the Anti-Castro Operation Zapata," June 13 1961, p. 1, Box 61A.
[70] Ibid., p. 3. [71] Ibid., p. 8. [72] Ibid.
[73] JFKPL, National Security Files, Cuba-Subjects, Folder: Para-Military Study Group, Taylor Report Part II, Meetings 19 and 20, "Memorandum for Record Paramilitary Study Group Meeting at the Pentagon 19th Meeting," May 22, 1961, p. 22, Box 61A.
[74] JFKPL, National Security Files: Cuba, Folder: Cuba Para-Military Study Group, Taylor Report, Part 1, Memorandum No. 1, Box 61A; Arthur Schlesinger, *A Thousand Days: John F. Kennedy in the White House* (Boston: Houghton Mifflin, 1965), pp. 229, 267.
[75] Draper, "Cuba and U.S. Policy," p. 22. [76] Ibid., p. 26.
[77] JFKPL, President's Office File, "Memorandum for the President," from McGeorge Bundy (February 8, 1961), Folder C, Security, 1961, Box 115.

Defense Robert McNamara presuming that the new administration was following a well-established previously developed policy.[78] However, others in the administration had reservations.[79] They felt that an invasion was unlikely to be effective and that it would damage US relations with allies. President Kennedy was among the skeptics. He had particular reservations about the air component of the plan,[80] which would make use of US-supplied napalm, bombs, machine guns, and rockets.[81] The president, along with Secretary of State Dean Rusk, worried that the Cuban government, and the broader international community, would attribute air attacks to the United States, rather than to exiles acting on their own, and that the United States, as a result, would be caught violating international law.[82] President Kennedy also worried about the superiority of Castro's forces and about Castro's popularity. Undersecretary of State Chester Bowles and Senator J. William Fulbright, Chair of the Senate Foreign Relations Committee, in turn, worried that a "beachhead operation" could turn Cuba into "our Hungary," and damage the United States even more than the Soviets were damaged by their invasion of the East European country.[83] No matter how Cuban the occupying force, the United States would be held accountable.[84]

Arthur Schlesinger, Special Assistant to the President, had a further concern. Although he opposed the invasion and felt it would "fix a malevolent image of the new administration in the minds of millions,"[85] he was reluctant to stop supporting "the brave men we have gathered in Guatemala." He was concerned that their demobilization would convey

---

[78] Schlesinger, *A Thousand Days*, p. 250.
[79] For an excellent discussion of the views toward the invasion held by high-level functionaries of different branches of the government, see Schoultz, *That Infernal Little Cuban Republic*, pp. 142–69; also, see Schlesinger, *A Thousand Days*, pp. 249–52.
[80] Draper, "Cuba and U.S. Policy," p. 26.
[81] JFKPL, National Security Files, Folder: Cuba-Subjects, Para-Military Study Group, "Narrative of the Anti-Castro Cuban Operation Zapata (June 13, 1961)," p. 23, Box 61A.
[82] Schoultz, *That Infernal Little Cuban Republic: The United States and the Cuban Revolution* (Chapel Hill: University of North Carolina Press, 2009), pp. 152–53. Secretary of State Rusk was particularly concerned that an intervention in Cuba would damage US relations with Latin America.
[83] JFKPL, President's Office Files, Countries-Cuba, Memorandum for the President, Subject: Cuba (April 5, 1961), Folder C: Security, 1961 (February 8, 1961), Box 115.
[84] Ibid.
[85] Cited in Stephen Kinzer, *The Brothers: John Foster Dulles, Allen Dulles, and Their Secret World War* (New York: Henry Holt, 2013), p. 298.

the impression that Washington was abandoning its anti-Castro fight.[86] "Having created the brigade ... its use against Cuba (w)as a necessity."[87] The CIA warned that demobilizing the exiles would create new problems. Exiles might forcibly resist and insist on keeping the CIA-allotted arms and equipment, and Washington would likely be discredited, such that disbandment would encourage pro-Castro revolutions around the Caribbean.[88] Schlesinger argued that the commitment to train exiles called for deploying them, whatever the costs. In essence, earlier commitment called for continued commitment. While Schlesinger recognized the risks of the invasion, he felt that the risks of abandoning the project were greater.[89]

Faced with the concerns, President Kennedy reserved the right to call off air support up to twenty-four hours before the scheduled exile landing in Cuba: a right he proceeded to exercise.[90] Nonetheless, the CIA went ahead with its planned landing of a 1,500-strong exile force, known as Brigade 2506, at the Bay of Pigs on April 17, 1961.[91]

The invasion was an unequivocal debacle, and US involvement was immediately transparent. Rather than the exiles instigating a mass uprising against Castro, Cubans defeated what they conceived as counter-revolutionary forces in a matter of days. Members of the invading brigade were scattered by Cuban artillery, attacked by Cuban bombers, and overwhelmed by Cuban troops.[92] Approximately one hundred exiles died in confrontations with Cuban forces, and the Cuban government took nearly twelve hundred Brigade 2506 members prisoners of war.[93]

Meanwhile, the invasion contributed to the consolidation, as well as radicalization, of the revolution. Within two weeks of the invasion, Castro declared the socialist turn of the initially nationalist revolution,[94]

---

[86] JFKPL, National Security Files, Cuba, Subjects, "Para-Military Study Group," Taylor Report Part 1, Memoranda 1–4, Memorandum No 3, "Conclusions of the Cuban Study Group," (June 13, 1961), p. 2, Box 61A.

[87] Schlesinger, *A Thousand Days*, p. 242.   [88] Ibid.

[89] JFKPL, President's Office Files, Folder: Cuba Security, 1962, Folder 1, Assessment by Arthur Schlesinger, Jr., Box 115.

[90] JFKPL, National Security Files-Cuba ... Narrative of the Anti-Castro Operation Zapata, p. 13, June 13, 1961.

[91] The brigade took its name from the assigned number of the first exile to die in the covert operation. He died in training, in Central America.

[92] Kinzer, *The Brothers*, p. 300.

[93] JFKPL, President's Office Files May 16, 1961–May 31, 1961, telegram FBIS May 21 LEM/RH, Box 114A; Kinzer, *The Brothers*, pp. 30, 302.

[94] Draper, "Cuba and U.S. Policy," p. 29.

and Cubans rallied patriotically against the "imperialists" and "counter-revolutionaries," in defense of the revolution. Further, in defeat, the invasion demoralized opponents of Castro, within as well as outside Cuba. In Cuba, the government crushed the underground with massive arrests. Castro emerged as a hero for having defended Cuba against the most powerful country in the world. And once the CIA's role in the invasion became known, it became a reviled symbol of imperialist intervention.[95] International opinion turned on the United States. Anti-US demonstrations broke out in cities around the world.[96]

The invasion was a costly debacle, financially as well as politically. The Kennedy administration spent markedly more than the $4.4 million that the CIA had projected for the "Program of Covert Action against the Castro Regime." The CIA spent $23 million just on training exiles for the invasion, and after the debacle it paid families of the brigade members who Cuba took hostage (through the to-be-described-later front organization, the Cuban Revolutionary Council) $311,500 monthly[97] It also paid $50,000 for medical treatment for sixty wounded brigade members who the Cuban government had returned to the United States.[98] The United States government, in turn, arranged for the Cuban government to receive approximately $60 million worth of food and medicine to release captured brigade members (paid with donations).[99]

Who was to blame for the costly debacle? The Kennedy administration, Congress, and the CIA were quick to blame the exiles involved in the invasion, rather than themselves, for a badly conceived intervention in the internal affairs of another country. Some US officials blamed exiles for immediately exhausting their ammunition supply in excessive firing on the first day, for failing to maintain discipline within their ranks, and for

---

[95] Kinzer, *The Brothers*, p. 303.
[96] *FRUS* 1961–1963, vol. X, Cuba, January 1961–September 1962, Office of the Historian, #160, "Memorandum," from the Acting Assistant Secretary of State for Inter-American Affairs to Secretary of State Rusk," April 20, 1961, p. 307.
[97] JFKPL, President's Office Files, Cuba General, January 1961–March 1961, "Memorandum for the President," subject: Howard Handleman on Cuba, March 31, 1961, from Arthur Schlesinger, Jr, Box 114A.
[98] JFKPL, National Security Files, Folder: Cuba, Subjects: Exiles-Brigade 2506, "Memorandum for the President," from Office of the Director of the Central Intelligence Agency, Subject: Payments to Dependents for Cuban Brigade Members, July 20, 1962. Open Box 48.
[99] Schoultz, *That Infernal Little Cuban Republic*, p. 169. The Cuban government referred to the deal as indemnification, the US government referred to it as ransom.

weak leadership and general incompetence.[100] They also criticized exiles for disobedience, for not dutifully following orders from Washington, and for failing to keep secret the invasion plans, such that Castro had ample time to plan a counter-attack.[101] In this vein, the director of the CIA Cuba Task Force complained that he had never encountered another group of people so incapable of keeping a secret as exiles.[102] Although the CIA had intended to catch Castro and his militia off-guard, informants within the exile community leaked plans of the invasion to the media.[103] Jacob Esterline of the CIA reported, at a meeting of the Paramilitary Study Group directed by General Maxwell Taylor, that "Cubans can not keep quiet ... (B)efore you knew it we had a Roman Circus on our hands – leaks to the press ... both in Miami and New York."[104]

Exiles, however, had their own grievances. Above all, they blamed the failed invasion on President Kennedy for not providing air support. They felt betrayed, and emerged from the invasion demoralized, disorganized, and disappointed.[105] In the words of a member of Brigade 2506, "We were sent in there to get slaughtered...(the) men running the boats didn't (even) know how to run them, [the] captain didn't know Spanish."[106]

Aside from the blaming, the Kennedy administration was divided about how the United States' Cuba policy ought to proceed in the aftermath of the failed invasion. Neither the Defense Department nor the CIA gave up on ousting Castro with the help of exiles. Within three weeks of the invasion, the Defense Department entertained a larger invasion force, involving 4,000 exiles, which it estimated would cost $100 million a

---

[100] JFKPL National Security Files, Cuba-Subjects, Para-Military Study, Taylor Group Report, Part I, Memorandum 1, June 13, 1961, Box 61A. Independently of the invasion, US officials complained that exile pilots who had been assigned responsibility for supplying arms for a popular uprising were so unqualified that they had difficulty locating the designated drop zone. JFKPL National Security Files, Cuba-Subjects, Para-Military Study Group, Taylor Report Part II, 2nd meeting of Green Study Group, April 24, 1961, General Maxwell Taylor, Memorandum for the Record, p. 8, Box 61A.
[101] Ibid., p. 15.   [102] Kinzer, *The Brothers*, pp. 289, 294.
[103] Schoultz, *That Infernal Little Cuban Republic*, p. 31.
[104] JFKPL Papers of President Kennedy, National Security Files, Cuba-Subjects, Para-military Study Group Taylor Report, Part II, Second meeting of Green Study Group, March 24, 1961, p. 15, Box 61A.
[105] JFKPL National Security Files-Countries, Cuba, Folder: Cuba, Subjects, Exiles, "U.S. Policy Toward Cuban Exiles," Annex III, May 3, 1961 p. 9, Open Box 48.
[106] JFKPL, National Security Files, Cuba-Subjects Para-Military Study Group, Taylor Report, Part II, Meeting 16, May 17, 1961, "Memorandum for Record," Paramilitary Study Group Meeting, p. 11, May 17, 1961, Box 61A.

year,[107] about twenty-four times the amount the CIA had initially projected for its covert undertakings. The Defense Department reasoned that with more exiles an invasion could succeed. However, it never implemented the more ambitious project.

The Secretary of the Army, in turn, proposed the formation of a "Freedom Brigade" within the Army, comprising Cuban "refugee" volunteers who would get Special Forces-type training. The Freedom Brigade was to be a highly trained flexible force that would undertake guerrilla and unconventional operations in Cuba in order to spearhead a US invasion and to assume occupation responsibilities in the post-combat phase. The idea was for US forces to intervene in Cuba but to get in and out of the country quickly, at which point the Freedom Brigade would take over.[108] Yearly costs for Freedom Brigade training were estimated at $23 million. This project was also quickly, as well as quietly, abandoned.

Less ambitiously, the Department of Defense offered qualified exiles career opportunities in the US Armed Forces on a volunteer basis, rather than as an independent unit. However, only eighty-eight exiles signed on.[109] Few exiles were interested once they realized that they would not be trained as a new invasion force that would fight in Cuba.[110] Given the small amount of exile interest, the Department of Defense also abandoned this initiative, in less than a year.

Nonetheless, the Department of Defense did not give up on the possibility of an exile invasion, even after President Kennedy agreed, in the context of the 1962 Missile Crisis, not to invade Cuba, in exchange for Soviet removal of their offensive missiles on the island.[111] In May 1963, for example, Secretary of Defense Robert McNamara informed the president that contingency plans for a Joint-Chiefs-of-Staff-approved invasion of Cuba were up-to-date. Plans were in place to introduce a large number

---

[107] Masud-Piloto, *From Welcomed Exiles to Illegal Immigrants*, p. 48.
[108] *FRUS*, "Action Memo," from NSC to HEW, CIA, State and Defense, p. 316
[109] According to another source that reported the termination of the US Armed Forces program to enlist Cubans, Cuban nationals joined the military between July 1961 and July 1962, 30 of whom were discharged soon after joining because they were either disqualified or lost interest once they learned that they would not serve in Cuban units. *FRUS*, 1961–1963, #426, "Memorandum," from Secretary of Defense McNamara to President Kennedy," September 13, 1962, p. 1060.
[110] *FRUS*, #299, "Memorandum," from the Deputy Secretary of Defense (Gilpatric) to President Kennedy, "Service of Cuban volunteers in U.S. Armed Forces," January 31, 1962, p. 734, and #313 to Chairman of the Joint Chiefs of Staff (Lemnitzer), March 13, 1962, p. 770.
[111] Schoultz, *That Infernal Little Cuban Republic*, pp. 185–89.

of troops and heavy combat equipment quickly.[112] McNamara also noted that the United States would provide military training to interested exiles, but within established units of the military, rather than in separate Cuban units.

The CIA, in turn, did not give up on involving exiles in efforts to oust Castro after the Bay of Pigs debacle. It turned to them for sabotage and underground activity,[113] and for covert intelligence and covert undertakings in Cuba, including for guerrilla operations.[114] With a planned budget of slightly under $14 million for fiscal year 1962, $10 million more than the CIA had initially proposed to President Eisenhower, the CIA focused on mobilizing opposition groups, disseminating propaganda, and overseeing exile paramilitary activity.[115] An ambitious covert project that President Kennedy authorized in November 1961, known as Operation Mongoose, or the Cuban Project, under the directorship of Air Force General Edward Lansdale, focused on undermining the island economy and on turning the population against Castro.[116] Operation Mongoose focused on deploying exiles to disperse anti-Castro propaganda over Cuba, to blow up strategic targets on the island,[117] and to destroy crop production, allegedly to help Cubans liberate Cuba.[118]

The White House and State Department, in contrast, were more tempered about how to proceed after the Bay of Pigs fiasco. They were apprehensive about continued covert engagement in Cuba, especially if it involved exiles. McGeorge Bundy, National Security Advisor to President Kennedy (and subsequently to President Johnson), informed the CIA director that, going forward, support should only be open and overt, and, in the context of the Missile Crisis, the White House mothballed Operation Mongoose. However, Schlesinger informed Secretary of State

---

[112] JFKPL, President's Office Files, Folder: Cuba Security 1963, Memorandum for the President from Robert McNamara, Secretary of Defense. "Contingency Plans for Cuba," May 7, 1963, Box 115.

[113] See FRUS, Ibid., #214, "Memorandum for the Record," May 9, 1961, p. 518, Subject: Meeting with the DD/P re Cuba Operations. The meeting affirmed continued commitment to sabotage and to "commo" training.

[114] JFKPL, Papers of President Kennedy, National Security Files-Cuba, Folder: Cuba, Para-Military Study Group, Taylor Report, Part 1, Memorandum No. 1, p. 1, Box 61A.

[115] FRUS, #251, "Memorandum," from the Deputy Under Secretary of State for Political Affairs (Johnson) to Secretary of State Rusk, July 22, 1961, Subject: Special Group Meeting, July 20, 1961, p. 633.

[116] Schoultz, That Infernal Little Cuban Republic, pp. 176–83.   [117] Ibid., p. 175.

[118] FRUS #377, "Memorandum," from the Chief of Operations, Operation Mongoose (Lansdale) to the Central Intelligence Agency Operations Officers for Operation Mongoose (Harvey)," August 16, 1962, Subject: Actions by Cuban Refugees, p. 939.

Dean Rusk that exiles could and should help oust Castro by mass infiltration of Cuba.[119]

The State Department proceeded to focus on dissident activity *in* Cuba by Cubans, with exile assistance. An internal State Department communication revealed concerns that the United States had been unsuccessful in creating an effective political base of internal opposition on the island, which was attributed to "our practice of 'controlling' and 'managing' the Cuban exiles as individuals" and not taking advantage of them as groups with assets in Cuba. "In effect, we (have) sought to make this a US. show using Cubans."[120] To correct the problem, exile groups with contacts in Cuba were to be nurtured.

In sum, the Eisenhower and Kennedy administrations turned to exiles to topple the Cuban government and conceal US involvement. After the Bay of Pigs debacle, the CIA, the Departments of Defense and State, and the White House did not give up trying to topple the Cuban government with exile assistance. However, they faced exiles with their own agenda, who resisted efforts to control them.

EFFORTS TO UNIFY AND CONTROL EXILES

Under both the Eisenhower and Kennedy administrations, the White House, the State Department, and the CIA tried to work with exile groups in order to unify them. In part, the CIA's "Program of Covert Action against the Castro Regime" addressed this concern, to control them, not to strengthen their power and influence.[121] Yet, exiles cooperated only in so far as they felt that it was in their interests to do so. They did not see themselves as puppets of Washington.

The Eisenhower administration tried to unify the exile community at-large in the FRD, the Frente Revolucionario Democrático. The FRD was to serve as a front organization that incorporated a broad range of Cubans, excluding communists, who were considered incompatible with US interests, and Batistianos, who were considered too tinged by their

---

[119] JFKPL, President's Office File, memo to Rusk from Schlesinger, Appendix A, April 24, 1961, Folder C, Security, 1961," Box 115.
[120] FRUS, #432 "Memorandum," from the Assistant Secretary of State for Inter-American Affairs (Martin) to the Deputy under Secretary of State for Political Affairs (Johnson)," September 19, 1962, pp. 1068–69.
[121] JFKPL, National Security Files, Cuba-Subjects, Para-Military Study Group, Taylor Report Part III, Annex 1, Paramilitary Study, "A Program of Covert Action against the Castro Regime," March 17, 1960, Box 61A.

association with the prerevolutionary government.[122] Organizationally, the FRD formally included five core groups, plus many small groups that were often little more than cliques with self-appointed leaders.[123] The Assistant Secretary of State worked closely with exiles to form the FRD, and to influence its selection of leadership, as well as the activities in which it engaged.[124] The FRD was to command and control its affiliated groups,[125] and provide a nucleus of a military force to spur uprisings in Cuba.[126]

The CIA, however, found the FRD unwieldy to work with.[127] Affiliated exile groups distrusted one another, and competed for power and for US funding. The FRD, moreover, faced difficulty recruiting members. Leaders of affiliated groups reached out mainly only to exiles who they believed would be loyal to them.[128] As a result, the FRD proved ineffective,[129] another failed US effort to use exiles for foreign policy gain.

When assuming office, the Kennedy administration, in turn, tried to unify exiles. During its first month in office it oversaw the formation of a new umbrella organization, the CRC, the Cuban Revolutionary Council. The CRC was more ambitious than the FRD. Headquartered in Miami, it appointed delegates in Latin American countries and Spain, and domestically across the United States.[130] The CRC even claimed to speak for the resistance movement *in* Cuba.[131] The CIA and State Department valued

---

[122] JFKPL National Security Files, Folder Cuba-Subjects, Para-Military Study Group, Taylor Report, Part II, May 22, 1961, "Memorandum for Record," Paramilitary Study Group Meeting at the Pentagon, 19th Meeting, Box 61A.
[123] Draper, "Cuba and U.S. Policy," p. 7.
[124] JFKPL National Security Files, Cuba-Subjects, Para-Military Study Group, Taylor Report, Part II, Annex 3, "Memorandum," Subject: Chronology of the Development and Emergence of the Revolutionary Council, May 17, 196, Box 61A.
[125] The CIA treated FRD leaders as puppets, with Howard Hunt, an intelligence officer who later plotted the Nixon Administration Watergate burglaries, being assigned responsibility for the unification effort. Schoultz, *That Infernal Little Cuban Republic*, p. 151.
[126] JFKPL National Security Files, Cuba-Subjects, Para-Military Study Group, Taylor Report Part II, 2nd Meeting of Green Study Group, General Maxwell Taylor, "Memorandum for the Record," April 24, 1961, Box 61A.
[127] Draper, "Cuba and U.S. Policy," p. 12.
[128] JFKPL, National Security Files, Cuba-Subjects, Para-Military Study Group, Taylor Report Part II, Meeting 21, "Memorandum for Record," Paramilitary Study Group Meeting at the Pentagon," 21st Meeting, May 30, 1961, Box 61A.
[129] Draper, "Cuba and U.S. Policy," p. 306.
[130] JFKPL, National Security Files, Countries-Cuba, Subjects Exiles October 1962, "Counter Revolutionary Handbook," p. II., Folder: Cuba, Open Box 48.
[131] JFKPL, President's Office Files, Cuba Security, 1962, Folder 1 of 2, Box 115, "Types of Covert Action against the Castro Regime," November 1961, Box 115. The goals of the

the organization to provide "singleness of guidance" and coordinated management.[132]

Initially, the CRC served the Kennedy administration well. Its leaders made speeches promoting United States' Cuba policy, and it provided a fig leaf for the invasion.[133] Following the failed invasion, the State Department, the Attorney General's office, and the White House, as well as the CIA, turned to the Miami office of the CRC to serve as a "focal point" through which exile groups would receive guidance, place requests, let off steam, *and* promote US foreign policy concerns.[134] Deputy Assistant Secretary of State for Inter-American Affairs Richard Goodwin made it known that the only exile group with which the State Department would work was the CRC, so as to simplify relations with exiles and unify them, and only on an open, not covert, basis.[135] Goodwin's claims notwithstanding, the CIA covertly funneled money through the CRC to Bay of Pigs Brigade members and their families,[136] and it worked through the CRC to recruit exiles for other subversive activity[137] as well as for the US Army.[138]

Yet, the CRC leadership promoted its own agenda, which included establishing an organizational footing in Cuba to serve as a bedrock for a provisional government that they planned to form following Castro's ousting.[139] In February 1962, they threatened to resign if the Kennedy

---

CRC included overthrowing Castro, reinstatement of the 1940 Constitution in amended form, a call for elections, incentivizing private investment, an agrarian reform that compensated landowners for expropriated land, restoration of properties that Castro's government had nationalized, and outlawing the Communist Party.

[132] *FRUS*, U.S. Department of State, Office of the Historian, *Foreign Relations, 1961–1963* Volume X Cuba (January 1961–September 1962), p. 812.
[133] Draper, "Castro's Cuba," p. 27.
[134] JJFKPL, National Security Files, "Memorandum for Mr. Bundy," Subject: "Cuban Focal Point in the Miami Area," December 29, 1962, Folder: Cuba, Subjects, Exiles-Brigade 2506, Box 48.
[135] *FRUS*, #220, Memorandum from the Secretary of Defense's Special Assistant (Yarmolinsky) to Secretary of Defense McNamara May 18, 1961, Subject: "Memorandum of Conversation," p. 529.
[136] JFKPL, President's Office Files, Countries-Cuba, "Memorandum," from General Godfrey McHugh, January 7, 1963, Box 56.
[137] JFKPL, President's Office Files, Cuba-General April 1, 1961–April 21, 1961, "Types of Covert Action against the Castro Regime," November 8, 1961, Box 115.
[138] JFKPL, National Security Files, Countries-Cuba, Folder: Cuba, Subjects Exiles-Brigade 2506, "White House Fact Sheet, Cuban Nationals in the United States," January 7, 1963, Box 48.
[139] JFKPL, National Security Files, Countries, Cuba, Subject: JMATE Political Events, March 21, 1961, Folder: Cuba, Subjects, Exiles, "Memorandum," for Director of Central Intelligence, Open Box 48.

The Making of Cuban Immigration Exceptionalism

administration refused to provide them with assistance for military action, commando raids, sabotage, and propaganda, all of which they argued were needed to oust Castro.[140]

Despite Kennedy administration backing, the CRC proved no more effective than the FRD. It failed to unify exiles, and it failed to bring about the change in Cuba that its leadership had hoped. Exiles became disillusioned with the CRC, as they had with the FRD. Because the CRC had invested heavily in the invasion, in defeat it lost cachet. Exiles became further disillusioned with the CRC when it stopped funding their affiliated groups, which occurred after it engaged in sabotage that the CIA had not sanctioned. The CIA, in disapproval, slashed CRC funding,[141] and went on to fund groups that were independent of the CRC,[142] which further intensified disunity within the exile community.

The factionalism even had ripple effects in Cuba. As early as February 1962, the White House had been informed that the disunity among exile groups demoralized anti-Castroites on the island.[143] After the Bay of Pigs invasion, the Cuban government contributed to the disunity, in repressing groups with ties to exiles in Miami. As a result, groups in Cuba constantly needed to rebuild and reorganize, which undercut anti-Castro resistance on the island.[144]

Indicative of how the factionalism preoccupied President Kennedy, in a December 29, 1962, speech to a large gathering at the Orange Bowl after Cuba had released exiles it had taken hostage at the Bay of Pigs, he asserted that it was "important that you submerge momentary differences ... to the united end that Cuba is free."[145] Out of concern for bringing order to the exile community, President Kennedy even called for the formation of a "formalized party." According to Kennedy, there

---

[140] *FRUS*, #308, "Memorandum of Conversation," February 27, 1962, Subject: "Cuban Revolutionary Council Spokesmen Stress Need for Military Action to Eliminate Castro Regime," p. 763.
[141] JFKPL National Security Files, Cuba-Subjects, Para-Military Study Group, Taylor Report Part II, "Memorandum for Record," Paramilitary Study Group Meeting at the Pentagon, 19th Meeting, May 22, 1961, Box 61A.
[142] *FRUS*, #259, "Recommendations," p. 650.
[143] JFKPL, President's Office Files, Cuba-General, January 1, 1962–October 22, 1962, "Cuba's Situation Up to February 6, 1962, Box 114A.
[144] JFKPL, National Security Files, Countries-Cuba, Folder: Cuba, Subjects Exiles, 1962, "Counter Revolutionary Handbook," Box 48.
[145] JFKPL, Remarks in Miami, Florida at the Presentation of the Flag of the Cuban Invasion Brigade, December 29, 1962 (www.jfklibrary.org/asset-viewer/archives/JFKPOF/042/JFKPOF-042-014).

were four major parties and about one hundred splinter groups. He may even have underestimated the factionalism in that a report released the following month, in January 1963, noted 415 exile organizations.[146] After the Bay of Pigs debacle, exile groups increased in number but decreased in effectiveness. Groups and organizations formed, broke up, disappeared, and reformed, "in a kaleidoscopic picture which varie(d) from week to week," according to a CIA memorandum.[147]

Groups were unified only in their commitment to oust Castro. They differed in their political and economic philosophy, the strategies that they advocated for overthrowing Castro, and the post-Castro society that they wanted.[148] They also competed for US support,[149] and never trusted one another.[150] A Counter-Revolutionary Handbook noted that rare was the refugee leader who had the selflessness to relinquish his group leadership position by integrating into a single unified group. Exile groups gladly took CIA funds, directly or through front organizations, but they resisted submitting to CIA control.

The CIA's failure to control exiles organizationally, as well as the failed Bay of Pigs invasion it had orchestrated, led the White House in 1963 to rethink the role that the CIA ought to play. McGeorge Bundy recommended to President Kennedy that its role be reduced.[151] At the time of Kennedy's assassination, in November 1963, the exile community remained fragmented and an ineffective instrument of United States' Cuba policy.

Subsequent administrations recognized how fractured the exile community was, but saw no gain in trying to unify it:[152] until Reagan's

---

[146] JFKPL National Security Files, Countries-Cuba, "Counter Revolutionary Handbook," Folder: Cuba, Subjects Exiles, 1962, Box 48.
[147] JFKPL, National Security Files, Countries-Cuba, Folder: Cuba, Subjects Exiles, January 1962–October 1962, CIA Memorandum for General Maxwell Taylor, Military Representative to the President, Subject: Principal Organizations and Personalities within the Cuban Exile Movement, Attachment 1, "Major Cuban Exile Organizations," Box 48.
[148] Ibid.
[149] JFKPL, National Security Files-Countries, Cuba, Folder: Cuba, Subjects: Exiles, "U.S. Policy Toward Cuban Exiles," p. 9, May 3, 1961, Annex III, Box 48.
[150] JFKPL, National Security Files, Cuba, Subjects, Exiles May 1963–June 1963, Memorandum from Department of State, Coordinator of Cuban Affairs, for Mr. McGeorge Bundy, the White House, p. 4, June 20, 1963, Subject: U.S. Position on Cuban Exile Unity, Box 48.
[151] JFKPL, President's Office Files, Folder: "Cuba Security 1963," Memorandum for the President, "Further organization of the Government for dealing with Cuba," from McGeorge Bundy, January 4, 1963, Box 115.
[152] "A Reappraisal of Autonomous Groups," June 1964, Digital National Security Archive, Item CUO1437.

administration, in the 1980s, as detailed in Chapter 4. President Johnson turned his foreign policy focus to defeating the "Communist specter" in Indochina, and, in the Americas, to an invasion of the Dominican Republic where he feared "another Cuba" was in the making. When Nixon assumed the presidency in 1969, Henry Kissinger, his national security advisor (and, subsequently, his, and then, President Ford's Secretary of State), wasted no time in arguing against engagement with exile groups. During Nixon's first month in office, Kissinger sent a memorandum to the president in which he noted that "the exile group is a highly fractionalized one with all kinds of axes to grind. It could be very embarrassing for the White House or you personally to get involved or become identified with any of the exile figures."[153] Similarly, a National Security study reported that exiles could not agree on fundamentals and work together, and no single entity spoke for a sizable segment of the exile community. It also noted that the politically active exiles "manifest egocentricity" and devote most of their efforts to building up their own position with a view to gaining power in a post-Castro Cuba,[154] and that exiles show themselves to be inept in carrying out operations.[155]

Thus, US efforts to control exiles overtly as well as covertly failed. Consequently, in due course Washington shifted from promoting Castro's overthrow to focusing on ways to strangulate the economy and limit Cuba's international influence.[156]

EXILE TERRORIST ATTACKS

Compounding problems from the United States vantage point, some exiles deployed terrorist tactics, which US sources referred to as "pinprick raids." Terrorist attacks initially focused on Cuba, but subsequently also on people in the United States and in Latin America with actual or presumed ties to the Cuban government. With time, presidents and their administrations came to consider the raids, especially those launched

---

[153] RNPL, WHCF, Subject Category CO, Folder [ex] 1039, Cuba (1969–1970), Memorandum for the President, from Henry Kissinger, Subject: Cuban Exiles, January 31, 1969, Box 23.
[154] RNPL, Presidential Materials Staff, National Security Council (NSC), Institutional ("H") Files, H-039, Meetings Files 1969-1974, Senior Review Group Meetings, Folder: Review Group NSSM 32, Cuba, "Annex to National Security Study Memorandum 32: Cuba, Factors Bearing on U.S. Policies," September 23, 1969.
[155] Ibid.
[156] RNPL, H-039, Presidential Materials Staff, NSC, Institutional ("H") Files, Meetings Files 1969-1974, Senior Review Group, Meetings, Folder: Review Group NSSM 32 Cuba, "Situation and Prospects."

from the United States, to be counterproductive to US national interests, and accordingly disapproved of them.

Raids took different forms. In 1959 and 1960 they included Florida-launched bombings of sugar mills that were intended to destroy production of the centuries-old mainstay of the island economy. Raids also involved anti-Castro leafleting over Havana, and delivery of weapons to rebels in Cuba, especially in the Escambray Mountains, where a counter-revolutionary movement organized in the early 1960s.[157]

Although the CIA initially backed exile raids, it did so increasingly less over time. In one memorandum written in 1963 it denied continued involvement in raids, while in another, written six days later, it admitted to directing two exile raids.[158]

Even without CIA support, exiles engaged in raids during Kennedy's presidency. In 1963, for example, the exile groups Alpha 66, the Second Front of Escambray, and the Revolutionary Student Directorate carried out at least seven aggressive hit-and-run raids.[159] They used the raids to transport arms to Cuba for sabotage, guerrilla activity, and uprisings. They struck an oil installation, a power plant, and a lumber mill. Some airstrikes dropped fifty to one hundred pound bombs on sugar *centrales*.[160] Miami-based Orlando Bosch was among the exiles involved in the 1963 bombings, as well as in leafletting Cuba to incite opposition to Castro (subsequently he engaged in other "terrorist" activities as well.[161] Although the raids caused economic damage, they left Castro's hold on power intact.

The disunity among exiles was reflected in the raids, and contributed to their limited impact. Exile groups that sponsored raids fought among themselves, and competed in raids "to earn the glory."[162] Had they joined forces they would likely have been more effective.

---

[157] Schoultz, *That Infernal Little Cuban Republic*, pp. 103–41; JFKPL, National Security Files, Countries, Cuba, Subjects Exiles, Memorandum for Mr. Bundy, from Gordon Chase, White House, Subject: "Pedro Morales: Detained Cuban Exile," April 15, 1963, Folder: April 1963, Box 48.
[158] See JFKPL, National Security Files, Countries, Cuba, Subjects: Exiles April 1963, Box 48.
[159] JFKPL, President's Office Files, Folder: Cuba General, April 1963–November 1963, "List of Raids," Box 115.
[160] JFKPL, President's Office Files, Al Burt, "Success in Secret War against Castro Revealed in Premier's Own Propaganda," *Washington Post* (November 12, 1963), Folder: Cuba, General, June 1963–November 1963, Box 115.
[161] JFKPL, National Security Files, Cuba, Box 61A.
[162] JFKPL, President's Office Files, Telegram Subject: Possible Raid by L-66 against Cuban Target at Cayo Frances on March 21, 1963, Folder: Cuba, Security 1963, Box 115.

The Making of Cuban Immigration Exceptionalism

The stance of the Eisenhower, but especially the Kennedy, administration toward exile raids was ambiguous and contradictory. President Eisenhower initially approved of raids, until advised by his Ambassador to Cuba, Philip Bonsal, that they damaged bilateral relations.[163] In turn, President Kennedy, along with his Secretary of State, became more disapproving of raids after terminating Operation Mongoose. They worried that the raids undermined US national interests in provoking armed reprisals, in convincing the Cuban government to step up repression,[164] and in serving to strengthen Soviet and Cuban Communist Party political control.[165] In 1963, the State Department became especially concerned about exile attacks on Soviet freighters near Cuba.[166] It worried that in retaliation the Soviets might fire on US ships and planes that were surveilling Cuba.[167] Concerned about Soviet retaliation, in September 1963 Kennedy's (and subsequently Johnson's) National Security Advisor, McGeorge Bundy, requested the Attorney General to stop exile "pin-prick raids,"[168] and the INS to prohibit exiles suspected of involvement in raids from leaving the United States, even from leaving Miami.[169] At the same time, though, the Kennedy administration approved covert CIA "low risk sabotage,"[170] and raids launched from third countries that were beyond "our control."[171]

The Kennedy administration, however, proved no more successful in stopping exile raids than in unifying and controlling exiles, or executing a

---

[163] Schoultz, *That Infernal Little Cuban Republic*, p. 111.
[164] JFKPL, National Security Files, "Briefing Paper for the President's Press Conference," September 12, 1963, Subject: Anti Castro Raids against Cuba, Box 61A.
[165] JFKPL, National Security Files, Folder: Cuba, Subjects, Exiles-March 1963, "Activist Exile Groups" Press Conference, March 21, 1963, Box 48.
[166] JFKPL, National Security Files, Folder: Cuba, Subjects, Exiles, Department of State, Director of Intelligence and Research, Memorandum to The Secretary, from Roger Hilsman, Intelligence Note, "Soviet Response to Two Attacks on Their Freighters off Cuba," March 27, 1963, Box 48.
[167] Ibid.
[168] JFKPL, National Security Files, Papers of President Kennedy, Cuba, White House, from Mr. Chase, to Mr. Hatcher, Subject: Raids on Cuba, September 14, 1963, Box 61A.
[169] JFKPL, National Security Files, Memorandum for Attorney General from Robert Hurwitch, Deputy Coordinator of Cuban Affairs, Subject: Actions and Recommendations to Prevent Pin-Prick Raids against Cuba, April 1, 1963, Countries: Cuba, Subjects Files, April 1963, Box 48.
[170] Schoultz, *That Infernal Little Cuban* Republic, p. 215.
[171] JFKPL, National Security Files, Countries: Cuba, subjects, "Memorandum" for Mr. Bundy from Gordon Chase, White House, Subject: Exile Raids from Non-U.S. Territories, September 30, 1963, Box 61A.

successful exile invasion of Cuba.[172] The Coast Guard assessed that it could not detect, much less stop, more than half of all raids.[173] President Kennedy himself acknowledged that the United States lacked the capability to prevent exile raids.[174]

After Kennedy's assassination, White House support for exile raids ended. President Johnson took a tough stance on them,[175] especially as he shifted his foreign policy focus elsewhere,[176] and prioritized domestically on his ambitious anti-poverty and civil rights agenda.[177] He rejected a CIA proposal to resume a Mongoose-like undertaking, and ordered the CIA to mothball its large Miami station, which had worked closely with exiles, including on raids.[178] Opened in 1961 after the shutdown of the US Embassy in Havana, at its peak the Miami station was second in size only to CIA headquarters in Langley, Virginia.

Despite Johnson administration disapproval, in 1968 small groups of exiles staged bombings and other terrorist acts under the label "Cuban Power." Their targets included consulates and airline offices throughout the hemisphere that dealt with Cuba, and ships of countries that traded with Cuba. With the arrest of ringleaders, terrorist acts continued, but less frequently. One of the arrested ringleaders was Bosch, who was associated with acts of sabotage not only, as previously noted, in Cuba, but also in the United States and other Latin American countries.[179]

The administrations of the Republicans Richard Nixon and Gerald Ford, as well as of Democrat Jimmy Carter, were no more supportive of exile raids than President Johnson had been.[180] Against the backdrop of,

---

[172] JFKPL, National Security Files, White House, Folder: Country: Cuba, Subjects: Exiles, July 1963–September 1963, Memorandum for Members of the Special Group, "Raids on Cuba," September 16, 1963, from Gordon Chase, White House, Box 48.

[173] JFKPL National Security Files, Folder: Cuba, Subjects: Exiles April 1963, Memorandum for the Attorney General, from Robert Hurwitch, Deputy Coordinator of Cuban Affairs, Subject: Actions and Recommendations to Prevent Pin-Prick Raids against Cuba, April 1, 1963, Box 48.

[174] JFKPL, National Security Files, Subjects: Exiles, Folder: Cuba, March 1963, Memorandum for the Record, from Carl Kaysen, White House, March 22, 1963, Box 48.

[175] Schoultz, *That Infernal Little Cuban Republic*, p. 239.

[176] For an excellent discussion of the Johnson administration's ambivalent stance on raids, and exile determination for their continuation, see Schoultz, *That Infernal Little Cuban Republic*, pp. 214–26.

[177] Ibid., pp. 202, 218–19.   [178] Ibid., p. 226.

[179] Indicative of exiles' support for terrorist undertakings was that they pressed for Bosch's release when he was arrested.

[180] RNPL, WHSF, Subject Files CO-137-14-2-7, Memorandum to John Ehrlichman, from Henry Kissinger, Subject: Letter from J. Edgar Hoover to John Ehrlichman, January 30, 1969, on Manuel Artime Buesa, Box 23.

The Making of Cuban Immigration Exceptionalism

reputedly, nearly three hundred terrorist acts committed by Cubans, more than half in the United States,[181] Kissinger conveyed to President Nixon that it was not in "our interest" to support or encourage activity that could not succeed and that foreign governments condemned.[182] Kissinger considered the raids to be petty and ineffective in shaking Castro's grip on Cuba, and a thorn in United States–Cuba relations, which he hoped to improve. He recommended that President Nixon not support them. For related reasons, he also advised President Nixon not to acquiesce to pressure from exiles to pardon Bosch, who, in addition to committing the noted terrorist acts, in October 1976 was implicated (though not charged) in the shooting down of a Cuban airliner in transit from Barbados to Jamaica (masterminded by Luis Posada Carriles) that killed all seventy-three passengers aboard.[183]

Against the backdrop of the shootdown, Carter, on assuming the presidency in 1977, issued a Presidential Directive that condemned freelance sabotage raids.[184] The Presidential Directive signaled official US disapproval of raids. However, that did not stop determined exiles from continuing to engage in terrorist acts, albeit with decreased frequency. In 1979, for example, exiles who were opposed to Carter's bilateral bridge-building efforts murdered two Cuban American members of the so-called Committee of 75 that met with Castro and other Cuban officials, in what became known as the Dialogue. Members of the Committee of 75 had successfully convinced Cuban authorities to permit Cuban Americans to be able to visit family in Cuba, which hardline exiles opposed, as well as to release political prisoners.

---

[181] Arboleya Cervera, *Cuba y los cubanoamericanos: El fenómeno migratorio Cubano* (Havana: Fondo Editorial Casa de las Américas, 2013), p. 161.
[182] See source in footnote 180.
[183] RNPL, WHCF: Subject: Cuba ExCo 39, Cuba (1969–1970), Memorandum to Kenneth Cole, from Henry Kissinger, Subject: Letter from J. Edgar Hoover on Orlando Bosch Avila, January 31, 1969, Box 23. The CIA allegedly had advance intelligence about the Cuban airliner bombing. Bosch, who was arrested in connection with the bombing, was acquitted in a trial in Venezuela, after which he moved to Miami, where he lived until his death in 2011. In 1990 President George H. W. Bush pardoned Bosch of all charges in the United States, in response to political pressure that had built up during Cuban American Ileana Ros-Lehtinen's congressional campaign. Jeb Bush, her campaign manager, requested his father to pardon Bosch. Posada Carriles, who was held for eight years while awaiting a final sentence, fled to the United States, where he was charged only for entering the country illegally. He was released on bail in 2007.
[184] Schoultz, *That Infernal Little Cuban* Republic, pp. 289, 290.

CONCLUSION

President Eisenhower set in motion a chain of immigration entitlements for Cubans. He bent entry rules and imagined Cubans in ways that circumvented immigration regulations set by Congress. He hoped thereby to undermine an anti-American nationalist revolution led by Castro ninety miles offshore. In the throes of the Cold War, President Eisenhower conceived Cuban immigration as a "soft power" foreign policy strategy to convince Cubans of the virtues of capitalist democracy. At the same time, the Eisenhower and then the Kennedy administrations turned to Cuban émigrés to carry out covertly a major "hard power" invasion to topple the Cuban government that concealed US involvement.

In a "path-dependent" manner, Presidents Kennedy and then Johnson built on President Eisenhower's outreach to Cuban immigrants. They extended additional entitlements to Cubans, and to ever more Cubans, as they faced new problems and new conditions: committed, as they were, to defeating communism, above all in America's "backyard."

Yet, they faced exiles who sought to use and not merely be used by the United States. Exiles resisted US government efforts to control them, and sponsored terrorist acts to advance the anti-Castro cause as they defined it to be.

Beginning in 1973, President Nixon, almost without exception, and then Presidents Ford and Carter during his first three years in office, appeared to shut the path of Cuban privilege that the Eisenhower, Kennedy, and Johnson administrations had, in succession, expanded. They granted Cubans almost no new immigration entitlements, and reined in entitlements that Cubans had enjoyed until then. The wind-down coincided with their efforts to lessen bilateral tensions and to build cross-border bridges. Presidents and their administrations privileged Cubans when they perceived it in their foreign policy interests to do so, but not otherwise.

With time, most of the Cubans who immigrated acquiesced to Castro's rule and opted to integrate into American society, but without forgetting where they came from and why. The next chapter details how Cubans adapted to what became their new homeland, with generous resettlement benefits.

2

The Privileging of Cuban Immigrants in the United States, 1959–1979

Cuban exceptionalism did not stop at the border, with unique entry rights. The Eisenhower, Kennedy, and Johnson administrations also entitled Cubans to unique benefits after they arrived. Each administration expanded benefits and the number of Cuban beneficiaries, in order to address problems that earlier entitlements had created or left unresolved, plus new issues that arose. While President Eisenhower established the norm of privileging Cubans, he did not make continued privileging inevitable. Rather, his outreach to Cubans predisposed Congress, and subsequent presidents, to follow suit. In the process, ever more Cubans who initially thought they had only temporarily moved to America stayed, aided in their adjustment to America by the special entitlements.

Most Cubans received benefits as "imagined refugees," that is, as persons who successive administrations defined as refugees so that they could qualify for entitlements for which they otherwise could not, and who, as imagined, qualified for more benefits even than "real refugees," that is, persons who had fled persecution or likely persecution, the near-universally agreed definition of refugees. No other immigrants, or even native-born people in need, received comparable entitlements to the incoming Cubans. This chapter describes the benefits that the Cuban arrivals received, and how the benefits helped them adapt, including in comparison to others into whose midst they moved: in the 1960s and 1970s. In turn, the privileging will be shown to have fueled resentments among the US-born, such that Cubans became a domestic and not merely foreign policy concern.

ENTITLEMENT TO UNIQUE REFUGEE BENEFITS AS IMAGINED REFUGEES

The United States entitled Cubans to the most generous benefits ever offered to immigrants. Eisenhower's Republican administration set the stage, but the administrations of Kennedy and Johnson, both Democrats, substantially expanded entitlements for incoming Cubans and expanded the number of Cuban beneficiaries. As in the case of admissions, Cubans received entitlements as imagined refugees: no questions asked, other than where they came from and when.

When Cubans first flocked to Miami in large numbers after Castro came to power, private charities very generously offered them a helping hand, especially the Catholic Church. Even private companies, such as Eli Lilly and Upjohn, helped out. They, for example, supplemented federal funds for a medical training program.[1] However, with the arrival of ever more Cubans, a citizens' committee in Miami appealed for federal assistance.

In October 1960, the Eisenhower administration responded. It funded a Cuban Refugee Emergency Center, modeled on its earlier program for Hungarian refugees. Eisenhower allotted $1 million from the Mutual Security Act Contingency Fund for the new center to cover costs of food, clothing, housing, medical care, and, if Cubans wanted it, relocation assistance.[2] With the Mutual Security Act intended to contain the spread of communism, the source of funding reflected how President Eisenhower viewed Cuban émigrés through Cold War lenses.

The former home of the *Miami News* became the headquarters of the new center for incoming Cubans. Cubans fondly referred to the building as El Refugio (the Refuge), and later as the Freedom Tower, their "Ellis Island." Incoming Cubans flocked there to register for assistance,[3] to which they felt entitled.

---

[1] Maria Cristina García, *Havana USA: Cuban Exiles and Cuban Americans in South Florida 1959–1994* (Berkeley: University of California Press, 1996), pp. 26, 27.

[2] Garcia, *Havana USA*, p. 21.

[3] While the federal government sold the building in 1972, at a time when the first major wave of Cuban immigration tapered off, its symbolic significance to Cubans lived on. Millionaire Jorge Mas Canosa, who led the Cuban American National Foundation until his death in 1997 (see Chapter 5), bought the building to preserve it as a monument to Cuban refugees. Soon after he died the building was sold. Subsequently, it was donated to Miami-Dade College and transformed into a gallery. Reflecting its continued symbolic significance to the Cuban community, when the salsa legend Celia Cruz, who moved to America shortly after the revolution, died, in 2003, she was memorialized at Freedom

When taking over as president, Kennedy built on Eisenhower's initiative, but on a grander scale. Kennedy established what he called the Cuban Refugee Program (CRP), for all Cubans who arrived in the United States in 1959 or subsequently. The CRP targeted more Cubans and offered them a broader range of entitlements than Eisenhower's Cuban Refugee Emergency Center had. Kennedy immediately increased four-fold the Mutual Security Act Contingency Fund monies for Cuban arrivals.[4] Then, in 1962 he signed into law the Migration and Refugee Assistance Act (P.L. 87-510), which, among its provisions, formalized assistance to Cubans. Kennedy relegated responsibility for administrating the CRP to the Department of Health, Education, and Welfare (HEW). HEW, in turn, allotted funds to state and local public agencies that worked with the incoming Cubans.

After the 1961 Bay of Pigs debacle President Kennedy further expanded assistance to Cubans. He proposed a near six-fold increase in funds for them for fiscal year 1962 and a nine-fold increase for the following year, compared to the amount President Eisenhower had allotted.[5] He hoped thereby to convince Cuban émigrés who had felt betrayed by his refusal to provide air support for the Bay of Pigs invasion of his commitment to them.[6] He envisioned that the CRP would both help Cubans adapt to America and, at the same time, train them for serving in a post-Castro government. His administration even envisioned that the CRP would serve as immigrant bait, to lure other Cubans to America, on

Tower. And Senator Marco Rubio, son of Cuban immigrants, who later in this book will be shown to become one of the most nationally influential Cuban Americans, in 2015 launched an unsuccessful presidential campaign there.

[4] "Revised Cuban Refugee Program, April 29, 1961" *Digital National Security Archive, collection: Presidential Directives PDOO687;* JFKPL (John F. Kennedy Presidential Library), Abba Schwartz Papers, Box 7, Folder: Statement by Dean Rusk, "Statement by Secretary of State Dean Rusk before the Senate Subcommittee on Refugees and Escapees," July 14, 1966, Box 7.

[5] "Revised Cuban Refugee Program"; John Thomas, "Cuban Refugees in the United States," *International Migration Review* vol. 1 no. 2 (Spring 1967): 49; Félix Masud-Piloto, *From Welcomed Exiles to Illegal Immigrants* (Lanham, MD: Rowman & Littlefield, 1996), p. 53; JFKPL, Abba Schwartz Papers, folder: Chapter 6, Drafts, Box 12; Silvia Pedraza-Bailey, *Political and Economic Migrants in America* (Austin: University of Texas Press, 1985), p. 42.

[6] "Revised Cuban Refugee Program." The CRP provided institutional as well as individual funding. In particular, it reimbursed public school systems with heavy concentrations of Cuban children (especially in Miami-Dade County, but also in Union City and West New York, New Jersey); JFKPL, National Security Files: Countries, Cuba, Folder: Cuba, Subjects: Exiles, "U.S. Policy toward Cuban Exiles, Annex B: Revised Cuban Refugee Program," May 3, 1961, Box 48; García, *Havana USA*, p. 37.

the presumption both that a large brain drain would cause the Castro-led government to collapse and a mass exodus would turn world opinion against the revolution. The mass exodus would temper international criticism of the United States for having imperialistically meddled in Cuba's internal affairs when invading Cuba.[7]

The CRP offered Cuban families as much as $100 in monthly cash assistance, plus food (surplus commodities), health care, funds for summer camps for children, courses in English, basic, vocational, and adult education, and grants and interest-free loans for college studies. In addition, it offered job training and job placement services, and professional retooling, especially for Cuba-trained doctors and lawyers, to enable them to qualify for licensing in the United States. No other immigrants or refugees received comparable entitlements.

On assuming the presidency, Johnson initially reduced, but then expanded, CRP funding. He decreased the funding when Cuban immigration briefly tapered off. However, when initiating the Freedom Flights he increased CRP funding beyond Kennedy administration levels. In his penultimate year in office, the budget allotted to the CRP reached $70.6 million,[8] and in his last year he issued Presidential Determination No. 68, which transferred an additional $1,800,000 funds to the CRP (drawing on the Foreign Assistance Act), to address "unexpected refugee and migration needs" of Cubans. In two years he allotted more than seventy times the funds that President Eisenhower had allotted to assist Cubans.[9] President Johnson expanded funding, including on a per capita basis, when 3,000 to 4,000 new Cubans began to arrive monthly on the Freedom Flights he initiated, with greater needs than the first Cubans who immigrated. The percentage of Cuban entrants, for example, who received public assistance rose from 14 to 21 under Johnson's presidency,[10] partly because the newcomers were, on average, older, less educated, and less fluent in English than the first Cubans who fled the revolution. Because many of the first arrivals were middle and upper

---

[7] Masud-Piloto, *From Welcomed Exiles to Illegal Immigrants*, p. 50; JFKPL, National Security Files: Countries, Cuba, Folder: Cuba, Subjects: Exiles, "U.S. Policy Toward Cuban Exiles."
[8] Thomas, "Cuban Refugees in the United States," p. 49.
[9] President Johnson allotted funds from the Foreign Assistance Act.
[10] Department of Health Education, and Welfare (HEW), Social and Rehabilitation Service, "Analysis of Federal Expenditures to Aid Cuban Refugees," Report to the Subcommittee to Investigate Problems Connected with Refugees and Escapees, Committee on the Judiciary, U.S. Senate, by the Comptroller General of the U.S., November 3, 1971, p. 13.

class,[11] they moved to America with more human and social capital, and, if they had been able to take savings with them, also with more financial assets.[12]

While he was fiscally (and politically) more conservative than Presidents Kennedy and Johnson, President Nixon, Johnson's Republican successor, initially continued the CRP. He even increased CRP funding beyond that of the Johnson administration, to approximately $145 million in 1973.[13] If the program initially had been driven by foreign policy concerns, Nixon envisioned it also to have domestic political payoff: to help solidify political support among recently enfranchised Cuban immigrants. He envisioned Cubans as serving his agenda of transforming the south into a Republican stronghold.[14] However, in his last year in office CRP funding was slashed, when the Freedom Flights ended. CRP expenditures had triggered heated debate in Congress that contributed to a cutback in the program's offerings.[15]

The CRP had been premised on a unique, inclusionary definition of a refugee: anyone who left Cuba after Castro assumed power, even if they came for economic reasons. All Cubans who registered at the Cuban Refugee Emergency Center in Miami qualified for CRP programs, including those who were admitted with temporary parole, student, and "indefinite voluntary departure" status.[16] Many more Cubans thereby qualified for CRP offerings than would have been the case if Washington had applied the near-universally accepted more restricted criterion for refugee status, namely someone who fled actual or likely persecution. Even the more than quarter million Cubans admitted to the United States on the Johnson administration-initiated Freedom Flights, on the basis of family reunification, as well as unauthorized Cuban entrants, qualified for the CRP. They benefited from America's historically most generous refugee program as imagined refugees, at a time when the United States offered no program to assist "real" refugees (or immigrants).

---

[11] Eckstein, *The Immigrant Divide*, p. 16.
[12] Ibid. and references therein; Alejandro Portes and Alex Stepick, *City on the Edge: The Transformation of Miami* (Berkeley: University of California Press, 1993).
[13] Pedraza-Baily, *Political and Economic Migrants in America*, p. 42.
[14] Maurice Labelle, "An Election Post Mortem," *Coral Gables Times* (November 12, 1970). RNPL (Richard Nixon Presidential Library), WHCF (White House Central Files), Subject Category CO, Folder: (ex)(039), Cuba (1969–1970), Box 23.
[15] Masud-Piloto, *From Welcomed Exiles to Illegal Immigrants*, p. 68.
[16] Thomas, "Cuban Refugees in the United States," p. 57.

CRP goals which, in principle, justified the generous offerings, were somewhat contradictory. On the one hand, the CRP focused on helping Cubans become self-supporting and adapt well to the United States. On the other hand, another of its goals was to prepare beneficiaries to assume leadership positions in a post-Castro US-friendly government. With time, the CRP addressed the first, but not the second, goal. The diversity of program offerings helped Cubans adjust to America, and adjust well, as detailed later in this chapter. It gave them a jump-start in the world of work. However, many of the first arrivals undoubtedly would have done well without the costly program, in light both of the assets with which they came and having settled in Miami, which offered extraordinary economic opportunities as the city transformed from a small tourist destination for "snowbirds" into a metropolis with global, especially hemispheric, reach.[17]

All told, the CRP provided approximately $1 billion in assistance to Cubans. The education, public assistance, and Freedom Flights components of the Program consumed 90 percent of the funds, with the cost of the airlift, alone, having doubled between fiscal years 1968 and 1972.[18] Over 700,000 Cuban immigrants benefited from the CRP.[19] They acquired skills and leadership training that they could draw on/in the United States, though not in a post-Castro Cuba, as initially conceived.

With the shutdown of CRP offerings, the era of exceptional entitlements for arriving Cubans appeared to have run its course: all the while that the Castro-led government became firmly entrenched in power, the revolution increasingly institutionalized. In 1976, Cuba implemented a new constitution and a new system of governance from the national to the local level, under the aegis of Cuban Communist Party rule, the only political party permitted since the mid-1960s.

ENTITLEMENT TO A UNIQUE PATH TO LAWFUL PERMANENT RESIDENCY AND CITIZENSHIP

While the CRP provided Cubans with unique access to resources to adapt to America economically, it did not entitle them to political rights. Presidents Eisenhower and Kennedy, and Johnson during his first years

---

[17] Eckstein, *The Immigrant Divide*, pp. 69–87.
[18] HEW, "Analysis of Federal Expenditures to Aid Cuban Refugees," pp. 1, 2.
[19] Masud-Piloto, *From Welcomed Exiles to Illegal Immigrants*, p. 54.

in office, officially only granted Cubans temporary residency rights, the only immigration authority they commanded.

In 1962, when Kennedy first paroled large numbers of Cubans into the country, the Senate did entertain a bill to permit the new arrivals to adjust their status and become lawful permanent residents. The bill would have given Cubans their own unique path to citizenship, distinct from that of other immigrants. However, it received insufficient support to pass.

Three years later, after Johnson assumed the presidency, Congress considered yet other legislation to permit Cubans to adjust their status, in the context of the omnibus Hart–Celler immigration bill. However, as described in Chapter 1, President Johnson agreed to delete the provision that would have allowed Cubans to become lawful permanent residents, in order to obtain sufficient congressional support for the omnibus immigration bill.

Concern with Cubans' in-limbo status nonetheless continued, including on President Johnson's part. By 1966 some 164,000 Cubans, more than half of those in the United States, were without permanent residency rights: approximately 71 percent of them held parole status, and 29 percent held "indefinite voluntary departure" status.[20] Then, beginning December 1965 the Johnson administration paroled 3,000 to 4,000 new Cubans into the country monthly on the Freedom Flights, with no rights to permanent residency. During the first year of the Freedom Flight program, 45,000 Cubans were paroled into the country, more than one-third the total number of Western Hemisphere immigrants that the Hart–Celler Act permitted entry in one year.

Against this backdrop, in 1966 Congress deliberated the Cuban Refugee Adjustment Act, P.L. 89-732.[21] The bill, which subsequently came to be known as the Cuban Adjustment Act (CAA), and how it is referred to in this book, allowed Cubans with temporary entry rights to adjust their status, without having to leave the country to apply from abroad. The Hart–Celler legislation, as noted in Chapter 1, required people from the Western Hemisphere to apply abroad for permanent residency rights.

---

[20] See *Congressional Record*, Volume 112, Part 14, U.S. Senate, August 10, 1966, p. 18930; *Congressional Record*, U.S. House of Representatives (September 19, 1966), pp. 22913–21.

[21] See Public Law 89-732, November 2, 1966 (HR 151831) "To adjust the status of Cuban refugees to that of lawful permanent residents."

Unlike when the Hart–Celler Act was under consideration, the Johnson administration determinedly lobbied for P.L. 89-732, to amend section 245 of the Immigration and Nationality Act, in order to enable Cubans admitted, inspected, or paroled into the United States to become lawful permanent residents (LPRs). Modeling the proposed law on special legislation passed under the Eisenhower administration for Hungarian refugees who had been paroled into the country, President Johnson had high-ranking members of his administration advocate for the bill. They advanced a range of arguments at congressional hearings to convince Congress to pass the bill,[22] which Secretary of State Dean Rusk defined as "high priority."[23] The CAA became Cubans' most exceptional and long-lasting entitlement. Passage of the bill was not inevitable, but it addressed a key problem that earlier Cuban privileging had generated and left unresolved: The long-term residency rights of Cubans admitted only with temporary entry rights. In backing the bill, the Johnson administration built on the precedent established by the Eisenhower and Kennedy administrations, of extending unique rights to Cubans. Alternatively, the Johnson administration might have kept Cubans in their in-limbo status until they could be repatriated without risk that they would face persecution.

Johnson administration cabinet members advanced a range of arguments to convince Congress to enact the bill. As with the CRP, the CAA privileged Cubans on the premise that they were refugees, without requiring them to provide evidence that they had fled actual or likely persecution.

One set of arguments made by testifying members of the Johnson administration at the hearings centered on foreign policy concerns that were consistent with the initial rationale for privileging Cubans. A Department of Justice spokesperson argued that Cubans should be granted the right to adjust their status, and be able to do so from within the United States, "because of the upheaval in their native country causing them to flee."[24] Secretary of State Rusk argued that the law implied

---

[22] Unless otherwise indicated, I draw on testimony presented at the 1966 Cuban Refugee Adjustment Act Congressional hearings.
[23] U.S. Congress, House of Representatives, "Adjustment of Status for Cuban Refugees," Hearings before subcommittee no. 1 of the Committee on the Judiciary, 89th Congress, 2nd session, H.R. 15182 & 15183, volume 112, part 14, and U.S. Senate, August 10, 1966: 18930 [testimonies by Ball, Heymann, Katzenbach, Hennessy, Winston, Thomas].
[24] Ibid.

neither recognition nor permanence of the Cuban government. He thereby preempted an argument that congressional opponents of Cuban status adjustment enabling legislation had made in the past.[25]

Other arguments that high-level Johnson administration officials made focused on domestic concerns, which highlighted how as early as 1966 Cuban privileging had come to be perceived as more than a foreign policy matter. In this vein, some Johnson administration personnel who testified at the hearings argued for passage of the legislation on practical and humanitarian grounds.[26] Ellen Winston, Commissioner of Welfare at the Department of Health, Education, and Welfare (HEW), for example, argued that Cuban parolees would benefit economically from the status adjustment. In her words, they experienced financial hardship because of the "underemployed position in which they were forced to work."[27] In that some states restricted professional licensing to lawful permanent residents, "green card" holders, and citizens, the proposed legislation would increase Cubans' employment options.[28]

Ramsey Clark, Deputy Attorney General, made a different pitch: to compassion. He argued that with LPR status more Cubans could attain higher education. They would be "in a position to enjoy the advantages of in-state resident students at various institutions of learning."[29] Lawful permanent residents qualified for subsidized, in-state college tuition rates.

In a further appeal to compassion, Ramsey Clark argued that it was time-consuming and a financial burden for Cubans to have to go abroad to apply for permanent residency rights. The Hart–Celler legislation requirement, that temporary entrants from Western Hemisphere countries needed to apply for permanent residency rights from outside the United States, imposed, in his words, a "useless burden" on Cubans, which, he claimed, lawmakers who supported the 1965 legislation had

---

[25] *Congressional Record*, House of Representatives September 19, 1966, pp. 22914, 22917.
[26] *Congressional Record*, House of Representatives September 19, 1966, p. 22914.
[27] U.S. Congress, House of Representatives, Adjustment of Status for Cuban Refugees: Hearings before subcommittee no. 1 of the Committee on the Judiciary., 89th Cong., 2nd sess., p. 19700; See also Roland Estevéz, "Modern Application of the Cuban Adjustment Act of 1966 and Helms-Burton: Adding Insult to Injury." *Hofstra Law Review* vol 30 (2002), p. 1278.
[28] Estevéz, "Modern Application of the Cuban Adjustment Act of 1966 and Helms-Burton."
[29] LBJPL, Personal Papers of Ramsey Clark, Folder: Personal papers August 16, 1966 Immigration-Cuban Adjustment Act "Statement of Ramsey Clark Deputy Attorney General (AG) before Immigration Subcommittee Senate Judiciary Committee on S. 3712 Immigration," Box 96.

not intended. While some 75,000 Cubans had taken on the "time consuming financial burden" of going abroad to apply for immigration visas, the proposed law, in Clark's words, would rectify "the capricious circumstance."[30] Nonetheless, neither Clark nor any other Johnson administration official who testified at the hearings argued that other Latin Americans in the United States who aspired to become lawful permanent residents should similarly be spared the costs and inconvenience of leaving the country to apply for immigration visas. The Johnson administration officials who testified focused their concern on entitlements for Cubans.

Members of the Johnson administration also argued that the CAA should be passed for reasons of justice, to correct an unjust immigration requirement.[31] In this vein, Commissioner of Welfare Winston argued in her testimony that it was "unfair" for Cubans to have to leave the United States to attain immigration visas.[32] Yet, she too voiced no concern that the proposed legislation would unfairly privilege Cubans over other Western Hemisphere people who, if they wanted to have their status adjusted, needed to leave the United States to apply.

Cabinet members even argued that Cubans had the *right* to in-country status adjustment. Secretary of HEW John Gardner noted, *after* enactment of the CAA, that Cubans had a unique right to lawful permanent residency. In his words, "The Cuban refugees ... well earned the right to become permanent residents." He added that he was pleased that the new law "makes it possible for (Cuban) refugees who so desire to establish permanent residence as a first step towards citizenship." However, he never specified why Cubans should be uniquely singled out for the right.[33]

High-ranking members of the Johnson administration also argued that the CAA would be fiscally wise. Ramsey Clark spoke to this matter as well. He argued that with permanent residency status, Cubans would reduce federal agency financial expenditures in that they would be better positioned to qualify for employment, and thus have less need for welfare

---

[30] Ibid.
[31] Estevéz, "Modern Application of the Cuban Adjustment Act of 1966 and Helms-Burton"; *Congressional Record*, U.S. House of Representatives September 19, 1966, p. 22914.
[32] *Congressional Record*, U.S. House of Representatives September 19, 1966, p. 22915.
[33] LBJPL, Collection: National Security-Defense Ex ND 19 Korean War Folder ND 19-2/CO, Memorandum for the President from Secretary Gardner, HEW November 29, 1966, Draft Release for the White House, Box 418.

or job training.³⁴ Like Commissioner of Welfare Winston, Clark focused on states that limited certain employment to permanent residents and citizens. Yet, while Winston argued that Cubans who were unable to attain professional licenses faced underemployment, Clark claimed that without passage of the CAA, Cubans would be a fiscal burden because they would not have work and thus would draw on costly government programs for the unemployed.

In turn, Undersecretary of State George Ball argued that the CAA would be useful from an administrative vantage point. He claimed that the American consulates in Mexico and Canada, the closest countries where Cubans could go to apply for immigration visas, were understaffed to handle Cuban requests for immigration applications. With the US Embassy in Havana closed since 1961, Cubans could not apply from Cuba before moving to the United States. However, Ball's claims about Mexico were questionable.³⁵

If the US Embassy in Mexico indeed faced difficulty processing visas for Cubans, the "Immigration Service," the Immigration and Naturalization Service, reported the situation differently. It informed the State Department that between 1963 and 1965 most Cubans needed to wait no more than six to eight weeks in Mexico for immigration visas, which the State Department considered "a relatively short period of time."³⁶ Then, in 1967, Hugh Whitaker of the Bureau of Security and Consular Affairs in the Department of State noted that Cubans who qualified for visas were accepted immediately. In his words, "There is no waiting period after they have all the required documents and clearances from the Department of State in Washington."³⁷ Were the bureaucratic hurdles manageable, the Undersecretary of State did not make that known when testifying.

Members of the Johnson administration who testified at the hearings also argued that the legislation would be good for America, not merely for

---

³⁴ LBJPL, Collection: Personal Papers of Ramsey Clark, Folder: Personal Papers Aug 16, 1966, Immigration: Cuban Adjustment Act, "Statement of Ramsey Clark."
³⁵ Between March 1963 and December 1964 over 1,000 Cubans were apprehended at the US–Mexican border. Under-staffing at US consulates in Mexico purportedly contributed to Cuban attempts to enter the United States visa-less, across the Mexican border.
³⁶ LBJPL National Security File, Country File Latin America, Cuba, Folder: "Refugees October 1963–January 1965, "Communication to Embassy Mexico from State Department, about Visas: Cuban Refugees," Dec 15, 1964, Box 30.
³⁷ LBJPL National Security-Defense Gen ND 19-2/CO, Folder: ND 19-2/CO 55, Letter from Hugh Whitaker, Special Assistant, Bureau of Security and Consular Affairs, to Max Santana of *El Cubano Libre*, Mexico City February 27, 1967, Box 419.

Cuban immigrants. Commissioner of Welfare Winston claimed that the United States would be the real benefactor since Cubans brought professional and occupational skills not fully utilized because of their parole status.[38] By way of example she noted that in states that restricted professional medical licenses to permanent residents and US citizens, Cuba-trained physicians could only work as interns. She considered that "tragic" for communities in great "need of increased medical facilities," a point Wilbur J. Cohen, Undersecretary of HEW at the time, also stressed.[39]

In arguing that the CAA would be good for America, Commissioner Winston alleged that the law would not jeopardize work opportunities for non-Cubans. Noting that the bill was directed at Cubans who were already in the United States, she claimed it would not "adversely affect employment opportunities of U.S. citizens who are unemployed."[40] This testimony was disingenuous in that the administration, at the time, was paroling some 3,000–4,000 Cubans a month into the country, many of whom needed work and would compete with non-Cubans in the labor market: a particular concern of African Americans in Miami, where incoming Cubans mainly settled, as detailed later in this chapter. Even if Cubans displaced native-born workers, they were to qualify for the proposed status adjustment rights.

The top-ranking Johnson administration officials who testified helped convince Congress to pass the Cuban status adjustment enabling legislation, their disingenuous claims notwithstanding. On November 2, 1966, Congress enacted the Cuban (Refugee) Adjustment Act. The vote in the House of Representatives was 300–25, and in the Senate the legislation passed by voice vote, unchallenged. The executive branch lobbying broadened the appeal of the law, in stressing domestic, and not merely foreign policy, pay-offs.

The CAA specified that Cubans who had been inspected and admitted, or paroled, into the United States since January 1, 1959, and had been physically present for at least two years, could become lawful permanent residents, at Attorney General discretion. Subsequent chapters will show that for the next fifty years the Attorney General's office used its

---

[38] U.S. Congress, House of Representatives, Adjustment of Status for Cuban Refugees: Hearings before subcommittee no. 1 of the Committee on the Judiciary, 89th Cong., 2nd sess., p. 19700.
[39] Estevez, "Modern Application of the Cuban Adjustment Act of 1966 and Helms-Burton," p. 1279.
[40] *Congressional Record*, House of Representatives September 19, 1966, p. 22915.

discretionary authority to permit Cubans admitted with temporary entry rights to adjust their status.

Thus, Cubans' unique temporary entry rights became bedrock for the new privileging. Nearly all Cubans who touched US soil were paroled into the country, and, then, on the basis of the CAA, awarded lawful permanent residency and associated rights. They did not need to compete with other foreign-born people for the limited number of immigrant visas the United States awarded annually, on the basis of the preference system.

UNIQUE RIGHTS FOR CUBANS EMBEDDED IN THE CUBAN ADJUSTMENT ACT

Remarkably, the CAA did not merely provide the basis for Cubans to transform their temporary into permanent residency rights. The law included a bundle of additional entitlements for Cubans.

First, as noted, the CAA exempted Cubans from the Hart–Celler legislation requirement that aspiring Western Hemisphere immigrants needed to apply for lawful permanent residence from outside the United States. Some legislators had supported the CAA specifically for this reason, out of concern that were Cubans in the United States to return to Cuba to apply they were likely to face persecution. While Cubans who had left for America might, at the time, indeed have faced persecution if they returned to Cuba, they could have applied for lawful permanent residence from Mexico or another country, as some 75,000 Cubans had. Moreover, the CAA remained in effect after Congress passed the 1976 INA Amendments that allowed peoples from the Western Hemisphere who were in the United States to apply for legal permanent residence without leaving the country. The 1976 Amendments, in essence, undermined a key rationale for the CAA, namely, to allow Cubans to adjust their status in the United States.

The CAA, in addition, exempted Cubans from the need for Labor Department certification that they would not displace native-born people in the work force. The Hart–Celler reform, which had been passed the preceding year, required immigrants to attain such certification.

In addition, in conjunction with the CAA the INS issued a precedent decision that held Cubans not to be statutorily precluded from eligibility for adjustment of status if a public charge, even though the INA denies public charges rights to lawful permanent residency. The CAA, as interpreted by the INS, thus exempted Cubans from a basis of exclusion to which all other nationals were subject.

In turn, until 1976 the CAA entitled Cubans to "first dibs" to Western Hemisphere immigration slots. Cubans who were granted lawful permanent residency were charged to the yearly regional admission quota of 120,000 that was specified in the Hart–Celler Act. Thus, the more Cubans that were granted lawful permanent residency on the basis of the CAA, the fewer people were eligible from other countries in the region. However, the 1976 INA amendments allowed for the admission of Cubans independently of the regional quota. Cubans thereby circumvented the multi-year immigration visa queue that other aspiring immigrants faced (involving more than a ten-year wait, for example, in the case of Filipinos, Mexicans, and Chinese).[41]

The CAA entitled Cubans to the unique rights on the premise that they were refugees, even though they were admitted independently of the seventh preference category of the Hart–Celler legislation that capped yearly global admissions of persecuted peoples at 10,200. The CAA imposed no cap on the number of Cubans that the United States admitted, and did not require Cubans to demonstrate that they had fled persecution.[42]

The CAA, in turn, was inclusionary in the Cubans it specified to be eligible for status adjustment. It entitled persons who came directly from Cuba, as well as persons of Cuban origin who immigrated to the United States from third countries, to the right to adjust their status. The CAA even entitled non-Cubans who were engaged or married to Cubans, and children of Cubans regardless of the country of their citizenship and place of birth, to lawful permanent residency rights, if inspected, admitted, or paroled into the United States. Here, the CAA built on the Johnson administration's "territorial stretching" of parole entry rights to relatives of Cubans in the United States who lived in third countries (described in Chapter 1). In essence, the CAA treated relatives of Cubans as if they were Cuban even when they were not, just as Cubans were imagined as

---

[41] David Abraham, "The Cuban Adjustment Act of 1966: Past and Future," Lexis 2015, Emerging Issues 7331 (2015).

[42] The CAA routed Cubans around the asylum process. Heather Kolinsky, "A Fine Line, Redefined: Moving toward More Equitable Asylum Policies," Baltimore Law Review vol. 40 (2010–2011), p. 660; Note (no author), "The Cuban Adjustment Act of 1966: Mirando por los Ojos de Don Quijote or Sancho Panza?," Harvard Law Review vol. 111 (2000–2001), pp. 906, 907. On the CAA, see also LBJPL, Collection: Administrative History Department of Justice Vol. 9, INS, Part 3, Folder: Cuban Refugees, Box 8/OR Office of White House Press Secretary, "Cuban Refugees," Statement by the President, November 10, 1966.

refugees even when they did not meet near-universally accepted criteria for refugee status.

The CAA packet of entitlements also included a fast-track to citizenship. Cubans could have their application date for immigration status adjustment set either to the date that they were paroled into the country or to a date thirty months prior to when they filed their application. They thereby were granted a retroactive starting date for the five-year waiting period for citizenship. In contrast, other nationals qualified for citizenship only after five years as lawful permanent residents. Cubans could even have half of the five-year waiting period for citizenship waived, which enabled elderly Cubans to qualify sooner for Medicare, made available only to US citizens,[43] and all Cubans over eighteen to vote sooner than would otherwise have been possible.[44]

To Cubans' further advantage, the CAA contained no expiration date. All earlier refugee legislation, described in Chapter 1, included end-dates. Representative William Cahill of New Jersey was one of the few congressmen to question the open-ended terms of the CAA. In his words, "There would be no termination, and there could be an unlimited number." He added that Cubans "will love the way we live and won't want to go back to their native land. We are really closing our eyes to reality if we expect that these people will return to the conditions from which they have come ... (and we are) setting a precedent which will have far-reaching effects in the future."[45]

Congressman Cahill's warning notwithstanding, Undersecretary of State Ball admitted that he deliberately left open whether the new legislation would apply to the thousands of Cubans that the Johnson administration was airlifting monthly into the United States.[46] Even President Johnson acknowledged, though only after signing the CAA, that he anticipated the bill would apply not only to the Cubans already in the United States but also to the 3,000–4,000 new Cubans his administration was admitting monthly on Freedom Flights: "as long," in his words, "as the stream of refugees continues ... "[47] In omitting an expiration date

---

[43] García, *Havana USA*, p. 42.   [44] Prior to 1971 the minimum age to vote was 21.
[45] U.S. Congress, House of Representatives, "Adjustment of Status for Cuban Refugees," Hearings before Subcommittee no. 1. of the Committee on the Judiciary, 89th Congress, 2nd session, pp. 18–19.
[46] Richard Eder, "Ball Urges Immigrant Status for Cuban Refugees," *New York Times* (August 11, 1966): 12.
[47] *Public Papers of the Presidents of the United States: Lyndon B. Johnson 1966* Book II, p. 1364.

legislators reinterpreted a law that Congress had initially conceived for Cubans who were already *in* the United States, not for newcomers. In essence, legislators crafted the law to entitle Cubans on an ongoing basis to a unique path to lawful permanent residency.

The CAA in its final form, inclusionary in the Cubans it entitled to adjust their status, was more exclusionary of the nationals to whom it applied than was the law when initially proposed and deliberated. First, in an early version of HR 15183, which became the basis of the CAA, Dominicans who moved to the United States between April 24, 1965 and June 2, 1966, displaced by the Johnson administration Dominican military intervention, also were to be granted the same status adjustment rights as Cubans: the intervention, noted in Chapter 1, ousted a popularly elected reformist president who President Johnson perceived as possibly becoming "another Castro" in America's "backyard." However, the Conference Committee that addressed differences between the House and Senate versions of the proposed legislation dropped the status adjustment entitlement for Dominicans. The committee argued for deferral of consideration of Dominican adjustment rights until Congress returned the following year. With Congress never readdressing the matter, Dominicans never received CAA entitlements.[48] Also, the State Department had initially proposed extending status adjustment rights to other Western Hemisphere peoples. Because the Justice Department argued to limit the rights to Cubans, the State Department proposal was also omitted from the final version of the bill.

Even after signing the legislation, President Johnson extended another CAA-related entitlement to Cubans. He exempted Cubans from the $25 fee that the INS charged other immigrants to process status adjustment requests. President Johnson added this fee-waiver to Cubans' parole-processing fee waiver.[49] He justified the added fee exemption on humanitarian grounds. In his words, "The ability of Cuban refugees to become permanent U.S. residents – without the imposition of any fees – makes

---

[48] U.S. Congress, House of Representatives, "Status of Cuban Refugees." Report 2334, 89th Cong., 2nd sess., Conference Report (To accompany H.R. 15183) October 21, 1966, p. 27963.

[49] JFKPL, Papers of the JFK White House, Central File ND 19-2. Folder: Displaced Persons Refugees, Box 636 "Caribbean Crisis" prepared by the Special Sub-Committee on Caribbean Refugee Problem, International Rescue committee, (January 30, 1961): 14, Box 636.

individuals eligible for many benefits."[50] Yet, even without the fee waiver Cubans received far more benefits than other immigrants, and he offered no evidence that Cubans were more economically needy and deserving of the fee-waiver than other foreign-born people applying for immigration status adjustment. Indeed, President Johnson singled out Cuba-trained professionals as key beneficiaries of the CAA, in enabling them to qualify for medical licenses that are limited to lawful permanent residents and citizens: far from the most economically needy immigrants. Moreover, the CAA in itself saved Cubans money, in enabling them to adjust their status without having to leave the country to apply from elsewhere, as people from other countries in the hemisphere were required to do until passage of the 1976 INA Amendments. His avowed humanitarian rationale notwithstanding, President Johnson probably envisioned political pay-off from the revenue loss: loyalty and votes, possibly for himself (had he decided to run for reelection in 1968), but, minimally, for the Democratic Party, as Cubans took out citizenship. If exiles felt betrayed by President Kennedy when he withheld air support for the Bay of Pigs invasion, they could not feel the same about President Johnson.

IMMEDIATE IMPACT OF CUBAN IMMIGRANT EXCEPTIONALISM

Cuban immigrants benefited both from the CRP and the CAA, partly at the expense of native-born people, and were perceived accordingly. African Americans, in particular, resented Cubans, who they believed benefited from the associated entitlements at their expense.

Impact on Cuban Immigrants

After passage of the CAA, Cubans in large numbers took advantage of their new right to lawful permanent residence. Some 41,000 Cuban immigrants applied to have their status adjusted during the first year that the law was in effect, and nearly 82,500 applied by the second year.[51] Once they were officially permanent residents, some of them, as

---

[50] *Public Papers of the Presidents of the United States: Lyndon B. Johnson 1966* Book II, p.1364.
[51] Oscar Trelles, "Cuba and the United States: A Review of the Immigration Laws of the Two Countries before and during the Castro Government," *Immigration and Nationality Law Review* vol. 25 (1979–1980): 46.

anticipated, qualified for jobs from which they previously had been excluded. At the same time, the CRP opened up education, job training, and job placement opportunities that gave Cuban immigrants labor market advantage. Then, once they became citizens they could use the ballot box to their ethnic group's advantage.

Beneficiaries of entitlements contributed to the transformation of the Cuban community in the United States, economically and politically. While Cubans with parole status enjoyed work rights that were denied visa-less immigrants from other countries, the CRP and the CAA, combined, contributed to the formation of a Cuban American professional class. The CRP offered Cubans training to meet US professional standards, while the CAA qualified Cubans for jobs that were reserved for LPRs and citizens. For example, half of Cuba's 6,000 doctors fled Cuba when the government nationalized health care, which reduced doctors' earning power, in the name of equality. Fortunately for them, the CRP,[52] together with the CAA, helped qualify them to practice in the United States. Some 1,700 "refugee doctors" who took CRP-funded courses at the University of Miami Medical School had been able to practice under the supervision of US doctors, but on attaining LPR status, thanks to the CAA, they could practice independently and take advantage of a growing demand for doctors with President Johnson's Great Society Medicare and Medicaid initiatives. From the US vantage point, the mainly Cuba-trained medical professionals minimized training costs. In the 1960s it cost over $40,000 to train a US doctor from kindergarten through medical internship, but only $300 to qualify a Cuba-educated doctor to practice in the United States.[53] Thus, the federal government, and not merely Cuban immigrant doctors, benefited from granting the status adjustment rights.

With lawful permanent residency, Cubans were also able to become licensed teachers. They addressed a growing demand for Spanish language instruction, which increased not only because ever more Cubans came to the United States but also because the Hispanic population of the country in general, and of Miami in particular, increased.[54]

Overall, it did not take long for Cuban immigrants to make impressive economic gains. Many of them earned more than they had in Cuba, and more than native-born people into whose midst they moved. Business

---

[52] Julie Feinsilver, *Healing the Masses: Politics at Home and Abroad* (Berkeley: University of California Press, 1993), p. 33.
[53] Thomas, "Cuban Refugees in the United States," p. 54.
[54] Ibid., p. 54; Eckstein, *The Immigrant Divide*, p. 46.

people, managers, and professionals, who accounted for almost a third of the nearly quarter million Cubans who immigrated during the first three years of Castro's rule,[55] on settling in Miami formed a vibrant ethnic community that created work and income-earning opportunities, not only for the high status arrivals but also for Cubans of more humble origins.[56] The Cubans further benefited from having settled in the right place at the right time, in Miami as it transformed from a small tourist community into a metropolis with global, especially hemispheric, reach[57]: a transformation they helped bring about. All the while, CRP entitlements helped Cuban arrivals get a jump-start in the world of work.

Both the assets with which they came and the benefits they received on arrival contributed, in Miami, to the percentage of 1960s arrivals with high status professional, managerial, and technical jobs doubling, and the percentage who came to rank among the top tercile of all income earners rising from 12 to 19, between 1970 and 1980.[58] Undoubtedly, many of the Cuban immigrants would have done well in America without the special entitlements, given that they had emigrated with impressive human and social capital assets, and some also with financial capital. However, the special entitlements they received gave them an economic boost.

Beginning in the 1970s, in Miami the 1960s arrivals, on average, even outperformed the native-born workforce. Whereas in 1970 a higher percentage of persons born in the United States than in Cuba held high-status jobs and ranked among the top tercile of income earners, by 1980 the converse was true.[59]

Washington's preoccupation with the Cold War even created economic opportunities for Cubans above and beyond those that were opened up by the CRP and CAA. In the 1960s, the CIA and other intelligence agencies employed some 12,000 to 15,000 Cubans in Miami as case officials and agents.[60] Concerned about preventing "other Cubas" in

---

[55] Ibid., pp. 12, 16.
[56] Kenneth Wilson and Alejandro Portes, "Immigrant Enclaves: An Analysis of the Labor Market Experiences of Cubans in Miami," *American Journal of Sociology* vol. 86 (September 1980): 295–319.
[57] Eckstein, *The Immigrant Divide*, pp. 69–87.   [58] Ibid., p. 71.   [59] Ibid., p. 71.
[60] At its peak, only the CIA headquarters in Langley, Virginia were larger than its Miami station operation. See "JMWAVE" (https://en.wikipedia.org/wiki/JMWAVE). See also www.maryferrell.org/php/cryptdb.php?id=JMWAVE, Joan Dideon, *Miami* (New York: Simon and Schuster, 1987), p. 90; and Guillermo Grenier and Alex Stepick, *Miami Now! Immigration, Race, and Ethnicity and Social Change* (Gainesville: University Press of Florida, 1992).

the Hemisphere, the agencies valued Cubans' command of Spanish, plus their aversion to Communism. Less explicitly politically driven, Cubans benefited from Small Business Administration (SBA) loans, a federal program that guaranteed private bank loans for those who were entrepreneurially ambitious.[61] In this case, an agency designed to promote business in general helped Cuban émigrés more than others in Miami, and independently of CRP entitlements.

Even among the unemployed, Cubans were at an advantage. On arrival, they immediately qualified for assistance through the CRP, which imposed no length-of-residence prerequisite. In contrast, in Florida, immigrants from other countries needed to reside five years in the state to be eligible for welfare.

In turn, the CAA had political payoff for Cubans. It provided the bedrock for them to become not merely a local but also a national political force, after taking advantage of their CAA-based LPR status to become citizens. As of 1970, four years after the passage of the CAA, 45 percent of Cubans in the United States lived in Miami, one-third of whom had become citizens. While Cubans then only accounted for 4 percent of the city's population, ten years later they accounted for over a fourth, half of whom had taken out citizenship. Once they were citizens, most age-eligible Cubans took advantage of their right to vote.[62] They then had votes to deliver to politicians who were attentive to their concerns.

Presidential candidates quickly recognized Cubans' potential political import in Florida. The state's population grew such that its electoral college votes surged from 10 in 1960 to 17 by the time of the 1972 election, and Miami-Dade County, with its large concentration of Cubans, picked up one congressional seat in the interim years. As of 1972, Florida held the eighth largest number of electoral college votes (tied with New Jersey).[63] With the state sometimes voting Democratic, while in other elections voting Republican, presidential candidates recognized how Cuban American voters could tilt the election outcome in their favor.[64] Accordingly, in an appeal for Cuban American votes, Gerald Ford, the Republican presidential candidate in 1976 (who had assumed

---

[61] Portes and Stepick, *City on the Edge*, pp. 132–40; Eckstein, *The Immigrant Divide*, p. 81.
[62] Eckstein, *The Immigrant Divide*, pp. 46, 91–94.
[63] "1972 United States Presidential Election" (https://en.wikipedia.org/wiki/1972_United_States_presidential_election).
[64] "Florida Elected Officials Look Up," *270toWin* (www.270towin.com/states/Florida).

the presidency in 1974 after Nixon resigned over the Watergate scandal), pledged to speed up the process of naturalization for Cuban immigrants and requested Congress to eliminate delays caused by immigration quotas.[65] He was targeting Cuban Americans who were already eligible to vote, on the presumption that they would be appreciative of "their people" attaining a new entitlement. However, he lost the election to Jimmy Carter, and before leaving office he never delivered on his promise to fast-track Cuban immigrant rights to citizenship. Nonetheless, even the promise of the entitlement reveals that as Florida's national electoral importance soared, and Cuban Americans' importance among voters in the state increased, owing to the CAA, Cuban immigrants had become a domestic political force to contend with.

Impact on Native-Born

The Eisenhower, Kennedy, and Johnson administration policies that were good for Cuban immigrants fueled resentment among the native-born populace. This was especially true in Miami. As early as October 1960, the City Manager of Miami declared that "an emergency situation exists ... caused by displaced people from Cuba."[66] Then, at a December 1961 hearing of a subcommittee of the Senate Judiciary Committee, invited speakers complained that Miami disproportionately bore the costs of incoming Cubans.[67]

Native-born resentment intensified when President Johnson announced his open-ended invitation to Cubans on October 3, 1965. In an October 19 (1965) memorandum, Harold Hunton, of the US Department of Commerce Community Relations Service, informed George Culberson of the Johnson administration that almost everyone he interviewed in Miami was bitter about the prospect of the arrival of unlimited numbers of new Cubans. He was informed that they had a bad experience with the first Cuban influx, in 1960, and worried that most

---

[65] James M. Naughton, "Ford, Stumping in Florida, Brands Castro an 'Outlaw'," *New York Times* (February 29, 1976) (www.nytimes.com/1976/02/29/archives/ford-stumping-in-florida-brands-castro-an-outlaw.html).

[66] JFKPL, White House Central File (WHCF), n.d., 19-2, Folder: Displaced Persons-Refugees, "Caribbean Crisis: A Danger and an Opportunity," prepared by the Special Sub-Committee on Caribbean Refugee Problem, the International Rescue Committee, New York City (January 30, 1961), p. 14, Box 636.

[67] U.S. Senate, "Cuban Refugee Problems," Hearings before the Subcommittee to Investigate Problems Connected with Refugees and Escapees of the Committee of the Judiciary (Washington DC: GPO, December 6, 7, 13, 1961), p. 2.

incoming Cubans would also settle in Miami even if the federal government tried to divert them elsewhere. Capturing the pulse of the community, Hunton reported that "(W)e have a very tense situation ... a potentially dangerous one ... Miami may have had it."[68]

The Executive Director of the Dade County Community Relations Board echoed Hunton's concern. He noted that Miami "has been near the brink for some time ... The arrival of large numbers of (additional) Cuban refugees might 'push it over'."[69] He reported that community leaders resented that the federal government was asking Dade County to solve a national problem without assurances of additional funds to absorb the community impact. They felt that assistance for the earlier influx was "too little and too late."

Top advisors to President Johnson, in turn, expressed concern about the domestic political costs of reaching out to Cubans. Undersecretary of State George Ball, for example, forewarned that although the "propaganda aspects (of the open-ended invitation to Cubans) ... are major," he felt that "the ramifications as far as (the) American scene is concerned are great" and the President needed to consider how "much heat" he was willing to take from Floridians. In another communique Ball noted that Miami will "go up in smoke if (the) President indicates too much hospitality to these people."[70] Similarly, McGeorge Bundy, President Johnson's National Security Advisor, spoke of the need to "soothe Floridians."[71]

Determined to take advantage of the "propaganda value" of welcoming Cubans, President Johnson tried to minimize domestic resentment and resistance by giving incoming Cubans incentives to settle away from Miami. His administration made Cuban entitlement to CRP benefits conditional on setting up roots elsewhere.

Tying benefits to settling elsewhere proved, however, no panacea.[72] When Cubans no longer needed or qualified for CRP benefits they

---

[68] LBJPL, Collection: National Security-Defense Ex ND 19 Korean War, Box 418, Folder ND 19-2/CO, Harold Hunton, "Growing Negro-Cuban Tensions, Miami, Florida." U.S. Department of Commerce, Community Relations Service, Memorandum to George Culberson. October 19, 1965, Box 418.

[69] Ibid.

[70] LBJPL, Collection: Papers of George Ball, Telcon Sec. Rusk/Mr. Ball October 1, 1965. Folder: Cuba II (December 12, 1963–May 30, 1966), Box 2.

[71] LBJPL, Collection: Papers of George Ball, Telcon Ball/Bundy October 1, 1965, about President's Press Conference Today, Folder: Cuba II (December 12, 1963–May 30, 1966), Box 2.

[72] Eckstein, *The Immigrant Divide*, p. 46. In justifying the Freedom Flights the Johnson administration claimed that nearly three-fourths of Cuban arrivals settled away from Miami. LBJPL, Collection: Files of Douglass Cater, Folder: Cater, Federal Task Force,

gravitated to Miami, where friends and family who previously immigrated lived, such that the city became known as "Havana USA."[73] In Miami, the Cubans exacerbated labor market tensions as well as problems in the schools.

To temper the brewing tensions, the Johnson administration designated the City of Miami an economic development zone, eligible for multi-million dollar grants and loans under the Public Works and Economic Development Act of 1965. In President Johnson's words, "We must make a concerted effort to help the Miami community ... (make) the fullest possible use of existing Federal programs to maintain and stimulate economic growth and to avoid an undue additional burden on the community as a result of the influx of refugees." Federally funded programs targeted public employment, job-training, employment service, and a small business development center, as well as new public housing and preschool programs.[74] In turn, a special Miami task force promoted what was known as "creative Federalism," involving a partnership between federal, state, and local governments, and between public and private institutions and individuals.[75] The expanded "economic opportunity pie" would, in principle, appease not only the incoming Cubans but also those who were born in the United States. The millions of dollars that the Johnson administration accordingly channeled to Miami were, in effect, indirect costs of his outreach to Cubans.

Despite Miami becoming an economic development zone, in the course of the 1970s native-born people became ever more disadvantaged relative to Cuban immigrants. In 1970, 19 percent of those who were US-born held high-status jobs, compared to 11 percent of Cuban immigrants. However, by 1980, the Cuba-born did better: 24 percent of them held high-status jobs, while only 16 percent of the US-born did. The percentage of native-born people with such jobs decreased, while the percentage of Cuba-born people with such jobs increased.[76]

June 28, 1966, Memorandum for the President from John Gardner, Secretary of HEW, accompanying Report to the President, Federal Task Force for Greater Miami, Box 95. In point of fact, only one-sixth of Cubans who were registered with the Cuban Refugee Center settled outside Miami. And many who settled elsewhere moved to Miami after they no longer received CRP benefits.

[73] García, *Havana USA*.
[74] LBJPL, Collection: Files of Douglas Cater, Report to the President, Federal Task Force for Greater Miami.
[75] Ibid.   [76] Eckstein, *Immigrant Divide*, p. 71.

Meanwhile, schooling became contentious. Miami residents resented that their local tax dollars went to educate Cuban children, who they felt the federal government had thrust on them. They felt that Cubans, living in rental units, benefited from the schools without having to pay the ad valorem tax that financed local education: Non-Cuban taxpaying property owners bore the costs, while their children suffered from the crowding of schools caused by the inundation of Cubans.[77]

The Johnson administration tried to temper the school-related tensions by absorbing some of the education expenses. It covered costs of temporary school construction and some operating costs of the schools that incoming Cuban children attended in large numbers.[78] In addition, the federally funded CRP channeled funds to the local school districts where many Cuban children attended: mainly in Miami-Dade County, but, secondarily, in Union City and West New York, New Jersey, home to the second largest Cuban settlement. However, federal dollars never covered all costs incurred by local school districts, and over time Washington reduced its contributions, which increased the financial burden that local taxpayers had to absorb.

Resentful of paying for a problem considered to be of Washington's making, the Miami-Dade school board refused to allow children who came on the Freedom Flights into local schools until the federal government agreed to pay all expenditures. Angrily, the Superintendent of Schools for Dade County echoed the school board. He reportedly said on television that the schools would not accept Cuban refugees unless additional funds were made available for them.[79] Faced with the

---

[77] HEW, "Analysis of Federal Expenditures to Aid Cuban Refugees," p. 13; LBJPL, Collection: National Security-Defense Ex ND 19 Korean War, Folder ND 19-2/CO, Harold Hunton, "Growing Negro-Cuban Tensions, Miami, Florida," U.S. Department of Commerce, Community Relations Service, Memorandum to George Culberson, October 19, 1965, Box 418. As early as 1964, Miami taxpayers complained that they were unfairly taxed to finance services for Cubans, at that time to finance health services for Cubans. LBJPL, National Security-Defense Gen ND 19-2/CO, Folder ND 19-2/CO55 11/22/63-10/19/65, letter from Deputy Clerk of Dade County to President Johnson April 23, 1964, Box 419.

[78] LBJPL, Collection: National Security-Defense Ex ND 19 Korean War Folder ND 19-2/CO, Folder: John Gardner, Secretary HEW, Memorandum for the President, November 4, 1965, Box 418. In order to allay local resentment, the Johnson administration also covered three months of hospitalization benefits for needy refugees.

[79] LBJPL, Collection: National Security-Defense Ex ND 19 Korean War, Folder ND 19-2/CO, Harold Hunton, "Growing Negro-Cuban Tensions, Miami, Florida," U.S. Department of Commerce, Community Relations Service, Memorandum to George Culberson, October 19, 1965, Box 418.

pushback, the Johnson administration agreed to absorb 60 percent of the costs. When it later tried to reduce the percentage to 45, Miami-Dade County officials insisted on a compromise: that Washington continue to pay 60 percent of the costs incurred for educating those "refugee students" whose families received financial aid.[80]

People born in the United States particularly resented Cubans who they believed not to be refugees. As early as 1961, a Miami-Dade County Commissioner questioned, when testifying before Congress, whether the incoming Cubans really were political refugees. He thought Cubans were taking advantage of an opportunity to better themselves economically.[81] This was all the truer of the more than quarter million Cubans admitted on the Freedom Flights.

In summary, Miami residents felt that Cubans were unfairly privileged at their expense. That Cubans were fleeing an increasingly Soviet-allied government in the throes of the Cold War did not convince them otherwise. Although the resentments did not stop President Johnson from massively expanding the number of Cubans admitted to the country on Freedom Flights, independently of Congress-regulated immigration admissions, he tried to temper tensions by expanding "the Miami economic pie," in principle for all, and by having the federal government absorb costs of schooling Cuban immigrant children. Nonetheless, resentments, remained, especially among native-born African Americans.

Impact Specifically on Native-Born African Americans

Although racial resentments had flared when the first Cubans flocked to Miami, that did not convince President Johnson to refrain from welcoming ever more Cubans, including with resettlement benefits. Nor did the mounting civil rights and Black Power movements that swept the country in the course of the 1960s, and the growing militancy of the then still-called "Negro" leadership, dissuade him.[82]

---

[80] See HEW, "Analysis of Federal Expenditures to Aid Cuban Refugees," p. 13, and LBJPL, National Security-Defense Files, Gen ND 19-2/CO, Folder: ND 19-2/CO55 11/22/63-10/19/65, Letter from Deputy Clerk of Dade County to President Johnson April 23, 1964, Box 419.

[81] US Senate, "Cuban Refugee Problems," Hearings before the Subcommittee to Investigate Problems Connected with Refugees and Escapees of the Committee on the Judiciary, 87th Congress, 1st session December 6, 7, and 13, 1961, p. 55.

[82] LBJPL, Collection: National Security-Defense Ex ND 19 Korean War, Folder: ND 19-2/CO, Box 418.

As early as December 1961, speakers at the hearing of the subcommittee of the Senate Judiciary Committee on "Cuban Refugee Problems" warned that Miami faced an explosive situation rooted in rising tensions between Americans, especially "Negroes," and the Cuban community.[83] "Negro" leaders complained about the flood of Cuban arrivals at a time of substantial unemployment,[84] and about Cuban displacement of "Negro laborers," particularly in the construction and hotel industries.[85] The "Negro displacement," in turn, reportedly fueled crime. Out of work, "Negroes" mugged and pickpocketed to feed themselves and their families.[86]

Before initiating the Freedom Flights, top advisors warned President Johnson in internal White House communications that interethnic/racial tensions were on the verge of exploding. Gordon Chase, assistant to McGeorge Bundy, National Security Advisor to President Kennedy (and then to President Johnson), noted that although there had been no serious incidents yet in Miami, the "breaking point is obviously not far away," especially because Cubans generally were unwilling to move from the Miami area.[87]

Senior advisors became particularly concerned after President Johnson announced in his 1965 Liberty Island speech the open-ended welcoming of Cubans. They warned him that the "Negro" leadership, which was more militant than when the first Cubans came, was determined that "Negroes" would not be "sacrificed" again to the special humanitarian needs of new refugees.[88] Reflecting on the mounting racial tensions, a SCLC, Southern Christian Leadership Conference, staff member warned a city official that if the Cuban refugees come a "resort-type Watts" will transpire.[89] The neighborhood of Watts, in Los Angeles, had experienced

---

[83] U.S. Senate, "Cuban Refugee Problems," Hearings ... p. 49.   [84] Ibid., p. 31.
[85] Ibid., p. 55.   [86] Ibid., p. 56.
[87] LBJPL, National Security File, Files of Gordon Chase, Folder: Cuba Coordinating Committee Progress Report, Memorandum for Mr. Bundy, Subject: Cuba Coordinating Committee Progress Report February 2, 1963, Box 5.
[88] LBJPL, Collection: National Security-Defense Ex ND 19 Korean War, Folder ND 19-2/CO, Box 418.
[89] LBJPL, Collection: National Security-Defense Ex ND 19 Korean War, Folder ND 19-2/CO, Memorandum from Samet, U.S. Department of Commerce, Community Relations Service to George Culberson, "Growing Negro-Cuban Tensions, Miami, Florida," October 19, 1965, Box 418; on African American resentments and actual violent reactions toward Cubans, and the entitlements they received, see RNPL, White House Special Files, Staff Member and Office Files, Harold Ziegler, Subject File, Foreign Affairs and Defense, Folder: Ronald Ziegler, "Cuba," Sam Jacobs, "Blacks Ask U.S. Program Probe," *Miami Herald* June 25, 1970, Box 28.

a violent riot earlier in 1965. Harold Hunton of the Department of Commerce Community Relations Service even reported widespread rumors that the Cuban community was arming in response to the negative reaction to their arrival.[90]

"Negroes" viewed the federal government as the villain.[91] Seymour Samet, also of the US Department of Commerce Community Relations Service, noted that the "Negro" community was angry that they, as American citizens, were not getting the same amount and quality of government assistance as "the refugees," namely, the Cubans. For one, in his words, "The federal government relief subsidy was greater for the refugees than the local relief moneys for Negro indigent."[92] Cuban families received up to $100 a month through the CRP, while "Negroes," as well as other needy Floridians, received a maximum of $81. Second, Cubans could secure cash assistance immediately on arrival, through the CRP, while the state required that others reside in Florida five years for welfare eligibility.[93] Third, unemployed "Negroes" received no assistance after their unemployment compensation ended, whereas Cubans received open-ended support through the CRP. In addition, "Negroes" resented that employment placement services offered Cubans jobs that they traditionally had held, for example, as bellmen, porters, chambermaids, and elevator operators.[94]

Angrily, some "Negro" leaders in Miami took their grievances directly to President Johnson. The director of the Miami branch of the NAACP, the National Association for the Advancement of Colored People, wrote to Johnson that "the average Negro citizen of this community who lost his job to a Cuban has ... borne his burden in silence as a sacrificial lamb for the extension of freedom and democracy to refugees from another land." He added that the federal government, "acting without pressure of an immediate crisis ... decided to further accommodate the Cuban people

---

[90] LBJPL, Collection: National Security-Defense Ex ND 19 Korean War, Folder ND 19-2/CO, Memorandum from Seymour Samet, to George Culberson.
[91] Ibid.
[92] LBJPL, Collection: National Security-Defense Ex ND 19 Korean War, Folder ND 19-2/CO, Harold Hunton, "Growing Negro-Cuban Tensions, Miami, Florida," U.S. Department of Commerce, Community Relations Service, Memorandum to George Culberson, October 19, 1965, Box 418.
[93] U.S. Senate, "Cuban Refugee Problems," Hearings before the Subcommittee to Investigate Refugees and Escapees of the Committee on the Judiciary, 87th Congress, 1st session (December 6, 7, 13, 1961), p. 15.
[94] LBJPL, Collection: National Security-Defense Ex ND 19 Korean War, Folder ND 19-2/CO, Box 418.

in their mass exodus from tyranny ... (N)ow is the time to look to the freedom of all our citizens from the economic oppression that will almost certainly be caused by this addition to our labor market."[95]

In another letter sent to President Johnson ten days after his Liberty Island speech, the Miami NAACP director expressed further dismay that Cubans were costing "Negroes" jobs. "There are many ... categories of employment ... that Negroes no longer enjoy as a direct result of the Cuban influx which apparently is about to be extended." He added that the Cuban influx has had its "most severe affect upon that group of citizens least able to afford it, the uneducated, non-highly skilled, non-professional Negro who prior to the Cuban influx could eke out a fairly decent standard of living."[96] Even before the flood of new arrivals on the Freedom Flights, "Negroes" had experienced an unemployment rate that was triple that of Cuban immigrants',[97] despite how recently the Cubans had come.

With Cubans benefiting at "Negroes'" expense, Florida Congressman Claude Pepper implored President Johnson to address "Negro" leaders' concerns.[98] The congressman noted that in many places only Cubans experienced no unemployment, which he attributed to bottom-line economics, not to racism. The new arrivals were cheaper to hire "than our local people." Pepper warned of likely protest, and urged job creation, especially for unskilled workers that were displaced by Cuban refugees.[99]

"Negro" resentments extended beyond the world of work, to the schooling of children, and beyond issues of federal versus local school funding: to race-based inequities. As early as the 1961 Senate hearings on Cuban refugees, "Negroes" complained that Cubans were treated with respect and assistance and admitted to "White" public schools from

---

[95] LBJPL, National Security File, Country File Latin America-Cuba, Folder: "Refugee: October 1963-1/65)," Box 30.
[96] LBJPL, Collection: National Security-Defense Gen ND 19-2/CO, Folder ND 19-2/CO55 (11/22/63-10/19/65), letter to President Johnson, October 13, 1965, from Donald Wheeler Jones, President Miami branch, NAACP, Box 419.
[97] LBJPL, National Security File, Files of Gordon Chase, Folder: Cuba Coordinating Committee Progress Report, Memorandum from Gordon Chase to Bundy, Box 419; see also Masud-Piloto, *From Welcomed Exiles to Illegal Immigrants*, p. 63.
[98] Pepper had served as a Florida senator between 1936 and 1951. Between 1963 and 1989 he served as a congressman from Miami. A New Dealer, he championed "Negro" rights. Although early in his political career he was pro-Soviet Union, he subsequently became outspokenly anti-Communist and anti-Castro.
[99] LBJPL, Collection: National Security-Defense Gen ND 19-2, Folder ND 19-2/CO 55 10/20/65–12/10/65, Box 419.

which mulattos and Negroes were excluded.[100] With President Johnson's introduction of the Freedom Flights, Samet, of the Department of Commerce Community Relations Service, spoke of "Negro" exclusion alongside Cuban inclusion. The "Negro community," he noted, begrudged the integration of Cubans into the public schools while their children remained segregated.[101] He also noted "Negro" resentment that their children were held back scholastically because of the inundation of new Cubans who were not proficient in English.[102]

Despite the warnings, the top-level Johnson administration officials who testified at the CAA hearings that were held after the start of the Freedom Flights were silent about how the status adjustment legislation might work to "Negroes'" disadvantage. Commissioner of Welfare Winston had claimed that the CAA targeted the under- rather than the un-employed. She focused on Cubans who worked "below" their capacity when lawful permanent residency was a job requisite. Others in the administration claimed that because Cubans settled outside Miami in order to qualify for CRP benefits, they would not adversely impact on "Negro'" employment in Miami. The high-ranking members of the Johnson administration who testified turned a deaf ear to evidence and warnings that Cubans gravitated to the city,[103] independently of the incentives to settle elsewhere to qualify for CRP benefits. Cubans preferred living among "their own," in a city they were remaking in their own image.[104] And with Cubans gravitating to live among "their own," during President Johnson's last year in office, and again in 1970, African Americans took to the streets in protest, fueling "resort-type Watts," as the SCLC staff member had previously forewarned. They rioted in Miami's largely African American Liberty City, angry over shortages of housing, poor job opportunities, substandard health, and inadequate welfare benefits, all the while that the Cubans received refugee relief.[105]

---

[100] U.S. Senate, "Cuban Refugee Problems," Hearings before the Subcommittee to Investigate Refugees and Escapees of the Committee on the Judiciary, 87th Congress, 1st session (December 6, 7, 13, 1961), p. 77.
[101] LBJPL, Collection: National Security-Defense Ex ND 19 Korean War, Folder ND 19-2/CO, Box 418.
[102] U.S. Senate, "Cuban Refugee Problems," p. 77.
[103] LBJPL, Collection: National Security-Defense Gen ND 19-2, Folder ND 19-2/CO 55 10/20/65–12/10/65, Box 419.
[104] García, *Havana USA*; Eckstein, *The Immigrant Divide*, Chapter Two; Portes and Stepick, *City on the Edge*.
[105] RNPL, White House Special Files (WHSF), Staff Member and Office Files, Harold Ziegler, Subject File, Foreign Affairs and Defense, Folder: Ronald Ziegler, "Cuba," Sam Jacobs, "Blacks Ask U.S. Program Probe," *Miami Herald* June 25, 1970, Box 28.

Fortunately for Miami African Americans, the Freedom Flights ended under President Nixon, which kept new Cuban arrivals from continuing to exacerbate labor market pressures and crowding in the schools. Yet, with Presidents Nixon, Ford, and Carter during his first three years in office doing little to redress interethnic/racial inequities and resentments, tensions persisted, particularly as the city became ever more Cuban. Between 1970 and 1980 the African American percentage of the Miami population increased slightly, from 14 to 18. However, Cubans' presence in the city soared, as previously noted, from 4 to 26 percent, as they defied government efforts to have them settle elsewhere.[106] They gravitated to where they wanted to live.

Against this backdrop, when faced in 1980 not only with an economic recession but also with a new wave of Cuban immigrants, racial tensions flared. Chapter 3 describes the surge in new Cuban arrivals, and the racial and other resentments it unleashed. Cuban immigration became all the more a domestic, as distinct from a foreign, policy concern.

CONCLUSION

Cuban privileging did not stop with unique entry entitlements. Successive presidents extended unique resettlement benefits to Cubans upon their arrival, on the presumption that they were refugees, and special refugees at that. Cubans received more generous benefits than native-born people in need, and more generous benefits than refugees and immigrants from other countries. Federal funds also helped Cubans get preferential access to business opportunities independently of their refugee status.

Presidents extended social and economic, plus political, entitlements to Cubans in a "path dependent" manner, under both Democrat and Republican administrations. Privileging Cubans was not a partisan matter. It began as a pan-partisan Cold War project to defeat global Communism, and then was expanded to address new problems that arose.

Entitlements helped Cubans adapt well to America, but they did not serve to spur regime change in Cuba, the instituting of a US-friendly capitalist-based democracy. Nonetheless, against this backdrop, US–Cuban tensions partially thawed in the course of the 1970s. Beginning with the Nixon administration, momentum built up to improve

---

[106] Eckstein, *The Immigrant Divide*, p. 46.

bilateral relations, with Washington coming to accept, however begrudgingly, Cuba's political transformation.

Meanwhile, Cubans that Washington privileged helped transform Miami into a major US city, although at considerable domestic political and economic costs. The privileging of Cubans fueled resentments that imploded in 1980, as an unprecedented number of new, unauthorized Cubans came ashore, as described in Chapter 3.

3

The Immigration Crisis of 1980

Carter Administration Privileging of Cubans Anew, Spillover Benefits for Haitians

By the mid-to-latter 1970s, the United States had welcomed more than 665,000 Cubans who had fled the radical transformation of their homeland, and helped them adapt well.[1] In showcasing virtues of capitalist democracy, US presidents had hoped that the Cuban immigrants would delegitimize the Castro-led government to the point of collapse. Instead, the exodus of disaffected Cubans helped consolidate the revolution. Against this backdrop, President Nixon reined in Cuban immigrant entitlements during his last year in office, and, for the remainder of the 1970s, Presidents Ford and Carter kept Cuban privileging at bay. The era of Cuban immigration exceptionalism seemed to have run its course.

The new stance was consistent with the unraveling of the Cold War consensus that Washington should take a hard-line stance on Cuba. Following Nixon's historic visit to China in 1972, the United States resumed economic and diplomatic relations with the communist-run country, and, in 1975, the United States accepted the communist victory in Vietnam. Against this backdrop, President Ford took "baby steps" to improve economic relations with Cuba. He removed restrictions on trade by overseas subsidiaries of US firms with Cuba. Jimmy Carter, his successor, went further. He lifted restrictions on US to Cuba travel; he permitted charter flights to facilitate the travel; and he took preliminary measures to

---

[1] Maria Cristina García, *Havana USA: Cuban Exiles and Cuban Americans in South Florida, 1959–1994* (Berkeley: University of California Press, 1996), p. 45.

reestablish diplomatic relations with Cuba, which included the US and Cuban governments opening Interests Sections in each other's country.[2] With the US Interests Section offering consular services, Cubans could, in principle, apply for visas in Cuba, which would allow them to emigrate with lawful permanent residency rights, and thereby eliminate the need (and rationale) for the Cuban Adjustment Act.

On his part, Castro made overtures to the United States. In the hope of convincing the Carter administration to relax its economic embargo of Cuba, he agreed to permit thousands of political prisoners to emigrate, some of whom had served long jail sentences for involvement in US-sponsored covert activity in Cuba.[3] He also agreed to a meeting with moderate Cuban Americans that became known as the Dialogue, which led him to release more political prisoners and to permit Cubans who had fled the revolution for the first time to visit family they had left behind.[4] With the Dialogue involving a conciliatory stance toward the Cuban government, hard-line exiles aggressively turned on their fellow émigrés who improved cross-border relations.[5]

However, when Castro sent military troops to Angola and Ethiopia, which the Carter administration perceived as advancing the Soviet interests Union's global bilateral tensions built up anew. Tensions built up further in 1980 when Castro opened the door for Cubans to leave for the United States without entry permission, as he had in 1965 from Camarioca. Some 125,000 new Cubans came ashore before Castro put

---

[2] Although the State Department favored improving relations with Cuba, President Carter's National Security Advisor, Zbigniew Brzezinski, a Cold War hawk, did not.

[3] Jimmy Carter Presidential Library (JCPL), Staff Offices, Special Assistant to President: Torres, Folder: Cuban/U.S. Issue/Briefing Book, April 8, 1980–May 22, 1980, Memorandum to Phil Wise, White House, from Bernardo Benes and Alfredo Duran, "The issuance of parole visas to 5,000 ex-political prisoners of Cuba," September 21, 1979, Box 17.

[4] García, *Havana USA*, pp. 49–50. The Miami banker Bernardo Benes headed the "Committee of 75." Indicative of deep divisions within the Cuban American community, thirty exile organizations denounced the Dialogue, and accused participants of being "Communists." Anti-Castro militants bombed the bank that Benes directed, firebombed the cigar factory owned by one of the "Committee of 75" who was photographed in Cuba with Castro, and assassinated two participants. In the mid-1960s, Benes had financed violent anti-Castro activity, but because he became disillusioned with prospects of overthrowing the Cuban government by force, he shifted his focus in the mid-1970s to helping Cuban political prisoners and to family reunification.

[5] On the Cuban perspective toward the Dialogue see Jesús Arboleya, *Havana Miami: The US–Cuba Migration Conflict* (Melbourne: Ocean Press, 1996), pp. 24–26.

a plug to the exodus.[6] If in years past most Cubans had immigrated with US approval, that was not the case in 1980.

This chapter describes the mass migration of 1980, the context in which it occurred, and how the Carter administration responded, in what President Carter described as one of the most difficult human problems he faced in the White House.[7] After initially breaking with past presidents, in taking measures to block unauthorized Cubans from coming, he proceeded to build on their precedent by extending special entitlements to yet more Cubans. Earlier Cuban immigrants, accustomed to special entitlements for "their people," "locked President Carter into" privileging yet more Cubans: at great economic, social, and political costs.

At the same time, President Carter will be shown to break with precedent in his treatment of Haitians. Rather than restrict their rights, as had previous presidents, and as he, himself, had done during his first three years in office, in 1980 he extended the same rights to unauthorized Haitians as to unauthorized Cubans.

PRELUDE TO THE MASS EXODUS FROM CUBA IN 1980

The mass exodus from Cuba began small. When Castro terminated the Freedom Flights in 1973, approximately 35,000 Cubans who the Cuban government had approved for emigration were unable to leave. In principle, the Nixon and Ford, as well as Carter, administrations could have screened them, and granted those who met US admission criteria visas to immigrate independently of the Freedom Flights. So too could they have admitted other Cubans, in accordance with immigration regulations set by Congress. Instead, in the mid to late 1970s, the Cubans who the United States authorized came mainly via third countries, Spain in particular. Blocked from direct lawful immigration, about one thousand Cubans risked their lives and took to small boats, hoping to reach the United States without entry visas.[8] The Carter Administration had been

---

[6] As I note in Chapter 4, some documents in the Reagan and Bush Presidential Libraries state that 129,000 Cubans came to the United States from Mariel. Since, more frequently, the figure 125,000 is cited, I use that number.

[7] Hideaki Kami, *Diplomacy Meets Migration: US Relations with Cuba during the Cold War* (Cambridge: Cambridge University Press, 2018), p. 145.

[8] David Engstrom, *Presidential Decision Making Adrift: The Carter Administration and the Mariel Boatlift* (Lanham, MD: Rowman & Littlefield, 1997), p. 43.

slow even to admit the political prisoners whose release and emigration it had negotiated with the Cuban government.[9]

Without the ability to emigrate legally, in 1980 some disaffected Cubans hijacked planes. Many more hijacked boats. Although they entered the United States without authorization and in violation of international law, on arrival they received heroes' welcomes from earlier émigrés. US officials, in turn, paroled them into the country and exempted them from prosecution.[10]

The hijackings reflected increased interest in immigration at a time when the United States permitted few Cubans to come lawfully. The Cubans who wanted to leave disliked aspects of their country's political and economic makeover. Dating back to the 1960s, the revolutionary government had tried to convince the populace to work for the collective good, not private gain: in order to build what it portrayed as an ideal communist society. Castro captured the hearts and minds of committed revolutionaries, especially youth. Others, however, resented and resisted working for little personal reward. As a result, productivity declined. To improve worker motivation, in the early 1970s the government made more consumer goods available. The economy improved somewhat as a result, helped by record high world sugar prices that drove up earnings of the country's main export. However, when world sugar prices dropped later in the decade, sugar earnings plummeted and the economy took a downturn. In response, the Cuban government introduced austerity measures that caused Cubans' living standards to deteriorate. Making matters worse, a swine flu decimated the pig population. Cubans were left without their beloved staple, pork.[11]

Cubans who sought to leave in 1980 wished for a different life. Many of them disliked the Marxist-Leninist turn of the revolution.[12] Some of

---

[9] Wayne Smith, *The Closest of Enemies* (New York: W. W. Norton, 1987), p. 200; Karen DeYoung, "Castro, Exiles Reach Accord on Release of 3,000 Cubans," *Washington Post* (December 10, 1978) (www.washingtonpost.com/archive/politics/1978/12/10/castro-exiles-reach-accord-on-release-of-3000-cubans/9633641d-b976-4457-9ba1-52b1ca3ca3d7/).

[10] William LeoGrande and Peter Kornbluh, *Back Channel to Cuba* (Chapel Hill: University of North Carolina Press, 2014), pp. 214–15.

[11] Carmelo Mesa-Lago, *Market, Socialist, and Mixed Economies* (Baltimore: Johns Hopkins University Press, 2000); William LeoGrande and Julie Thomas, "Cuba's Quests for Economic Independence," *Journal of Latin American Studies* vol. 34, part 2 (May 2002): 325–64.

[12] See Mirta Ojito, *Finding Mañana: A Memoir of a Cuban Exodus* (New York: Penguin Press, 2005) and Reinaldo Arenas, *Necesidad de Libertad: Testimonios de un intellectual disidente* (Mexico City: Kosmos Editorial, 1986).

them had never approved of the country's makeover but, for one reason or another, had not previously packed their bags and left. Others who had initially supported Castro turned against the revolution as it allied with the Soviet Union. There also were young men who wished to escape the draft and avoid fighting in the liberation wars in Africa that the Cuban government supported. Still others sought refuge from persecution: from religious persecution, as the revolution officially became atheist, and from political persecution, when opposing the revolution's radicalization. Homosexuals, in turn, sought refuge from persecution for their sexual orientation.[13]

Further fueling interest in emigration were the return visits that the Cuban government permitted following the Dialogue.[14] Some émigrés had not seen their relatives in Cuba for twenty years, while communication by mail and telephone had been minimal. The Cuban government had restricted ties between the Cubans who stayed and those who fled, and turned those who stayed against their family "turncoats." It rallied regime loyalists to stigmatize and ostracize those who rejected the revolution and uprooted, at the same time that many Cubans who had resettled in America resented their relatives who had sided with the revolution and stayed.

Cubans' feelings toward those who left changed, however, with the return visits. Estranged family members bonded, while visiting émigrés made a point of vindicating their decision to leave. They deliberately tried to impress their island relatives, with jewelry, clothes, and other goods that were no longer available in Cuba, and with embellished stories of their good life on the other side of the Florida Straits. In so doing, they convinced some of their island relatives to follow their example and immigrate: less to flee communism than to enjoy a consumer lifestyle that was no longer possible in Cuba. Revolutionary rhetoric had not convinced these Cubans otherwise.

Against this backdrop, in January of 1980 the CIA's Cuba Analytic Center warned the White House that new emigration pressures were building up on the island and that the Cuban government might unleash another Camarioca-type boatlift to defuse domestic discontent.[15]

---

[13] Arenas, in *Before Night Falls* (London: Serpent's Tail, 2001), addresses the persecution he and other homosexuals suffered during the first two decades of the Cuban revolution.
[14] Smith, *The Closest of Enemies*.
[15] Alex Larzelere, *The 1980 Cuban Boatlift: Castro's Policy, America's Dilemma* (Washington, DC: National Defense University Press, 1988), p. 219.

As noted in Chapter 1, in 1965 the Cuban government had permitted over 5,000 Cubans to leave from Camarioca in small boats without US entry permission: unauthorized arrivals who convinced the Johnson administration to negotiate the airlift with the Cuban government that authorized the immigration of over a quarter million new Cubans to the United States.

Giving credence to the CIA warning, in February, Carlos Rafael Rodríguez, Cuba's then deputy prime minister, told Wayne Smith, chief of the United States' newly opened Interests Section in Havana, "Our patience is running out ... If your government wants people in small boats, we can give you more than you bargained for."[16] Rodríguez expressed displeasure that the United States had refused to grant Cubans visas to immigrate legally, but welcomed Cubans who arrived illegally: in essence, that the United States manipulated its immigration policy to its own advantage.

The Cuban government had tried to convince the Carter administration to permit authorized immigration and to cooperate in preventing illegal immigration and hijackings. However, the Carter administration insisted that until Cuba removed its military forces from Africa it would only admit political prisoners.[17] It accordingly tried to leverage the United States' Cuban immigration policy for foreign policy gain: in this instance, to restrict immigration until Cuba curtailed its overseas involvements as an alleged "Soviet proxy."[18] Rejecting the conditionality, the Cuban government sacrificed the right of Cubans to immigrate lawfully rather than contain its global influence.

With the Carter administration unresponsive to the Cuban government efforts to open up legal immigration, Castro, on March 8, went public on Rodríguez's warning. He noted that "(I)f Washington continued to look the other way," with respect to hijackings, "we might have to take our own measures ... We once had to open the Camarioca port ... We hope we don't have to take such measures again."[19] Following up, on March 27 the chief of the Cuban Interests Section in Washington D. C., Ramón Sánchez Parodi, told State Department officials that the Cuban government was entertaining "another Camarioca" if the United States did not admit more Cubans and deter hijackings.[20]

---

[16] LeoGrande and Kornbluh, *Back Channel to Cuba*, p. 215.
[17] Engstrom, *Presidential Decision Making Adrift*, p. 44.
[18] Brzezinski, President Carter's National Security advisor, insisted on the prerequisite.
[19] LeoGrande and Kornbluh, *Back Channel to Cuba*, pp. 215–16.
[20] Engstrom, *Presidential Decision Making Adrift*, p. 50.

The specter of "another Camarioca" did not, however, convince the Carter administration to grant Cubans visas to come lawfully. Four thousand Cubans were on a waiting list for visas, some of them for more than two years.[21] In frustration, 700 Cubans protested in front of the US Interests Section in Havana, and nearly 400 Cubans forced their way into the building. Once they had applied to their government for exit visas, they lost their rights to work and to a ration card entitling them to affordably priced food.[22]

Small numbers of other Cubans sought asylum at Latin American embassies in Havana.[23] Most significantly, on April 1 a few Cubans crashed a bus through the gates of the Peruvian embassy to request asylum. Cuban guards fired on the bus. Inadvertently, a guard was killed in the crossfire, which incensed Castro and led him three days later to order the guard posts at the embassy to be torn down and the grounds left unguarded to enable asylum-seekers to enter. Undoubtedly, he was surprised when 10,000 Cubans stormed the embassy over a period of two days. They jammed themselves inside, shoulder to shoulder.

The Cuban government faced a crisis. Aside from revealing widespread discontent, the embassy occupants were without adequate food, water, toilet facilities, and beds for sleeping. To address the immediate problems, Cuban authorities told the asylum-seekers to return home, with the promise that arrangements would be made for them to be able to leave the country. While the asylum-seekers waited to leave, neighbors, mobilized by the Communist Party-controlled block organization, aggressively chastised them and made their lives uncomfortable.

Because most Cubans who occupied the Peruvian Embassy wanted to go to the United States, where friends and family had previously moved, Washington became directly involved in finding a solution to the Embassy crisis. In collaboration with the Cuban and Peruvian, as well the Costa Rican, governments, the Carter administration offered to have the

---

[21] JCPL, Collection Staff Offices, Special Assistant to President: Esther Torres Coopersmith, September 26, 1979–November 11, 1979, through Department of Education September 5, 1979–August 25, 1980, Folder: "Cuba: December 7, 1979 to February 14, 1980, White House, from Susan Gómez-Collins to Bob Pastor, February 14, 1980, Box 17."

[22] JCPL, Collection: Domestic Policy Staff, Civil Rights and Justice White, Refugees: Cubans and Haitians (6), Folder: Refugees: Cubans and Haitians (3), "Cuban Refugee Crisis May Prompt Introduction of Special Legislation," *Congressional Quarterly*, Special Report: Refugees, May 31, 1980, Box 22.

[23] JCPL, Staff Offices Hispanic Affairs: Armando Rendon Collection, Folder: Cuban–Haitian Refugees 1979–1980, Brian Atwood, "Foreign Affairs Memorandum: The Cuban Exodus," May 1980, Box 1.

asylum-seekers flown to Costa Rica, where up to one-third of them, 3,500, would be screened, along with their families, for admission to the United States as refugees.[24] Here, President Carter built on President Johnson's successful airlift that had brought Cubans who had been screened abroad to the United States.

The Carter administration expected other governments to accept the remaining 6,500 Peruvian Embassy asylum-seekers. Few countries, however, rose to the occasion, and the 500 asylum-seekers who the Peruvian government accepted resented the United States for passing them over.[25] In June, they staged a hunger strike in Peru, to press for admission to the United States.

In admitting the Cubans as refugees, the Carter administration could circumvent the congressionally mandated preference system that had officially guided immigrant admissions since passage of the 1965 immigration reform. The administration claimed that the Cubans were refugees on the grounds that they had sought asylum in a foreign embassy, even though few of them met the near universally agreed criteria for refugee status to which the United States had subscribed as a signatory to the 1967 Protocol Relating to the Status of Refugees (ratified by the US Senate in 1968). The Carter administration knew full well that Castro had opened the embassy to any Cuban who wanted to leave, regardless of reason.

President Carter even went a step further in his outreach to the 3,500 Cubans. In a Presidential Determination, he claimed that it was in the foreign policy interests of the United States to designate the Peruvian Embassy asylum-seekers as refugees entitled not merely to entry but also to resettlement assistance.[26]

---

[24] Shortly before the Peruvian Embassy occupation, President Carter had committed the United States to admit 16,000 Cuban refugees, in conjunction with the Refugee Act of 1980 (to be described later in the chapter). JCPL, Collection: Domestic Policy Staff, Civil Rights and Justice White, Refugees: Cubans and Haitians (6), Folder: Refugees: Cubans and Haitians (3), "Cuban Refugee Crisis May Prompt Introduction of Special Legislation," *Congressional Quarterly*, Special Report: Refugees, May 31, 1980, Box 22. The United States eventually took in 6,200 of the Embassy occupants. Garcia, *Havana USA*, p. 57.

[25] JCPL, Collection: Staff Offices Hispanic Affairs: Rendon Collection, Office of the White House Press Secretary, Folder Cuban: Haitian Refugees 1979–1980, Atwood, "Foreign Affairs Memorandum: The Cuban Exodus."

[26] JCPL, Collection: Staff Offices Special Assistant to President: Torres, Folder: Cuban/U.S. Issue/Briefing Book, April 8, 1980–May 22, 1980, Memorandum from Peter Tarnoff (Department of State) for Secretary of Defense, Attorney General, Director of Central Intelligence, Chairman Joint Chiefs of Staff, Director Office of Management and Budget,

The Peruvian Embassy occupation proceeded to generate problems for the Carter administration. Two days after the first asylum-seekers arrived in Costa Rica, Castro abruptly suspended the airlift, after the arrival of only seven hundred Cubans.[27] Irate about the negative international publicity that the Costa Rican president gave to the arriving Cubans, Castro announced that Cubans needed to be flown directly from Cuba to their final destination. Costa Rica could not serve as a waystation. The new requirement put President Carter in a bind, in that a refugee act that he had signed into law just a few weeks before the stampede on the Peruvian Embassy specified that persons needed to be screened abroad and demonstrate that they fled persecution in order to be admitted to the United States as refugees.

THE MASS EXODUS FROM MARIEL

Complicating matters for President Carter, before he had time to arrange an airlift direct from Cuba Castro acted on his Deputy Prime Minister's warning that the Cuban government might allow people in small boats to pick up family, "more than you bargained for." On April 20, two days after stopping the airlift, the Cuban government announced that Cubans who wished to emigrate to the United States were free to board boats at the port of Mariel, some twenty miles from Havana.[28] He thereby unleashed a replay of Camarioca, this time, though, on far grander scale, at a different port. While typically limiting departures, Castro manipulated the new exodus to Carter administration disadvantage. He deliberately fueled bilateral tensions anew, over emigration.

Earlier Cuban émigrés immediately seized the opportunity to have their family in Cuba join them in the United States. They commissioned boats to go from Florida to Mariel. By April 25, approximately one thousand boats set off for Mariel.[29] Compliance with official Washington immigration regulations did not concern them.

Assistant to the President for National Security Affairs, Subject: Mini-PRC Meeting on Cuban-Peruvian Situation, April 8, 1980, Box 17.

[27] Gilburt Loescher and John Scanlan, *Calculated Kindness: Refugees and America's Half-Open Door 1945–Present* (New York: Free Press, 1986), p. 182.

[28] Smith, *Closest of Enemies*, p. 212.

[29] JCPL, Collection: Staff Offices, Special Assistant to President: Torres, Folder: Cuban/U.S. Issue/Briefing Book, April 8, 1980–May 22, 1980, Office of the Vice President, Memorandum for Secretary of State, Seretary of Defense, Secretary of the Treasury,

The Cuban government opened the Mariel port not merely to the Peruvian Embassy asylum-seekers – those it had promised could leave – but also to other Cubans. In so doing it triggered a far larger exodus than would have been the case had the Carter administration accepted all of the Peruvian Embassy asylum-seekers. By the end of September, some 125,000 Cubans had come to the United States from Mariel: over thirty-five times more than the 3,500 Peruvian Embassy occupants that President Carter had agreed to admit, and over ten times more than had he accepted all of the embassy occupants. More Cubans came during the first week of what came to be known as the Mariel boatlift than had come from Camarioca in 1965,[30] and, in May, more Cubans came to the United States via Mariel than in any previous year.

The Carter administration immediately faced the problem that the boatpeople had not been screened abroad and admitted in accordance with US immigration and refugee regulations. Also, their numbers far exceeded the 20,000 yearly Western Hemisphere country quota that Congress had instituted four years earlier, in INA immigration amendments. Compounding problems for the Carter administration, the Cuban government reserved the prerogative to load four people of its choosing on to the boats for every one family member picked up.[31] Spitefully, Cuban authorities loaded drug addicts, alcoholics, prostitutes, criminals, and mental patients, as well as Jehovah Witnesses, homosexuals, and others they considered undesirable, on to the boats. Twenty-six thousand of the Cubans had criminal records, although mainly for minor crimes. Approximately two thousand had committed serious felonies.[32]

In early July, the Cuban government proceeded to nearly provoke a military confrontation with the United States over the Mariel exodus. It ordered a large Cuban freighter, the Blue Fire, to transport three thousand Cubans to Florida. The scale of the undertaking so infuriated the Carter Administration that it insisted the Blue Fire be stopped, militarily if necessary. It accordingly ordered naval forces to blockade the Mariel port.[33] Fortunately, successful diplomacy on the part of Secretary of

---

Attorney General, and Secretary of Health, Education and Welfare, Subject: Meeting on Cuban Refugees, the White House, April 26, 1980, Box 17.

[30] Engstrom, *Presidential Decision Making Adrift*, p. 138.
[31] Larzelere, *The 1980 Cuban Boatlift*, p. 133.
[32] García, *Havana USA*, p. 64; Rafael Hernández and Redi Gomis, "Retrato del Mariel: el ángulo socioeconómico," *Cuadernos de Nuestra América* vol. 3 no. 5 (January–June 1986): 124–51.
[33] LeoGrande and Kornbluh, *Back Channel to Cuba*, p.221, fn 259.

State Edmund Muskie, the Chief of Mission of the US Interests Section in Havana, Wayne Smith,[34] President Carter's director for Latin America at the National Security Council, Robert Pastor, and Executive Secretary of the Department of State Peter Tarnoff convinced the Cuban government to withdraw the boat.[35]

Meanwhile, in Cuba Castro tried to manipulate the mass migration to his political advantage, by discrediting and stigmatizing those who sought to leave. He portrayed departing Cubans as unpatriotic and "scum," and, with his blessing, the Communist Party called on neighborhood groups and unions to stage *actos de repudio*, repudiation acts, against the "turncoats." In night-time rampages, regime loyalists attacked the homes of their neighbors who had requested exit permits.[36] And before Cubans could leave they were required to sign documents confessing to be social deviants and to have committed crimes against the state.[37] Thus, while the Cuban government officially allowed Cubans to leave, it did not let them depart with dignity.[38] In turning neighbors against each other, the Mariel migration became a low point in the history of the revolution. At the same time, the government rallied patriotism to the anti-migration cause. It organized a million-strong demonstration on May 1, and other rallies subsequently.[39]

Finally, on September 25, Castro shuttered the Mariel port to emigration: in part to help President Carter's reelection prospects against the conservative Republican presidential candidate Ronald Reagan.[40] By then, however, Castro had caused President Carter too much political damage, as detailed later in this chapter. In November, President Carter

---

[34] In 1977 the Carter and the Cuban governments established Interests Sections that fell short of full diplomatic relations.

[35] Kami, *Diplomacy Meets Migration*, pp. 169–71; Smith, *Closest of Enemies*, pp. 233–34.

[36] Susan Eckstein, *The Immigrant Divide: How Cuban Americans Changed the US and Their Homeland* (New York: Routledge, 2009), p. 25. For portrayals by Cubans who left from Mariel, seeMirta Ojito, *Finding Manana: A Memoir of a Cuban Exodus* (New York: Penguin Press, 2005) and Reinaldo Arenas, *Before Night Falls* (New York: Viking, 1993).

[37] García, *Havana USA*, p. 65; Arenas, *Before Night Falls*.

[38] In my book, *The Immigrant Divide* (pp. 24–27), I cite indignities that Cubans faced when leaving, and when trying to leave, from Mariel.

[39] Kami, *Diplomacy Meets Migration*, pp. 155–56.

[40] Lars Schoultz, *That Infernal Little Cuban Republic: The United States and the Cuban Revolution* (Chapel Hill: University of North Carolina Press, 2009), p. 361; LeoGrande and Kornbluh, *Back Channel to Cuba*, pp. 222–23; Engstrom, Presidential Decision-Making Adrift, p. 79.

lost his bid for reelection, with the mass arrival of unauthorized Cubans contributing to his defeat.

With the Cuban government controlling who could leave, Mariel Cubans were socioeconomically and racially more diverse than earlier Cuban émigrés.[41] There were professionals and persons in the arts in the mix but also more working class and dark-skinned Cubans. Meanwhile, the "undesirables" who the Cuban government had loaded on to the boats that Cuban émigrés commissioned smeared the image of all the new Cubans. The media focused on the "undesirables." As a consequence, President Carter could not claim the new migration as a victory of capitalist democracy over communism. Outraged by the media portrayals, the American public for the first time opposed Cuban immigration.[42]

CARTER ADMINISTRATION RESPONSE TO THE MARIEL MIGRATION

The Carter Administration could not passively stay at the sidelines as the Cuban government permitted Cubans to leave for the United States without entry authorization. Did it treat arriving Cubans the same as other unauthorized immigrants, and deny them legal rights to stay, to work, and to citizenship, or did it follow the precedent of previous presidents and grant them special entitlements?

In 1980, conditions in the United States did not favor welcoming yet more Cubans. The country was in a restrictionist mood. Since the mid-1970s over two million unauthorized immigrants from other countries were estimated to have entered the United States. In addition, several thousand Indochinese refugees who had sided with the United States in

---

[41] See Eckstein, *The Immigrant Divide*, pp. 16, 19, 23–28. On Mariel émigrés, see also García, *Havana USA*, chapter 2; Ernesto Rodríguez Chavez, "El patrón migratorio cubano: cambio y continuidad," *Cuadernos de Nuestra America* vol. 9l, no. 1 (January–June 1996): 77–95; R. Bach, J. Bach, and T. Triplett, "The Flotilla 'Entrants': Latest and Most Controversial," *Cuban Studies* vol. 11 (1981): 29–48; Jesús Arboleya, *Havana Miami: The US–Cuba Migration Conflict* (Melbourne: Ocean Press, 1996); Silvia Pedraza, *Political and Economic Migrants in America: Cubans and Mexicans* (Austin: University of Texas Press, 1985). On the adaptation of Mariel Cubans in their first few years, see Alejandro Portes, Juan Clark, and Robert Manning, "After Mariel: A Survey of the Resettlement Experiences of 1980 Cuban Refugees in Miami," *Cuban Studies/Estudios Cubanos* vol. 15 (Summer 1985): 37–59.

[42] Scanlan and Loescher, "U.S. Foreign Policy, 1959–80: Impact on Refugee Flow from Cuba," p. 127.

the Vietnam War came, at a time when the American economy was in recession and jobs were scarce. Running for reelection that year, President Carter had his own political interest in not exacerbating labor market pressures and in demonstrating command over the country's borders. The Iranian hostage crisis, involving Americans who Iranian students held in captivity, had already made President Carter look politically weak in the eyes of Americans.

Despite the unwelcoming milieu, earlier Cuban immigrants were deeply committed to having family in Cuba join them in the United States. They were willing to defy US immigration regulations and the restrictionist mood of the time. President Carter accordingly faced conflicting pressures.

Strategies Considered

Top members of the Carter administration immediately deliberated alternative ways in which the President might deal with Castro's opening of the Mariel port to emigration.[43] On April 25, the Office of the Vice President drafted a report outlining options for the Secretaries of State, Defense, Treasury, and Health, Education and Welfare, and the Attorney General to consider.[44] A high level group of consultants that was convened by the Vice President's office discussed the options at a meeting the following day. Three of the four alternatives focused on blocking entry of the new Cubans: a reversal of the United States' until then inclusionary stance toward Cubans, but consistent with domestic economic and political concerns at the time.

The one inclusionary option that the Vice President's group considered involved *welcoming the Mariel Cubans*. While appreciated from a human rights vantage point, the group worried that the option had three main drawbacks: (a) it would be costly, were the new arrivals to receive comparable benefits to earlier Cubans; (b) it would defy the Refugee Act that President Carter had just signed into law; and (c) it would expose a contradiction in US treatment of Cubans and Haitians who were seeking refuge in the United States at the same time.

---

[43] For an excellent description of meetings held to discuss the Mariel crisis, see Engstrom.

[44] JCPL, Collection: Staff Offices, Special Assistant to President: Torres; Folder: Cuban/US/Issue/Briefing Book April 8, 1980–May 22, 1980; Office of the Vice President, Memorandum for Secretary of State, Secretary of Defense, Secretary of the Treasury, Attorney General, and Secretary of Health, Education and Welfare, Subject: Meeting on Cuban Refugees, the White House, April 26, 1980, April 25, 1980, Box 17.

The second option that the group proposed was to *discourage Cubans from coming*: with tighter enforcement of existing laws and cooptation of Cuban Americans to stop the boatlift. US diplomats were ordered to oppose the boatlift because it violated US law.[45] To discourage unauthorized Cubans from immigrating, the group also proposed that the President rally *international pressure to convince Castro to resume the airlift*, which would allow for safe, orderly immigration.[46]

The third option that the committee considered involved the President invoking *national emergency powers*. He might take all possible steps to prevent boat departures and fine boat captains on their return from Cuba.

The fourth option was to *order a ship to transport Cubans to a third country*. This option invoked memories of the Blue Fire, although the passengers were not to be brought to the U.S. However, the advisory group worried that Cubans would resist being sent anywhere but to the United States, and that other governments would be unlikely to accept many Cubans. The Carter administration had already struggled to find countries that were willing to accept the Peruvian Embassy asylum-seekers.[47]

Exclusionary Initiatives

The Carter administration immediately concerned itself with how to stop boats from illicitly transporting Cubans to the United States: already prior to, but also after, deliberation of the April 25 memorandum. US officials considered stopping boats in Cuban waters and on the high seas, imposing a naval blockade, and diverting boats to Guantanamo. However, they concluded that such interventions would be legally and politically problematic, as well as inhumane.[48]

Reflecting the administration's concern with exclusion, immediately after Castro opened the Mariel port for Cubans to leave, the National

---

[45] David Scott FitzGerald, *Refuge beyond Reach: How Rich Democracies Repel Asylum Seekers* (New York: Oxford University Press, 2019), p. 105.
[46] JCPL, Collection: Cuban/Haitian Task Force, "Cubans Seek Asylum in United States," United States Department of State, Bureau of Public Affairs, May 14, 1980, Box 11. At least seven Cubans had died during the Mariel boatlift on the high seas.
[47] JCPL, Collection: Staff Offices, Special Assistant to President: Torres, Folder: Cuban/US. Issue/Briefing Book, April 8, 1980–May 22, 1980, Meeting on Cuban Refugees, The White House, Memorandum from A. Denis Clift, Assistant to the Vice President for National Security Affairs, for Secretaries of State, Defense, Treasury, and Health, Education and Welfare, and Attorney General, Subject: Options for Cuban Refugees, April 26, 1980, Box 17.
[48] Kami, *Diplomacy Meets Migration*, p. 147.

Security Council recommended that the administration stop the boatlift. In turn, on April 23, the State Department warned that anyone traveling to Mariel to pick up Cubans would be committing a felony, and be subject to up to five years imprisonment, fines of $1,000–$2,000, and forfeiture of their boats. Under US law it is a felony to bring an alien into the country if they are not duly admitted by an immigration officer.[49] In this vein, the US Customs Service seized some boats that were returning from Mariel.[50]

Consistent with the second option, the administration also set about to coopt Cuban Americans: to convince them not to go to Mariel to pick up family. The day after the Vice President's committee deliberated the four options, a group was commissioned to meet with Cuban American leaders, in a get together that Jack Watson – Assistant to the President for Inter-Government Affairs, and, later, Carter's White House Chief of Staff – described as a disaster.[51] Subsequent to the "disastrous" meeting, Eugene Eidenberg, President Carter's pointman in Miami, continued to try to dissuade Cuban Americans from going to Mariel, without, in his own estimation, success.[52]

The administration also took preliminary steps to divert Mariel Cubans to third countries, in line with the fourth option considered. On May 6, INS Acting Commissioner David Crosland sent a memorandum to the Office of Legal Counsel at the Department of Justice specifying that a foreigner apprehended within US territory who had not landed does not appear to have a right to apply for asylum under terms of the Refugee Act, and could be towed to a third country where he or she would not face persecution.[53]

Then, on May 14 President Carter announced new "get tough" enforcement measures that included a five-point program to end the boatlift.[54] The Attorney General was instructed to begin exclusion proceedings, and the INS was instructed both to fine persons unlawfully bringing Cubans to the United States and seize their vessels. New criminal violations and criminal prosecutions were introduced.[55]

[49] JCPL, Staff Offices Hispanic Affairs: Rendon Collection, Folder: Cuban–Haitian Refugees 1979–1980, "Mini-PRC on Cuban Refugees," April 22, 1980, Box 1.
[50] Larzelere, *The 1980 Cuban Boatlift.*   [51] Ibid., pp. 79–80.
[52] Ibid., p. 81; Kami, *Diplomacy Meets Migration*, p. 147.
[53] FitzGerald, *Refuge beyond Reach*, p. 106.
[54] JCPL, Cuban–Haitian Task Force, "Briefing Materials, Senate Appropriations Subcommittee Hearings," March 6, 1981, Box 11.
[55] JCPL, Office of the White House Press Secretary, White House Briefing by Benjamin Civiletti, Attorney General and Stuart Eizenstat, Assistant to the President for Domestic Affairs and Policy, and Jack Watson, Secretary to the Cabinet and Assistant to the President for Intergovernmental Affairs on Cuban Refugee Policy, May 14, 1980;

The exclusionary measures, however, were ineffective. By the third week of the opening of the Mariel port to emigration, tens of thousands of Cubans had made their way to the United States, no boat captains had been arrested, and customs agents had seized only six vessels carrying Cubans.[56] The fines had not dissuaded boat skippers from transporting Cubans from Mariel because the profits they could make as illicit human couriers far exceeded the fines; because local INS and Customs officials in Florida resisted enforcing penalties, accustomed as they were to welcoming Cubans; and because juries in South Florida rarely convicted the boat operators who were brought to trial, siding, instead, with Cuban Americans who sought family reunification.[57]

By June, though, enforcement policies did seem to take effect. Federal authorities had seized more than 400 boats,[58] and the Coast Guard had issued over 1,600 citations for infractions of maritime law. Two large cutters, supported by helicopters, were commissioned to patrol the Florida Straits,[59] and the Treasury Department amended Cuban Assets Control regulations to prohibit both the transporting of visa-less Cubans and financial transactions at Mariel between US-based boat owners and Cuban authorities.[60] From June 9 to September 26, when back channel Carter administration negotiations convinced the Cuban government to reseal the Mariel port to emigration,[61] only 13,400 Cubans came to the United States. In contrast, over 100,000 Cubans had come from Mariel prior to June 9.[62]

Inclusionary Initiatives

At the same time that the Carter administration initiated exclusionary measures to block Cuban immigration from Mariel, in line with three of the four options that the Vice President's committee recommended for

---

Larzelere, *The 1980 Cuban Boatlift*, p. xxi; "White House Statement on the Administration Policy toward the Refugees," May 14, 1980, *Public Papers of the Presidents of the U.S.: Jimmy Carter, 1980-1981 Book 1*.

[56] Engstrom, *Presidential Decision Making Adrift*, p. 82.
[57] Ibid.; JCPL, Federal Records: Records of Cuban–Haitian Task Force, Fort Indiantown Gap Camp File, Consolidation (File #2) (2) Funding, Folder: Cuban Refugees, Memorandum from Paul Michel, Associate Deputy Attorney General, to Victor Palmieri, Refugee Coordinator, U.S. Department of State and David Aaron, National Security Council, "Cuban Refugees," Box RG220.
[58] Engstrom, *Presidential Decision Making Adrift*, p. 111.
[59] FitzGerald, *Refuge beyond Reach*, p. 106.   [60] Ibid.
[61] LeoGrande and Kornbluh, Back Channel to Cuba, Chapter 5.
[62] Engstrom, *Presidential Decision Making Adrift*, p. 114.

policy consideration, it reached out to the Cubans who had managed to come ashore.[63] It processed them for admission, and granted them special entry rights and resettlement benefits above and beyond the entitlements associated with the one inclusionary option the Vice President's committee had considered. The Carter administration increasingly built on inclusionary initiatives of past presidents.

Outreach to Mariel Cubans who made it ashore began almost immediately, at the same time that the administration tried to block Cubans from coming. By the end of the first week that the Cuban government opened the port to emigration, the Carter administration agreed to grant those who came ashore sixty-day parole.[64] Then, in an oft-cited speech to the League of Women Voters in Philadelphia on May 5, President Carter hinted that the Mariel Cubans would be treated differently than other unauthorized immigrants. He made it known that he welcomed Cubans who sought "freedom from Communist domination" with "an open heart and open arms": as if he were guided by Cold War foreign policy concerns. Borrowing from President Johnson's framing of his "Freedom Flights," he spoke of the entourage of boats that left from Florida to pick up Cubans at Mariel as a Freedom Flotilla, and after the speech he commissioned the Coast Guard to issue safety instructions for boat owners who made the round trip to Mariel.[65] He also ordered the Navy, along with the Coast Guard, to assist the flotilla.[66] Even before the speech, the Coast Guard had assisted over 360 vessels.[67]

Jody Powell, President Carter's press secretary and closest, most trusted aide, affirmed at a May 6 news conference that the administration had decided not to turn boats from Mariel around or tow them to Cuba.[68] He signaled that the administration planned to treat Mariel Cubans differently

---

[63] On the conflicting Carter Administration policies, see Ibid., especially chapters 4 and 5; Scanlan and Loescher, "U.S. Foreign Policy, 1959–80."

[64] Ronald Copeland, "Cuban Boatlift: Strategies in Federal Crisis Management," *Annals of the American Academy of Political and Social Science* (1983), p. 146.

[65] Scanlan and Loescher, "U.S. Foreign Policy, 1959–80." p. 137; Engstrom, *Presidential Decision Making Adrift*, pp. 81–87.

[66] Juan Clark, Jose Ignacio Lasaga, and Rose Reque, *The 1980 Mariel Exodus: An Assessment and Prospects* (Washington, DC: Council on Interamerican Security, 1981), p. 4.

[67] FitzGerald, *Refuge beyond Reach*, p. 105.

[68] JCPL, Staff Offices Hispanic Affairs: Rendon Collection, Office of the White House Press Secretary, Folder: Cuban–Haitian Refugees 1979–1980, News Conference with Jody Powell, May 6, 1980, Box 1.

than other unauthorized immigrants (other than the Haitians, described later in this chapter, who arrived at the same time as the Cubans).[69]

Victor Palmieri, President Carter's Coordinator for Refugee Affairs, in turn, justified President Carter's special welcoming of Cubans as an extension of past policy. He explained at a May 12 Judiciary Committee hearing on the Caribbean crisis that when the President spoke of "open arms" it was in reference to twenty years in which the United States had a special relationship with Cubans who fled Castro.[70]

Even when announcing the five-point program on May 14 to stop the boatlift, President Carter called for an orderly sealift, if not an airlift. His administration made it known that it would prioritize admitting the Cubans who had sought refuge at the US Interests Section in Havana, political prisoners, Peruvian Embassy occupants, and close family of Cuban American permanent residents.[71] Building on President Johnson's Memorandum of Understanding associated with the Freedom Flights, the sealift was to allow for an orderly migration of Cubans who had not only been cleared to leave by the Cuban government but had also been approved for entry by the US government. If the Carter administration had been sparing in the number of Cubans it admitted during its first three years, it now proposed to welcome the flood of new unauthorized Cubans traversing the Florida Straits. However, the Cuban government insisted that cooperation with a sealift be contingent on bilateral talks about a range of issues, including about US spy overflights and US operations at its military base in Guantanamo Bay.[72] Because the Carter administration refused to accept the contingent conditions, an orderly sealift never transpired.

Then, in a further inclusionary gesture, in June the White House extended new entitlements to the Mariel Cubans who by then had come

---

[69] Ibid.; JCPL, Collection: Domestic Policy Staff, Civil Rights, and Justice White, Refugees: Cubans and Haitians, Folder: Refugees: Cubans and Haitians (6), Memorandum for the President, from James McIntyre, Jack Watson, and Stu Eizenstat, Subject: Strategy for dealing with status and benefits of Cuban and Haitian arrivals, n.d., Box 22.

[70] U.S. Senate, Committee on the Judiciary, *Caribbean Refugee Crisis: Cuban and Haitians*, Hearings before the Committee on the Judiciary, 96th Congress, 2nd session, May 12, 1980.

[71] Larzelere, *The 1980 Cuban Boatlift*, p. 276.

[72] JCPL, Staff Offices Hispanic Affairs: Rendon Collection, Folder: Cuban Refugees 1980, Office of the White House Press Secretary, The White House, Briefing by Benjamin Civiletti, Attorney General, Stuart Eizenstat, Assistant to the President for Domestic Affairs and Policy, and Jack Watson, Secretary to the Cabinet and Assistant to the President for Intergovernmental Affairs on Cuban Refugee Policy, May 14, 1980, Box 1.

ashore. It announced that the Cubans would be considered to be asylum seekers, and qualify for a new temporary status created especially for them, that of "Entrants: Status Pending" (described in more detail later in this chapter), which entitled them to resettlement assistance. President Carter subsequently extended the Entrant status rights to all Cubans who arrived until Castro shuttered the Mariel port to emigration in late September. In turn, his Attorney General extended Cubans' temporary rights to parole until January 1981, by which time the White House assumed Congress would enact legislation to entitle Entrants to lawful permanent residency.[73]

WHY THE CARTER ADMINISTRATION SHIFTED FROM EXCLUDING TO PRIVILEGING MARIEL CUBANS

In view of the economic recession, record unauthorized immigration from other countries, and "undesirables" in the Mariel mix, why did President Carter increasingly shift from an exclusionary to an inclusionary stance toward the new Cubans? Earlier Cuban immigrants, who had been beneficiaries of entitlements in the past, were key to the shift.

Earlier Cuban immigrants had not been passive bystanders since the days when Cubans stormed the Peruvian Embassy. At the time, they staged parades and demonstrations in Miami to pressure the White House to accept the asylum-seekers, and they collected money, food, and clothing for Cubans at the embassy that they planned to deliver in a flotilla of small boats.[74] Among the demonstrators were sanitation workers in Hialeah, a city within Miami-Dade County that came to be home to the largest percentage of people of Cuban origin of any city in the United States. Also, a motorcade of 50,000 Cuban Americans paraded through the streets of Miami to demand that the Carter administration admit the asylum-seekers.[75]

Then, when Castro halted the airlift of Peruvian Embassy asylum-seekers to Costa Rica and announced, on April 19, that Cuban

---

[73] Copeland, "Cuban Boatlift of 1980," p. 148.
[74] Ibid., p. 144; Engstrom, *Presidential Decision Making Adrift*, p. 61; Larzelere, *The 1980 Cuban Boatlift*, p. 27.
[75] JCPL, Staff Offices Special Assistant to President: Torres, Folder: Cuban/U.S. Issue/Briefing Book, April 8, 1980–May 22, 1980, Memorandum to Phil Wise, White House, from Bernardo Benes and Alfredo Duran, Subject: The issuance of parole visas to 5,000 ex-political prisoners of Cuba, September 21, 1979, Box 17.

Americans could come by boat to Mariel to pick up relatives, Cubans in Miami shifted their strategy. They defied US immigration regulations, and seized the opportunity to retrieve relatives. Key leaders in Miami warned the White House of likely riots in Miami if it blocked Cubans from coming.[76]

Earlier Cuban émigrés who, in the main, by 1980 were more economically established than when Castro opened the Camarioca port to emigration in 1965, roamed the Key West waterfront with fistfuls of cash. Boatowners took advantage of the situation and charged exorbitant fees, as much as $5,000 per person they picked up at Mariel.[77] So committed were some of the earlier Cuban immigrants to have family join them in the United States that they mortgaged their homes, sold their cars, and drew on their life savings to pay boat owners.[78] Thus, while the Cuban government opened the door for Cubans to leave, earlier Cuban immigrants were the new immigrant enablers, together with boat owners that they commissioned.

The Carter administration had tried to restrain the Cuban immigrant enablers by seeking the cooperation of influential Cuban Americans: or, in the less polite language of the "in-house" April 25 memorandum of the Office of the Vice President, by coopting Cuban American leaders. Esteban Torres, a Mexican American who served as special assistant to President Carter, led the effort to coopt Cuban Americans. However, he returned discouraged from meeting with a key group of them. In an April 29 note to Jack Watson, he bemoaned, "Frankly, we lost control." He added that more effort was essential to "bring the community in. We simply must take the offensive."[79]

The administration faced Cuban Americans who were divided in their views and imposed conflicting demands. One faction wanted the administration to intervene forcefully, in order to destabilize the Cuban government. This faction did not want Cubans to leave the island, but, rather, to form a nucleus on the island to overthrow Castro with US support. After twenty years, these émigrés had not given up on toppling the Castro-led

---

[76] Larzelere, *The 1980 Cuban Boatlift*, pp. 239–40.
[77] John Goshko, "State Department Seeks to Halt Sealift," *Washington Post* (April 24, 1980) (www.washingtonpost.com/archive/politics/1980/04/24/state-dept-seeks-to-halt-sealift/e13bcoab-1434-40ec-8141-75e7bc76181e/).
[78] Kami, *Diplomacy Meets Migration*, p. 147.
[79] JCPL, Staff Offices Special Assistant to President: Torres, Folder: Cuban-Peruvian Situation, Memorandum from Esteban Torres, the White House, to Jack Watson, Subject: Cuban Situation, April 29, 1980, Box 17.

government with US assistance. A second faction, in contrast, wanted the United States to accept all Cubans who wished to come, consistent with the one inclusionary strategy outlined in the April 25 memorandum. They wanted all Cubans to enjoy the "open arms" that they experienced when they came. Yet another faction was wary about subversive and criminal elements among the Cubans coming from Mariel.[80]

Palmieri, the Carter administration coordinator of refugee affairs, understood that determined Cuban Americans could not easily be stopped. He considered it "one of the greatest jokes" that the group of high ranking government officials thought they could coopt the "crazed Cuban freedom fighters."[81] From the start, influential Cuban Americans warned senior State Department officials that they would not support the administration's efforts to terminate the boatlift.[82] In essence, they resisted cooptation.

The strategy advocated by the second faction, to accept all Cubans who wished to come, won out, but not by convincing the administration of the merits of their stance. Rather, while high-ranking members of the administration focused on coopting influential Cuban Americans,[83] rank-and-file Cuban Americans took it on themselves to commission boat pickups in Mariel. They had strength in numbers. They even refused the administration's promise to find a safe and orderly alternative way for their relatives to come to the United States, unconvinced that it would deliver on its promise. As a result, the boatlift continued until Cuban Americans retrieved the relatives they wanted and whose trip they willingly financed, and Castro shuttered the port to emigration.

In essence, high-ranking members of the administration had underestimated the collective force of ordinary Cubans. Scholarly analysts of the boatlift have done little better. Their studies have focused on state actors. For example, David Engstrom, in his book on the boatlift, focuses on strategies that were recommended by different state actors, their stature and influence, and the speed, consistency, and timing of their decision-making: all the while that ordinary Cuban Americans took history into their own hands, unconcerned about policymakers. Engstrom highlights how state-based dynamics account for Johnson administration success

---

[80] Ibid.   [81] Engstrom, *Presidential Decision Making Adrift*, p. 80.
[82] Goshko, "Leaders Seek Admission of All," *Washington Post* (April 27, 1980): 1.
[83] Lars Schoultz, in *That Internal Little Cuban Republic*, p. 295, notes, "the Carter archives are dotted with discussions about how to use U.S. policy toward Cuba to bolster the (A) dministration's standing among Florida's Cuban American community."

and Carter administration failure in handling the Cuban boatlifts under their respective watches. Although Engstrom does not ignore rank-and-file Cuban Americans, they are not the focus of his concern. In a sense, they are portrayed as an exogenous force with which the state actors needed to contend.[84] Moreover, in his emphasis on statecraft accounting for President Johnson's success and President Carter's failure to rein in unauthorized migration from Cuba, Engstrom ignores that some 270,000 Cubans came on the Freedom Flights that President Johnson instituted to rein in a mass exodus in the making from Camarioca. President Carter's inability to similarly transform the Mariel exodus into an organized sealift, if not an airlift, resulted in roughly half as many Cubans immigrating. Nevertheless, the 1980 boatlift that Cuban Americans determinedly undertook on their own will be shown, later in this chapter, to have been far more costly than President Johnson's outreach to Cubans.

While Engstrom, in essence, insightfully addresses intrastate dynamics that led, in his words, to Carter's, but not Johnson's, presidential decision-making going "adrift," he inadequately accounts for how the Cuban American community had changed since the days of the Camarioca boatlift. By 1980, the Cuban American community was far larger, owing, in part, to the more than one-quarter million Cubans that had come on the Freedom Flights: a larger force for the Carter administration to deal with, especially in Florida. By 1980, Cuban Americans also were wealthier, having taken advantage of assets they came with, the unique entitlements they received on arrival, and opportunities to be had in Greater Miami as the city transformed into a vibrant metropolis that Cuban Americans helped to make. They therefore were better able than Cuban Americans in 1965 to pay boat owners to transport family from Cuba and more confident in asserting their will and way. Also by 1980, more Cuban émigrés had votes to parlay, as beneficiaries of the 1966 Cuban Adjustment Act which provided them a path to citizenship. They thus were better positioned to pressure for family from Cuba to be able to join them in the United States.

By the same token, the Carter administration faced a more recalcitrant Castro than had the Johnson administration. By 1980, the Cuban revolution had officially become institutionalized, and Castro had consolidated power. He was better positioned then than in 1965 to resist US pressure

---

[84] See, for example, Engstrom, *Presidential Decision Making Adrift*, pp. 202–4.

and to leverage migration to his own advantage. A full understanding of the Mariel migration thus needs to take into account Cuban state dynamics, as well as dynamics among ordinary Cubans with transnational ties.

Hideaki Kami, in his study of US Cold War Cuban migration policy, adds to Engstrom's intrastate analysis: in his focus on what he defines as the interaction between diplomacy and migration. He elucidates US–Cuba diplomatic struggles over control of Cuban migration in 1980. Like Engstrom, he focuses on state institutions and state actors, though more in a transnational context. While recognizing how Cuban Americans, in his words, "ignored Washington," he barely describes, much less analytically accounts for, the role that ordinary Cuban émigrés played in the 1980 migration crisis. The Mariel migration stopped when the number of Cuban émigrés seeking to bring family from Cuba tapered off, in which context Castro plugged the Mariel port to emigration.

James C. Scott, in his analysis of "weapons of the weak," highlights – though not in the Cuban/Cuban American context – how "ordinary people" with limited formal power can evade demands made of them, and, in the aggregate, bring about change that powerful people oppose.[85] The ordinary Cuban Americans who took history into their own hands to retrieve family from Cuba contributed to a mass migration that high level policymakers, including President Carter himself, tried to avert and contain: much as Cuban émigrés in the 1960s resisted US efforts to unify and control them. While acting in their own (family) interests, they will be shown to have unleashed a multitude of consequences even they had not imagined.

PROBLEMS PROCESSING MARIEL CUBANS

Difficulties dealing with Mariel Cubans did not stop with their defiance of administration efforts to block their entry. Any foreign policy gain from admitting Cubans who rejected their country's Soviet-allied government became overshadowed by domestic problems that they unleashed.

Immediately, the administration faced the problem of how to deal with Cubans' illegal status. US law calls for exclusion or incarceration of

---

[85] James C. Scott, *Weapons of the Weak: Everyday Forms of Peasant Resistance* (New Haven, CT: Yale University Press, 1985) and *Domination and the Arts of Resistance: Hidden Transcripts* (New Haven, CT: Yale University Press, 1990).

persons who arrive without documentation and entry permission. The administration might have deported them but run the risk of committing the diplomatic sin of *refoulement*, that is, of subjecting returnees to persecution. Alternatively, it might have incarcerated them, but, as detailed later in the chapter, Mariel Cubans were quick to protest even temporary detention for admission processing. Also, earlier Cuban immigrants constrained the administration's options, having already pressured for the admission of Peruvian Embassy asylum-seekers.

Once "opting" to allow Mariel Cubans to stay, the Carter administration needed to screen them, and deny entry to those who immigration authorities deemed inadmissible. Yet, the processing generated new problems for the administration. In order to deal with the tens of thousands of arrivals who had not been pre-screened before coming ashore, President Carter declared a state of emergency in Florida. He assigned to FEMA, the Federal Emergency Management Agency, the responsibility for dealing with the new arrivals. However, FEMA proceeded to generate its own set of problems. It had insufficient Spanish-speaking staff; it was plagued by personnel turnover; it lacked a clear sense of direction; and it clashed with other federal agencies that also dealt with the Mariel Cubans.

Given the problems with FEMA, in July President Carter created a new bureaucracy, the Cuban–Haitian Task Force (CHTF), to deal with the processing and resettlement of Mariel Cubans, as well as Haitians who arrived at the same time (described later in the chapter). The CHTF reported directly to Palmieri, President Carter's coordinator for refugee affairs at the State Department, and to Eugene Eidenberg, Deputy Assistant to the President for Intergovernmental Affairs. In mid-November, after the Mariel door had been shut, the Carter administration transferred responsibility for the CHTF to the Department of Health and Human Services (HHS).[86]

Because Cubans arrived in such large numbers, immigration officials could not process them all immediately in Florida where they came ashore. Thus, after setting up makeshift processing centers in the state, the Carter administration opened processing centers elsewhere in the country, on military bases, where it faced yet new problems: in Eglin, Florida; Fort Chaffee, Arkansas; Indiantown Gap, Pennsylvania; and Fort McCoy, Wisconsin.[87]

---

[86] In June of 1981 the Reagan Administration disbanded the CHTF.
[87] Three of the four centers had previously been used for processing Indochinese refugees.

The administration had intended to open a fifth processing center, at Fort Allen, Puerto Rico. However, it dropped the plan when confronted with local political opposition. Puerto Ricans feared greater competition for jobs and greater crime, swayed by the media portrayals of Mariel Cubans as criminals. Faced with the opposition, the governor of Puerto Rico intervened to block the detention of Mariel Cubans on the island. Given that he was running for reelection later in the year, he did not want to turn voters against him. Putting his political interests first, he found a basis for suing the federal government: failure to prepare an adequate assessment of the environmental impact that internment of Mariel Cubans would have. The local district judge responded by issuing a temporary injunction that halted the transfer of Cubans to Fort Allen.[88]

Then, after sending the new arrivals to the processing centers that it had successfully set up, the Carter administration faced problems finding sponsors for some of the Cubans that families did not claim. Without sponsors, the new arrivals could not be released. Making matters worse, 30–40 percent of the federally funded placements that voluntary agencies, known as VOLAGS, contracted, broke down because host families found the Cubans problematic.[89]

The Carter administration faced yet more problems, with the criminals and mental patients that the Cuban government had spitefully loaded onto boats at Mariel. The INS deemed some 2 percent of the arrivals "inadmissible," either because they had committed violent crimes in Cuba or because they needed institutionalization for psychiatric disorders.[90] After the administration closed other processing centers, it assigned all of the "inadmissibles" to the Fort Chaffee detention center in Arkansas. However, the Cubans who were sent to Fort Chaffee did not quietly acquiesce to their internment. Some of them escaped the facility, and committed robberies and other crimes in surrounding communities. Their escape contributed to Bill Clinton, the incumbent Arkansas governor at the time, losing his reelection bid. His Republican opponent

---

[88] JCPL, Office of Chief of Staff Cuba-Haiti [3], Cuban–Haitians, Statement by the Honorable Hernan Padilla, mayor of San Juan, presented to Secretary of State Edmund Muskie, October 16, 1980, "Puerto Rico and the Refugee Issue" [3] FOIA Kate Moore, Box 2.

[89] Silvia Unzueta, "The Mariel Exodus: A Year in Retrospect," Cuban Information Archives, document 0033 (Metropolitan Dade County Government, Office of the County Manager, Special Projects Administrator for Refugee Affairs, April 1981).

[90] Schoultz, in *That Infernal Little Cuban Republic*, p. 360, describes how arbitrary some of the classifications of Mariel Cubans as criminals were.

campaigned on the promise to shut the facility: a promise he acted on when elected. The Mariel Cubans who were interned in Fort Chaffee were then sent to the federal penitentiary in Atlanta and to a federal prison in Oakdale, Louisiana, where they caused yet more havoc, as described in Chapter 4.

Thus, if President Eisenhower set in motion a precedent of welcoming Cubans to discredit and undermine Castro's rule, Mariel Cubans generated problems that discredited Carter's presidency, while accomplishing no foreign policy goal. The problems for the Carter administration did not stop with processing the new arrivals for admission.

REFUGEES OR NOT REFUGEES, THAT IS THE QUESTION: THE NEED FOR AN IMMIGRATION STATUS TO ADMIT MARIEL CUBANS

Along with determining which Mariel migrants were "admissible," the Carter administration needed a basis for authorizing their stay in the United States. The Hart–Celler Act (described in Chapter 1), which regulated immigration, could not serve as the basis for admitting so many Cubans, especially those without family in the United States to sponsor them.[91] Complicating matters, the INA Amendments of 1976 capped yearly Western Hemisphere country admissions at twenty thousand, and the State Department had such a backlog of immigration applications that no one who applied in 1980 could receive a residency visa.[92] In that President Carter happened to have signed into law the Refugee Act of 1980 just a few weeks before the first Mariel migrants came ashore, could the new legislation provide a basis for their admission? The applicability of the new refugee act became controversial and embroiled in domestic politics.

The Refugee Act of 1980

The Refugee Act of 1980 marked the first significant refugee legislation passed by Congress in decades.[93] How applicable was it to Mariel

---

[91] In some cases, the INS assigned the designation on the basis of hearsay reported by fellow arrivals. JCPL, Collection: Domestic Policy Staff, Civil Rights and Justice White, Refugees: Cubans and Haitians (6), Folder: Refugees: Cubans and Haitians (3), "Cuban Refugee Crisis May Prompt Introduction of Special Legislation," *Congressional Quarterly*, Special Report: Refugees, May 31, 1980, Box 22.
[92] Ibid.
[93] Congress passed the refugee act against the backdrop of President Carter's Attorney General having paroled approximately 290,000 Indochinese refugees into the United

Cubans? The law addressed broadly defined victims of persecution, not merely those living under communism. Thus, Cubans might qualify for admission on the basis of the new, broader refugee criterion, as well the older, narrower criterion, "victims of communism." Since Castro had come to power, Cubans had benefited more than any other group from the presumption that they were refugees.

Yet, the new refugee act called for reining in presidential parole authority, the basis on which most Cubans had been admitted into the United States. Members of Congress had felt that presidents had abused their parole authority, especially in admitting Cubans.[94] Nonetheless, recognizing that presidents needed parole authority to grant temporary entry rights under certain circumstances, when in the national interest and when humanitarian considerations were compelling, Congress agreed to permit presidential parole authority on an individual case-by-case, but not group, basis. If President Carter believed that admission of Mariel Cubans met these criteria, he might parole them into the country. However, it would be difficult to assess the merits of over one hundred thousand Cubans from Mariel case by case. Also, parole provided no basis for lawful permanent residency.

Complicating matters more, the Refugee Act set the cap of annual refugee admissions from all countries in the world until 1983 at 50,000, 19,500 of them from Cuba.[95] Yet, some 125,000 Cubans arrived from Mariel.

The Refugee Act did allow for admission of asylees, as distinct from refugees. Like refugees, asylees were defined as persons who had fled persecution and would likely suffer persecution if they returned to their homeland.[96] They differed only in where they applied for admission. Asylees apply in the United States; refugees apply abroad. Thus, once they were in the UnitedStates, technically, Mariel Cubans needed to be admitted as asylees. However, the Refugee Act only allowed five thousand

---

States. The Carter administration felt an obligation to admit the Indochines after the Vietnam War ended and the United States withdrew from the region. Kenneth Brill, "The Endless Debate: Refugees Law and Policy and the 1980 Refugee Act," *Cleveland State Law Review* vol. 32, issue 1 (1983): 124.

[94] Edward Kennedy, "Refugee Act of 1980," *International Migration Review* vol. 15 no. 1–2 (Spring–Summer 1981): 144.

[95] Felix Masud-Piloto, *From Welcomed Exiles to Illegal Immigrants: Cuban Migration to the U.S., 1959–1995* (Lanham, MD: Roman & Littlefield), p. 84.

[96] JCPL, Staff Offices Hispanic Affairs: Rendon Collection, Folder: Cuban–Haitian Refugees 1979–1980, Atwood, "Foreign Affairs Memorandum."

asylees to be awarded lawful permanent residency status in any one year,[97] and on the basis of a time-consuming vetting process, which was unfeasible for the large number of Mariel arrivals.[98]

Thus, even if Mariel Cubans had fled actual or likely persecution, they could not all be admitted either as refugees or as asylees. The Refugee Act of 1980 did, nonetheless, include one provision that was advantageous to Cubans: if they were paroled into the country. It specified that paroled Cubans could have their status adjusted to that of lawful permanent residents after one year, on the basis of the Cuban Adjustment Act. Until then, Cubans needed to wait two years. The modification put paroled Cubans on par with refugees in terms of the period they needed to wait to qualify for lawful permanent residence.

Contested Refugee Status

The Refugee Act of 1980 thus left the question of whether Mariel arrivals qualified for admission as refugees or asylees unresolved. President Carter had consulted with the Senate and House Judiciary Committees to admit the 3,500 Peruvian Embassy asylum-seekers that he promised US entry as refugees.[99] As refugees, they were to be screened for admission abroad, although his administration did not require them to demonstrate that they had fled actual or likely persecution, a requisite for refugee status under the new law; it would admit them as *presumed refugees*, on the grounds that they had sought refuge in a foreign embassy, even though the Cuban government had allowed any aspiring immigrant to go to the Peruvian Embassy, no questions asked. Thus, in admitting the Peruvian Embassy occupants as refugees, President Carter bent the rules of the refugee act almost immediately after signing it into law.

---

[97] JCPL, Collection: Domestic Policy Staff, Civil Rights and Justice White, Refugees: Cubans and Haitians (6), Folder: Refugees: Cubans and Haitians (3), "Cuban Refugee Crisis May Prompt Introduction of Special Legislation," *Congressional Quarterly*, Special Report: Refugees, May 31, 1980, Box 22.

[98] JCPL, Collection: Records of Cuban Haitian Task Force: RG220, Folder: Fascell/Stone, Memorandum from Assistant Attorney General, Office of Legal Counsel, USDJ, to Honorable Stuart Eizenstat, "Applicability of the Refugee Act of 1980 to Arriving Cubans and Haitians," May 27, 1980, Box 3.

[99] Scanlan and Loescher, "U.S. Foreign Policy, 1959–80," p. 136; B. E. Aguirre, "Cuban Mass Migration and the Social Construction of Deviants," *Bulletin of Latin American Research* vol. 13 no. 2 (1994), p. 165.

In contrast, President Carter argued that the Cubans arriving from Mariel were ineligible for admission as refugees, unlike those from the Peruvian Embassy. Most Mariel Cubans had not fled persecution; rather, they came to the United States to reunite with family, and – as key advisors to the President acknowledged – to improve their economic well-being.[100] The US also did not screen them abroad, as required for refugee admissions.

Against this backdrop, the question of whether to grant Mariel Cubans refugee status became highly contentious and politicized. Candidates in the 1980 election took issue with President Carter. During the primaries, both Republican candidates, George H. W. Bush and Ronald Reagan, as well as Edward Kennedy, a Democrat who challenged President Carter, argued that the Mariel Cubans qualified for admission as refugees. Kennedy's stance was particularly notable in that he chaired the Senate Judiciary Committee that was responsible for the new refugee act. He argued that the Mariel crisis did not involve a new refugee situation; rather, it evolved from the Peruvian Embassy occupation from which President Carter had admitted over three thousand Cubans as refugees. Kennedy expressed no concern about whether the Mariel Cubans had indeed fled actual or likely persecution.

The candidates across the partisan divide who took issue with President Carter argued less on principle than politics.[101] They wanted to appeal to earlier Cuban immigrants in the key "swing" state of Florida with votes to cast. Cuban American voters were expected to favor a candidate who promised to admit the new Cubans and assist their resettlement. While President Carter also had his eyes on the Florida electoral prize, he claimed that his stance was one of principle: the new Cubans did not meet the refugee admissions criteria that were specified in the new refugee act.

---

[100] JCPL, Collection: Domestic Policy Staff: Civil Rights and Justice White, Folder: Refugees: Cubans and Haitians (5), "Questions and Answers for Hearing on May 13 and 14, 1980," and Folder: Refugees: Cubans and Haitians (6), Memorandum for the President, from James McIntyre, Jack Watson, and Stu Eizenstat, "Strategy for dealing with status and benefits of Cuban and Haitian arrivals," Box 22.

[101] See JCPL, Collection: Domestic Policy Staff, Civil Rights and Justice White, Refugees: Cubans and Haitians, Folder: Refugees: Cubans and Haitians (3), Memorandum for the President from Frank Moore, Bob Schule, and Terry Straub, of the White House, Subject: Congressional Consultation on the Cuban/Haitian Situation, June 6, 1980, Box 22; JCPL, Collection: Cuban–Haitian Task Force, Memorandum for John White, Subject: Comments on the Draft Memorandum to the President on the Status of Cubans and Haitians, Box 11; Engstrom, *Presidential Decision Making Adrift*, pp. 146–47, 156.

Doris Meissner, Deputy Associate Attorney General at the time, offered a race-based explanation of President Carter's stance. She claimed that President Carter would indeed have treated the Mariel arrivals as refugees if Haitians had not come ashore in large numbers at the same time.[102] Although, arguably, the Haitians were better qualified than the Mariel Cubans for admission as refugees, because they were dark-skinned, their admission was more controversial. They were likely to fuel a racial backlash. Meissner thus implied that President Carter was also politically motivated in refusing to admit the Cubans as refugees, and not merely principled in his stance.

CIRCUMVENTING IMMIGRATION *AND* REFUGEE ADMISSION BARRIERS: CREATION OF A NEW UNIQUE BASIS TO ADMIT CUBANS

After President Carter won the Democratic primary, the matter of admitting Mariel Cubans remained unresolved. Building on precedent set by previous presidents, he proceeded not only to admit them, but to entitle them to benefits to assist their resettlement, though not as refugees.[103]

In June, President Carter drew on his discretionary authority to create the previously noted new immigration status for the Mariel Cubans, under the Attorney General's parole authority: that of "Entrants: Status Pending."[104] The Vice President's committee that deliberated options for the president had not even considered inventing a new, inclusionary basis for their admission. In admitting the Cubans, as well as Haitians who came ashore at the same time, as Entrants, President Carter circumvented congressional control over immigration. Cubans who arrived between April 21 and June 19 (and Haitians involved in immigration proceedings

---

[102] Mark Hamm, *The Abandoned Ones: The Imprisonment and Uprising of the Mariel Boat People* (Boston: Northeastern University Press, 1995), p. 54.
[103] Members of Congress were divided in their stance, not entirely on partisan lines. See JCPL, Collection: Domestic Policy Staff, Civil Rights and Justice White, Refugees: Cubans and Haitians, Folder: Refugees: Cubans and Haitians (3), "Cuban Refugee Crisis May Prompt Introduction of Special Legislation," *Congressional Quarterly Special Report: Refugees*, May 31, 1980, and Memorandum for the President, from Frank Moore, Bob Schule, Terry Straub (the White House), Subject: Congressional Consultation on the Cuban/Haitian Situation, June 6, 1980, Box 22.
[104] JCPL, Collection: Federal Records: Records of Cuban–Haitian Task Force, Fort Indiantown Gap Camp File, Briefing Book: Senate Appropriations Subcommittee (1) through Consolidation (File #2) (1), Folder: Briefing Book; Senate Appropriations Subcommittee [1], CHTF Data Book (4), Box 34.

as of June 19) were to be eligible for the special temporary immigration status, for six months.[105]

As Entrants, the Haitians, along with the Mariel Cubans, attained rights to work. They also were exempted from possible deportation as unauthorized immigrants, and eligible for SSI (Supplementary Security Income), Medicaid, AFDC (Aid to Families with Dependent Children), and emergency assistance. Carter's Cuban-Haitian Task Force specified that state and federal governments were to cost share;[106] local governments were to cover 25 percent of expenses. However, Cubans, as well as Haitians, who arrived after June 19 were to be ineligible either for the Entrant status or for the entitlements.[107]

The Carter administration proceeded both to renew Mariel arrivals' parole rights beyond the initial six months and to extend "Entrant: Status Pending" rights to more Cubans (as well as to more Haitians), namely, to those who came ashore up until October 10. An additional 11,000 visa-less Cubans, along with 5,500 visa-less Haitians, thereby attained Entrant status. In total, the approximately 125,000 unauthorized arrivals from Mariel, together with 25,000 unauthorized Haitians, thereby became newly imagined lawful, if temporary, immigrants.[108]

While the new Cuban (and Haitian) arrivals accordingly secured rights that were denied to other unauthorized immigrants, their entitlements fell short of those that were extended to persons admitted as refugees, who were granted permanent residency rights. Congress needed to enact special legislation for Entrants to attain such rights.

The coordinator of refugee affairs, Palmieri, approved of extending parole rights to the new Cubans, but felt that Congress should not be called on to legislate a unique path for them to attain lawful permanent residency until after the election. He feared that domestic politics, namely, election ambitions, would influence how members of Congress voted. He sensed that after the November election there would be a "less aggravated

---

[105] JCPL, Collection: Staff Offices Domestic Policy, Civil Rights and Justice White, Folder: Immigration and Refugee Policy, Select Commission (no. 2) (1), Office of Media Liaison, The White House Press Office, "Cuban and Haitian Arrivals: Crisis and Response: Background Report," June 30, 1980, Box 12.

[106] JCPL, Staff Offices Hispanic Affairs Rendon Collection, Folder Cuban–Haitian Refugees 1979–1980, "Cuban–Haitian Fact Sheet," June 20, 1980, Box 1.

[107] Ibid.

[108] Ruth Wasem, "U.S. Immigration Policy on Haitian Migrants," *CRS Report for Congress* (Washington, DC: Congressional Research Service, January 21, 2005), p. 1; JCPL, Collection: Cuban/Haitian Task Force, Folder: Briefing Materials: Senate Appropriations Subcommittee Hearings, March 6, 1981, Box 11.

environment."¹⁰⁹ At the same time, he did worry about extending unique entitlements to yet more Cubans because it would be

> locking ourselves into a posture where we will probably be accepting in the future all who happen to make their way here from Cuba. It is time instead to move decisively away from the special treatment Cubans have enjoyed for twenty years and toward parity with Haitians and all other asylum seekers.¹¹⁰

Notwithstanding Palmieri's advice to defer calling on Congress to pass enabling legislation until after the election, on July 31 President Carter arranged for his Attorney General's office to submit the Cuban–Haitian Entrant Act of 1980 to Congress for approval. The legislation was to formalize Entrant entitlements to resettlement benefits on the basis of federal–local government cost sharing, and permit Entrants to adjust their status after two years. The proposed legislation would have allowed, in one year, six times more Cubans than nationals of any other country to become lawful permanent residents, and the admission of over twice as many Cubans as refugees from all countries, in accordance with the Refugee Act of 1980.¹¹¹ At the same time, the legislation called for repealing the Cuban Adjustment Act, which, since 1966, had enabled Cubans – and only Cubans – to use temporary entry rights as a springboard for attaining lawful permanent residence.¹¹²

Congress was not, however, persuaded. It did not enact the proposed legislation. Under the circumstances, the administration had several options. It could submit new legislation to the next session of Congress; it could reclassify the Mariel Entrants as refugees, and thereby entitle them to adjust their status on the basis of the Cuban Adjustment Act (and submit separate legislation to Congress to enable the Haitian Entrants to adjust their status); it could let the Entrant status expire, in which case the Mariel Cubans would (re)join the ranks of unauthorized immigrants; or it could renew Cubans' (and Haitians') Entrant status while leaving their

---

¹⁰⁹ JCPL, Records of Cuban–Haitian Task Force—RG220, Subject File: Ada Merritt School through Cuban Situation, Folder: Cuban Reports to White House, Memorandum to John White, Office of Management and Budget, from Victor Palmieri, Subject: Options on the Status of Cubans and Haitians, June 12, 1980, Box 1.
¹¹⁰ Ibid.
¹¹¹ JCPL, Collection: Staff Offices Domestic Policy, Civil Rights and Justice White, Refugees: Cubans and Haitians, Folder Refugees: Cubans and Haitians (3), letter to the Vice President from Alan Parker, Assistant Attorney General, Legislative Affairs, Department of Justice, July 31, 1980, Box 22.
¹¹² JCPL, Staff Offices Hispanic Affairs, Rendon Collection, Folder: Cuban–Haitian Refugees 1979–1980, Cuban–Haitian Fact Sheet.

long-term status unresolved.[113] The Carter administration opted to extend Mariel Cubans' rights as Entrants until July 15, 1981, under the presumption that by then Congress would pass enabling legislation for them to adjust their status.[114] It never embraced the idea of deporting them or forcing them to join the ranks of illegal immigrants (whose numbers, especially from Mexico, and from Nicaragua following the Sandinista revolution of 1979, were on the rise). Thus, after having tried to block Mariel Cubans from coming, the administration opted for a strategy that extended new, unique rights to them.

Meanwhile, amid the migration crisis, the newly established US Interests Section in Havana stopped issuing immigration visas. The Carter administration extended rights to unauthorized immigrants from Mariel while shutting down legal immigration options. It stopped processing visa applications after a Cuban government-orchestrated mob attacked hundreds of ex-political prisoners who were applying for US immigration visas. The Cuban government provoked the confrontation to pressure the United States to tie bilateral discussions on a range of issues to US admission of the former political prisoners.[115] It sought a quid pro quo for conceding to let the once political prisoners leave the country.

THE BATTLE OVER FINANCING ENTITLEMENTS FOR THE NEWLY IMAGINED ENTRANTS

When it created a unique status for admitting the Mariel Cubans, the Carter administration also arranged for them to receive resettlement benefits similar to the exceptionally generous benefits that had been offered to earlier Cuban immigrants, who were imagined as refugees. There was little dispute about providing the new Cubans with benefits, but considerable disagreement about who should pay how much of the costs. The question of whether or not the Mariel Cubans deserved unique entitlements got lost in the political struggle over federal versus local funding.

---

[113] See U.S. House of Representatives (H.R.) 7978, Cuban-Haitian Entrant Act of 1980, 96th Congress (1979–1980).
[114] Ibid.
[115] William LeoGrande, "From Havana to Miami: U.S. Cuba Policy as a Two-Level Game," *Journal of Interamerican Studies and World Affairs* vol. 40 no. 1 (Spring 1998): 67–86.

As unauthorized entrants, the new Cubans qualified for few federal benefits. Yet, determined to entitle them to assistance, President Carter drew on disaster relief funds and on the Emergency Refugee and Migration Assistance Fund.[116] In declaring a state of emergency in southern Florida, his administration was also able to draw on a number of federal agency budgets.[117] It estimated the immediate costs of assisting the Mariel arrivals at nearly half a million dollars for FY 1980 (for five months), and $1,200,000 for FY 1981.[118]

The Carter administration arranged for the new Cuban arrivals to receive similar entitlements to those the earlier Cuban immigrants had received through the Cuban Refugee Program (CRP), America's most generous immigrant assistance program ever: job and language training; Medicaid-based health care; food stamps; financial assistance; and social services. It established the previously noted State Department-based Cuban–Haitian Task Force, the CHTF, to coordinate ten federal agencies that were involved in providing the benefits to the Cuban, along with Haitian, Entrants. The CHTF was authorized to reimburse states and localities 75 percent of their costs.

Yet, in providing the unique set of benefits to the latest Cuban arrivals, the Carter administration faced a series of problems. The CHTF was plagued by bureaucratic infighting, and political battles emerged between federal and state/local authorities, as well as between members of Congress and the White House. Local agency budgets had to be raided in order to finance the portion of expenditures that needed to be locally funded. Turf battles ensued.[119]

In Florida, where most of the incoming Cubans and Haitians settled, local cost sharing fell on resentful taxpayers. Faced with resentment about paying for an immigration problem that was not of their making, the state's Congressional delegation pressed for full federal funding of resettlement assistance. The legislators from the state argued that

---

[116] JCPL, Staff Offices Hispanic Affairs, Rendon Collection, Folder Cuban–Haitian Refugees 1979–1980, Atwood, "Foreign Affairs Memorandum."

[117] JCPL, Staff Offices Hispanic Affairs, Rendon Collection, Folder Cuban–Haitian Refugees 1979–1980, "News Conference" at the White House with Jody Powell, May 6, 1980, Box 1.

[118] JCPL, Staff Offices Special Assistant to President: Torres, Folder: Cuban/U.S. Issue/Briefing Book April 8, 1980–May 22, 1980, Note to Victor Palmieri, from Roger Winter, Office of Refugee Resettlement, Department of Health, Education, and Welfare, "Fact Sheet: Estimated Domestic Assistance Costs for Newly Arriving Cubans," Box 17.

[119] Aguirre, "Cuban Mass Migration and the Social Construction of Deviants," p. 169.

Carter's cost-sharing arrangement imposed an unfair tax burden on Florida residents, and that the Mariel émigrés were a national, not local, immigration matter.

Some members of Congress pressed to have the newly arrived Cubans classified as refugees, not because they felt the new arrivals had fled persecution, but because, if admitted as refugees, Floridians would not be taxed to finance assistance. The Federal government would cover all expenses. In this vein, the Senate Judiciary Committee (chaired by Kennedy) called on the administration to draw on the recently enacted Refugee Act of 1980 to reimburse 100 percent of the costs that states incurred in administering CHTF entitlements.

With President Carter insistent that most Mariel Cubans were not refugees, in that they demonstrated no evidence of fleeing persecution or likely persecution, the House of Representatives passed the 1981 foreign aid authorization bill on June 5 with a floor amendment proposed by the Florida Democrat Dante Fascell. The amendment called on the federal government to fully reimburse localities for the cash and medical assistance that they provided the new Cubans, whether or not they were refugees. Twelve days later the Senate approved a similar amendment, proposed by another Florida Democrat, Richard Stone. Miami-Dade County officials worked with the Florida Congressional delegation and the governor to lobby for passage of the amendment.

Despite Congress not approving the proposed amendment to the foreign aid authorization bill, the Florida legislators refused to put the matter to rest. Under pressure from them, on August 5 Senator Edward Kennedy introduced S. 3013, which considered the new Cubans to be refugees and thereby eligible for 100 percent federally reimbursed assistance under terms of the Refugee Act. Kennedy accused President Carter of proposing Mariel Cubans to be "75 percent, not 100 percent, refugees."[120]

When the Senate bill did not gain sufficient traction, determined legislators pursued another way to force the federal government to absorb all costs of assistance to the new Cubans: incorporation of the so-called Fascell–Stone Amendment into Title V of the Refugee Education Assistance Act (REAA) of 1980 (PL 96-422), which passed by voice vote on October 1. The Fascell–Stone Amendment entitled Cuban–Haitian Entrants to 100 percent federally financed Medicaid, SSI, food stamps, AFDC, English language courses, and job training for up to three

---

[120] Kennedy, "Refugee Act of 1980," p. 142.

years,[121] comparable to the federally funded benefits that refugees received, provided that the Entrants did not receive a final nonappealable order of removal.[122] In addition, the REAA entitled school districts to receive $450 federal dollars per new Cuban student.[123]

Thus, with the passage of the REAA, Congress finally agreed to treat the Mariel Cubans the same as refugees, while cognizant that they did not meet official criteria for refugee status. Building on the Cuban Refugee Program, which had entitled earlier Cuban arrivals to an exceptional range of full federally funded benefits as imagined refugees, Florida politicians fought for similar entitlements for the recent, unauthorized Cuban arrivals. However, they were motivated by local political considerations, not Cold War concerns. They sought to appeal to their growing Cuban immigrant political base, though not at Florida taxpayers' expense. With the Title V amendment, they accomplished their mission. No other unauthorized immigrants besides the Haitians who were fortunate enough to have arrived by sea at the same time as Mariel Cubans were entitled to comparable REAA benefits.

Title V of the REAA even extended certain benefits that earlier Cuban immigrants had not received to Entrants. The additional entitlements included rights to health care and cash benefits after becoming lawful permanent residents. Earlier émigrés lost special rights to these benefits once they adjusted their immigration status.

President Carter initially opposed the Fascell–Stone Amendment on budgetary grounds. He was not averse to the new Cubans receiving special entitlements, but wanted local cost sharing, as outlined in the legislation he had proposed in July.[124] With Congress having refused to pass the Cuban–Haitian Entrant Act, he accepted the Fascell–Stone

---

[121] Ronald Reagan Presidential Library (RRPL), White House Staff Member & Office Files, Francis (Frank) S.M. Hodsoll Files, 1981, Series II, President's Task Force on Immigration and Refugees (13): Immigration and Refugees (General) (11), Folder: Immigration and Refugees (13), Box 11. The Refugee Act called for the final phasing out of the Cuban Program authorized under the Migration and Refugee Assistant Act of 1962.

[122] Wasem, *U.S. Immigration Policy on Haitian Migrants* (Washington, DC: Congressional Research Service, Report for Congress, 2011), p. 9.

[123] JCPL, Collection: Domestic Policy Staff, Civil Rights and Justice White, Refugees: Cubans and Haitians, Cubans and Haitians, Folder Refugees: Cubans and Haitians (3), memorandum for the President, from Stu Eizenstat, Ellen Goldstein (White House), Subject Enrolled Bill H.R. 7859, Refugee Education Assistance Act of 1980, Box 22.

[124] Copeland, "Cuban Boatlift of 1980," p. 147.

Amendment, which considered Entrants as refugees for purposes of benefit eligibility.[125] While holding steadfastly that Mariel Cubans were not refugees, he agreed to *imagine* them as if they were refugees to entitle them to the same benefits as persons officially admitted as refugees. No other unauthorized immigrants were similarly imagined and, thus, similarly entitled to entirely federally funded benefits.

EXTENSION OF CUBAN ENTITLEMENTS TO HAITIANS

The United States had a shameful history of discriminating against Haitians. President Carter was part of that history until 1980, when he extended similar entitlements to Haitians as to Cubans if they arrived at the same time by sea. He extended the entitlements to Haitians when faced with stepped-up advocacy on their behalf.

Discrimination against Haitians Prior to 1980

During the course of the 1970s, economic and political conditions in Haiti went from bad to worse. Yet, the United States granted few Haitians immigration visas. As of 1977, the United States had admitted a mere 7,000 Haitians, almost all officially as economic migrants. Because Haitians had difficulty immigrating lawfully, those determined to relocate in the United States sought refuge without authorization. Their numbers soared from less than 300 in 1977 and 3,000 in 1979, to approximately 25,000 in the year of the Cuban exodus from Mariel.[126]

Haitians suffered the worst poverty in the hemisphere, as well as the despotic rule first of the kleptocrat Francois Duvalier, known as "Papa Doc," between 1957 and 1971, and then of his son, Jean-Claude "Baby Doc," beginning in 1971 (until 1986, when he was overthrown by a popular uprising). Despite both Duvalier governments killing and torturing thousands of Haitians, US presidents considered the Haitians who immigrated and who aspired to immigrate as seeking a better economic life, not refuge from persecution.

---

[125] JCPL, Federal Records: Cuban-Haitian Task Force, Fort Indiantown. Briefing Book, Senate Appropriations, Folder: CHTF: Legislative Action, comparisons of special status legislation, Refugee Act of 1980, Fascell-Stone Amendment, and Current Policy as of October 10 (1980), Box 34.

[126] Wasem, "U.S. Immigration Policy on Haitian Migrants," *CRS Report for Congress* (Washington, DC: Congressional Research Service, January 21, 2005), p. 1.

Few Haitians had come to the United States before 1980 because immigration authorities blocked their entry, and detained and deported many of those who made it ashore. Haitians briefly fared better when President Carter appointed Leonel Castillo as INS Commissioner, in 1977. Castillo, the first ethnic minority (Chicano) to serve as Commissioner, ordered the INS to release imprisoned Haitians without bond and grant them rights to work while they awaited asylum and deportation hearings. He ended years of bonded detention.[127] However, confronted with opposition from INS staffers and others in Miami, Castillo went on to retract rights that he had granted Haitians.[128] As a result, the Justice Department proceeded to deny Haitian asylum-seekers the right to work; it prevented them from fair hearings for asylum claims; and it expedited their deportation hearings. It did so in conjunction with what became known as the Haitian Program.[129]

Relevance of the Refugee Act of 1980

With the Refugee Act of 1980 officially ending Washington's Cold War bias in refugee admissions, Haitian prospects of admission as refugees should have improved, given the continued brutality of the Haitian government. Yet, 90 percent of US refugee admissions in 1980, as well as in 1981, were communist escapees (from Indochina, the Soviet Union, and Eastern Europe).[130] Thus, while Washington's refugee policy officially changed with the passage of the Refugee Act, in practice Cold War admission biases continued, which worked to Haitians' disadvantage. The longstanding racial biases in US admissions also worked to their disadvantage.

By 1980, Haitians, however, benefited from advocates on their behalf. They also more actively pressed for rights on their own.

Legal Advocacy on Haitians' Behalf

Faced with the history of earlier discrimination against Haitians, the Carter administration initially treated Haitians and Cubans differently.

---

[127] Alex Stepick, "Haitian Boat People: A Study with Conflicting Forces Shaping U.S. Immigration Policy," *Law and Contemporary Problems* vol. 45 (Spring 1982): 182; Jeffrey Kahn, *Island of Sovereignty: Haitian Migration and the Borders of Empire* (Chicago: University of Chicago Press, 2019), p. 71.

[128] Stepick, "Haitian Boat People," p. 182.   [129] Ibid., p. 183.   [130] Ibid., p. 173.

While Cubans who arrived before the Mariel exodus had been quickly processed for entry, classified as asylum applicants, and given cash and other assistance, Haitians were put in exclusion proceedings and detained.[131]

Fortunately for Haitians, they benefited from committed lawyers who filed legal cases on their behalf. The most celebrated case, the Haitian Refugee Center v. Civiletti (President Carter's Attorney General), was filed in May 1979, in the southern district of Florida.[132] The class action case argued that the Haitian Program had violated Haitian rights, that the US government had unfairly prejudged Haitian requests for political asylum (denying their claims), and that the INS had improperly handled Haitian asylum claims.

On July 2, 1980, Judge James Lawrence King issued his opinion on the case. He concluded that "Haitians who came to the United States seeking freedom and justice did not find it." "(T)hey were confronted with an Immigration and Naturalization Service determined to deport them."[133] Judge King added that "The decision was made among high INS officials to expel Haitians, despite whatever claims to asylum individual Haitians might have … This program (the Haitian Program), in its planning and executing, is offensive to every notion of constitutional due process and equal protection."[134] Believing that INS officials had been motivated, in part, by racial prejudice,[135] Judge King imposed a temporary injunction against the INS for denying Haitians fair representation and due process in deportation hearings. He also called for a stay of exclusion proceedings and enjoined the INS from executing deportation orders. Also finding that Haitians were denied work rights, in violation of the United Nations Protocol and the Administrative Procedure Act,[136] the court ordered their rights to be recognized. In addition, Judge King found the INS bureaucracy (but not Castillo) guilty of unfair treatment of Haitians.

Furthermore, Judge King concurred with plaintiff claims that Haitians had "well-founded fear of persecution" in Haiti, and that beyond economic motivations for immigrating they had political reasons for seeking refuge in the United States. In that they had fled persecution, grounds for refugee admission, Judge King issued a plan for reprocessing Haitian asylum claims.

---

[131] Ibid., p. 187.   [132] Ibid., pp. 185–87.   [133] Ibid., p. 186.
[134] JUSTIA:US Law, *Haitian Refugee Ctr.* v. *Civiletti*, 503 F. Supp. 442 (S.D. Fla. 1980), https://law.justia.com/cases/federal/district-courts/FSupp/503/442/1467096/.
[135] Stepick, "Haitian Boat People," p. 186.   [136] Ibid.

Subsequently, however, the fifth circuit court reversed Judge King's ruling. Nonetheless, the Carter administration codified King's opinion in regulatory texts. Haitians, accordingly, acquired legal basis for contesting INS exclusion.[137]

Political Advocacy on Haitians' Behalf

Independently of court cases, Haitians, together with their advocates, turned to political strategies to press for rights. Angered at what they considered unfair and discriminatory race-based treatment, they mobilized politically.

Haitians, for one, turned to the streets to press for rights they felt unfairly denied to them. In Miami, New York, and Washington they staged marches and hunger strikes.

Haitians also pressed for rights through institutional channels. They approached members of Congress, including the Black Caucus, as well as high-ranking members of the Carter administration. In April of 1980, they organized a letter-writing campaign to the president that the civil rights activist Vernon Jordan, union leaders, the executive vice president of the Synagogue Council of America, leaders of civil rights groups, and some members of Congress endorsed.[138]

Criticism of Haitian exclusion intensified after President Carter announced plans to admit Cubans who had stormed the Peruvian Embassy,[139] and more so after his administration began to admit unauthorized Cubans from Mariel. Key domestic policy advisors of President Carter were responsive to the mounting advocacy on Haitians' behalf. Stuart Eizenstat, chief domestic policy adviser, along with Jack Watson, who coordinated the president's domestic policy, recommended that both the Haitian and Cuban migrant situation be similarly resolved.[140] They argued that it was discriminatory to grant asylum

---

[137] Kahn, *Island of Sovereignty*, p. 61.   [138] Stepick, "Haitian Boat People," p. 188.
[139] JCPL, Collection: Domestic Policy Staff: Civil Rights and Justice White, Refugees: Cubans and Haitians, Folder: Refugees: Cubans and Haitians (4), Memorandum for Stu Eizenstat, from Frank White, Subject: Haitian Refugees, April 18, 1980, Box 23.
[140] JCPL, Collection: Domestic Policy Staff: Civil Rights and Justice White, Refugees: Cubans and Haitians, Folder: Refugees: Cubans and Haitians (10), Memorandum for the President, from Jack Watson, Stu Eizenstat, Subject: Cuban–Peruvian Situation and Implication for the Haitian in Florida, Box 23. For an excellent discussion of the debate within the Carter administration over admission of both the Haitians and Cubans as Entrants entitled to comparable benefits, see Engstrom, *Presidential Decision Making Adrift*, chapter 6, 156. The administration advocated for legislation, in order that Haitians be treated equally to Cubans.

automatically to the Cubans, but not to the Haitians, despite the Cubans having no stronger claim to refugee admission.[141] In a memorandum to the president they noted

> No one seriously argues that all of the 10,000 persons in the Peruvian Embassy (or, indeed, the 3,500 we will ultimately take) fled because of their personal political activities or beliefs ... It is far more likely that the vast majority wish to leave because they do not like their quality of life in Cuba ... Haitians who have left Haiti for the same reasons are being turned away.[142]

Amid the mounting political pressure, in May 1980 the Senate Judiciary Committee held hearings on the Cuban–Haitian crisis. There, Palmieri was grilled about the Administration's double standard toward Cubans and Haitians.[143] Criticism of the inequitable treatment of Cubans and Haitians contributed to President Carter's decision to extend comparable entitlements to both groups of aspiring immigrants, as "Entrants: Status Pending."

Although the Carter administration responded to Haitian rights advocates by officially linking Haitians' fortunes to Cubans' when the Mariel door was open, after Castro closed the door it rebuffed new unauthorized Haitian arrivals. Moreover, even when the Mariel door was open, Cubans and Haitians were not treated entirely equally. VOLAGS, the voluntary agencies charged with arranging sponsorships for the new arrivals, for example, had more funds for their placements of Cubans than Haitians. Also, unlike Cubans Haitians were not offered political asylum.[144]

COSTS INCURRED IN ADMITTING THE UNAUTHORIZED MARIEL CUBANS

The welcome mat extended to Mariel Cubans and piggy-backed Haitians helped the Carter administration to defuse domestic political pressure for immigrant equity, but it was socially and politically, as well as

---

[141] JCPL, Collection: Domestic Policy Staff—Civil Rights and Justice White, Refugees: Cubans and Haitians, Folder: Refugees: Cubans and Haitians (10), Memorandum for the President, from Jack Watson, Stu Eizenstat, Subject: Cuban-Peruvian Situation and Implication for the Haitian in Florida, Box 23.
[142] Ibid.
[143] Jon Sawyer, "Refugee Policy Draws Fire in Hearing," *Washington Post* (May 12, 1980): 6.
[144] Carl Lindskoog, *Detain and Punish: Haitian Refugees and the Rise of the World's Largest Immigration Detention System* (Gainesville: University of Florida Press, 2018), pp. 42–43.

economically, costly. From the vantage point of the Carter administration, many of the costs were unanticipated and unwanted. Past privileging of Cubans locked the administration into continued privileging of Cubans, the costs notwithstanding.

Fiscal Costs

Washington spent more on Cubans than on any other immigrant group, and more on Cubans in 1980 than in years past. A sampling of Mariel Cuban-related expenditures is illustrative.

Expenditures began offshore, with the stampede of asylum-seekers at the Peruvian Embassy in Havana. The Carter administration committed $4.5 million from the Emergency Refugee and Migration Assistance Fund to fly asylum-seekers to Costa Rica,[145] from where they were to be processed for admission to the United States.

After Castro opened the port of Mariel to allow Cubans to leave, US expenses soared. The US Navy and Coast Guard spent at least $1 billion on Cubans at sea, to try to block them from coming.[146] Unsuccessful in keeping them away, the Carter administration proceeded to incur costs in screening them for entry. Initially, the INS set up two processing centers in South Florida, one beneath an elevated interstate overpass off of I-95 in Key West, the other on the Orange Bowl football field in Miami. Agents of the INS, the FBI, the Pentagon, and the CIA interviewed the unauthorized arrivals there. The Cubans who were believed to pose no public threat were released on parole, if they had family to sponsor them.

However, with the South Florida facilities inadequate for accommodating the tens of thousands of arrivals from Mariel, FEMA set up the previously mentioned resettlement facilities around the country. The federal government spent more than a billion dollars on the Cubans at the camps where they were interned and on helping them adapt.[147] Aside from expenses associated with the housing and screening of the new Cubans, the federal government paid $2,000 per entrant to the VOLAGS that arranged sponsors for those without family who claimed

---

[145] Gastón Fernández and Leon Narvaez, "Refugees and Human Rights in Costa Rica: The Mariel Cubans," *International Migration Review* vol. 21 no. 2 (Summer 1987): 408.
[146] Clark, Lasaga, and Reque, *The 1980 Mariel Exodus: An Assessment and Prospects*, p. 15.
[147] Denise Blackburn, "Cuban/Haitian Entrant Program," *International Migration Review* vol. 6 (1983), pp. 189–99.

them: a total of approximately $120 million, for placement of some 60,000 Cubans.[148] Until sponsors were found, the federal government had to cover Cubans' living expenses. On September 26, 1980, when Castro closed the Mariel port to migration, there still were 16,000 Cubans without sponsors.[149]

The INS kept the Fort Chaffee facility open the longest, to house not only the Cubans without sponsors but also those it deemed "inadmissible." Only in 1982, after Reagan assumed the presidency, was Fort Chaffee finally closed: after having cost the federal government $100,000 a day to intern Cubans there: $36,500,000, for each of two years.[150]

Costs to American taxpayers continued after the Mariel door shut, the result of Castro spitefully loading "undesirables" on to the boats sent by Cuban Americans to pick up relatives from Mariel. After closing Fort Chaffee, tax dollars were spent on interning the Mariel "excludables" at the federal prison in Oakdale, Louisiana and at the federal penitentiary in Atlanta. As of December 1982, the government had spent $10,000 per prisoner a year on 2,555 interned Cubans.[151] Had the Carter administration been able either to screen the Cubans before their arrival or to convince the Cuban government to accept the return of the "inadmissibles" it would have been spared the expenses.

Furthermore, the Fascell–Stone Amendment to the REAA, which entitled the unauthorized Mariel Cubans (as well as the unauthorized Haitians who came ashore at the same time) to benefits otherwise only offered refugees, also came with a significant pricetag, one that continued for years. The Fascell–Stone Amendment committed the federal government to spend approximately $10,000 a year on each Cuban from Mariel,

---

[148] Clark, Lasaga, and Reque, "The 1980 Mariel Exodus," p. 11. Agencies involved in finding sponsors included the International Rescue Committee and church-affiliated groups. Family could also serve as sponsors if they committed to help asylum applicants until they were self-supporting.

[149] Peter Smeallie, "The Mariel Boatlift." PO's UMW Blogs. (Masterpo.umwblogs.org/2009/12/08/the-mariel-boatlift).

[150] RRPL, WHSO (White House Staff and Office) Files, T. Kenneth Cribb Jr. Files, Office of Cabinet Affairs OA 3809, 4821, Cabinet Affairs Series 1, Memorandum to C. Fuller, from Ed Harper (Executive Office of the President, Office of Management & Budget), subject: Closeout of Ft Chaffee, Arkansas Cuban Detention Camp, Folder: Immigration and Refugee Policy OA 4821.

[151] Jorge Domínguez, "Cooperating with the Enemy?," in Christopher Mitchell (ed.), *Western Hemisphere Immigration and United States Foreign Policy* (University Park: Pennsylvania State University Press, 1992), p. 78; see also Aguirre, "Cuban Mass Migration and the Social Construction of Deviants," pp. 159, 169.

more than $100 million in total: for health care, education, welfare, AFDC, Supplementary Security Income (SSI), and food stamp expenses. As a result, the federal government spent, in the aggregate, more on the Mariel Cubans in 1981 than on refugees admitted from other countries, in that the Refugee Act set the yearly cap on US global refugee admissions at 50,000 (until 1983). The Carter administration admitted more than twice that number of Cubans as Entrants.

State and local governments, in turn, bore Mariel Cuban-related expenses, especially in Florida, in Miami-Dade County above all. While the federal government did reimburse Florida nearly half a billion dollars to cover expenses related to the Fascell–Stone Amendment between April 1980, when the first Mariel boatpeople arrived, and December 1981, the end of the first year of the Reagan administration, Florida's unreimbursed outlays during this period more than doubled, from $31,600,000 to $68,292,000.[152] Costs to Florida rose especially after President Reagan took office and slashed federal assistance. For example, Miami-Dade County Jackson Memorial Hospital incurred $6 million in bills for treatment of Entrants after the Reagan administration cut back reimbursements. The county also spent over $5 million on criminal-justice related expenses on Cuban and Haitian Entrants, plus approximately $17 million on the schooling of children of Cuban and Haitian Entrants.[153]

The noted expenditures, an underestimate of total expenditures on Mariel Cubans, far exceeded the federal outlays for the well-funded Cuban Refugee Program between 1961 and 1972. Taxpayers paid dearly for Carter administration efforts first to block Mariel Cubans from coming, then to process them for admission and intern those without sponsors, and then to provide the new Cubans with benefits that were not offered to other unauthorized immigrants (except the Haitians who had the good fortune to arrive alongside Mariel Cubans). Taxpayers also had

---

[152] RRPL, WHSO Files, T. Kenneth Cribb: Files, Office of Cabinet Affairs OA 3809, 4821, "Memorandum for Richard Darman," from Faith Ryan Whittlesey [White House] subject: Approval of Paper on Refugees as a "White House Digest," Christina Bach Files OA 12740, 12741, Folder: Refugees and Immigration (1) OA 12740, November 23 1983, Box 2 [of 7].

[153] RRPL, WHSO Files, Michael Uhlmann Files OA 11593, Memorandum to Dewey Knight, Assistant County Manager, from Eileen Maloney, Intergovernmental Coordinator, November 12, 1981, Subject: Impact of Cuban/Haitian Entrants on Services provided by Metro-Dade County, Folder CCLP: Immigration: Cubans/Haitians OA 11593, Box 7.

to bear the long-term costs of imprisonment of the "excludables" whose return to Cuba was refused by Havana authorities.

Social Costs: Unrest, Crime, and Racial and Nativist Backlash

The Mariel migration also came with social costs. Some of the newcomers caused havoc in the facilities where they were detained and imprisoned, and in surrounding communities: not only, as previously noted, at Fort Chaffee. Meanwhile, native-born people resented the criminals in the Mariel mix, and, in Miami, the added labor market competition in the world of work, plus the hispanization of a city to which they felt long-standing claims. Mariel Cubans fueled the domestic tensions while serving no foreign policy objective.

Unrest in Detention Facilities

Having fled Cuba on the presumption that they would be welcomed – as had Cubans in the past – Mariel arrivals resented their detention and imprisonment, and conditions thereof. On numerous occasions they rebelled.

The Carter administration almost immediately faced difficulty in maintaining "law and order" in the facilities where it detained Mariel Cubans. Already in May of 1980, not long after the first of the Cubans arrived, those detained at the Eglin Air Force Base rioted. They protested physical and psychological abuse, and rape.[154] A week later, nearly 1,000 of the Cubans detained in Fort Chaffee went on a rampage,[155] rebelling at a facility that a government report described as a modern-day concentration camp.[156] Hundreds of them jumped barriers, staged a roadblock, and burned down buildings. Forty-five people suffered injuries.[157]

In August, Mariel Cubans rioted at Fort Indiantown Gap, Pennsylvania,[158] and, on larger scale, at Fort McCoy, Florida, where violence occurred daily. Inmates were stabbed, and detainees who

---

[154] Unzueta, "The Mariel Exodus."
[155] Copeland, "The Cuban Boatlift of 1980," p. 147.
[156] Unzueta, "The Mariel Exodus."   [157] Kami, *Diplomacy Meets Migration*, p. 165.
[158] JCPL, Collection: Federal Records: Records of Cuban-Haitian Task Force, Fort Indiantown Gap Camp, After Action Report, Folder: After Action Report, Public Affairs and Intergovernmental Relations, July 25, 1980–October 15, 1980 (2) and Memorandum to Assistant Director, Public Affairs and Intergovernmental Relations, from Public Information Officer, Cuban–Haitian Task Force, Fort Indiantown Gap,

escaped broke into nearby homes.[159] In a letter to President Carter, the Florida governor described Fort McCoy as a prison camp that had devolved into a state of constant siege, plagued by physical and psychological assaults, stabbings, beatings, robberies, suicide attempts, gang warfare, and escapes.[160]

The Mariel Cubans who subsequently were sent to the federal penitentiary in Atlanta and to the federal prison in Oakdale, Louisiana, were even more rebellious. Their protests continued after Reagan assumed the presidency, as detailed in Chapter 4.

In sum, the Carter administration's need to screen the new arrivals because they were not prescreened before arrival, and to lock up the criminals and mental patients that Castro foisted on the United States, spurred social unrest. Mariel Cubans did not passively acquiesce to confinement. Expecting better treatment in America, they protested.

Racial and Ethnic Nativist Backlash

Native-born Americans, in turn, resented the flood of new arrivals and the "misfits" in their midst: especially, but not only, in Miami. They blamed the new Cubans for a surge in crime, and resented the preferential treatment that the new Cubans received. In Miami, native-born people also resented the Cuban cultural makeover of "their" city.

In 1980, crime in Miami soared. Native-born Americans blamed the new Cubans for the breakdown in law and order. The city became known as the murder capital of the United States, as well as the drug capital. Cubans, along with Colombians, controlled the cocaine market,[161] though not necessarily Cubans from Mariel. Mariel Cubans were accused of committing half of all violent crimes in the city, and in 1981 they accounted for one-third of the city's apprehended murderers.[162]

Subject: After Action Report on Operations of Cuban–Haitian Task Force, FIG, Public Information Office and Task Force Spokesman, October 21, 1980, Box 33.

[159] JCPL, Records of Cuban-Haitian Task Force: RG220, Fort Indiantown Gap Camp File, AP and UPI Wire Copies, August 24, 1980 to August 31, 1980 through After Action Report, Folder: AP and UPI Wire Copies August 24, 1980 to August 31, 1980, Box 32; Kami, *Diplomacy Meets Migration*, p. 174; Nick Nichols, "Castro's Revenge," *Washington Monthly* vol. 14 (March 1982): 39–42.

[160] JCPL, Staff Offices Hispanic Affairs Miriam Cruz Files, Folder: Cuban Refugees August 15, 1980–November 28, 1980, letter to President Jimmy Carter, from Governor of Wisconsin, September 3, 1980, Box 2.

[161] James Kelly, "Trouble in Paradise," *Time* (November 23, 1981), pp. 22–32.

[162] Unzueta, "The Mariel Exodus"; Nichols, "Castro's Revenge."

Mariel Cubans, however, arrived before the surge in crime,[163] and they were responsible for only 16 percent of felony arrests.[164] The crime rate among the American population-at-large was roughly seventeen times greater than among the Cuban newcomers.[165] Mariel Cubans, in essence, were blamed for crime not entirely of their doing.

At the same time, Mariel Cubans unleashed new racial tensions. On May 17, 1980, African Americans in Miami rioted, in another "resort-type Watts." Eighteen people lost their lives.[166] Although police brutality and the acquittal of four White Miami-Dade police officers associated with the death of an African American ignited the 1980 unrest, underlying the rage was pent-up African American resentment of Cubans, whose presence in the city had soared since the 1960s. African Americans particularly resented what they perceived to be Cubans' preferential treatment in the world of work. Although census data show non-Hispanic Whites to have been pushed aside in the labor market more than African Americans, and African American public sector employment to have increased substantially in the 1970s, including relative to other racial and ethnic groups,[167] and although the economist David Card found the Mariel newcomers neither to have driven down wages nor to have caused an uptick in the unemployment rate in the city,[168] African Americans saw the situation differently.[169] Their unemployment rate was three times higher than Cuban immigrants'.

African Americans were not alone in resenting the Mariel influx. The newcomers fueled the first xenophobic English Only movement in the country, a movement predominantly involving Whites. As the Cuban population spiraled from 4 percent to approximately one-fourth of

---

[163] Aguirre, "Cuban Mass Migration and the Social Construction of Deviants," pp. 175–76.

[164] RRPL, Edwin Meese III Files OA 9451-9452, Memorandum from Michael Uhlmann [White House], to Edwin Meese III Subject: Meeting with Senator Hawkins, May 24, 1983, Letter from Hawkins to President, May 18, 1983, Folder: Immigration and Refugee Matters (1) OA 9451, Box 31; Aguirre 1994: 175–76; Hamm, *The Abandoned Ones*, p. 88.

[165] Ibid., p. 59.   [166] Kelly, "Trouble in Paradise."   [167] Ibid.

[168] David Card, in "The Impact of the Mariel Boatlift on the Miami Labor Market," *Industrial and Labor Relations Review* vol. 43 no. 2 (1990): 245–57, argues that African American earnings did not suffer from the arrival of Mariel Cubans. Even if Card is objectively correct, African American perceptions were real in their consequences. Furthermore, had Mariel Cubans not come, African Americans may well have done better.

[169] ABC News–Harris Survey, "Americans Uneasy about U.S. Policy on Accepting Cuban Refugees," May 26, 1980.

Miami's population over a mere ten year period, between 1970 and 1980,[170] Cubans turned Spanish into the language of the streets, workplaces, and government offices. Against this backdrop, a nativist backlash included calls for repeal of a 1973 bilingual-bicultural ordinance that had been implemented when the city was more welcoming of Cubans, and for an amendment to the Florida Constitution to establish English as the official language of the state. Amid the anti-immigrant backlash, some political candidates based their campaigns on nativistic appeals, in calling, for example, for language tests for citizenship. In so doing they heightened hostility toward the new Cubans.

As is typically the case, in Florida economic insecurities fueled the nativist turn.[171] Cubans took over jobs that both Whites and Blacks had previously monopolized, especially in the garment, construction, hotel, and restaurant industries.[172] Displaced and resentful, non-Hispanic Whites left Miami in droves. Unlike the African Americans who rioted, the non-Hispanic Whites packed their bags and left, such that their percentage of the city's population plunged from 79 to 45 between 1970 and 1980 (and to 31 and then 21 percent in 1990 and 2000, respectively).[173] They took advantage of the greater residential options they had in comparison to African Americans, owing to racial discrimination in the housing as well as labor market.[174]

The timing of Mariel Cubans' arrival magnified hostility toward them. Coming during a recession-linked uptick in unemployment, most Americans, nationwide, and not merely in Miami, felt immigration should be curtailed until job opportunities improved.[175] While President Carter claimed to welcome the new Cubans as "freedom lovers," and "with open arms," the American people felt differently, in view of their own interests and vision of America. In the main, they felt that Mariel immigrants should not be allowed to stay, that Washington should discourage Cubans from coming, that fewer Cubans and other refugees

---

[170] Eckstein, *The Immigrant Divide*, p. 46.
[171] John Higham, *Strangers in the Land: Patterns of American Nativism, 1860–1925* (New Brunswick, NJ: Rutgers University Press, 2002).
[172] Alejandro Portes and Alex Stepick, *City on the Edge: The Transformation of Miami* (Berkeley: University of California Press, 1993), pp. 41–42, 46.
[173] Eckstein, *The Immigrant Divide*, p. 46.
[174] Albert Hirschman, *Exit, Voice, and Loyalty: Responses to Decline in Firms, Organizations, and States* (Cambridge, MA: Harvard University Press, 1970).
[175] RRPL, Collection: Frances (Frank) S.M. Hodsoll Files, 1981, FAIR Fact Sheet, Federation for American Immigration Reform, Folder: Immigration and Refugees [17]. February 1981, Box 11.

should be allowed into the country, that the United States had been too willing to accept refugees from Cuba, and that Washington provided Cubans with too much assistance.[176] As early as May of 1980, a Newsweek-Gallup poll reported that 59 percent of Americans nationwide disagreed that it was good for the United States to permit so many Cubans to come because it demonstrated widespread dissatisfaction with Castro's government. Most of those canvassed in the survey considered it "difficult and expensive to take in so many refugees."[177] In another national survey the same month, two-thirds of those interviewed felt President Carter was "more wrong than right" in allowing the Cubans into the United States. Almost as many of them believed "Castro made us look foolish" when he forced the United States to admit criminals, mental patients, and other misfits.[178] The criminals and mental patients, although they were a minority of the new arrivals, turned Americans as never before against all Cubans. Moreover, even after the number of Cuban arrivals tapered off, Americans remained unwelcoming of Cubans. In late August (of 1980), a Harris poll found 81 percent of Americans still opposed to Cuban migration,[179] and the outreach to Cubans not to be a foreign policy asset.

The aversion to unauthorized immigrants and refugees that Mariel Cubans unleashed continued after Castro closed the Mariel port to emigration in September. Shortly thereafter, a national poll found 91 percent of Americans to favor an "all out effort" to stop illegal immigration.[180] Resentment toward all immigrants, especially toward unauthorized immigrants,[181] but also toward refugees, continued during Reagan's

---

[176] RRPL, Michael Deaver: Files, Series VI Political Material, Polling Information 1982: Dick Wirthlin, 1983-84 (1), Prepared by Reagan–Bush 1984 (1), Folder: (Reagan–Bush 1984) Attitudes on Immigration, Box 65; Aguirre, "Cuban Mass Migration and the Social Construction of Deviants," p. 175.

[177] RRPL, Collection: Frances (Frank) S.M. Hodsoll Files 1981, FAIR Fact Sheet, Federation for American Immigration Reform, Folder: Immigration and Refugees [17], February 1981, Box 11.

[178] RRPL, Collection: Frances (Frank) S.M. Hodsoll Files 1981, ABC News: Harris Survey, "Americans Uneasy about U.S. Policy on Accepting Cuban Refugees," May 26, 1980, and FAIR Fact Sheet, Federation for American Immigration Reform.

[179] Kami, *Diplomacy Meets Migration*, p. 165.

[180] RRPL, Immigration and Naturalization, WHSO Files, Martin Anderson Files CFOA 84, President's Task Force (3 of 3), June 26, 1981, Subject: Report of the Task Force on Immigration and Refugee Policy, from Attorney General, "Memorandum for the President," Folder: Immigration and Refugee Policy.

[181] RRPL, Michael K Deaver Files, WHSO Files, Edwin Meese III Files OA 6512, 6518, Attorney General, "Report of the Task Force on Immigration and Refugee Policy,"

presidency. When asked by pollsters in the early 1980s whether the United States should let in all of the refugees it could handle because it shows the world that people living under Communism do not like living under such a system, few Americans, nationwide, answered in the affirmative.[182]

Mariel émigrés even unleashed tensions within the Cuban community. They did not experience the warm welcome that they anticipated. Earlier arrivals had pressed the Carter administration to admit the Cubans who occupied the Peruvian Embassy and they generously offered Mariel Cubans food and clothing on arrival. However, more upper and middle class, and near-uniformly White (by self-definition, in the census), they looked down on the working class and mixed-race newcomers.[183] They also sought to distance themselves socially from the Mariel Cubans who were held in disrepute.

Thus, while President Eisenhower started the precedent of privileging Cubans over other immigrants with the intent of containing the Communist "specter" in America's backyard, in 1980 the American people, nationwide and not merely in Florida, opposed admitting Cubans and entitling them to special resettlement benefits: even though the United States was still in the throes of the Cold War.[184] The majority of Americans even envisioned the new Cubans to be a foreign policy liability, in serving Cuban more than the US government interests.

Political Costs

For President Carter, the timing of the Mariel immigration crisis could not have been worse, politically as well as economically. The Cubans came

---

Memorandum for the President. June 26, 1981, Folder: Immigration and Refugee Matters [3], Box 22.

[182] RRPL, WHSO Files, Frances [Frank] S.M. Hodsoll Files, 1981, Series II President's Task force on Immigration and Refugee Policy, Folder: Immigration and Refugee Policy Development (1), Box 9; Michael K Deaver Files, White House Staff Member and Office Files, Series VI Political Material, Polling Information 1982: Dick Wirthlin, 1983-84[1], Folder: [Reagan–Bush 1984] Attitudes on Immigration. Prepared by Reagan–Bush 1984 [1]. Box 65; and Collection: Frances (Frank) S.M. Hodsoll Files 1981, FAIR Fact Sheet, Federation for American Immigration Reform.

[183] I discuss tensions between the different émigré waves in *The Immigrant Divide*, chapter 1.

[184] A Harris poll found that over 80 percent of the people surveyed disapproved of President Carter's handling of the Cuban refugee situation. RRPL, Michael K Deaver Files, White House Staff Member and Office Files, Series VI Political Material, Polling Information 1982.

ashore in large numbers in an election year, when the economic recession fueled hostility toward immigrants in general, but especially toward unauthorized immigrants.

President Carter focussed on the Florida vote when responding to the Mariel crisis. At the time, the state had the eighth largest number of electoral college votes (tied with New Jersey, each with 17). He had won Florida in 1976, but he recognized when running for reelection in 1980 that the state was no shoo-in. It had voted Democrat only one other time since 1948.[185] He hoped his support of the Fascell–Stone Amendment, which he very deliberately signed into law in Tallahassee, Florida's capital, would help him win the state's electoral college vote: in having spared residents of the state from being directly taxed to finance entitlements for the Cubans and Haitians that had been admitted as Entrants.

While President Carter might have done worse at the polls had he not supported the amended REAA, most Cuban Americans favored Ronald Reagan, the Republican candidate, who took a tough stance against Castro.[186] In 1980, Reagan won 86 percent of the Cuban American vote in Dade County. Cuban Americans resented President Carter's initiatives to improve US–Cuba bilateral relations, and what they perceived as a mishandling of the Mariel crisis. President Carter's generous program for Mariel Cubans did not persuade them otherwise.

Nationwide as well, Reagan won the election by a landslide.[187] President Carter's outreach to Mariel Cubans backfired badly, in fueling anti-Cuban and anti-immigrant sentiment. If there had been foreign policy gain from welcoming Cubans in years past, President Carter faced neither domestic political nor foreign policy gain from admitting the Mariel Cubans and granting them special entitlements.

Voters turned on President Carter, disillusioned with what they considered his poor handling not only of the Mariel crisis but also of the Iranian hostage crisis and the economy at the time.[188] Carter himself considered the Mariel crisis – which preoccupied him for half of

---

[185] www.270towin.com.
[186] Edward Cody, "In Miami, It's 'Reagan, Si,'" *Washington Post* (May 21, 1983) (www.washingtonpost.com/archive/politics/1980).
[187] Ibid.
[188] The Iranian hostage crisis involved fifty-two Americans who an Iranian student group took hostage and the Carter administration failed to rescue.

1980 – such a low-point in his presidency that the museum documenting his administration at his presidential library in Atlanta makes no note of it. No doubt, President Carter hoped history would forget the Mariel crisis.

CONCLUSION

Cuban privileging appeared to have ended as Castro's second decade of rule drew to a close. The United States admitted few Cubans and slashed federal funding for Cuban entitlements. However, in 1980 an onslaught of new unauthorized Cubans arrived, more than in any previous year. Return visits that the Carter and Cuban governments agreed to permit backfired on both governments, in convincing over one hundred thousand new Cubans that they wanted to emigrate. After initially blocking their arrival, the Carter administration admitted them and entitled them to benefits that it did not offer other unauthorized entrants.

The Carter administration admitted them not by design but in response to the Cuban government's decision to let them leave and earlier Cuban immigrants' determination to have island family join them in the United States. Even though Congress officially regulates immigration, with Presidents having certain discretionary power over admissions, in 1980 neither Congress nor the President had the upper hand. President Carter responded defensively, to conditions not of his making or choosing. In principle, he might have interdicted, detained, deported, and repatriated Mariel Cubans, in order to block them from entering the United States, as the Reagan administration will be shown to have done when faced with an onslaught of new, unauthorized Haitians. Although President Carter initially took steps to exclude Mariel Cubans, it did not take him long before he reopened the path of privilege that Cubans had trodden in the past. He found himself locked into privileging Cubans anew.

While past became prologue, the reason for continued Cuban privileging changed in 1980. Domestic politics became a driving force. By 1980, earlier Cuban immigrants felt empowered to press for continued privileging of "their people." Settling in Florida, the largest "swing state" in presidential elections, worked in their favor. Florida politicians, sensitive to the growing Cuban American electorate, pressed for entitlements for the new Cubans, though not at local taxpayers' expense. In that he was running for reelection, President Carter was responsive. However, the very admission of the Mariel Cubans contributed to his electoral defeat. Voters resented the problems that the new Cubans generated.

Chapter 4 details how Reagan, upon assuming the presidency, further privileged Cuban immigrants. He even helped transform them into a political force that influenced Washington's Cuba policy, including its Cuban immigration policy.

4

Delinking Cubans from Haitians

The Deepening of Cuban Privileging and the Turn against Haitians under the Reagan and Bush I Administrations

Ronald Reagan inherited the issue of what to do about the 125,000 unauthorized Cubans and 25,000 unauthorized Haitians with temporary entry rights granted by the Carter administration that were scheduled to expire a half year into his presidency.[1] At the same time, he faced mounting unauthorized immigration not only from Haiti but also from Mexico and Central American countries. If he was "locked in" by precedent, he would be expected to extend new rights to the Cubans, and privilege them over the other unauthorized immigrants, especially since he had campaigned on an anti-Communist, anti-Castro foreign policy platform. Yet, he also sought support of so-called Reagan Democrats, fiscally conservative working class Whites turned nativist amid an onslaught of new arrivals during an economic downturn.

Both the Reagan administration, and that of George H. W. Bush, his vice president and presidential successor, will be shown indeed to continue privileging Cubans, even against the backdrop of the anti-immigrant backlash: though more sparingly than previous administrations. They also turned to Cuban exiles to assist their foreign policy preoccupation with suppressing Leftist movements that were challenging US hegemony at the time in Central America. President Reagan even helped transform the Cuban immigrant community into a domestic political force that came to influence US Cuba policy independently, including regarding immigration. Meanwhile, both the Reagan and Bush administrations turned

---

[1] Although some documents at the Reagan and Bush Presidential Libraries state that 129,000 Cubans came to the United States from Mariel, since most frequently the number cited is 125,000, I use that number.

viciously on Haitians, especially on new Haitians who sought refuge in the United States. While they expanded the Cuban path of privilege, they reopened the Haitian "path of disprivilege."

ADDRESSING THE CARTER LEGACY: REAGAN ADMINISTRATION INITIATIVES TO EXTEND NEW ENTITLEMENTS TO HAITIAN AND CUBAN ENTRANTS "YOKED TOGETHER"

When President Reagan took office in January 1981 he faced the upcoming expiration, in July, of the special temporary entry rights, as "Entrants: Status Pending," that President Carter had granted to the unauthorized Cuban and Haitian boatpeople who came ashore in 1980. Should he renew their temporary status, or compel them to (re)join the ranks of unauthorized immigrants, and possibly detain and deport them? Or, should he try to convince Congress to pass special legislation that would allow them to become lawful permanent residents, hopefully with greater success than President Carter? President Reagan faced the dilemma against the backdrop of, by then, an estimated three-and-a-half to six million undocumented immigrants living in the country, half to one million of whom had come in 1980.[2]

President Reagan's advisors resented the dilemma they faced. They viewed the "Entrant" status that the Carter administration created as a legal fiction, in that persons so classified were presumed not to have entered the country. They claimed the Entrants not to be officially in the United States, to be living in "legal limbo" and in a "legal void."[3]

Against this backdrop, President Reagan considered two options recommended by a task force that he had commissioned to resolve the problem of Entrants' future status. One option involved seeking legislation to enable all but serious criminal offenders and the mentally ill (who were to be held in custodial facilities until repatriated) to become lawful permanent residents. At the same time, the administration would urge Congress to repeal the Cuban Adjustment Act (CAA), which, since 1961, had provided Cubans with their own unique path to permanent

---

[2] RRPL (Ronald Reagan Presidential Library), White House Staff and Office Files (WHSO), Frances Hodsoll Files, 1981. Series II, President's Task Force on Immigration Reform Policy, U.S. Department of Justice, "U.S. Immigration and Refugee Policy."

[3] Bridget O'Brian, "Despite Agreement, Cuban Detainees Exist in 'Legal Limbo,'" *The National Law Journal*, and letter to Jeb Bush, from Rafael Penalver, of Penalver & Penalver, February 19, 1988, GHWBPL, Office of the Chief of Staff, Philip Brady Files, Subject Files, Folder: Cuban/Nicaraguan Immigration (3), ID 14831-004.

residency.[4] The other option involved granting the Entrants a new temporary status with a path to permanent residency after five years, if they demonstrated at least minimal English proficiency and interest in continuing to be part of the community where they lived.[5]

In that Congress did not enact the legislation that the task force proposed, President Reagan drew on his discretionary authority to grant the Haitian, along with the Cuban, Entrants a new basis for remaining in the United States. He requested the Justice Department to assign them indefinite parole rights, which would spare them detention and possible deportation and allow them legal rights to work. He thereby granted the Mariel Cubans, as well as the Haitians who arrived at the same time, more secure rights than had President Carter, who had granted them time-bound, though potentially renewable, residency rights. However, President Reagan granted them long-term parole rights in defiance of an objective of the Refugee Act that Congress enacted the preceding year. The Refugee Act aimed at reining in presidential parole-granting, and permit parole only on an individual, rather than group, basis.

President Reagan proceeded to propose another new, invented immigration status for both the Cubans and Haitians that President Carter had admitted as Entrants, in line with the second option recommended by the task force: that of Temporary Residents. In this vein, he requested his Attorney General's office to submit legislation to create Cuban/Haitian Temporary Resident Status: "The Cuban/Haitian Temporary Resident Status Act of 1981." The new status was to resolve the long-term rights of the Cubans and Haitians to whom President Carter had only extended short-term rights.

The new Temporary Resident status was to be incorporated into the Omnibus Immigration Control Act of 1982 that was before Congress at the time,[6] which addressed unauthorized immigration in general. According to the proposed legislation, Cubans and Haitians who had

---

[4] Clara Germani, "Immigration Bill Hits Welfare Snag," *Christian Science Monitor* August 14, 1984 (www.csmonitor.com/1984/0814/081419.html).
[5] RRPL, White House Staff and Office (WHSO) Files, Frances Hodsoll Files, 1981, Series II, President's Task Force on Immigration and Refugees (13), Immigration and Refugees (general) (11), Folder: Immigration and Refugees, memorandum to Ed Gray, Office of Policy Development, and Frank Hodsoll, Office of Chief of Staff, from Joe Ghougassian, Subject: Clarification points concerning the Cuban/Haitian Options, April 28, 1981, Box 11, and Folder: Immigration and Refugee Policy Development (3), "Cuban/Haitian Options," Box 9.
[6] RRPL, Kenneth Cribb Files, Cabinet Affairs Series I, Folder: Immigration Control (3 of 5), OA 4821, memorandum from the Office of the Attorney General to the Speaker of the House of Representatives, October 20, 1981, Box 1.

been paroled into the United States between April 20 and December 31, 1980 were to be entitled to the new status, if they were not held in detention or deemed "inadmissible." Temporary Residents were to have work rights, be permitted to renew their status every three years, and be eligible for lawful permanent residence after five years of continuous living in the United States, if they were self-sufficient and had some fluency in English, and were not otherwise excludable. The December cutoff for eligibility for the new status would entitle yet more unauthorized Cuban, as well as Haitian, immigrants to the special rights. October 10 had been the cutoff date for rights to Entrant status. Moreover, the Temporary Residents who adjusted their status and became lawful permanent residents were not to be counted against the country and regional quotas that the Immigration and Nationality Act 1976 Amendments had set for Western Hemisphere yearly admissions. They were to be entitled to lawful permanent residency status independently of the preference system that had guided immigration admissions since 1965.[7] The Reagan administration accordingly proposed new bases for privileging Cubans, and, in this case, also Haitians.

Yet, President Reagan limited the benefits to which the newly imagined Temporary Residents were to be entitled, consistent with his "leaner and meaner" fiscal belt-tightening approach to governance, known as "Reaganomics." They were to be ineligible for refugee benefits that had been extended to Mariel Cubans under Title V of the Refugee Education Assistance Act (REAA) (described in the previous chapter), which included AFDC (Aid to Families with Dependent Children), SSI (Supplementary Security Income), food stamps, aid to the elderly, disabled, and blind, and housing assistance.[8] The proposed legislation thereby included a mix of new inclusionary and exclusionary measures: in effect, "taking with one hand while giving with another." As Temporary Residents, Cuban, as well as Haitian, Entrants would continue to be privileged over other unauthorized arrivals, but less so, and in a less costly manner than under the Carter administration. In reimagining the Cubans and Haitians as Temporary Residents, President Reagan

---

[7] RRPL, T. Kenneth Cribb Files, Office of Cabinet Affairs, Cabinet Affair Series I, Folder: Immigration Control (2of 5), OA 4821, memorandum for Fred Fielding, Counsel to the President, from H. P. Goldfield, of the White House, Subject: Status of Immigration Policy, Legislative Proposals, October 20, 1981, Box 1.

[8] RRPL, T. Kenneth Cribb Files, Cabinet Affairs Series I, Folder: Immigration Control (4 of 5) OA4821, "Cuban/Haitian Temporary Resident Status Act of 1981."

could deny them benefits to which they had been entitled as Entrants. President Reagan proceeded to use the occasion of the expiration of their rights as Entrants, in July 1981, to narrow their economic and social entitlements.

The Senate version of the bill, S.2222, called for a better deal for Entrants than President Reagan's Attorney General had proposed. It called for a temporary resident status that permitted the Cuban and Haitian Entrants to be eligible for permanent residence after three, not five, years.[9] S.2222 also called for entitling Entrants, alone among immigrants, to public assistance before they became lawful permanent residents.[10] They were to remain eligible for REAA benefits. The Senate, in essence, sought to continue to treat the Entrants as a protected class of initially unauthorized immigrants, amid a mounting "war on illegals" on the Administration's part.

Congress never, however, enacted the proposed omnibus immigration bill during its 1981–1982 session. With its sponsors determined to push the legislation through, with some modifications, during the following session of Congress Representative Romano Mazzoli (Democrat, Kentucky) proposed a new bill: H.R.1510, the Immigration Reform and Control Act of 1983. H.R.1510 established procedures for most unauthorized immigrants who arrived before January 1, 1982 to adjust their status, not only the Entrants.[11]

Yet, the administration refused to support H.R.1510. It wanted legislation that included greater enforcement measures, to crack down on the unauthorized immigrants who were entering the United States in mounting numbers. It also wanted restrictions on immigrant rights to welfare.[12] It preferred the Senate to the House version of the bill, in that the Senate version called for less federal assistance to unauthorized immigrants. Because Congress approved neither version of the proposed 1983 legislation, Entrants' long-term rights remained unresolved.

---

[9] Congress.gov, "S.222-Immigration Reform and Control Act of 1982," 97th Congress (1981–1982) (www.congress.gov/bill/97th-congress/senate-bill/2222).
[10] Temporary Residents, other than Cuban–Haitian Entrants, were to be ineligible for federal public assistance until after three years as lawful permanent residents.
[11] Congress.gov, "H.R.1510-Immigration Reform and Control Act of 1983," 98th Congress (1983–1984) (www.congress.gov/bill/98th-congress/house-bill/1510).
[12] RRPL, Andrew Card Files, OA 8198, 12425, Folder: Immigration and Refugees (2), letter to Congressman Peter Rodino, Committee on the Judiciary, from William French Smith, Attorney General, July 27, 1983., Box 1.

"REAGANOMIC" CUTBACKS, EXCEPT FOR CUBANS

While he was concerned about resolving the long-term rights of the Cubans to whom President Carter had granted temporary "Entrant: Status Pending" rights, President Reagan sought to slash expenditure on Entrants. He did so partly in conjunction with slashing refugee entitlements: consistent with his "Reaganomic" cutback in taxes and promotion of free-market activity, but not with the tradition of privileging Cuban immigrants. However, after slashing federal-financed benefits for incoming Cubans, he reinstituted them.

Cuban immigrant entitlement cutbacks had already begun before Reagan took office. In 1980, before his election, Congress had used the occasion of passage of the Refugee Act to phase out entirely the exceptionally generous Cuban Refugee Program (CRP), which by then had cost the federal government $1.4 billion.[13] Yet, on taking office President Reagan speeded up the CRP shutdown.

In 1982 the Reagan administration focused on reducing benefits for all refugees: a mere two years after passage of the Refugee Act that for the first time in US history entitled refugees to resettlement assistance. It proposed that the federal government reduce the period of refugee entitlements from 36 to 18 months, that it reduce the entitlements it funded, and that it restrict eligibility for refugee entitlements, to cash and medical assistance, to which only persons who qualified for the AFDC program would be entitled.[14] During President Reagan's second term of office he slashed assistance even more: by 48 percent per refugee.[15]

The Reagan administration did not spare Entrants from the cutbacks.[16] It restricted the number of Entrants who were eligible for

---

[13] Norman Zucker, "Refugee Resettlement in the United States: Policy and Problems," *Annals of the American Academy of Political and Social Science* vol. 467, The Global Refugee Problem: U.S. and World Response (May 1983): 172–86.

[14] RRPL, Michael Uhlmann Files, Folder: CCLP: Immigration, Cubans/Haitians OA 11593, Memorandum from J. Steven Rhodes, White. House, to Richard Williamson, Subject: Impact Aid to Dade County, Florida for Cuban/Haitian Entrants to be Raised at Senior Staff, January 15, 1982, Box 7.

[15] Anastasia Brown and Todd Scribner, "Unfulfilled Promises, Future Possibilities: The Refugee Resettlement System in the United States," *Journal of Migration and Human Security* vol. 3, no. 3 (2014): 101–20.

[16] Germani, "Immigration Bill Hits Welfare Snag"; RRPL, Michael Uhlmann: Files, various folders, especially William French Smith, Attorney General, Letter to Peter Rodino, Committee on Judiciary, House of Representatives, July 27, 1983 and Memorandum for Edwin Meese from Joseph Wright, December 20, 1983, Subject: Legislative Strategy on Immigration Legislation, Folder: Immigration, Box 4: OA 9445; RRPL, Kenneth

entitlements, and it revised cash and medical assistance requirements such that 22,000 fewer of the 85,000 Entrants in Florida qualified. It also reduced federal funding for the English language courses and employment training program that the Carter Administration had made available to Entrants: and did so while raising the bar for lawful permanent residency and citizenship to include English language proficiency and economic self-sufficiency, namely, no dependence on welfare.[17] The Reagan administration thereby made it more difficult for Entrants to adapt to their new land.

However, the Reagan administration proceeded to acquiesce to political pressure. It awarded Florida $31 million in federally funded "impact aid" to cover costs of refugee equivalent benefits for Cubans in the state. Florida politicians pressed for the funding, building on their success at having convinced the Carter administration to fully fund Entrant entitlements in 1980 (through the Refugee Education Assistance Act). As a result, Florida continued to receive 100 percent federal reimbursement for assistance to Entrants. In this instance, Cuban privileging involved exemption from federal cutbacks, rather than new entitlements.

In turn, the Reagan administration broadened benefits for certain of the Cuban Entrants, beyond those specified in Title V of the REAA: despite the costs involved. It arranged for full federally funded refugee benefits for Mariel Cubans in government custody. They were to be eligible for Title V benefits even if they received a final nonappealable deportation or exclusion order, until the Cuban government accepted their repatriation. A spokesperson for the Attorney General argued that this extension of benefits was in keeping with the original intent of the Fascell–Stone amendment, even though the amendment specifically had noted that Cubans with final orders of exclusion were ineligible for federal benefits.

The Reagan administration also prioritized Cubans in the refugees it admitted and entitled to refugee benefits, in accordance with the Refugee Act that Congress passed in 1980. For fiscal year 1981, for example, it allotted Cubans over half of the 4,000 refugee admission slots set aside for Latin Americans. It even allowed Cubans who did not meet the criteria

---

Cribb Files, Cabinet Affairs Series I, Folder: Immigration Control (4 of 5), OA 4821, memorandum from the Office of the Attorney General to the Speaker of the House of Representatives, October 20, 1981.
[17] Kenneth Cribb Files, Ibid.

for refugee status to qualify for the admission slots. It allotted half of the slots reserved for Cubans to Cubans living in Spain, even though in so doing it made a mockery of a law intended for persons whose lives were at risk.[18] Cubans who had relocated in Spain experienced no persecution. Moreover, the Reagan administration admitted the Cubans residing in Spain independently of Spain's refugee allotment, and it entitled them to refugee benefits, for no reason other than that they were Cuban. Even *if* the Cubans had fled persecution in Cuba, they were living safely in Europe. Meanwhile, the Reagan administration prioritized Cubans over not only Haitians but also the growing number of Central Americans who were fleeing violence and persecution in their homelands.

Then, in February 1984, the Reagan administration floated the idea of reclassifying the Mariel Cubans who had been living safely in the United States since 1980 as refugees, despite President Carter's insistence that they were not. As refugees, the Mariel Cubans could adjust their status on the basis of the Cuban Adjustment Act. Joe Ghougassian had floated the idea already in a White House memorandum to the Office of Policy Development and the Office of the Chief of Staff in 1981, three months after Reagan had assumed the presidency. Ghougassian argued that the Haitians who President Carter admitted as Entrants, in contrast, did "not qualify as refugees under the law," and that they therefore should only receive work permits.[19] As refugees, Mariel Cubans would qualify not only for refugee benefits but, once lawful permanent residents, also for additional entitlements, including a path to citizenship. The administration, however, did not immediately act on the proposal.

Advocates for equal rights for Haitians expressed opposition, ultimately to no avail. For example, when the administration floated the plan, the Miami Metro Dade county manager wrote a letter to the Attorney General in which he noted that the County Board would not tolerate a double standard in treatment of the Cubans and Haitians that were currently classified as Entrants. He argued that they both arrived under similar circumstances and the federal government had accorded them the

---

[18] RRPL, Immigration and Naturalization, WHSO Files, Cicconi, "Intra-agency Task Force on Immigration and Refugee Policy Decision Paper" (State Working Group Draft) March 26, 1981, Folder: Immigration and Refugees [1], Box 10. The State Department agreed to allow up to 4,000 privately sponsored refugees annually from Cuba, and others from a religious Iranian group that had fled persecution and relocated in Pakistan and India.

[19] RRPL, WHSOF, Francis S.M. Hodsoll Files, 1981, Series II, President's Task Force on Immigration and Refugees (3): Immigration and Refugees (general) (11), Folder: Immigration and Refugees (13), memorandum to Ed Gray from Joe Ghougassian.

"same dubious immigration status." He argued that any change in status should be offered to Haitians as well as Cubans.[20]

CONGRESSIONAL EFFORT TO KEEP HAITIAN AND CUBAN ENTITLEMENTS "YOKED TOGETHER"

Days before the Reagan administration suggested, in February 1984, a reimagining of the Cuban, but not the Haitian, Entrants as refugees, Representative Peter Rodino of New Jersey proposed legislation to keep entitlements of the two groups of Entrants "yoked together:" H.R.4853, the Cuban/Haitian Adjustment Act. H.R.4853 would offer both groups of Entrants, plus other unauthorized arrivals from the two countries who came to the United States before January 1, 1982, a path to permanent residence and citizenship. No other unauthorized arrivals were to be covered by the legislation.

The proposed legislation included several new unique entitlements for Haitian as well as Cuban Entrants. For one, it specified that the Secretary of State would exempt the Cubans and Haitians from the 20,000 annual country cap on immigrant admissions that Congress instituted with the 1976 INA Amendments. The exemption would be especially advantageous for the 125,000 Cuban Entrants but also for the approximately 25,000 Haitian Entrants.[21] The Cubans and Haitians were also to be exempt from the status adjustment fees that were typically charged to immigrants. This entitlement built on President Johnson's status adjustment fee-waiver for Cubans who became lawful permanent residents on the basis of the Cuban Adjustment Act (CAA). In addition, Entrants who applied for permanent residence under H.R.4853 were to be exempt from the need to comply with the labor certification and good-public-standing requirements for lawful permanent residence that were specified in the 1965 Hart–Celler legislation governing immigrant admissions.[22]

H.R.4853 even proposed a unique fast-track for Entrants to attain citizenship. They were to be able to apply two-and-a-half years of US residence, going back to 1982, to the typical five-year lawful permanent

---

[20] RRPL, Christina Bach Files, Folder: Refugees and Immigration (1) OA 12740, Letter to Attorney General William French Smith from M.R. Stierheim, Dade County Manager, February 16, 1984, Box 2 (of 7).
[21] U.S. House of Representatives (USHR), Committee on the Judiciary: Hearing before the Subcommittee on Immigration, Refugees, and International Law, 96th Congress, 2nd session on H.R. 4853 Cuban/Haitian Adjustment, Serial no. 64 (May 9, 1984), p. 29 (www.loc.gov/law/find/hearings/pdf/00183878840.pdf).   [22] Ibid., p. 15.

residency requirement for naturalization. The United States did not offer unauthorized entrants from other countries comparable years-of-living-in-the-United States credit toward citizenship. Moreover, the previously noted omnibus immigration bill before the very same session of Congress, H.R.1510, did not offer comparable retroactive residency credit toward citizenship for unauthorized immigrants.[23]

However, high-ranking Reagan administration officials fought the proposed legislation. While claiming to do so on the basis of principles, it did so in ways that in effect, if not stated intent, discriminated against Haitians (building on previously instituted Haitian exclusionary policies). The INS Commissioner, a State Department representative, and the assistant Attorney General all testified against the bill at the Cuban/Haitian Adjustment Act hearings in May 1984, on the grounds that relief should not be "piecemeal" or for specific groups.[24] They argued that piecemeal legislation would serve as a precedent for other immigrant groups, such as for the Nicaraguans and Salvadorans who at the time were fleeing to the United States to escape civil wars in their homelands.[25] None of the high-ranking officials who testified acknowledged that the Reagan administration had previously promoted piecemeal rights for Cuban and Haitian Entrants when advocating that they be granted Temporary Resident Status. They also did not acknowledge that there was a long-standing precedent for "piecemeal" status adjustment enabling legislation: for Hungarian, East European, and Indochinese parolees in 1958, 1960, and 1975, respectively, as well as for Cubans in 1966.

The Reagan administration representatives were all the more disingenuous in arguing against "piecemeal" legislation in that it had announced plans the same month that Congressman Rodino proposed H.R.4853 to allow, as noted earlier, Mariel Cubans to adjust their status on the basis of the CAA: "piecemeal" legislation of the highest order.[26] INS Commissioner Alan Nelson even acknowledged when testifying at the H.R.4853 hearings that the proposed legislation was not necessary for Cubans because the CAA entitled them to permanent residency rights.[27]

---

[23] Ibid., p. 12. While never enacted during the session of Congress, HR1510 called for repeal of the Cuban Adjustment Act.
[24] Ibid., p. 16.   [25] Ibid., p. 29.
[26] No Author, "Floridians Seek Residency Status for Haitians, Along with Cubans," *New York Times* (February 13, 1984) (www.nytimes.com/1984/02/13/us/floridians-seek-residency-status-for-haitians-along-with-cubans.html).
[27] Ibid.

Commissioner Nelson also argued that H.R.4853 was not necessary because Haitians and Cubans could qualify for status adjustment under H.R.1510, which Congress was deliberating at the time. He expressed no concern that Haitians would be left without a path to lawful permanent residence if Congress did not enact H.R.1510, which indeed proved to be the case.

Commissioner Nelson added that he preferred the CAA to H.R.4853 because, as amended in 1980, it allowed Cubans to adjust their status after one year on parole. H.R.4853 required a two-year waiting period. While Nelson had noted that he favored sunsetting the CAA, he never pressed for it. Instead, he argued that since it remained on the books, it should be drawn on.[28]

Commissioner Nelson, in addition, argued against specific aspects of the Cuban/Haitian Adjustment Act that would have worked to Haitians' advantage. In particular, he opposed the cutoff date that the proposed legislation specified for qualification for status adjustment.[29] The law was to apply to Cubans and Haitians who arrived in the United States before January 1, 1982. Nelson argued that the cutoff date should instead be mid-1981. On the face of it, a difference of half a year seems inconsequential. However, while the earlier cutoff date would exclude few Cubans – since hardly any came to the United States after the Cuban government shut the Mariel port to emigration in September 1980[30] – ten thousand unauthorized Haitians who had come ashore between mid-1981 and January 1982 would be denied residency rights with the earlier cutoff date.[31]

At the same time, Commissioner Nelson had the INS take several steps to limit Haitian qualification for status adjustment should H.R.4853 be enacted. The INS called many Haitians who had arrived after October 1980 to exclusion and deportation hearings, which would disqualify them from consideration for permanent residency rights were H.R.4853 enacted.[32] The INS also restricted status adjustment rights for Haitians who were "known to the INS" and "in proceedings." Haitians who had presented themselves to the INS but who never were assigned to exclusion

---

[28] USHR, Committee on the Judiciary, Hearing ... on H.R. 4853 Cuban/Haitian Adjustment ... p.115. In the spirit of immigrant equity, even the more comprehensive White House-promoted immigration bill before Congress at the time, the Immigration Reform and Control Act (IRCA) (HR1510), called for repeal of the CAA. See Ibid., p. 124. Not passed during the 1984 session of Congress, the repeal-proviso was dropped from the version of the legislation.

[29] Ibid., p. 35.   [30] Ibid., pp. 128, 135.   [31] Ibid., p. 35.   [32] Ibid, p. 13.

proceedings, as well as Haitians who had not filed for asylum, were to be ineligible for H.R.4853 status adjustment rights.[33] Some Haitians had not filed for asylum because they were told it unnecessary once granted Entrant status, others because they feared dealing with the INS after earlier abusive experiences with the Haitian Program (described in Chapter 3). Still other Haitians were to be disqualified for immigration status adjustment through no fault of their own, because INS personnel had lost their files when implementing detention assignments.[34]

Representative Rodino argued that he deliberately introduced H.R.4853 to prevent a delinking of Haitian from Cuban rights for reasons of common sense, compassion, and fair play.[35] He said the need for justice and fairness was so compelling that the special legislation should be enacted.[36] It would keep lawful permanent resident rights for Haitians and Cubans "yoked together," and "right the wrong." The "wrong" included the Reagan administration's unlawful detention of Haitians (described later in this chapter).[37] In Rodino's words, "No group in recent history had been subjected to more injustices by the immigration service."

At the H.R.4853 hearings, Congressman George Crockett, an African American Michigan Democrat dedicated to civil rights, echoed Rodino's concerns. He noted that the administration did not want Haitians to be given the fair treatment that the bill would grant.[38] He added that the Haitians should be eligible for immigration status adjustment to correct the Reagan administration's unlawful and discriminatory treatment of them.[39] While Rodino claimed that "To treat the two groups differently ... would violate fundamental fairness," Crockett argued that the State Department's representative and the INS Commissioner were "opposed to bringing about ... equality of treatment ... (d)espite ... (their) impassioned denials of racial discrimination against Haitians." Rodino's and Crockett's reasoning, however, fell on deaf ears.

At the hearings, Miami community leaders – who by the 1980s included some Cuban Americans – also argued in favor of the Cuban/Haitian Adjustment Act, to protect and advance Haitian rights, to lessen Cuban–Haitian tensions, and to address the discrimination Haitians perceived. Florida Democrat Congressman Claude Pepper, along with Reverend Thomas Wenski, and Monsignor Bryan Walsh who had directed Operation Peter Pan, plus the Cuban Americans Eduardo

[33] Ibid., p. 140. [34] Ibid., p. 138. [35] Ibid., pp. 39, 115. [36] Ibid., p. 29.
[37] Ibid., p. 128. [38] Ibid., p. 44. [39] Ibid., p. 60.

Padrón and Paul Cejas, all advocated for the proposed legislated rights for Haitians as well as Cubans. Padrón served as chair of Greater Miami United (and in 1995 became president of Miami-Dade Community College); Cejas, a successful businessman, served as chair of the Miami Dade School Board (and as ambassador to Belgium under President Clinton). Monsignor Walsh argued that "to act only for the Cubans is an invitation to divisiveness," and Reverend Wenski argued that President Reagan's interest in entitling Cubans to adjust their immigration status on the basis of the CAA, after having denied them the right for the first three years of his administration, was an electoral ploy to get Hispanic votes for his reelection.[40] For these reasons, the Miami community leaders recommended that the Reagan administration endorse the Rodino bill.

REAGAN ADMINISTRATION DELINKING OF CUBAN AND HAITIAN ENTRANT RIGHTS

There was enough controversy among legislators, in addition to the opposition from the administration, that Congress never passed H.R.4853. Congress also did not pass H.R.1510, the Immigration Reform and Control Act of 1983, which the administration had supported. H.R.1510 called for a crackdown on unauthorized immigrants, including prohibition of employers to hire unauthorized immigrants, and for greater expenditures on immigration enforcement. While H.R.1510 also allowed for unauthorized immigrants who arrived before 1982, including both Cuban and Haitian Entrants, to legalize their status, enough Democrats opposed H.R.1510 to prevent its passage. They were responsive to Hispanics who were worried that employers would discriminate against them, fearful of fines for hiring "illegals."

Against this backdrop, in October of 1984 the Reagan administration acted on the plan it had floated in February, to reimagine the Cuban Entrants as refugees, and, as refugees, to permit them to adjust their status and become lawful permanent residents. It re-envisioned the Mariel Cubans in the absence of new evidence revealing that they indeed had fled persecution. President Carter, as previously noted, had refused to admit them as refugees in the absence of evidence that they had fled persecution. President Carter's reasoning notwithstanding, President Reagan's INS Commission argued that the delays in congressional

---

[40] No author, "Floridians Seek Residency Status for Haitians, Along with Cubans."

attention to the Simpson–Mazzoli bill, the Immigration Reform and Control Act of 1983, "forced the Administration" to consider Cuban applications for legal status under the CAA (for which, if they were refugees, they would qualify).[41] He expressed no concern that the "delays" left Haitian Entrants without the possibility to adjust their status.

An INS spokesperson admitted that the (Immigration and Naturalization) Service planned to process Cuban applications for residency under the CAA if H.R.1510 were not enacted. When Congress did not enact the legislation, the Reagan administration determinedly bent existing law to Mariel Cubans' advantage. If the Cubans were refugees, the Reagan administration did not need Congress to pass legislation to enable them to qualify for lawful permanent residence.

The Reagan administration reconceived the Mariel Cubans as refugees against the backdrop of a lawsuit filed on Cuban immigrants' behalf.[42] The lawsuit claimed that the government discriminated against the 1980 Cuban boatpeople in denying their requests for permanent residency to which the CAA entitled them. When faced with the lawsuit, Commissioner Nelson concluded that the Cubans indeed were entitled to relief under the CAA and that it would be very unfortunate if the government had to engage in protracted litigation that would lead to a court-directed legalization program.[43] He defended drawing on the CAA despite the Reagan administration having proposed, early on, that Congress sunset it!

Notably, President Reagan announced definitive plans to allow the Cuban Entrants to adjust their status the month before the November election, consistent with Reverend Wenski's claim that the granting of Cuban Entrants status adjustment rights was an "electoral ploy." The Cuban Entrants would be ineligible to vote in the upcoming election since they were not yet citizens, but the announcement of the new entitlement endeared naturalized Cubans to vote for him, in the key state of Florida. With far fewer Haitian votes at stake, President Reagan could leave Haitian Entrant rights unresolved with little political pushback. There were far fewer Haitians than Cubans in Florida, and far fewer Haitians

---

[41] Robert Pear, "Reviews on Cuban Aliens Shifted to Justice Department," *New York Times* (December 11, 1984), p. 28.

[42] Reginald Stuart, "Immigration Bill May Bring End to Long Wait of Boat People," *New York Times* (June 26 1984) (www.nytimes.com/1984/.../26/.../immigration-bill-may-bring-end-to-long-wait-of...).

[43] Pear, "Reviews on Cuban Aliens Shifted to Justice Department."

with citizenship and therefore votes to cast. Rights of the Cuban and Haitian Entrants became embedded in domestic politics.

THE REAGAN ADMINISTRATION'S "WAR" ON ILLEGAL IMMIGRANTS

While President Reagan slashed benefits for Entrants as well as refugees, and denied Haitian Entrants the same long-term residency and citizenship rights as Cuban Entrants, he also reduced the annual global cap on authorized immigrant admissions: from 290,000 to 270,000 (plus immediate family). He also aggressively blocked unauthorized immigrants from entry, in a range of ways.

INS Commissioner Nelson took pride in what he described as President Reagan's "fair, firm, and consistent" immigration policy. He contrasted it, in his words, with President Carter's "inconsistent and vacillating policies" of 1980.[44] "Firm and consistent" President Reagan's policies were; however, in denying asylum to persons fleeing for their lives, "fair" the policies were not.

Reagan Administration Exclusion of Unauthorized Immigrants Arriving by Land as Well as by Sea

"Firm and consistent," President Reagan claimed that, going forward, Cubans who came without authorization would be treated the same as other unauthorized arrivals. Here, he was less committed to immigrant equity than avoiding "another Mariel." He was helped by Castro, who, for his own reasons, closed the Mariel port to emigration and commanded his coast guard to block new Cubans from leaving. Aside from a continued exodus of "his people" not reflecting well on the revolution, it would stand in his way of negotiating an agreement with the United States to allow safe, lawful immigration.

At the same time, the Reagan administration aggressively blocked unauthorized Haitians who continued to seek refuge in the United States after the Mariel door closed. President Reagan showed no residue of goodwill to Haitians, following President Carter's welcoming of them

---

[44] GWHPL (George H. W. Bush Presidential Library), National Security Council (NSC), Nicholas Rostow Files, Subject Files, Folder: Refugees, "Report to the Attorney General and the National Security Council on Immigration Issues, prepared by the INS," January 12, 1989, CFO1063–025.

in 1980. As detailed later in this chapter, President Reagan secured the cooperation of the repressive Haitian government to keep Haitians from departing. He also ordered the US Coast Guard to interdict them on the high seas, as well as in US waters, which his Attorney General admitted violated international law.[45]

In an indication of how aggressively the Reagan administration intervened to keep Haitians out, it interdicted and repatriated over 16,000 Haitians between 1982 and 1988, two-thirds the number of Haitians that the Carter administration had admitted as Entrants: despite little difference between the two sets of Haitians other than the time at which they left their home country.[46] In addition, the Reagan administration expanded detention facilities to lock up unauthorized Haitians who managed to come ashore, and then had them deported.

The Reagan administration also tried to block unauthorized land immigrants from Mexico and Central America. In the course of the 1980s, Mexicans in stepped-up numbers sought refuge from their country's 1982 debt crisis and subsequent neoliberal restructuring that impoverished many. In turn, Central Americans sought refuge from the state violence, repression, and civil strife in their homelands,[47] to which the Reagan administration contributed in providing governments in the region billions of dollars of aid for their "dirty wars" against Left-leaning movements for greater justice.

President Reagan justified the aid as "help(ing) our neighbors resist the Soviet-Cuban assault" and suppress a "string of anti-American Marxist dictatorships."[48] The White House claimed there would be an inundation of immigrants should the region "fall to the Communists."[49] It projected that the Cubans and Haitians who came ashore in 1980 would barely amount to 5 percent of the number of Central Americans who would flock to the United States in the event of communist takeovers in the

---

[45] Mary Thornton, "Bars to Immigration Sought," *Washington Post* (October 22, 1981) (www.washingtonpost.com/archive/politics/1981/10/22/bars-to-immigration-sought/a82 18377-0eef-46df-a744-755cceefc3c6/).
[46] GHWBPR, NSC, Rostow, Subject Files, "Report to the Attorney General and the National Security Council on Immigration Issues."
[47] Ibid. While guerilla and other grass-roots movements also deployed violent tactics, US-trained and financed military were responsible for most civilian deaths during the civil wars (93 percent in Guatemala).
[48] Cited in David Scott FitzGerald, *Refuge beyond Reach* (New York: Oxford University Press, 2019), p.125.
[49] Although it is impossible to know how many would have sought refuge in the United States had the "Left" won in Guatemala and El Salvador, millions from the Central American countries fled to the United States in the decades that followed.

region. Appealing to nativist anti-immigrant sentiments, President Reagan warned of "a tidal wave of refugees – and this time they'll be 'feet people' and not boat people – swarming into our country seeking safe haven from communist repression."[50] When a "tidal wave of refugees" from the region indeed came, they fled, in the main, repressive Right-wing, not Marxist, dictatorships. And when they arrived, the Reagan and then the Bush administrations immediately reimagined them as economic migrants, not refugees, and unauthorized economic migrants at that. Between 1984 and 1990 the United States granted asylum to less than 3 percent of Salvadoran and Guatemalan asylum seekers,[51] years during which the two administrations admitted thousands of Cubans as refugees who had not fled persecution and whose lives were not at risk.

The Great Compromise: The Reagan Administration Convinces Congress to Block Future Unauthorized Immigration from All Countries in Exchange for Agreeing to Officially Admit Unauthorized Immigrants Already in the Country

As part of what the INS Commissioner described as a "firm and consistent" strategy, the Reagan administration also turned to Congress to enact legislation to finance greater securitization of the US–Mexican border and a clampdown on illegal entrants. After Congress did not pass the previously noted Omnibus Immigration Control Act of 1982 or the Immigration Reform and Control Act of 1983, it did pass legislation in 1986, similarly entitled the Immigration Reform and Control Act (IRCA). IRCA mandated enhanced border enforcement; criminalization, for the first time, of employer hiring of illegal aliens; and denial of welfare rights to unauthorized entrants.[52] So committed was the Reagan administration to a crackdown on undocumented entrants that it proceeded to recommend to the incoming Bush administration, in 1989, that it block congressional efforts to repeal employer sanctions and other restrictive measures of IRCA.[53]

---

[50] Quoted in the *Washington Post* (June 21, 1983), and cited in Douglas Massey, Jorge Durand, and Nolan J. Malone, *Beyond Smoke and Mirrors: Mexican Immigration in an Era of Economic Integration* (New York: Russell Sage Foundation, 2002), p. 86.
[51] Ibid., p. 126.
[52] For a summary of immigration and immigration policies, see GHWBPR, NSC, Rostow, Subject Files, "Report to the Attorney General and the National Security Council on Immigration Issues," Ibid.
[53] Ibid.

In order to get support of members of Congress who were opposed to the immigrant-unfriendly components of the proposed legislation, the bill allowed for the largest legalization program in US history: for nearly three million undocumented entrants who had come to the United States before 1982, provided they could demonstrate at least minimal knowledge of the English language and US history and government, and pay a fine and back taxes. While mainly interested in the restrictive components of IRCA (including requiring employers only to hire authorized immigrants), President Reagan took the high ground when signing the bill into law. In his words, the legalization "will go far to improve the lives of a class of individuals who now must hide in the shadows, without access to many of the benefits of a free and open society. Very soon many of these men and women will be able to step into the sunlight and, ultimately, if they choose, they may become Americans."[54] Unauthorized immigrants who arrived after 1982 received no comparable welcome. They were subject to arrest, detention, and deportation, rather than the "sunlight" of which President Reagan spoke.

Cubans were not among the immigrants who were granted amnesty with IRCA. This was because in October 1984 the Reagan administration had already reimagined the Cuban Entrants as refugees, eligible for lawful permanent residence on the basis of the CAA, and because few Cubans had emigrated since the Cuban government shut the Mariel port to departures. However, with IRCA, Congress entitled the Haitian Entrants, plus other Haitians who had come to the United States without authorization before 1982, to lawful permanent residence. Some 35,000 Haitians took advantage of the opportunity to adjust their status.[55] Congress thus advanced Haitian equity that President Reagan had denied.

As part of its "firm and consistent" treatment of unauthorized immigrants the Reagan administration, in turn, stopped congressional efforts to grant "extended voluntary departure" and "safe haven" status to the Central American arrivals after 1982 who were ineligible for IRCA amnesty. "Extended voluntary departure" or "safe haven" status would have granted the asylum-seekers temporary immigration rights, which would have spared them from detention and deportation, though not

---

[54] Ronald Reagan, "Statement on Signing the Immigration Reform and Control Act of 1986," November 6, 1986 (www.reaganlibrary.gov/research/speeches/110686b).

[55] GHWBPL, NSC, Nancy Bears Dyke, Subject Files, Folder: Refugees: Haiti, 1992 (1), "Fact Sheet on Legal Immigration from Haiti," CF 01074-005.

entitle them to social and economic assistance. The INS advised the White House to oppose the temporary immigration statuses because they would likely become stepping stones to permanent residency.[56] In that the Central Americans were fleeing Right-wing governments, the Reagan administration envisioned no ideological pay-off to admitting them.

After succeeding Reagan as president, Bush did sign the Immigration Act of 1990 into law, which granted Temporary Protective Status (TPS) rights to unauthorized entrants who were unable to return to their home country because of ongoing armed conflict, environmental disaster, or other extraordinary conditions.[57] Granted on a country-of-origin basis, Salvadorans were the main initial recipients of TPS: the result of grassroots advocacy on their behalf, after Congress denied them "extended voluntary departure" or "safe haven" status. The unauthorized entrants could attain TPS for potentially renewable eighteen month periods.

However, President Bush, like President Reagan, refused to admit the Central Americans, as well as the Haitians, as refugees. Bush's administration denied nearly all their asylum claims. It did admit more refugees than had the Reagan administration,[58] but mainly Indochinese who had allied with the United States in its war in Asia against communism. Annual refugee admissions increased from 60,000 to 78,000 under President Reagan to between 110,000 and 130,000 under President Bush.[59] Meanwhile, the Bush, like the Reagan, administration allotted most admission slots set aside for Latin American and Caribbean refugees, in accordance with the Refugee Act of 1980, to Cubans. Only 500 Nicaraguans and Salvadorans were admitted as refugees, despite the vast number fleeing violent civil wars in their homelands.[60]

---

[56] The Immigration and Naturalization Service recommended to the Attorney General and the National Security Council that because history has shown people with temporary statuses to tend to become permanent residents, the administration should oppose legislation granting Central Americans "extended voluntary departure" or "safe haven" status. GHWBPL, NSC, Rostow, Subject Files, Folder: Refugees, "Report to the Attorney General and the National Security Council on Immigration Issues."

[57] The Act also introduced a diversity visa and ended exclusion of homosexuals.

[58] "Refugee Admissions by Region Fiscal Year 1975 through January 31, 2020" (www.wrapsnet.org/documents/Refugee%20Admissions%20by%20Region%20since%201975%20as%20of%201-31-20.pdf).

[59] U.S. Annual Refugee Resettlement Ceilings and Number of Refugees Admitted, 1980–Present (www.migrationpolicy.org/programs/data-hub/charts/us-annual-refugee-resettlement-ceilings-and-number-refugees-admitted-united).

[60] Brown and Scribner, "Unfulfilled Promises, Future Possibilities," p. 108.

Meanwhile, President Bush slashed refugee benefits even more than President Reagan had, and he reduced the period of eligibility for benefits, from 36 months, when the Refugee Act went into effect, and from 18 months under President Reagan, to 8 months.[61] President Bush, in turn, opposed granting refugees cash and medical assistance, which he viewed as forms of welfare. While it was cost-saving, the world's wealthiest country, as a result, backtracked on assisting victims of persecution to which it had committed with passage of the Refugee Act in 1980.

Detention and Deportation

The Reagan administration's "firm and consistent" policy, expanded on by the Bush administration, also included a build-up of immigration detention facilities: across the country, and at the US naval base in Guantanamo Bay, Cuba. Combined with the restrictive policies initiated with IRCA, the Reagan administration contributed to what became enduring changes in US immigration enforcement. Its initially controversial detention of immigrants became a routinized feature of the country's immigration system. And consistent with its neoliberal "Reaganomics," the administration privatized detention facilities, which operated with minimal government oversight.

In conjunction with his "war on drugs," President Reagan, in turn, increased deportations of unauthorized immigrants and strengthened border security. His administration deported an average of 21,000 immigrants a year.[62] Thus, while extending permanent residency rights to the 125,000 unauthorized Cuban entrants that President Carter admitted on a temporary basis, the Reagan administration blocked other unauthorized immigrants from entry: or locked them up in detention facilities.

President Bush further increased deportations: to about 35,330 a year. Among those deported by his administration were poor youth who had affiliated with inner-city gangs, especially in Los Angeles. When they were deported, they transnationalized the US gangs: most famously, Mara

---

[61] Ibid.
[62] Douglas Massey, "The Bipartisan Origins of White Nationalism," paper presented at the Annual Meeting of the Eastern Sociological Society, February 29, 2020, Philadelphia, based on data of the U.S. Office of Immigration Statistics, *2020 Yearbook of Immigration Statistics*, Table 39: "Aliens Removed or Returned: Fiscal Years 1892 to 2018" (Washington, DC: U.S. Department of Homeland Security, available at www.dhs.gov/immigration-statistics/yearbook/2018/table39.

Salvatrucha, MS-13. The gangs made life in their homelands, especially in El Salvador, even more violent and unsafe than before.

EXTENSION OF ENTITLEMENTS TO CUBAN IMMIGRANTS: IN PRINCIPLE VERSUS PRACTICE

During his 1980 presidential campaign, Reagan promised Cubans another airlift, similar to President Johnson's Freedom Flights. While quietly burying the proposal once elected, in 1984 he signed a bilateral agreement that officially committed the United States to routinely admit Cubans. The Reagan administration thereby seemed to commit to a new immigration entitlement for Cubans, against the backdrop of official US immigration policy since 1965, of admitting foreign-born people only on the basis of the preference system, not country of origin.

With access to immigration through legal channels, Cubans would be less likely to enter without authorization, and the United States would be able to screen which Cubans came. Most importantly to the Reagan administration, in conjunction with the agreement the Cuban government agreed to the return of the Mariel "inadmissibles," who were costly to the United States to keep locked up.

However, in 1985 the Reagan administration suspended the accord. While reinstating it in 1987, his administration proceeded to issue immigration visas only sparingly. At the same time, it turned to earlier Cuban émigrés to help contain the Left-leaning movements that were gaining momentum in Central America, much as the Eisenhower and Kennedy administrations had turned to them for the ill-fated Bay of Pigs invasion. At the same time, the Reagan administration helped transform Cuban émigrés into influential ethnic lobbyists. As president, Bush carried through on the policies that Reagan had put in place.

Promises Made, Promises Not Kept: Shutting the Door to New Cuban Immigrants

During his 1980 presidential campaign, Reagan gave a speech to a large Miami-Dade County audience, packed with Cuban Americans, in which he criticized his opponent, incumbent President Carter, who was running for reelection, for mishandling the Mariel crisis. He called for a new, massive Cuban airlift, in which the federal government shared the financial burden to assist Cubans "in their flight to freedom." In addition, Reagan criticized the Carter administration for having been "irresponsible and indifferent" toward Cuban émigrés. His speech resonated with Cuban Americans who wanted family still in Cuba to join them in the United States, and also with other Floridians who resented being taxed to cover expenditure on Cuban immigrants. Reagan complained that President Carter had ducked the issue, and tried "to shift the burden to the backs of Florida residents" even though the Mariel Cubans were a national problem.[63]

By the time Reagan won the election – with the Cuban American and general Florida vote – immigration from Cuba had slowed to a trickle. The newly established US Interests Section in Havana that the Carter administration had instituted had stopped processing visa applications when Castro opened the Mariel door for Cubans to emigrate without US authorization, and it continued to issue few visas after Castro closed the Mariel door. President Carter insisted that before his administration would resume issuing visas the Cuban government needed to accept the return of the Mariel arrivals who US immigration authorities deemed inadmissible. Cubans who wished to immigrate legally thus paid the price for a US–Cuban government bilateral feud. Ironically, President Carter instituted barriers to authorized immigration when extending unique entitlements, as Entrants, to unauthorized Cuban immigrants who had arrived under his watch!

Before President Carter left office, Havana authorities did agree to take back the "excludables." However, they agreed to take back only the Mariel Cubans who wished to return, which was unacceptable to President Carter. Carter insisted that Cuba take them all. The "inadmissibles," mainly criminals and mentally disturbed people who the Cuban government had loaded on to the boats that Cuban Americans had sent to Mariel to pick up relatives, were, as detailed in Chapter 3, a difficult group to deal with and costly to maintain in US prisons and mental institutions.

Upon becoming president, Reagan never implemented the massive airlift he had promised during his campaign, and his administration responded to few Cuban requests for visas to immigrate with authorization. In 1983 and 1984, for example, his administration denied immigration visas to 15,000 immediate relatives of Cubans who were lawful US permanent residents, and it ignored 26,000 Cuban requests for preference

[63] GHWBPL, Vice President (VP) Records, Office of National Security Affairs, Donald Gregg Files, Subject Files, Folder CHTF, OA/ID 19854-016, "Cuban/Haitian Fact Sheet."

system-based visas.⁶⁴ Like President Carter, President Reagan insisted that the Cuban government accept the return of the "excludables" before the United States would honor visa requests.⁶⁵ In addition, his administration made its commitment to admit political prisoners contingent on the Cuban government accepting the return of the "excludables."⁶⁶ His administration even had claimed that one reason it refused to support the Cuban/Haitian Adjustment Act was that Section 2 called for the United States to resume visa-granting to Cubans.⁶⁷ It prioritized the return of the "excludables" over family reunification, legal immigration, and admission of Cubans who had suffered persecution in Cuba: all the while that it reimagined the unauthorized Mariel Cuban "admissibles" as refugees, to grant them a path to lawful permanent residence and citizenship.

Extension of New Unique Immigration Entitlements to Cubans

In December 1984 the Reagan administration signed a bilateral migration agreement with Cuba, known as the Mariel Accord. The accord committed the United States to issue up to 20,000 immigration visas to Cubans yearly, a maximum set for admissions from all other countries, as well as to admit former political prisoners and their families.⁶⁸ In return, the Cuban government agreed to accept the return of the approximately 2,700 Mariel Cubans that US immigration officials had deemed inadmissible, a key concern of President Reagan. On its part, Cuba hoped the accord would become a stepping stone to talks on a broader set of issues: a hope that never materialized.⁶⁹

At the same time, the migration accord included provisos entitling Mariel Cubans to new unique rights. For one, it entitled them to a fast-track to citizenship. It made their residency status retroactive to the time they arrived in the United States nearly five years prior,⁷⁰ thereby entitling

---

⁶⁴ USHR, Committee on the Judiciary, Hearing ... on H.R. 4853 Cuban/Haitian Adjustment, Serial no. 64 (May 9, 1984), p. 159.
⁶⁵ Ibid., p. 168.
⁶⁶ William LeoGrande and Peter Kornbluh, *Back Channel to Cuba: The Hidden History of Negotiations between Washington and Havana* (Chapel Hill: University of North Carolina Press, 2014), p. 239.
⁶⁷ Ibid., p. 136.
⁶⁸ The Mariel Accord (and an accompanying Communique) also committed the United States to admit 3,000 Cuban political prisoners.
⁶⁹ LeoGrande and Kornbluh, *Back Channel to Cuba*, p. 241.
⁷⁰ GHWB VP Records, Office of Policy, Mary Gall Files, Subject Files, Folder: Domestic Policy Office Files, Cuban Immigration (1985), OA/ID 15259-006, Final Report of

them to qualify almost immediately for citizenship. Also, the accord allowed Mariel Cubans, after one year as lawful permanent residents, to arrange for the immigration of spouses and children that were still in Cuba.[71] Thus, the special rights that President Carter had granted the unauthorized Mariel arrivals, as Entrants, became, under President Reagan, a springboard for additional entitlements. Noteworthy, the Mariel Accord marked the first country-specific immigration agreement to which the United States committed since the 1965 immigration reform ended national origins basis of admission.[72]

Retraction of Cuban Immigration Entitlements

Nonetheless, within a year after the Migration Accord took effect and after the return of only 201 "excludables," the Reagan administration broke its commitment to admit up to twenty thousand Cubans yearly: in response to a new bilateral feud. Reagan administration-funded Radio Martí had just begun to broadcast programs to Cuba to promote regime change. In anger, Castro announced that his government would not accept any more "excludables," and that it would cease to allow Cuban Americans to visit the island.[73] In a tit for tat, the Reagan administration suspended the migration agreement. It refused to issue any more immigration visas to Cubans, other than to Cubans in third countries.[74] Lawful migration ground to a halt. Thus, immigration rights became embroiled, anew, in broader US–Cuba Cold War tensions.

In August 1986, President Reagan went a step further. He banned visa-granting to Cubans who had recently emigrated to third countries,[75] after the Interests Section in Havana stopped issuing visas. He claimed that he did so to stop Cuban government "trafficking in human beings," but,

---

Greater Miami Chamber of Commerce, Committee on Immigration, "Cuban Immigration into Dade County: The Next Phase," May 7, 1985.

[71] Ibid.

[72] For FY 1989, Congress, in turn, targeted over $10 million to assist communities affected by the unauthorized Cuban and Haitian entrants. In helping to defray local costs, local resentment could be tempered. GHWBPL, Presidential Records, National Security Council, Nancy Dyke Subject Files, Folder: Refugees: Domestic Considerations, Conference Report to Accompany H.R. 2990.

[73] LeoGrande and Kornbluh, *Back Channel to Cuba*, p. 247.

[74] Kenneth Skoug, *The United States and Cuba under Reagan and Shultz: A Foreign Service Officer Reports* (Westport, CT: Praeger, 1996).

[75] Carlos Harrison, "U.S.-Cuba Agreement Bolstered: Immigration Rights Written into the Law," *Miami Herald* (December 25, 1987).

more significantly, to block the Cuban government from profiting from fees it charged Cubans who left for third countries (from where they could immigrate to the United States). Here, President Reagan prioritized strangulating the Cuban government economically over family reunification. Harkening back to the 1960s, the Reagan administration sought to leverage immigration policy to debilitate the Cuban government, in this case by withholding, rather than by granting, Cuban rights to immigrate.

Thus, while granting new entitlements to Mariel Cubans, the Reagan administration retracted immigration rights to other Cubans, in Cuba as well as in third countries. If the Eisenhower, Kennedy, and Johnson administrations had granted Cubans special immigration entitlements in pursuit of their Cold War foreign policy agenda, the Reagan administration retracted Cuban immigration entitlements, committed to the same foreign policy agenda (though also to pressure the Cuban government to accept the return of the "inadmissibles").

CONGRESSIONAL EFFORT TO REINSTATE CUBAN IMMIGRATION RIGHTS THE REAGAN ADMINISTRATION BLOCKED

In the course of the 1980s, Cuban Americans became increasingly well organized, influential, and politically connected, as detailed later in this chapter. Feeling that "their people" should be entitled to continued special entry prerogatives, they did not passively accept the Reagan administration shutdown of Cuban immigration, from Cuba and third countries. Some members of Congress proposed legislation to address their concerns.

Senator Frank Lautenberg, Democrat from New Jersey, took the lead. He proposed legislation to allow Cuban immigration that the White House prohibited. With New Jersey being home to the second largest Cuban community in the United States, he was especially attuned to Cuban immigrant yearnings. He proposed a bill to commit the United States *by law* to issue up to 20,000 visas yearly to Cubans,[76] irrespective of whether the Cuban government accepted the return of the "excludables." The Mariel Accord had made Cuban visa-granting a matter of Executive Branch discretion that allowed President Reagan to withhold visas from Cubans.

Cuban Americans lobbied especially for reinstating third country immigration, to enable an estimated 12,000 Cubans who were "stranded" in

---

[76] GHWBPL, VP Records, Office of Chief of Staff, Philip Brady Files, Subject Files, Folder: Cuban/Nicaraguan Immigration [3], "Cuban Immigration," ID14831-004.

countries where they had expected to get US visas after the Reagan administration shut down visa-granting in Cuba. Indicative of Cuban American concern, a subgroup of the Cuban American Democratic Association collected 10,000 signatures requesting that Cubans in third countries be allowed to immigrate.[77] A Miami radio station, in turn, publicized that several hundred exiles would go to Washington to lobby for third-country Cuban immigration rights.[78]

Senator Lautenberg's proposed legislation had bipartisan support. For example, at the House of Representatives hearing about the legislation, the Massachusetts Democrat Barney Frank called the administration's shutdown of Cuban immigration perverse and crazy, and punishing of innocent victims of Castro's oppression. The Illinois Republican Henry Hyde, in turn, argued that the policy punished good and decent people who would make great US citizens.[79]

Nonetheless, the Reagan administration opposed the proposed legislation. Both the State and Justice Departments lobbied members of Congress not to support it. The State Department Principal Deputy Legal Adviser Michael Kozak, along with Kenneth Skoug, the State Department's Coordinator for Cuba, insisted that the migration agreement had to be restored, unchanged, with the Cuban government accepting the return of the "excludables," before US–Cuban relations could improve.[80] Faced with the administration's opposition, Congress never enacted Lautenberg's bill.

REINSTATEMENT OF CUBAN IMMIGRATION RIGHTS: DE FACTO VERSUS DE JURE

Amid pressure from Cuban Americans and legislators, the Reagan administration went on to renegotiate the migration accord, in November 1987. Kozak and Skoug had met in private with Cuban officials in Mexico City

---

[77] GHWBPL, VP Records, Office of Chief of Staff, Phil Brady Files, Subject Files, ID 14831-003, Folder: Cuban/Nicaraguan Immigration, Tina Montalvo, "Senate Votes to Ease Cuban Immigration," *Miami Herald* (October 8, 1987).

[78] Ibid.

[79] Linda Greenhouse, "U.S. Assailed Again on Curbing Cuban Immigrants," *New York Times* (October 27, 1986) (www.nytimes.com/1986/09/27/world/us-assailed-again-on-curbing-cuban-immigrants.html).

[80] GHWBPL, VP Records, National Security Affairs, Donald Gregg Files, Country Files, Folder: Cuba 1988: Mariel/Detainees/Human Rights [1], Testimony of Michael Kozak, Principal Deputy, Legal Adviser, Department of State, before Subcommittee on Courts, Civil Liberties and the Administration of Justice of the Committee on the Judiciary, House of Representatives, February 4, 1988, OA/ID 19869-023.

to work out details.⁸¹ In the new accord, the United States again agreed to admit up to 20,000 Cuban immigrants a year, from third countries as well as from Cuba,⁸² while, most importantly to the Reagan administration, the Cuban government agreed to the return of "inadmissibles." Notably, the Cuban negotiators did not insist that Radio Martí stop beaming programs to Cuba, even though Castro had claimed he had suspended the Mariel Accord because of the broadcasts. The United States did agree to future talks about Radio Martí, but with no strings attached.⁸³ In principle, lawful immigration thus was back on track.

In practice, the Reagan administration took advantage of its discretionary authority. Although the bilateral agreement committed the United States to admit *up to* 20,000 Cubans annually, it specified no minimum. Taking advantage of the wording of the accord, between 1985 and 1994 the Bush as well as the Reagan administrations, and the Clinton administration during its first two years, in total issued only 11,222 immigration visas to Cubans.⁸⁴ The Bush and Clinton administrations, in essence, followed Reagan administration precedent of only sparingly admitting Cubans lawfully. The Reagan administration rejected some 80 percent of the Cubans who solicited visas.⁸⁵ The three administrations violated the spirit, though not the legal specifications, of the accord. During these years the United States could have issued sixteen times as many visas.⁸⁶ Meanwhile, between 1988 and 1992 the Cuban government agreed to accept the return of slightly more than one thousand "inadmissibles" who the Reagan and Bush administrations wanted deported.⁸⁷

The Reagan administration leveraged Cuban immigration for foreign policy gain, but on the basis of a new foreign policy logic. Turning the

---

[81] Ibid.
[82] GHWBPL, VP Records, Office of Chief of Staff, Phil Brady Files... Harrison, "U.S.-Cuba Agreement Bolstered," ID 14831-003.
[83] GHWBPL, VP Records, National Security Affairs, Donald Gregg Files, Country Files, Folder: Cuba 1988: Mariel/Detainees/Human Rights [1], OA/ID 19869-023, Testimony of Michael Kozak, Principal Deputy, Legal Adviser, Department of State, before Subcommittee on Courts, Civil Liberties and the Administration of Justice of the Committee on the Judiciary, House of Representatives, February 4, 1988.
[84] Félix Masud-Piloto, *From Welcomed Exiles to Illegal Immigrants: Cuban Migration to the U.S., 1959–1995* (Lanham, MD: Rowman & Littlefield, 1996), p. 135.
[85] Jesus Arboleya Cervera, *Cuba y los cubanoamericanos: El fenomeno migratorio Cubano* (Havana: Fondo Editorial Casa de las Americas, 2013), p. 58.
[86] Meanwhile, between 1989 and 1992 the United States granted approximately 122,000 nonimmigration visas to Cubans, 10 percent of who overstayed their visas and went on to become lawful permanent residents on the basis of the CAA.Ernesto Rodríguez Chavez, *Emigración Cubana Actual* (Havana: Editorial de Ciencias Sociales, 1997), pp. 69–71.
[87] Rodríguez Chavez, Emigración Cubana Actual, p. 73.

logic of previous administrations "on its head," the top Reagan policy advisor, Joe Ghougassian, suggested as early as April 1981 that it might be good to "shut off the safety-valve" in Cuba, namely emigration, so that "eventually, population growth, unemployment and underemployment" may cause internal unrest ... and destabilize Castro's regime."[88] Ghougassian's strategy even called for blocking immigration of Cubans more than other nationals. The Reagan, followed by the Bush and early Clinton, administrations admitted few Cubans besides those they officially admitted as refugees, who highlighted regime persecution of its people.[89] The three administrations reinterpreted how immigration might help topple the Cuban government.

REAGAN ADMINISTRATION TRANSFORMATION OF CUBAN IMMIGRANTS INTO LOYAL REPUBLICANS, AGENTS OF ITS FOREIGN POLICY, AND A POLITICAL FORCE IN THEIR OWN RIGHT

While only sparingly admitting new Cubans, President Reagan reached out to Cubans who were already in the United States to transform them into an important base of the Republican Party in Florida, a state of growing political importance as it became a magnet for ever-more Americans.[90] He also reached out to Cuban immigrants to assist in containing "Communist infiltration" in the hemisphere, especially in Central America. He recognized that in view of their shared antipathy to communism and shared interest in containing Castro's international influence, he could turn to them to help defeat the Left-leaning political movements that were gaining ground at the time in the region. Meanwhile, President Reagan also helped Cuban immigrants become an organizational force in their own right who could lobby for policies they wanted. President Reagan's vice president and presidential successor, George Bush, along with his son, Jeb, assisted in solidifying ties with the

---

[88] RRPL, White House Staff Member and Office Files, Francis S.M. Hodsoll Files, 1981, Series II, President's Task Force on Immigration and Refugees (3): Immigration and Refugees (general) (11), Folder: Immigration and Refugees (13), memorandum to Ed Gray from Joe Ghougassian.

[89] For example, the Bush administration admitted twice as many Cubans with refugee as with immigration visas, even twice as many unauthorized immigrants as Cubans with visas to move to the United States. Rodríguez Chavez, *Emigración Cubana Actual*, p. 93.

[90] By way of illustration, Florida's electoral college votes rose from ten in 1960, to seventeen in 1980. (www.270towin.com/states/Florida).

Cuban American community: ties that spanned business and politics, in Miami and beyond.

Formation of a Cuban American Republican Party Political Base

Since 1966 Cubans could become lawful permanent residents, even if they had come without authorization or if admitted only with temporary, parole rights. Thanks to the CAA, Cubans thereby enjoyed a path to citizenship that came with voting rights. By 1980, 60 percent of Cubans nationwide, and 51 percent of those in Miami, were citizens, 56 and 47 percent of whom, respectively, were of voting age.[91] The Cubans who became citizens took their voting rights seriously. Nearly all of them registered to vote.[92] When casting their ballots, they took candidates' stance on Cuba into account. They supported candidates who opposed the Castro-led government.[93]

Beginning in the 1980s, the Cuban émigré community successfully elected "their own" to political office, with their votes but also campaign contributions. In Miami, the hub of "Cuba, USA," they elected mayors of municipalities, as well as state legislators, who either were born in Cuba or whose parents were born there. In 1989 Ileana Ros-Lehtinen became the first Cuban immigrant elected to Congress, in an election to fill the seat vacated by Claude Pepper, who had died in office. Then, in 1992, Lincoln Díaz-Balart, also from South Florida, and Robert Menendez, a former mayor of Union City, New Jersey, the hub of "Havana North, USA," won House of Representative seats as well (with Menendez, in 2006, elected to the Senate).

The two South Florida Cuban immigrants elected to Congress ran on the Republican ticket,[94] as President Reagan worked to make the Republican Party Cuban immigrants' "natural" political home.[95] Together with the help of Vice President Bush, a business partner of

---

[91] Eckstein, *The Immigrant Divide*), pp. 91–92.
[92] Ibid., p. 93. Florida International University Miami surveys report high citizen and voter registration rates among Cuban Americans, with the rates being highest among those who emigrated before 1974.
[93] Ibid.
[94] Ibid., pp. 94–95. Although Menendez was a Democrat, from heavily Democrat northern New Jersey, he voted as a bloc with the South Florida Cuban American Republican members of Congress on all Cuba-related issues.
[95] Merle Black and Earl Black, *The Rise of Southern Republicans* (Cambridge, MA: Belknap Press/Harvard University Press, 2003).

Armando Codina – a Miami-based real estate developer who became one of the wealthiest Cuban Americans, a local Republican Party operator, and key member of the Cuban American National Foundation, described later in the chapter, the South Florida politicians turned the émigré community into Republican Party stalwarts. Vice President Bush's Spanish-speaking son Jeb, who became vice president of Codina's real estate investment firm as well as chair of the Dade County Republican Party, also helped. Florida had been heavily Democratic, but during Reagan's presidency the percentage of Republicans among registered party members in Dade County soared, from 39 to 68.[96] Many of the Republican Party's new members were Cuban American, some of whom had switched their party loyalty.[97] Díaz-Balart, whose father had served as majority leader in the House of Representatives in Batista's government, and who became one of the most influential Cuban Americans, served as an example. He had entered politics as a Democrat.

As of 1980, Cuban Americans, who by then accounted for over a quarter of Miami's residents,[98] cast an estimated 8 to 10 percent of the Republican vote in Florida. Over the course of the 1980s they helped elect Republicans in general, not merely Cuban Americans, to office.[99] President Reagan appealed to Cuban Americans with his outspoken anti-Communist and anti-Castro stance.

Cuban Immigrant Agents of Reagan–Bush Foreign Policy

President Reagan, in turn, courted Cuban Americans to advance his foreign policy agenda. He revived Washington's Cold War concern with defeating communism on the world stage, with a new twist: a focus on the Americas. The Reagan administration focused especially on defeating the Leftist movements that were gaining force at the time in Central America. With congressional constraints on invading countries, President Reagan worked with Vice President Bush, a former director of the CIA, to undermine, covertly, challenges to US hegemony in the region: and called on Cuban exiles for assistance.

---

[96] William Finnegan, "The Political Scene: Castro's Shadow," *New Yorker* (May 19, 2004), p. 74.
[97] Peter Schweizer and Rochelle Schweizer, *The Bushes: Portrait of a Dynasty* (New York: Anchor, 2005), p. 309.
[98] Eckstein, *The Immigrant Divide*, p. 46.
[99] Bernard Weinraub, "Wooing Cuban-Americans in G.O.P," May 22, 1987 (www.nytimes.com/1987/05/22/us/wooing-cuban-americans-in-gop.html).

Although Central American politics never engaged and enraged Cuban immigrants as much as did their antipathy to Castro, the Reagan administration turned to veterans of the Bay of Pigs invasion to assist in suppressing leftist movements in the region, including to help topple the Left-leaning Sandinistas, who in 1979 successfully ousted Anastasio Somoza. Somoza was an unpopular, corrupt, long-time US ally whose family had ruled Nicaragua since 1936. To undermine the Sandinistas, the Reagan administration funded, and covertly trained, the so-called Contras (Counterrevolutionaries). It did so after Congress passed the Boland Amendment (in 1984), which prohibited a military invasion of the country. Refusing to accept the Sandinista challenge to US regional hegemony, the Reagan administration circumvented congressional restrictions by trying to oust the Sandinistas covertly.[100] High-level members of the Reagan administration masterminded a covert operation which, when uncovered, became known as the Iran–Contra affair. It nearly took down Reagan's presidency. Senior officials secretly facilitated the sale of arms to Iran to fund the Contras.

While the Bay of Pigs invasion had been an unequivocal debacle, it proved a CIA training ground for Cuban exiles who assisted the Contras. The 2506 Brigade, the association of veterans of the Bay of Pigs invasion, financed Cuban exiles to help topple the Sandinistas.

Approximately two dozen of the veterans served as military advisers to the Contras. Other Cuban exiles participated in firefights in Nicaragua.

The involvements of a few key exiles are illustrative. Among the most notorious exiles to whom the Reagan administration turned was Félix Rodríguez. A Bay of Pigs veteran who worked for the CIA for more than a decade, Rodríguez ran an air resupply mission for the Contras in the 1980s.[101] Reputedly the main coordinator of the clandestine Contra arms mission, he worked with Vice President Bush's national security adviser.

---

[100] See Julia Preston and Joe Pichirallo, "Cuban Americans Fight for Contras," *Washington Post* (October 25, 1986), for a superb analysis of Cuban American involvement with the Contras (www.cia.gov/library/readingroom/docs/CIA-RDP90-00965R000605070018-8.pdf).

[101] Joe Pichirallo, "Contra Supply Figure Says He Warned North of Possible Scandal," *Washington Post* (May 28, 1987) (www.washingtonpost.com/archive/politics/1987/05/28/contra-supply-figure-says-he-warned-north-of-possible-scandal/4eb94bd9-5e87-4069-84fc-80adade60885/). When working for the CIA, Rodríguez also played an instrumental role in the 1967 manhunt to kill Ernesto (Che) Guevara, who left Cuba to promote revolution in Bolivia.

Also, in consultation with the Vice President he advised the Salvadoran military on how to repress leftist insurgents in their country.[102]

Another exile, Francisco José ("Pepe") Hernández, who was also CIA-trained and involved in the Bay of Pigs invasion, became a Contra combatant. He went on to become president of what evolved into the largest and most influential Cuban American organization, the Cuban American National Foundation, known as "the Foundation." While working with the Foundation, he collaborated with the Reagan administration to subvert the Sandinista government.[103]

Hernández's cousin, Luis Posada Carriles, another Bay of Pigs veteran and former CIA operative, received explosives training at the notorious School of the Americas. He served as a quartermaster for the Contras in El Salvador, and advised the Salvadoran security forces in their scorched-earth counterinsurgency campaign against the leftist Farabundo Martí National Liberation Front (FMLN). Posada Carriles was also involved in the secret arms resupply mission for the Contras, associated with the Iran–Contra scandal. He lived much of his life on the run, off the largess of Cuban exiles, and on the CIA payroll.[104] Before working with the Contras, he had masterminded the 1976 bombing of the Cubana airplane, noted in Chapter 1, that killed all seventy-three passengers aboard.[105]

---

[102] Ibid.; GHWBPR, Office of Policy Development, White House, Emily Mead Files, Folder: Nicaragua, 23344-021. As Vice President, Bush noted that he met with Rodriguez three times but never discussing the exile's work for the Contras, only his work advising the Salvadoran military to quell leftist insurgents. Ibid.

[103] Larry Rohter, "An Exile's Empire: A Special Report," *New York Times* (May 8, 1995) (www.nytimes.com/1995/05/08/us/exile-s-empire-special-report-with-voice-cuban-americans-would-be-successor.html).

[104] Hilary Goodfriend, "Death of a Cold War Supervillain"(www.jacobinmag.com/2018/06/luis-posasa-carriles-cold-war-supervillain); Frances Robles, "Luis Posada Carriles, Who Waged Quest to Oust Castro, Dies at 90," *New York Times* (May 23, 2018) (www.nytimes.com/2018/05/23/obituaries/luis-posada-carriles). Posada Carriles pr oceeded, in the 1990s, to mastermind a string of hotel bombings in Havana, to try to undermine Cuba's newly developed tourist industry; to attempt to kill Castro when attending a presidential summit in Panama, in 2000; and to enter the United States illicitly, in 2005. In 2011, he was acquitted of charges of lying to US immigration author ities about the bombings and of illicitly entering the United States.

[105] Also, Orlando Bosch, after he was convicted for plotting a bazooka attack on a Polish freighter docked in Miami, fled the United States, after which he plotted efforts to overthrow Castro in other countries. He illicitly returned to the United States, where Jeb Bush convinced his father's administration to grant the terrorist safe haven, whereupon a federal judge ordered his release from federal custody. GHWBPL, VP Records, Chief of Staff Office, Philip Brady Files, Subject Files, Folder: Cuban Community Issues-

The Cuban émigré community stood behind these and other of their "patriots" who fought to defeat the Left in Central America. They helped finance their operations and their escapes from prison. They, for example, raised at least $1 million in radio campaigns and private contributions for the Contras. As chair of the Miami Republican Party, Jeb Bush cultivated close relations with them. Although he admitted to supporting the Contras, he denied any role in the resupply mission.

The Cuban exiles were no more successful in Nicaragua than in the Bay of Pigs invasion. They failed to topple the Sandinista government. However, in 1990, after George Bush assumed the presidency, the Sandinistas were voted out of office. Nicaraguans had become disillusioned with Sandinistas who had not delivered on promised social and economic reforms, once they focused on defeating the Contras. Contributing to the Sandinista defeat, the United States threatened to continue to enforce an economic embargo of Nicaragua that it had previously imposed, unless the opposition won. With the embargo contributing to the poor performance of the Nicaraguan economy, voters wanted it lifted.

Thus, the Reagan and Bush administrations turned to Cuban exiles to help debilitate the Left in Central America. Drawing on exiles' earlier CIA training, the Reagan administration, in particular, sought to subvert progressive movements that challenged US economic and political interests in the region.

The Transformation of Cuban Americans into an Independent Nationally Influential Political Force

President Reagan also helped transform Cuban exiles into a political force in their own right. Although Cubans had been politically engaged since they arrived on American soil, during the Reagan years they became more unified and organized, and more focused on influencing US politics, especially on matters pertaining to Cuba.

Jorge Mas Canosa, who participated in the Bay of Pigs invasion and who worked closely with the exiles who were involved in violent and covert undertakings both in Central America and Cuba, in the course of the 1980s modified how he pursued his anti-Castro conviction. He became a "born-again" influence peddler. In 1981, President Reagan's

---

Miami-1988 [1], "Anti-Castro Militant Bosch Ordered Released in Miami," *Washington Post* (March 2, 1988), ID 14828-011.

national security advisor and director of the CIA encouraged him to help found the Cuban American National Foundation, which, as previously noted, became known as "the Foundation." Through the Foundation, Mas Canosa redirected his anti-Castro activism from militant covert to institutional political channels, in close collaboration with the Republican Party.[106]

President Reagan strengthened Mas Canosa's stature within the Cuban American community,[107] in helping to arrange for early funding for the Foundation, in praising him on numerous occasions publicly, and in granting him White House access. Florida Congressman Dante Fascell, the Democrat who had lobbied for Title V of the REAA to entitle Cuban Entrants to the same benefits as refugees, also helped give the Foundation its initial financial boost. He introduced legislation that established the National Endowment for Democracy (NED), of which he became the first director. Through the NED, the Reagan administration channeled hundreds of thousands of federal dollars to a Foundation-affiliated organization. Drawing on the funds, the Foundation made campaign contributions, demanding support for its anti-Castro crusade as a quid pro quo.[108]

Mas Canosa convinced fellow Cuban immigrants to contribute to the Foundation, such that it quickly established its own revenue base. Within a decade, the Foundation came to claim 50,000 members, with some 170 directors, trustees, and associates who amassed fortunes in the United States contributing $1,000 to $10,000 to the organization annually (some of them reputedly acquiring their wealth in drug trafficking, with Miami at the time becoming a hub).[109] Mas Canosa led by example. Having

---

[106] Mas Canosa never entirely convinced militant exiles to shift to more institutional channels to influence US Cuba policy. In 1989, for example, the FBI declared Miami the terrorist capital of the United States, with exiles responsible for many murders. Cuban American Committee Testimony, Hearing by subcommittee on International Economic Policy and Trade, March 13, 1990. GHWB Presidential Record, White House Office of Public Liason, Shiree Sanchez Files: Folder: Cuban American Committee. Cuban Americans who promoted dialogue with the Cuban government were assassinated, and had their homes and businesses bombed, 08236-023. For a Cuban perspective, see also Arboleya Cervera, *Cuba y los cubanoamericanos*, pp. 178–82.

[107] Mas Canosa acquired a small construction firm that under his tutelage became one of the two largest Hispanic-owned businesses: a telephone cable company, Mastec.

[108] Gaeton Fonzi, "Who Is Jorge Mas Canosa?," *Esquire* (January 1993); Patrick Haney and Walt Vanderbush, *The Cuban Embargo: The Domestic Politics of an American Foreign Policy* (Pittsburgh: University of Pittsburgh Press, 2005), pp. 43–44.

[109] "CANF Members and Directors through 1994," Cuban Information Archives Document 0239 http://cuban-exile.com/doc_226–250/doc0239.html; Juan Tamayo, "CANF Affirms Power Despite Struggles," *Miami Herald* (March 28, 2002) (http://64.21.33.164/CNews/y02/mar02/28e5.htm. On Cuban American ties to drug-trafficking,

acquired a small construction firm that, under his leadership, became, for a period, the largest Latinx-owned business in the United States, he helped finance the Foundation. The Foundation became one of the two best-funded ethnic lobbying groups in the United States, second only to the American Israel Public Affairs Committee, on which the Foundation was modeled.

Under the sway of its forceful leader, the Foundation wielded influence beyond its territorial base in Florida and across the partisan divide, even as most members voted Republican. The Foundation promoted Cuban American concerns, independently of members' private party preferences. Through political contributions and lobbying it rallied support for Cuba-related legislation among both Democrats and Republicans. Moreover, with the force of the Foundation behind him, Mas Canosa gained White House access not only under President Reagan but, subsequently, under President Bush and, initially, also under President Clinton. President Bush met with Mas Canosa in his first month in office. Decades later, the content of the meeting remained classified.[110]

Mas Canosa masterfully leveraged Foundation funds for the agenda he and his close collaborators set. Formally, the Foundation's main goal was to advance freedom and democracy in Cuba.[111] With that goal in mind, Mas Canosa and Foundation affiliates lobbied for legislation they envisioned would foment regime change on the island.

To leverage political influence in Washington, Mas Canosa oversaw the formation of a formally autonomous lobbying organization, the Cuban American Foundation (CAF), and a political action committee (PAC), the Free Cuba PAC. He formed the spin-off groups to comply with US regulations. The Free Cuba PAC accounted for all but 1 percent of Cuban American PAC contributions through the turn of the century.[112]

---

see Peter Dale Scott and Jonathan Marshall, *Cocaine Politics: Drugs, Armies, and the CIA in Central America* (Berkeley: University of California Press, 1998) especially pp. 24–35, 117–26.

[110] See GHWBPL VP Records, Press Office, Meredith Armstrong, Subject Files, Task Force on South Florida, Folder: Cubans (OA 169), Talking Points-VP Meeting with Jorge Mas, February 14, 1989, 20550-018.

[111] Cuban American National Foundation (www.canf.org).

[112] See the superb data compiled by the Center for Responsive Politics (www.opensecrets.org), including in separate files at ubsl/cubareport.asp, pubs/cubareport/appendix.asp, and pubs/cubareport/legislation.asp.

In 1983, in response to Foundation lobbying, Congress allotted $10 million in federal funds for Radio Martí, to beam anti-Castro messaging to Cuba that, when first aired, so angered Castro that, as previously noted, he withdrew Cuba's commitment to the bilateral migration agreement signed with the Reagan administration.[113] President Reagan had urged Congress to approve the Radio Martí-enabling legislation with no idea that it would lead the Cuban government to stop accepting "inadmissible" Mariel Cubans he wanted removed from the United States. Cuban authorities had come to see what they called the "anti-Castro lobbies" as a new, reconfigured "ultra-Right" source of opposition to Cuba in the United States.[114] Yet, President Reagan's promotion of exile interests backfired. Two years passed before his administration successfully negotiated reinstatement of the migration agreement, including Cuba's commitment to accept the return of "inadmissibles." The main congressional sponsor of the radio-funding bill had been Senator Paula Hawkins, a Florida Republican. Although she was not Cuban American, she was one of the top ten recipients of Cuban American campaign funds between 1979 and 2000.

Under Bush's presidency, Congress passed another Foundation-backed bill, to establish federally funded TV Martí, to complement the work of Radio Martí. Congressman Fascell, who was also not Cuban American but an active advocate for Cuban immigrant interests, advocated for TV Martí. Like Hawkins, Fascell received substantial campaign contributions from the Foundation-linked PAC.

Jeb, in turn, had urged his father – already when his father was vice president – to support TV Martí, for his own political reasons. Jeb claimed that Cuban Americans were "close to abandoning the Administration" out of anger about the renegotiated migration agreement, which they feared would result in the repatriation not only of the Mariel "inadmissibles" but also of Cubans who violated terms of their parole status.[115] Jeb envisioned TV Martí to be a Cuban American vote-getting issue for his father. Persuaded by his son, Vice President Bush

---

[113] GHWBPL, White House Office, Public Liaison, Files: Shiree Sánchez, Folder: CANF, "Losing an Air War with Castro," *New York Times* (March 24, 1990), ID 08236-017. As Chair of Radio Martí's advisory board, Mas Canosa promoted programs that advanced his own personal agenda (and not to all Cuban Americans' liking), as well as critiques of the Cuban government.

[114] Arboleya Cervera, *Cuba y los cubanoamericanos*, chapter 3.

[115] GHWBPL, VP Records, Office of National Security Affairs, Donald Gregg Files, Country Files, Folder: Cuba-1988, Mariel/Detainees/Human Rights [1], OA/ID 19869-

announced at a Foundation meeting in June 1988 that he supported TV Martí, and, on winning the presidential election later that year, signed the enabling legislation. In the newly elected president's words, "thousands of pictures are worth a single word – freedom."[116] Supporting TV Martí helped garner Cuban American votes, at American taxpayers' expense. The costly project proved to be a white elephant. The Cuban government blocked its reception.[117]

While Radio and TV Martí focused on destabilizing Castro's rule through the airwaves, the Foundation subsequently lobbied for the Cuban Democracy Act (CDA), to close loopholes in the Cuban embargo that the United States had instituted in 1962. It hoped thereby finally to destabilize the Cuban government to the point of collapse.[118] The Foundation-associated PAC contributed to the campaigns of the key sponsors of the enabling legislation in both the House of Representatives and the Senate. The sponsors were Democrats, New Jersey's Robert Torricelli and Florida's Bob Graham, the second and sixth largest recipients of Foundation political donations through 2000. While they were also not Cuban American, they represented the states with the largest concentrations of Cuban Americans.

During the 1992 Presidential campaign, the CDA was a key political issue in Florida, just as TV Martí had been during the campaign four years earlier. The Foundation helped secure the support of both the Democratic and Republican presidential candidates for the pending legislation. President Bush, when running for reelection, was the fifth largest recipient of Cuban American political donations. Bill Clinton, his Democratic challenger, received far fewer dollars, but he was very

---

023, Office of the Vice President, Memorandum for the Vice President, from Don Gregg/ Sam Watson, Subject: Cuba: Additional Things You Could Do-TV Martí.

[116] GHWBPL, VP Records, Office of National Security Affairs, Donald Gregg Files, Country Files, Folder: Cuba-1988, OA/ID 19869-022, Office of the Press Secretary, Vice President, "Excerpts of Remarks for Vice President George Bush," Cuban-American National Foundation Congress, Washington, DC, June 13, 1988.

[117] During the decades that followed, Radio and TV Martí were wracked by scandals and financial problems. For example, thirty years after initiating TV Martí, former mayor of Miami Tomas Regalado resigned as head of the parent agency because of scandals and budget problems. "U.S.-Cuba News Brief" (Washington, DC, Center for Democracy in the Americas September 27, 2019).

[118] The Cuban Democracy Act prohibited foreign-based subsidiaries of US companies from trading with Cuba; banned ships that landed in Cuba from US ports for six months; called for the withholding of US aid to countries that traded with Cuba; and restricted US-to-Cuba remittance-sending, other than to cover cost of Cuban travel to the United States. The bill also called for increased cross-border people-to-people contact.

transparent in his quid pro quo. After receiving $275,000 at two Miami Foundation-associated fundraising events during his campaign, he announced that he supported the CDA. President Bush – who initially had opposed the legislation because of its extra-territorial reach, which angered US allies – shifted his stance after Clinton publicly backed the bill. President Bush proceeded to sign the bill very publicly in Florida a few weeks before the election. He succeeded in winning the Florida vote with Cuban American support, but not the national election.[119] The CDA was not a concern to the broader electorate.

With the backing of the Foundation, Mas Canosa also convinced the Reagan administration in its last year to extend one new unique immigration entitlement to Cubans that did not require congressional approval: indeed, a program permitting circumvention of congressional control over immigration. It involved granting the Foundation the right to admit Cubans to the United States independently of official immigration and refugee channels:[120] through a Foundation-formed Cuban Exodus Relief Fund (CERF), which was established in 1988. The Foundation organized media marathons to raise funds so that CERF could finance the transportation of the Cubans, and to provide them with financial and medical assistance, and jobs, on their arrival.[121] In coordination with the State Department, the office of the US Coordinator for Refugee Affairs, and the Immigration and Naturalization Service (INS), the Reagan administration agreed to allow the CERF to bring up to 1,500 Cubans a year to the United States from third countries, from the very countries to which Cubans had gone in hopes of immigrating to the United States after the Reagan administration began to only sparingly issue immigration visas in Cuba (and from where it subsequently suspended issuing visas to Cubans).[122] As a Reagan administration Private Sector Initiative (PSI)[123]

---

[119] Disgruntled that its lobbying left Castro entrenched in power, a faction that was affiliated with the Foundation broke off to promote terrorist tactics, such as bombing of tourist facilities in Havana. See Rohter, "An Exile's Empire: A Special Report."

[120] Ibid.; Skoug, *The United States and Cuba under Reagan and Shultz*, pp. 151–72; GHWBPL, White House Office, Public Liaison, Files: Shiree Sanchez, Folder: CANF, Letter to Andrew Card, Assistant to the President, from Jacqueline Tillman, CANF, March 22, 1990, ID 08236-017.

[121] Rodríguez Chavez, Emigración Cubana Actual, pp. 51–58.   [122] Ibid.

[123] On President Reagan's PSI program, see Rénee Berger, "Private-Sector Initiatives in the Reagan Administration," *Proceedings of the Academy of Political Science*, vol. 36, no. 2, Public–Private Partnerships: Improving Urban Life (1986): 14–30; on the Cuban American National Foundation Private Sector Initiative Program, see GHWBPL, White House Office of National Service, Karen Barnes Files, Folder: CANF (1988),

that, in principle, only involved privately funded refugee resettlement,[124] CERF furthered the administration's commitment to neoliberal development and a reining in of state expenditures. While the Reagan administration approved the Foundation-run program, the Bush administration oversaw its implementation. By the end of President Bush's second year in office, the CERF was estimated to have saved the federal government over $30 million in refugee resettlement expenses.[125]

When he was vice president, Bush, along with Attorney General Meese, presided over the signing of the PSI-enabling directive at a Foundation congress.[126] Although it was officially a nonpartisan program, Jeb Bush, as chair of the Republican Party in Miami-Dade County, worked to promote the Foundation-run PSI. In a letter sent through official channels in February 1988, Jeb advised his father, who was in the throes of his presidential campaign, to be prepared to discuss with Cuban Americans when visiting Miami not only TV Martí but also the status of the Foundation-linked immigration program.[127] The program was popular among Cuban Americans who wanted family "stuck" in third countries to join them in the United States.

Once the CERF was up and running, the Foundation chartered flights to transport Cubans that it selected. All Cubans admitted through the program were assured authorization to work and medical insurance for two years, but no rights to welfare or other REAA entitlements.[128]

"Cuban American National Foundation Private Sector Initiative Program," ID 08276-014.

[124] GHWBPL, VP Records, White House Office of Public Liaison, Shiree Sánchez Files, Folder: CANF June 13, 1989, Memorandum to Shiree Sanchez, from Jacqueline Tillman.

[125] GHWBPL, NSC, Nancy Dyke Files, Subject Files, letter to Jewel LaFontant-Mankarious, Coordinator for Refugee Affairs, Department of State, from Diego Suarez, CANF, December 18, 1990, ID CFO1074-005(006).

[126] GHWBPL, White House Office of Public Liaison, Shiree Sánchez Files, Folder: CANF June 13, 1989, memorandum to Shiree Sanchez from Jacqueline Tillman, CANF Executive Director, Subject: CANF Congress 1989, June 1, 1989, ID 08236-017.

[127] GHWBPL, VP Records, Office of Chief of Staff, Philip Brady files, Subject Files, Folder: Cuban Community Issues Miami 1988. In a memorandum to the vice president, dated February 29, 1988, Phil Brady of the Office of the Vice President, alluded to Jeb Bush's suggestion that if the vice president were asked during his visit to Miami about the Private Sector Initiative he should mention that it is a promising undertaking.

[128] GHWBPL, White House Office of National Service, Karen Barnes Files, Folder: CANF (1988), George Volsky, "Cuban Exiles Land in U.S. Amid Families' Jubilation," *New York Times* (September 11, 1988); GHWBPL, White House Office of National Service, Karen Barnes Files, Folder: CANF (1988), Bonnie Anderson, "Latest Arrival of Cubans Ends Cruel Joke of Destiny," *Miami News* (September 12, 1988), ID 08276-014.

While the program participants lived safely in third countries, they were officially admitted as refugees. The US Coordinator for Refugee Affairs noted that the administration and the Foundation were cooperating to make the first test of a "permanent private refugee sponsorship program," despite equity and other concerns.[129] Such "outsourcing" of "refugee" admissions was without precedent.

Before the program ended (following a corruption scandal),[130] the Foundation had admitted 9,500 Cubans from third countries, nearly equivalent to the 11,222 immigration visas that the Reagan, Bush, and Clinton administrations, combined, had issued between 1985 and 1994[131]: and over 1,000 more a year, on average, than the initial 1,500 to which the Reagan administration had committed.[132] Furthermore, in FY1991 the Bush administration had set a refugee admission ceiling of 6,000 Cubans, in conjunction with the Refugee Act, 3,000 of whom it permitted the Foundation to resettle, allegedly at no cost to the government.[133] However, with the CERF drawing on an estimated $2 million in federal funds,[134] the Bush administration subsidized Foundation-controlled immigration that was supposed to have been entirely privately funded.

Wayne Smith, the top Carter administration-appointed diplomat at the Interests Section in Havana after its opening in 1977, criticized the privatization of Cuban admissions. In his words

I do not know of any other political organization in the United States that has ever received this kind of privilege (to independently admit immigrants). It is one they (the Foundation) have clearly used to their advantage, saying to people, 'We can get your uncle in Madrid to the U.S. and, oh, by the way, you do support the foundation, don't you?'[135]

---

[129] GHWBPL, VP Records, Office of Chief of Staff, Philip Brady Files, Subject Files, Folder: Cuban Community Issues-Miami (1988) [1], U.S. Coordinator for Refugee Affairs, "Status of the Cuban American Foundation's Private Sector Initiative," ID 14828-011.
[130] Arboleya Cervera, *Cuba y los cubanoamericanos*, p. 184.
[131] Masud-Piloto, *From Welcomed Exiles to Illegal Immigrants*, p. 135.
[132] Rodríguez Chavez, *Emigración Cubana Actual*, pp. 51–60.
[133] GHWBPL, NSC, Nancy Dyke Files, Subject Files, Folder: Refugees: Private Sector Initiative, Memorandum to Ambassador Jewel Lafontant-Mankarious, from Chris Gersten, Office of Refugee Resettlement, Subject: Expansion of Cuban American National Foundation's Private Sector Initiative, n.d., CF 01074-005(006).
[134] David Hancock, "1,728 Third Country Cubans Have Arrived Under Program," *Miami Herald* March 13, 1989; Masud-Piloto, *From Welcomed Exiles to Illegal Immigrants*, p. 133.; Rohter, "An Exile's Empire."
[135] Rohter, "An Exile's Empire."

The Foundation, through CERF, oversaw admission of Cubans until the Clinton administration slashed funding for CERF. While the Foundation by then had stopped accepting resettlement applications, for six years Mas Canosa awarded immigration visas to build up his own political following: initially with private Cuban American, but ultimately also with federal, funds. Cubans were admitted in accordance with his preference system, not that set by Congress, which officially controls immigrant admissions.

INADMISSIBLE CUBANS: EXCEPTION TO THE EXCEPTIONALISM

In principle, once the United States and Cuba agreed, in 1987, to reactivate the migration accord, the United States would admit as many as 20,000 Cubans a year, and Cuban authorities would accept the return of Mariel Cubans who US authorities considered inadmissible. However, the reactivated agreement immediately generated new, unanticipated problems for the White House, from Cubans who were fearful that they would be repatriated. While Mariel Cubans all along had resented and resisted their internment, in an ironic twist they rebelled anew, in 1987, when plans were announced that they might be repatriated, as "excludables." They wanted to stay in the United States, though not locked up.

By the time the migration accord was reactivated, the Reagan administration had consolidated most Cuban "excludables" in the federal penitentiary in Atlanta, which was considered the worst of the federal prison facilities and was slated for closing before the Mariel Cubans arrived, and at a federal prison in Oakdale, Louisiana. Oakdale accommodated Cubans who were believed to have committed serious crimes either in Cuba or in the United States but also Mariel Cubans held beyond the time of their sentencing who were waiting to be deported as excludable aliens or to be sent to halfway houses when there were openings.[136] In 1987, 7,600 imprisoned Cubans were considered for deportation: 5,000 more than at the time the 1984 migration agreement had been suspended.[137]

---

[136] GHWBPL, VP Records, Office of Chief of Staff, Phil Brady Files, Subject Files, Folder: Cuba/Nicaragua Immigration (2), Robert McFadden, "Cubans in 2D Jail Riot Over Fears of Deportation," *New York Times* (November 24, 1987), ID 14831-003.

[137] GHWBPL, VP Records, Office of Chief of Staff, Phil Brady Files, Subject Files, Folder: Cuba/Nicaragua Immigration (2), Inquirer Wire Services, "1,149 Cubans Get Approval to Leave Jails," *Philadelphia Inquirer*, January 5, 1987, ID 14831-003.

However favorably the Reagan administration treated the Mariel "admissibles," the same cannot be said of its treatment of the "inadmissibles" who it wanted repatriated to Cuba. It subjected the Mariel "inadmissibles" to deplorable conditions. Angrily, some of them had tried over the years to get released through legal channels. An Atlanta legal aid attorney, Gary Leshaw, filed a class action lawsuit on their behalf that addressed the intolerable and inhumane conditions thrust on them: overcrowding, inadequate lighting and recreation facilities, and lack of privacy, including toilet privacy.[138] Indicative of how distraught Mariel Cubans were, between 1982 and 1987 nine detainees committed suicide, and another 158 tried to do so. In addition, there were over 2,000 serious incidents of self-mutilation.[139]

In 1982, a US district judge in Atlanta indeed found the Reagan administration's review procedures to violate the Cubans' rights to due process. They were held in indefinite detention, without representation by an attorney and without the right to a meaningful appeal.[140]

However, the judicial system did not consistently rule in the Cubans' favor. In 1984, the 11th US Circuit Court of Appeals ruled that Cubans' parole could be denied or revoked without infringing on their constitutional rights. Three years later, the INS did agree to a new hearing policy for those who felt unfairly incarcerated: but without the right to an attorney, and, thus, adequate defense.

It was against the backdrop of resentment about their confinement and conditions therein, and about their deprival of a fair defense, that imprisoned Cubans staged a well-organized rebellion at the Oakdale prison, and immediately afterward at the Atlanta penitentiary, when the migration agreement was reinstated. In Oakdale, 1,000 Cubans seized control of the facilities for two weeks,[141] the longest prison takeover in US history.[142] Inmates broke windows, set buildings on fire, and took prison officials hostage. They also took over the institution's public

---

[138] Hamm, *The Abandoned Ones*, p. 87; GHWBPL, VP Records, Office of Chief of Staff, Philip Brady Files, Subject Files, Folder: Cuba/Nicaragua Immigration (3), Hon. Steven Trott, US. Department of Justice and Hon. J. Michael Quinlan, Director, Bureau of Prisons, "Press Conference," Washington, DC, December 10, 1987, 14831-004.

[139] Hamm, *The Abandoned Ones*, p. 88.

[140] GHWBPL, VP Records, Office of National Security Affairs, Donald Gregg Files, Country Files, Folder: Cuba 1988, Mariel/Detainees/Human Rights [3].

[141] GHWBPR, VP Records, Office of Chief of Staff, Phil Brady Files, Subject Files, Folder: Cuban/Nicaraguan Immigration (2), Art Harris, "Meese Offers to Delay Cuban Deportations," *Washington Post* (November 24, 1987), ID 14831-003.

[142] Hamm, *The Abandoned Ones*, pp. 176–77.

address system and broadcast what they called "Radio Mariel," a play on Radio Martí. One Cuban died in the takeover, and forty of them were seriously wounded. The Cubans wanted to be released, not repatriated.[143] Meanwhile, in Atlanta, Cubans rebelled for eleven days.

Defiant inmates released personnel they were holding hostage only after the US Attorney General's office agreed to a moratorium on deportations, and a "full, fair, and equitable" review of their cases. They had broad support for their demands. Not only did Leshaw advocate on their behalf.[144] Atlanta Congressman John Lewis – the esteemed civil rights leader who had been critical of how the Reagan administration handled imprisoned Cuban immigrants – helped broker a solution.[145] Also, Mas Canosa and the revered Cuba-born Auxiliary Bishop Agustín Román of Miami intervened on their behalf.[146] Román noted in a December 31 (1987) letter to Attorney General Meese that many detainees were held for seven years in indefinite detention without charges, and that others remained in indefinite imprisonment long after having served their sentences for offenses committed in the United States.[147] In response to the political pressures, a congressional report called for each detainee's case to be (re)assessed, possibly sparing them deportation.

The Mariel rebels insisted that the INS be barred from involvement in the review panels that the Justice Department agreed to set up. They perceived the INS to be a biased arbiter, and its review process to lack the most fundamental elements of fairness.[148] The Department of Justice, accordingly, established panels to review the cases that the INS turned down (but without guaranteeing the Cubans full assistance of counsel).

As early as 1986, before the rebellions, a Congress-commissioned inspection of the Atlanta penitentiary concluded that not only the INS

---

[143] GHWBPL, VP Records, Office of National Security Affairs, Donald Gregg Files, Country Files, Folder: Cuba 1988, Mariel/Detainees/Human Rights [3].

[144] GHWBPL, VP Records, Office of Chief of Staff, Phil Brady Files, Subject Files, Folder: Cuban/Nicaraguan Immigration (2), Ruth Marcus, "Plan for 7,600 Cubans Unveiled," *Washington Post* (December 2, 1987), ID 14831-003.

[145] GHWBPL, VP Records, Office of Chief of Staff, Phil Brady Files ... McFadden, "Cubans in 2d Jail Riot over Fears of Deportation."

[146] GHWBPL, VP Records, Office of Chief of Staff, Phil Brady Files, Subject Files, Folder: Cuban/Nicaraguan Immigration (2), Guillermo Martínez, "Cuban Community Has Come of Age," *Miami Herald* (December 8, 1987), ID 14831-003.

[147] GHWBPL, VP Records, National Security Affairs, Donald Gregg Files, Country Files, Folder: Cuba 1988: Mariel/Detainees/Human Rights [1], OA/ID 19869-023, Letter to Attorney General Edwin Meese from Agustín Roman, Auxiliary Bishop Miami, December 31, 1987.

[148] Pear, "Reviews on Cuban Aliens Shifted to Justice Department," p. 28.

but also the Department of Justice had treated many of the Mariel immigrants unjustly, and in a manner that drove up expenses. It found many of the "excludables" either to have already served sentences for crimes they committed or to be detained for crimes they never committed. As a result, hundreds of millions of federal dollars were unnecessarily and unjustly squandered on maximum security confinement. The investigation concluded that the Justice Department had overseen a deliberate disinformation campaign to turn the American people against Mariel Cubans, at taxpayers' expense.[149]

For many of the Cubans, the uprising paid off. In January 1988, the Justice Department agreed to release more than 1,100 of the interned Cubans, and announced plans to release more. The Reagan administration was found to have mistreated Cubans that it considered "inadmissible." However, only when imprisoned Mariel Cubans staged the takeovers of the facilities where they were interned did the administration right its wrongdoing.

Against the backdrop of the protests in Atlanta and Oakdale, in 1991, under the Bush administration, Mariel Cubans who were imprisoned for a variety of criminal charges in another federal correction institution, in Talladega, Alabama, also rebelled. They too protested the migration accord, which made them subject to deportation. By then over 450 Cuban detainees had been sent back to Cuba. The protesters demanded not to be returned to Cuba. In this case, though, following a ten-day standoff, the Bush administration speeded up Cuban deportations.[150]

REINSTITUTION OF EXCLUSIONARY HAITIAN POLICIES

The Reagan as well as Bush administrations took a different stance toward Haitians than toward Cubans: toward both the Haitians who President Carter had admitted as Entrants, and, especially, toward those who arrived after eligibility for the Entrant program ended. Haitian success at securing special rights did not last long. Even before the Reagan administration delinked entitlements for Cuban and Haitian Entrants, it had aggressively turned on Haitians who tried immigrating

---

[149] Hamm, *The Abandoned Ones*, p. 69.
[150] Ronald Smothers, "U.S. Agents Storm Prison in Alabama, Freeing 9 Hostages," *New York Times* (August 31, 1991) (www.nytimes.com/1991/08/31/us/us-agents-storm-prison-in-Alabama-freeing-9-hostages.html).

without authorization under its watch. It blocked them from the United States, and subjected those who managed to enter illicitly to harsh, cruel treatment: to detention and deportation. The Reagan administration also admitted few Haitians as refugees, including if they fled repression and persecution. In his determined effort to exclude Haitians, President Reagan even set his fiscal belt-tightening principles aside. Already in 1981, his administration had expended an estimated $96 million to block Haitians from entry.[151] President Reagan reopened the Haitian path of "disprivilege" that President Carter had set aside during his last year in office. President Bush followed suit, except when legally challenged.

An "imperfect storm" worked to Haitians' disadvantage. In the 1980s, Haitians faced presidents who treated them unfairly and inhumanely. They suffered from blatant racism, and from not serving the Reagan and Bush administrations' Cold War foreign policy agenda. Furthermore, they had few votes to parlay for favors, in part because they enjoyed no law comparable to the Cuban Adjustment Act to enable those who arrived without authorization rights to lawful permanent residence, and to citizenship, in turn. They also lacked the resources to become influential lobbyists. Fortunately for them, human rights advocates and dedicated lawyers convinced the courts to put a halt to some of the Reagan and Bush administrations' most egregious abuses.

An internal Cabinet memorandum written eight months after Reagan assumed the presidency is telling of his administration's preoccupation with blocking Haitians from the United States. Mike Horowitz, who became director and general counsel of the Office of Management and Budget, noted that the "Administration policy is to warehouse them (Haitians) in detention facilities and then to exclude them after hearings ... Unfortunately, a small coterie of Haitian defense lawyers has contrived to tie the exclusion process up in knots, preventing their exclusion and transportation back to Haiti." Horowitz also expressed concern about detention costs that "rise with every day and every boatload." He compared the strategy of the Haitian Refugee Center, which defended Haitians, to that of the Welfare Rights Organization that Reagan had fought as governor of California, before assuming the presidency. Horowitz claimed that the Haitian Refugee Center tied up the system with class action suits and procedural delays, to pressure the

---

[151] RRPL, Kate Moore Files, Office of Chief of Staff, "Point Paper: Consolidation of Cuban and Haitian Aliens at a Central Location," Cuban-Haitians [5] Cuba-Haiti [3] FOIA, Box 2.

administration to grant Haitians legal immigration status.[152] He bemoaned that the administration faced pressure to admit them, but expressed no concern that they were unfairly treated.

Interdiction and Repatriation

President Reagan's turn on Haitians began almost immediately after he assumed office, even as he supported legislation to allow the Haitian, along with the Cuban, Entrants to become lawful permanent residents. The Haitian asylum seekers who had the misfortune of trying to immigrate after the Entrant program ended and after President Carter left office were interdicted at sea and repatriated, and denied immigration and refugee rights.

During his first year as president, Reagan issued an Executive Order to authorize the US Coast Guard to stop and search vessels suspected of transporting undocumented Haitians to the United States in the high seas, outside US territorial waters.[153] He then asked Congress to pass an Emergency Interdiction Act to provide statutory authority for high-seas interdictions. However, he faced legislators who argued that the Simpson–Mazzoli immigration bill then before Congress did not empower a president to seize ships in international waters.[154]

Rebuffed by Congress, but nonetheless determined to block unauthorized Haitians from US entry, President Reagan proceeded to sign an interdiction agreement with Haiti's corrupt, repressive president, "Baby Doc" Duvalier, an anti-Communist ally. The agreement, together with an Executive Order President Reagan issued in September 1981, allowed the US Coast Guard to board and inspect private Haitian vessels on the high seas and repatriate those believed to be en route to the United States without entry permission. This marked the first use of a bilateral interdiction agreement to block unauthorized immigrants from the United States (which became precedent for subsequent agreements with other governments).[155]

---

[152] RRPL, T. Kenneth Cribb: Files, Cabinet Affairs Series I, Memorandum to Ed Harper, Glenn Schleede, Annelise Anderson from Mike Horowitz, September 16, 1981, Subject: Haitian Refugees, Folder: Immigration Control (3 of 5) OA4821, Box 1.

[153] Ruth Wasem, *CRS Report for Congress: U.S. Immigration Policy on Haitian Migrants* (Washington, DC: Congressional Research Service, February 1, 2010), p. 3.

[154] Kenneth Brill, "The Endless Debate: Refugees Law and Policy and the 1980 Refugee Act," *Cleveland State Law Review* vol. 32 issue 1 (1983): 119.

[155] Carl Lindskoog, *Detain and Punish: Haitian Refugees and the Rise of the World's Largest Immigration Detention System* (Gainesville: University of Florida Press, 2018), p. 59.

President Reagan's approach toward Haitians was far more draconian than Carter's toward Mariel Cubans when he tried, at first, to block their US entry. President Carter clamped down on the enablers – the boat captains – not on the Cubans seeking refuge; he mandated the Coast Guard to intervene in US, rather than international waters; and he did not require repatriation of interdicted Cubans. Although unjust and, in part, illegal, Reagan's exclusionary interventions were, however, more effective than Carter's. The Coast Guard did not succeed in intercepting all boats transporting Haitians, but the interdictions, plus the deterrent effect of Reagan's detention policy, described later in this chapter, reduced the number of unauthorized Haitian arrivals from 8,000 to about 120 between January and October 1982. Conditions in Haiti had not improved in the interim to account for the drop-off.[156]

Officially, even though US authorities were to interview Haitians on the Coast Guard cutters and grant asylum to those demonstrating well-founded fear that they would suffer persecution if returned to Haiti, State Department and INS interviewers prejudged Haitian claimants without interviewing them.[157] US officials concluded that most of the Haitians were economic migrants, even though the Duvalier government was reputed to be the most repressive regime in the Americas. Over a ten-year period that spanned the Bush as well as Reagan administration, the United States granted asylum to only twenty-eight interdicted Haitians.[158] The Reagan administration repatriated 16,000 Haitians, and the Bush administration repatriated approximately 23,500 Haitians.[159] The two administrations made a mockery of fair process.

---

[156] Stepick, "Haitian Boat People: A Study with Conflicting Forces Shaping U.S. Immigration Policy," *Law and Contemporary Problems* vol. 45 (Spring 1982), p. 190.

[157] No author, "Haitian Boat People," *Immigration in America* (December 21, 2011) (immigrationinamerica.org/536-haitian-boat-people.html); Christopher Mitchell, "U.S. Policy toward Haitian Boat People, 1972–93, *Annals of the American Academy of Political and Social Science* vol. 534 (July 1994): 73.

[158] Philippe Girard, *Haiti: The Tumultuous History: From Pearl of the Caribbean to Broken Nation* (New York: Palgrave Macmillan, 2010), p. 140. The Reagan administration, alone, interdicted and repatriated over 16,000 Haitians. GHWBPL, NSC, Rostow Files, Subject Files, Folder: Refugees. Report to the Attorney General and the National Security council on Immigration, prepared by Immigration and Naturalization Service, January 12, 1989, CF 01063-025.

[159] GHWBPL, NSC, Nancy Dyke Subject Files, Folder: Refugees: Haiti, 1992 (1), Press Guidance, "Haitian Boat People," July 30, 1992, CF 01074-006/5/006.

Indicative that Haitians typically sought refuge for political and not merely or mainly for economic reasons, when Jean-Bertrand Aristide became Haiti's first democratically elected president, in February 1991, the number of asylum seekers dropped markedly. Then, when a violent military coup ousted Aristide eight months later, the number of asylum seekers picked up anew. Fortunately for Haitians, in July 1992 a court decision prevented the repatriation of Haitians who the Coast Guard had interdicted in the high seas.

Building on President Reagan's discriminatory policies toward Haitians, President Bush claimed that the military who ousted Aristide committed no human rights violations. However, as the level of political violence in Haiti soared, and persecution of Haitians became transparent, his administration conceded to grant over 10,000 Haitians political asylum in the United States, half the number he repatriated. The Haitians admitted were believed to have a credible fear of persecution if returned to Haiti.[160]

With the Bush administration's admission of Haitians inspiring other Haitians to seek refuge in the United States, it reimposed a hardline stance. It proceeded to issue immigration visas to Haitians only sparingly, and to order the Coast Guard to once again interdict visa-less Haitians at sea, this time, however, not to repatriate them but to intern them under deplorable conditions at an offshore detention facility that the United States constructed in Guantanamo Bay, Cuba, on the land that the United States had convinced the Cuban government, after gaining independence from Spain, to lease it for a coal and naval station.[161] President Bush diverted Haitians to Guantanamo after the Haitian Refugee Center won a court case that put a temporary restraining order on the forced repatriation of Haitians. His administration interned some 34,000 Haitians in Guantanamo, more than the number of Haitians that the Carter Administration had admitted as Entrants, despite little difference between the two groups of Haitians and the conditions from which they had fled. One-third of the Guantanamo detainees did proceed to win asylum claims and were admitted to the United States, but the others were repatriated.[162]

---

[160] Rodríguez Chavez, *Emigración Cubana Actual*, pp. 67–68.
[161] Castro tried unsuccessfully to terminate the treaty that allows the United States to lease the land in Guantanamo Bay, which was signed shortly after Cuba gained independence from Spain.
[162] Girard, *Haiti: The Tumultuous History*, p. 140.

In order to make it yet more difficult for Haitians to attain asylum in the United States, in May 1992 President Bush transferred the refugee review process to Haiti, such that asylum seekers needed to make their claims under the watch of their repressive government. Haitians who evaded the new review policy and tried to make their way to the United States by sea without entry visas were to be repatriated without a hearing.[163] Only in three other countries did the United States establish in-country refugee-solicitation services (although subsequently in Cuba as well).[164]

President Bush turned on Haitians in no small part for his own opportunistic political reasons. Allowing large numbers of Haitians to come ashore would be unpopular in Florida, where most of them landed, and could cost him votes in his upcoming reelection bid. Floridians stereotyped Haitians as poor and AIDS-inflicted, and Whites in the state extended their prejudice against African Americans to Haitians. In interning unauthorized Haitians at Guantanamo, they were far from Florida.

Detention

The visa-less Haitians who escaped Coast Guard detection and reached the United States were also not welcomed. Under both the Reagan and Bush administrations, immigration authorities placed unauthorized Haitians in detention facilities for extended periods of time. In contrast, Mariel Cubans had been detained only briefly, until sponsors were found to assume responsibility for them (except those with criminal records and assessed to be mentally ill).

As early as July 1981, half a year into President Reagan's first term, a task force that he had commissioned to address general immigration and refugee matters recommended an expansion of detention camps to accommodate Haitians. Allegedly, the administration would thereby align its policy toward Haitians with its policies toward other illegal entrants, whose numbers from Mexico and Central America, in particular, were on the rise. The task force argued that detention would demonstrate a major commitment to enforcement, and prevent unauthorized Haitians from disappearing prior to exclusion hearings. The task force did, however, worry that the camps would overflow with detainees because of procedural delays and that there would be political problems

---

[163] Ibid., p. 141.
[164] GHWBPL, NSC, Nancy Dyke, Subject Files, Folder: Refugees: Haiti, 1992 [1] "Fact Sheet on Legal Immigration from Haiti," CF 01074—005/006.

in the communities where detention facilities were set up, as had happened in Arkansas when the Carter administration interned Mariel Cubans at Fort Chaffee. The task force also worried that the detention facilities would be seen as "concentration camps" filled with Blacks.[165]

Despite the concerns that the task force raised, the INS interned Haitians awaiting deportation hearings in overcrowded detention centers.[166] The most notorious was the Krome North Processing Center outside Miami. Krome North was built of barbed wire and concrete on an old missile site. Haitians were detained there indefinitely under substandard conditions, without entitlement to parole. Some 1,600 Haitians were assigned to Krome North, which was designed for a capacity of 1,000 inmates.[167]

Irate with their prolonged detention, and the conditions of their detention, in 1981 Haitians at Krome North staged a stone-throwing demonstration. Some of the Haitians broke through the barbed-wire fence and fled to the Everglade swamps. Others subsequently staged a hunger strike, backed by Haitians in Miami.[168]

Conditions in Krome North were so inhumane that the State of Florida filed a lawsuit against the Reagan administration for violating health and environmental standards, and for neglect and indifference by federal officials. Dade County mayors, African Americans, religious and human rights groups, along with dedicated lawyers, contested the administration's detention as well as interdiction policy. They argued that the policies were abusive, unfair, and racist, and advocated that, for such reasons, the Haitians should be released.[169]

---

[165] RRPL, Edwin Meese Files, OA 95409944, 9945, Folder: Immigration and Refugee Matters CM-62 (Task Force Report)) OA 9945, memorandum for the Cabinet from Craig Fuller, Office of Cabinet Administration, Subject: Immigration Issues, July 10, 1981.

[166] RRPL, T. Kenneth Cribb Files, Cabinet Affairs Series I, Folder: Immigration Control (2 of 5) OA 4821, Mary Thornton, "Haitian Refugee Dilemma," *Washington Post* (October 19, 1981).

[167] RRPL, Kate Moore Files, Office of Chief of Staff, "Point Paper: Consolidation of Cuban and Haitian Aliens at a Central Location," Box 1: Cubans-Haitians.

[168] George Volsky, "Haitians Flee Amid Protest at Holding Center in Miami," *New York Times* (September 4, 1981) (www.nytimes.com/1981/09/04/us/haitians-flee-amid-protest-at-holding-center-in-miami.html); Pear, "It's Time for Immigration Law Reform: Or Is It?," *New York Times* (January 3, 1982) (www.nytimes.com/1982/01/03/weekinreview/it-s-time-for-immigration-law-reform-or-is-it.html).

[169] RRPL, Office of Cabinet Affairs, Department of Justice, Office of Deputy Attorney General, "Memorandum to Craig Fuller," from David Hiller, Associate Deputy Attorney General, Subject: Dade County May 19, 1982 and Mary Thornton, "Haitian Refugee Dilemma: Lawyers Frustrate U.S. Illegal Immigration Policy," *Washington Post* (October 19,1981), pp. 1, 10.

Denial of Fair Judicial Treatment

The abusive treatment of Haitians did not stop with their detention. Haitians who filed for asylum – more than 11,000 in the first month of Reagan's presidency – faced unfair hearings.[170]

In June (of 1981), for example, the INS subjected the Haitians to mass exclusion hearings. The INS arranged for as many as forty handcuffed Haitians to be brought to its hearing rooms at the same time.[171] Moreover, on at least one occasion, an attorney from the Haitian Refugee Center was blocked from the courtroom.[172] Denied fair defense, only 1 percent of Haitians won their asylum claims.[173] Adding insult to injury, in July President Reagan's Attorney General announced new detention procedures that resulted in more Haitians than other nationals being detained unfairly and for longer.[174]

In a September 16 memorandum, Horowitz, of the Office of Management and Budget, spoke against the detention of Haitians: but for their deportation, not admission. He recommended that the Reagan administration concentrate its "resources on the exclusion process." In his words, "Present policy is the worst of all possible options. We create inhumane and politically unpopular quasi-concentration camps, and produce a new fugitive class of undocumented aliens ... (T)he only long-range solution is to get fair exclusion hearings underway, with enough due process to withstand court challenges." While admitting that Haitians were detained under abysmal conditions, he sought to expedite their deportations. Horowitz felt that INS Commissioner Nelson, who advocated for delinking rights for Cuban and Haitian Entrants, would cooperate.[175]

In general, Haitians were treated so poorly that the Reagan administration was besieged by lawsuits for neglect, inhumane conditions of detention, and more. Haitian Refugee Center lawyers, who sued the administration, insisted that some of the Haitians were political refugees

---

[170] Stepick, "Haitian Boat People," p. 189.   [171] Ibid.
[172] Thornton, "Haitian Refugee Dilemma."
[173] USHR, Committee on the Judiciary, Hearing ... on H.R. 4853 Cuban/Haitian Adjustment, Serial no. 64 (May 9, 1984), p. 92.
[174] Ibid., p. 58.
[175] RRPL, T. Kenneth Cribb: Files, Cabinet Affairs Series I, Memorandum to Ed Harper [White House Domestic Council], Glenn Schleede, Annelise Anderson, from Mike Horowitz, September 16, 1981, subject: Haitian Refugees, Folder: Immigration Control [3 of 5] OA 482.

from the repressive Duvalier government and that they therefore were entitled to full asylum hearings and due process. The administration responded by scheduling concurrent hearings for Haitians represented by the same lawyer in three different courtrooms to limit rulings in Haitians' favor.

Some legal cases filed in Haitians' defense stopped the most egregious Reagan administration policies. In most of the cases, the administration was found to have violated Haitians' rights to fair exclusionary hearings, to fair proceedings, and to fair legal representation. The administration was also found to have dealt with Haitians in a prejudicial, discriminatory, unlawful manner, and to have subjected them to closed-door kangaroo courts.[176] In addition, the administration's detention policy was found to violate UN protocol, in denying Haitians parole. In turn, an INS district director was found to have been motivated by a desire to discriminate against Haitians.[177]

The US District Court for the Southern District of Florida found the administration's treatment of Haitians so abusive that it enjoined any exclusion proceedings anywhere in the United States except where Haitians were represented by counsel.[178] Judge James Lawrence King, who had been appointed by President Nixon, determined that the Reagan administration was guilty of violating Haitians' rights: that Haitians were fleeing the most repressive government in the Americas, that they would be persecuted if they were returned to Haiti, and that INS abusive procedures violated the Constitution and must stop.[179]

The dedicated lawyers who sued the government on Haitians' behalf included Miami-based Ira Kurzban, who worked as a lead lawyer on a series of Haitian class action cases that accused the federal government of denying Haitians adequate presentation of their asylum claims and of depriving Haitians full and fair consideration. The INS was accused of deliberately sending Haitians to far-off places where there were few Creole-speaking translators and few lawyers offering free legal

[176] USHR, Committee on the Judiciary, Hearing ... on H.R. 4853 Cuban/Haitian Adjustment, serial no. 64 (May 9, 1984), pp. 4, 58–60; Stepick, "Haitian Boat People," p. 189. The Haitian Refugee Center, for example, filed legal cases on behalf of Haitians.
[177] Stepick, "Haitian Boat People," pp. 189, 191.
[178] Ibid., p.189; RRPL, WHSo Files, Kate Moore: Files, Office of the Chief of Staff Cubans-Haitians [2], White House Memo November 3, 1981, for James Baker III and Edwin Meese III, from Kate Moore, Kathy Collins, Subject: Selection of an Immigration Detention Site, Box 1.
[179] RRPL, T. Kenneth Cribb: Files, Cabinet Affairs Series I, Memorandum to Ed Harper ... from Mike Horowitz.

representation, such as to Lake Placid, New York; Big Springs, Texas; and Fort Allen, Puerto Rico. Reagan's strategy was designed to maximize prospects that Haitians would be deported, while technically granting them rights to immigration hearings.

Unfortunately for Haitians, they experienced a juridical setback in June 1982, when the Second Circuit Court of Appeals ruled that denial of parole to detained Haitians fell within the discretionary power of an INS district director.[180] Fortunately for Haitians, though, during the same month, Judge Eugene Spellman of the US District Court for the Southern District of Florida ordered approximately 1,800 Haitians to be released from detention facilities, on grounds that they had been unlawfully imprisoned for up to 18 months and detained on the basis of invalid criteria.[181] The INS was forced to grant the Haitians parole status.[182]

Legal battles continued under the Bush administration. President Bush exacerbated problems for Haitians when refusing to grant them Temporary Protective Status (TPS), the new temporary immigration status incorporated into the Immigration Act of 1990 that he signed into law for nationals of countries experiencing problems that made return to their homelands unsafe. His administration argued that thousands more Haitians would attempt to immigrate without authorization if it awarded TPS to Haitians in the United States.[183] It was more concerned about keeping Haitians out of the country than about extending rights to them.

CONCLUSION

In sum, the Reagan administration resolved the immigration problem it inherited from the Carter administration regarding Mariel Cubans' long-

---

[180] Stepick, "Haitian Boat People," p. 191.
[181] USHR, Committee on the Judiciary, Hearing ... on H.R. 4853 Cuban/Haitian Adjustment, serial no. 64 (May 9, 1984), pp. 58–60, 98.
[182] Stepick, "Haitian Boat People," p. 191.
GHWBPL, NSC, Nancy Dyke Files, Subject Files, Folder: Refugees: Haiti, 1992 [1], Letter to Walter Jones, Chairman, Committee on Merchant Marine and Fisheries, from Office of Legislative Affairs, U.S. Department of Justice, September 11, 1992, CF 01074-005/006.
Muzaffar Chishti, Doris Meissner, and Claire Bergeron, "At Its 25th Anniversary, IRCA's Legacy Lives On," *Migration Policy Institute*, November 16, 2011 (www.migration policy.org/article/its-25th-anniversary, ircas-legacy).
[183] GHWBPL, NSC, Nancy Dyke Files, Subject Files, Folder: Refugees: Haiti, 1992 [1], Letter to Walter Jones, Chairman, Committee on Merchant Marine and Fisheries, from Office of Legislative Affairs.

term rights. It did so by following precedent that had been set by previous administrations. Rather than deport them for having immigrated without authorization or extend temporary entry rights to them, President Reagan reimagined them as refugees. He thereby entitled them to lawful permanent residency, welfare, and other benefits, and a path to citizenship that included voting rights. His privileging of Cubans, and its timing, was politically motivated. He sought thereby to bolster support for his reelection, and for his controversial covert Central American policy.

Left at the sidelines were the Haitians. The Reagan administration refused to reimagine the Haitian, along with the Cuban, Entrants as refugees, and not because they were less deserving. Fortunately for the Haitian Entrants, and other unauthorized Haitians who had come to the United States before 1982, in 1986 Congress granted them, along with other unauthorized immigrants, rights to lawful permanent residency, and associated entitlements. However, the Bush, as well as Reagan, administration turned viciously on Haitians who came ashore after 1982. They subjected them to long-term detention and repatriation.

There was a "path dependency" to the Cuban privileging and Haitian disprivileging. Regarding Cubans, new entitlements built on earlier entitlements, and addressed problems that earlier entitlements had created or left unresolved. Both Presidents Reagan and Bush envisioned Cuban immigrants as serving the Cold War crusade against communism that President Carter had brushed aside in order to improve US relations with Cuba. They also envisioned Cuban immigrants as advancing their domestic political interests in winning election and reelection, and in strengthening the Republican Party's political base in a state with growing electoral importance that had historically leaned Democrat. The cumulative privileging contributed, in turn, to the transformation of Cuban immigrants into a political force that independently influenced US Cuba policy, including in ways that backfired on both presidents. Meanwhile, they interdicted and repatriated Haitians, and detained and deported those who managed to come ashore, denying them comparable rights to Cubans.

The Reagan–Bush era came to an end as the Soviet Union collapsed, more from its own internal weaknesses than from the foreign policy of the two Republican Presidents. In the new global context, the Left-leaning movements that took hold in Central America in the 1980s fizzled out. They suffered from loss of Soviet funding and from the discrediting of Marxism-Leninism that was implicit in the Soviet Union's collapse. Meanwhile, Cuba plunged into a deep depression when Soviet support subsided. However, rather than follow the example of their former Eastern European comrades and press for a democratic-market transition, Cubans in stepped up numbers followed the example of the Mariel Cubans and sought refuge in the United States, without authorization, since Washington granted few visas to Cubans to move to America lawfully. Against this backdrop, Clinton assumed the presidency.

5

Taking with One Hand, Giving with the Other

Clinton Administration Retraction and Expansion of Cuban Immigrant Entitlements

Beginning in 1989 the world changed, and, as a result, so did Cuba. Ordinary Germans in the then East Germany took history into their own hands and brought down their Soviet-allied communist government. Other East Europeans followed their example and brought down their respective communist governments, and by 1991 the Soviet superpower joined the dustbin of history. Thousands of miles away, the dissolution of the Soviet Union and the Soviet bloc dramatically impacted on Cuba. Cuba had been heavily dependent on Soviet aid and trade since the early years of the revolution. The sudden cut-off of Soviet ties caused the Cuban economy to contract, by 1994, more than 30 percent.[1] With scarcities driving up the cost of living, the peso lost much of its former value. People faced near-starvation.

In its effort to adapt to the crisis it faced, the Cuban government reached out to the country's diaspora, a potential source of hard currency essential for it reintegrating into the global market economy. Cuban authorities organized two conferences that involved Cubans living abroad, to encourage cross-border bridge-building;[2] they eased conditions for Cuban émigrés to visit and send remittances; and they

---

[1] Carmelo Mesa-Lago, *Market, Socialist, and Mixed Economies* (Baltimore: Johns Hopkins University Press, 2000); Carmelo Mesa-Lago, "Economic and Ideological Cycles in Cuba: Policy and Performance, 1959–2002," in Archibald R. M. Ritter (ed.), *The Cuban Economy* (Pittsburgh: University of Pittsburgh Press, 2004), pp. 25–41; William LeoGrande and Julie Thomas, "Cuba's Quests for Economic Independence," *Journal of Latin American Studies* vol. 34, part 2 (May): 325–64.

[2] On the 1994 conference, see *Conferencia*, "*La nación y la emigración*' (Havana: Editora Política, 1994).

authorized Cubans' right to possess and use dollars.³ Recognizing a silent majority of moderate Cubans in the United States, which Cuban scholars who visited the United States confirmed,⁴ the Cuban government lowered barriers it had previously imposed on Cuban ties with those who had emigrated. Ideological purity became a luxury Cuba no longer could afford.

Meanwhile, increasing numbers of Cubans envisioned emigration as their best hope, especially after Castro gave a green light in 1994 for people to leave (without US entry permission). From the Cuban government vantage point, the departure of disgruntled Cubans would defuse domestic tensions amid the economic crisis. Furthermore, Cubans who left would likely remit some of their earnings to family they left behind, and accordingly infuse much-needed hard currency into the economy.⁵

In turn, from Washington's vantage point, US foreign policy concerns changed with the Cold War's end, despite communism not having entirely disappeared from the world stage. China, Vietnam, and North Korea, as well as Cuba, continued under Communist Party rule. However, with Cuba ceasing to "export revolution" once faced with its domestic economic crisis, the Castro-led government no longer posed a national security threat to the United States. Thus, if there once had been a foreign policy justification for singling Cubans out for exceptional entitlements, to discredit the revolution, that ended with the Soviet Union's collapse. Under the circumstances, did Bill Clinton, the first president to serve entirely in the post-Cold War era, rein in the more than three decades of Cuban privileging?

This chapter details the Clinton administration's response to the surge in unauthorized Cubans taking to the Florida Straits. With no Cold War rationale to treat them differently than other unauthorized arrivals, his administration will be shown initially to break with precedent and block them from coming ashore. Yet, it then proceeded to admit them, to grant them special entitlements, and to reinstate entitlements it previously had

---

³ Antonio Aja Díaz, "El proceso migratorio externo de Cuba: Un balance de los años noventa," *Emigración Cubana: Anuario CEAP 1996* (Havana: Universidad de la Habana, Centro de Estudios de Alternativas Políticas, 1997), pp. 27–28.
⁴ See Hedelberto López Blanch, *La emigración cubana en Estados Unidos: Descorriendo Mamparas* (Havana: Editorial SI-MAR, 1998).
⁵ Susan Eckstein, *The Immigrant Divide: How Cuban Americans Changed the US and Their Homeland* (New York: Routledge, 2009) and Susan Eckstein, "Dollarization and Its Discontents: How People Are Remaking Cuba in the Post-Soviet Era," *Comparative Politics* (Spring 2009): 313–30.

retracted. It also exempted Cubans from new regulations that Congress legislated to crack down harshly, in general, on unauthorized immigrants. Like President Carter, President Clinton tried to rein in Cuban privileging, only to privilege Cubans anew.

This chapter then addresses congressional resistance to bills proposed by some legislators to rein in unique entitlements for Cubans: Congress, thereby, reinforcing the Clinton administration's continued privileging of Cubans. In turn, the chapter highlights how, in the post-Cold War foreign policy void, domestic politics increasingly came to shape Cuban immigration policy, including in the context of two immigration-linked incidents that came to haunt the Clinton administration. More than three decades of entitlements led Cuban exiles who were still deeply committed to reclaiming Cuba to take history into their own hands. They drew on earlier entitlements. In the process, they reflamed US–Cuban tensions and influenced the outcome of two presidential elections.

THE BUILD-UP OF NEW CUBAN IMMIGRATION PRESSURES

Faced with no prospects of immediate recovery from the impact of the Soviet Union's collapse, Cubans in increasing numbers followed the example of disgruntled Cubans before them: those who took off for the United States, visa-less, from the ports of Camarioca and Mariel, in 1965 and 1980, respectively. They left without US entry permission because, as previously noted, authorized entry was not an option for many. Until then, the Clinton administration, like the Reagan and Bush administrations, had only sparingly issued immigration visas, the 1984 migration agreement notwithstanding. In 1993 and 1994, for example, the Clinton administration issued only 2,700 visas. In line with the agreement, it could have issued eighteen times that number in the two years.[6]

With lawful immigration near-impossible, a replay of Mariel took hold, with theme and variation. In May and June of 1994 Cubans sought asylum in foreign embassies, as they had in 1980. Approximately 130 asylum seekers stormed German, Belgian, and Chilean ambassador residencies and embassies.[7] However, having learned from the 1980

---

[6] Matias Travieso-Díaz, "Immigration Challenges and Opportunities in a Post-Transition Cuba," *Berkeley Journal of International Law* vol. 16 (1998): 234–42.

[7] Aja Díaz, "La crisis de los balseros: una mirada al tema migratorio veinte años despues," *Temas* (2014) (Havana).

experience, this time Castro intervened to keep embassy stampedes at bay. He announced that whoever entered an embassy by force would never receive permission to leave the country.[8]

In a replay of 1980, Cubans also confiscated vehicles to take them to the United States: boats, an airplane, and a military vessel.[9] However, in June of 1994 police, in their effort to stop hijackings, shot and killed a hijacker.[10] Then, the following month a Cuban coast guard intervention caused a hijacked tugboat to sink. Forty-one Cubans drowned. And on August 4th, a police officer died in an encounter with hijackers who had seized two ferries in Havana harbor. Meanwhile, earlier Cuban immigrants greeted hijackers who successfully reached Miami with heroes' welcomes.

More significantly, on August 5th more than one thousand Cubans gathered in Havana harbor. They had heard rumors that a flotilla of boats commissioned by Cuban émigrés was *en route* from Florida to pick people up, and that a ferry would be hijacked to transport asylum seekers to the United States. Radio Martí, the US-funded radio station that Mas Canosa had founded to beam anti-Castro messages to Cuba, announced such plans.[11] When no boats arrived, the assembled Cubans chanted anti-Castro epithets and looted stores where only Cubans with access to dollars could purchase essentials that were no longer available in the peso economy.[12]

---

[8] Lars Schoultz, *That Infernal Little Cuban Republic: The United States and the Cuban Revolution* (Chapel Hill: University of North Carolina Press, 2009), p. 467.

[9] Geoffrey Hymans, "Outlawing the Use of Refugees as Tools of Foreign Policy," *ILSA Journal of International & Comparative Law* vol. 3 (1996–97): 153; Félix Masud-Piloto, *From Welcomed Exiles to Illegal Immigrants: Cuban Migration to the US, 1959–1995* (Lanham, MD: Rowman & Littlefield, 1996), p. 137.

[10] Jarrett Barrios, "People First: The Cuba Travel Ban, Wet Foot-Dry Foot and Why the Executive Branch Can and Should Begin Normalizing Cuba Policy," *Connecticut Public Interest Law Journal* vol. 11, no. 1 (Fall–Winter 2011), p. 7; Christina Frohock, "'Brisas del Mar': Judicial and Political Outcomes of the Cuban Rafter Crisis in Guantanamo," *Harvard Latino Law Review* vol. 15 (2012), p. 42.

[11] Robert Sandels and Nelson Valdés, "The Cuban Adjustment Act: The Other Immigration Mess," Counterpunch (August 2015): 9 (www.counterpunch.org/2015/08/28/the-cuban-adjustment-act...).

[12] LeoGrande, "From Havana to Miami: U.S. Cuba Policy as a Two-Level Game," *Journal of Interamerican Studies and World Affairs* vol. 40 no. 1 (Spring 1998): 67–86; LeoGrande and Peter Kornbluh, *Back Channel to Cuba: The Hidden History of Negotiations between Washington and Havana* (Chapel Hill: University of North Carolina Press, 2014); Maria Sartori, "The Cuban Migration Dilemma: An Examination of the United States' Policy of Temporary Protection in Offshore Safe Havens," *Georgetown Immigration Law Journal* vol. 15 (2000–2001): 319–55; Morris

The gathering morphed into the biggest anti-government demonstration held under Castro's rule. It suggested that without the ability to "exit," Cubans, in the words of Albert Hirschman, would take the political risk of "voice," and protest.[13] Preferring "exit" over "voice," Castro made it known that Cubans could leave. He announced that if the United States refused to stop hijackings, he would let asylum seekers go.[14] When the Clinton administration did not respond to his ultimatum, Castro announced that police would no longer patrol Cuba's coast. Again, faced with emigration pressures, he craftily made his problems also America's: as he had in 1965 and 1980.

Aware of the government's new permissiveness, Cubans took to small boats, makeshift rafts, and rubber dinghies that they constructed with the meager materials they could afford and obtain. An unknown number of them died at sea. According to the Clinton administration, in August alone dozens drowned.[15] Unseaworthy vessels capsized, and some of the rafters, *balseros*, as they came to be known, died of dehydration and starvation. They also became fodder for sharks.

Unlike in 1980, though, in 1994 the Cuban government made no effort to screen Cubans who sought to leave. Anyone could leave from anywhere. Some 33,000 rafters took advantage of the Cuban government's new permissiveness before the Clinton administration agreed to clamp down on hijackers, and Castro, in exchange, agreed to clamp down on departures.[16] Most importantly, the two governments proceeded to negotiate a new migration agreement, described later in the chapter, that was intended to make immigration between the two countries safe, legal, and orderly.

Morley and Chris McGillion, *Unfinished Business: America and Cuba after the Cold War, 1989–2001* (Cambridge: Cambridge University Press, 2002), p. 71.

[13] Albert Hirschman, *Exit, Voice, and Loyalty: Responses to Decline in Firms, Organizations and States* (Cambridge, MA: Harvard University Press, 1970).

[14] Barrios, "People First"; Frohock, "'Brisas del Mar'," p. 42.

[15] Steven Greenhouse, "Flight from Cuba: The Overview; U.S., in New Policy, Intends to Detain Cuban Immigrants," *New York Times* (August 19, 1994), p. 1 (www.nytimes.com/1994/08/19/us/flight-cuba-overview-us-new-policy-intends-detain-cuban-immigrants.html).

[16] Tad Szulc, "Castro's China Model," *New York Times* (February 29, 1996) (www.nytimes.com/1996/02/29/opinion/castro-s-china-model.html). For an analysis of the socioeconomic background of rafters, their reasons for emigration, the likelihood of Cubans with family abroad to leave, and changes in views of the Cuban population toward emigration during the Special Period, see Aja Díaz, "La crisis de los balseros," p. 199.

RETRACTION OF IMMIGRATION ENTITLEMENTS: OFF-SHORE DETENTION, REPATRIATION, AND DENIAL OF ENTRY WHEN ARRIVING IN "IRREGULAR WAYS"

As Castro orchestrated a repeat of 1965 and 1980, in allowing Cubans to leave without US entry permission, President Clinton at first commissioned the Coast Guard to bring Cubans they interdicted in the Florida Straits to the United States, as they had in the past.[17] However, he soon shifted his stance and ordered the Coast Guard to block them from coming ashore. He also announced that Cubans who managed to reach the United States in "irregular ways" would no longer be admitted. After more than thirty years, a US president appeared to close down Cubans' path of privileged entry.

Offshore Detention of Unauthorized Boatpeople

President Clinton acknowledged that the Cuban Adjustment Act (CAA) remained in effect.[18] However, he restricted its application. He announced that Cubans found at sea were not covered by the law, and were thus without rights to permanent residence. Until the summer of 1994, the Coast Guard, following presidential orders, had brought Cubans who they interdicted to the United States, whereupon they were paroled into the country, and, subsequently, awarded lawful permanent residency and associated entitlements on the basis of the CAA.[19]

President Clinton also sought to block so-called rafters from coming ashore, to avoid "another Mariel" that might jeopardize his reelection prospects. He thus announced on August 19 that "Today, I have ordered that illegal refugees from Cuba will not be allowed to enter the United States." Consulting with Janet Reno, his Attorney General, and Lawton Chiles, governor of Florida, where most incoming Cubans were headed,[20]

---

[17] Hymans, "Outlawing the Use of Refugees as Tools of Foreign Policy," p. 153.
[18] Jonathan Wachs, "The Need to Define the International Legal Status of Cubans Detained at Guantanamo," *American University Journal of International Law and Policy* vol. 11 no. 1 (1996), p. 85.
[19] Between 1966 and 1980, Cuban immigrants who were paroled into the country could become lawful permanent residents after two years. After 1980 they could adjust their status after one year in the United States.
[20] With much of the Florida electorate averse to yet another onslaught of Cubans, the Florida governor, running for reelection later that year, felt adamantly that the rafters should be blocked from entry. Luis Ortega, *Cubanos en Miami* (Havana: Editorial de Ciencias Sociales, 1998), p. 28.

he mandated the Coast Guard to take Cuban rafters (as well as unauthorized Haitian boatpeople) to "our naval base at Guantanamo, while we explore the possibility of other safe havens within the region."[21] Guantanamo again served the United States well, not as a military outpost, as in pre-revolution times, but as a place to intern unwelcomed immigrants off-shore, Cubans (though not Haitians) for the first time. President Clinton added that the rafters could not become lawful residents unless they returned to Havana and applied at the US Interests Section for immigration visas (with no a priori assurance that they would be granted visas).[22] By the end of August the Coast Guard had diverted over 30,000 Cubans to Guantanamo, and by the year's end an additional 5,000 Cubans.[23] Ironically, President Clinton ordered Cuban rafters to be detained on Cuban territory, many of them under conditions far worse than those they fled, and under conditions they had not anticipated, having assumed that the United States would admit them.[24]

Although President Clinton tried to convince other countries to accept rafters as Guantanamo filled beyond its official capacity, he had no more success than had President Carter when he tried to get other governments to accept Cuban Peruvian Embassy asylum seekers. Only the Panamanian government agreed to accept rafters, and only for six months. Furthermore, the Panamanian government required the United States to assume full responsibility for the financing and management of the facilities where the Cubans would be detained, at the US Howard Air Force Base in the Panama Canal.[25]

Per its agreement with Panama, after six months the Clinton administration transferred the 8,500 rafters it had detained in the Central

---

[21] Cited in Berta Esperanza Hernández-Truyol, "On Becoming the Other: Cubans, Castro, and Elian: a Critical Analysis," *Denver University Law Review* 78 no. 4: (2000–2001): 689.

[22] US General Accounting Office (USGAO), Report to Congress, "Cuba: U.S. Response to the 1994 Cuban Migration Crisis," NSIAD-95-211 (September 18, 1995) (www.gao.gov/assets/230/221797.pdf).

[23] Arthur Helton, "Securing Refugee Protection in the Americas: The Inter-American System on Human Rights and the Rights to Asylum Seekers," *Southwestern Journal of Law and Trade in the Americas* vol. 6 (1999): 130.

[24] The United States acquired rights to maintain a naval base in Guantanamo after intervening to establish a military government in Cuba following Cuba's independence from Spain.

[25] Although Suriname, the Turks and Caicos Islands, and several small countries in the East Caribbean agreed to accept Cubans if the United States assumed all costs and responsibility for running the operations, the United States never took them up on their offers. Sartori, "The Cuban Migration Dilemma," p. 329.

American country to Guantanamo.[26] By then, it had repatriated the Haitians there, which opened up space for Cubans. Additional space had become available by then also because it had quietly paroled into the United States Cuban rafters it deemed at-risk, namely the sick, the elderly, and children.

While internment of rafters offshore enabled President Clinton to block unauthorized Cubans from the United States, it was a financially costly endeavor: another Cuban immigrant expense that the United States incurred, this time, though, to keep Cubans away, not to admit them. For example, the Coast Guard and the Department of Defense spent nearly half a billion dollars between August 1994 and the end of 1995 to interdict and then accommodate Cubans outside the United States.[27]

Costs notwithstanding, the Clinton administration announced that the Cubans would be detained offshore indefinitely,[28] and, while offshore, they could not apply for asylum or enjoy rights comparable to persons in the United States.[29] In this vein, Attorney General Reno, commander of parole authority, made it known that rafters would neither be paroled nor admitted into the country.[30] In similar vein, INS Commissioner Doris Meissner, the chief Clinton administration officer in charge of immigrant admissions (who served as Deputy Associate Attorney General in the Carter Administration, as noted in Chapter 3), declared on August 22 (1994) that rafters detained in Guantanamo stood no chance of being admitted to the United States.[31] Reno and Meissner hoped their hardline stance would both convince detained rafters to return to Cuba where they could apply for visas to immigrate legally and deter other Cubans from trying to emigrate without authorization. However, they had no such luck. Between August 21 and 25 the Coast Guard picked up three times as many rafters as it had in all of 1993, and on August 23, more Cubans headed for the United States than on any day during the Mariel exodus.[32]

---

[26] Frohock, "'Brisas del Mar'," p. 45; Helton, "Securing Refugee Protection in the Americas," p. 134.
[27] David FitzGerald, *Refuge beyond Reach: How Rich Democracies Repel Asylum Seekers* (New York: Oxford University Press, 2019), p. 110.
[28] Sartori, "The Cuban Migration Dilemma." p. 329.
[29] FitzGerald, *Refuge beyond Reach*, p. 112.
[30] Morley and McGillion, *Unfinished Business*, p. 328.
[31] Sartori, "The Cuban Migration Dilemma," p. 328.
[32] Morley and McGillion, *Unfinished Business*, pp. 75, 77. At most, about 850 Cubans arrived in one day from Mariel in 1980. Kelly Greenhill, *Weapons of Mass Migration: Forced Displacement, Coercion, and Foreign Policy* (Ithaca, NY: Cornell University Press, 2010), p. 112.

Trying to demonstrate his control over immigration, President Clinton, in turn, proclaimed, "(T)he Cuban government will not succeed in any attempt to dictate American immigration policy."[33] Yet, not sufficiently confident of Cuban compliance, he asked the former Mexican president Carlos Salinas to intervene on his behalf. He asked Salinas to inform Castro that he would get a different US response than from the Carter administration in 1980 if he continued to let Cubans leave for the United States without authorization.

Exclusion of Unauthorized Cuban Boatpeople

President Clinton recognized that he needed Cuban government cooperation to prevent more rafters from seeking refuge in the United States, as well as to allow the return of "excludables," unauthorized Cuban immigrants who did not meet Washington's admission standards. He thus arranged to have Principal Deputy Assistant Secretary of Inter-American Affairs Michael Skol lead a US delegation to meet with Ricardo Alarcón, president of the Cuban National Assembly and a former foreign minister, to negotiate a new immigration agreement. The bilateral migration agreement that the Reagan administration negotiated had proven ineffective in containing unauthorized Cuban immigration, and ineffective in getting the Cuban government to accept the return of all Cubans that the United States deemed inadmissible.

When negotiating a new migration accord, Castro had hoped to gain concessions from the Clinton administration. Most of all, he wanted the United States to lift its trade embargo on Cuba, as well as recently instituted restrictions on US–Cuba travel and remittance-sending.[34] Cuban exiles had lobbied for the new restrictions, for what they called a "personal embargo": a ban on cross-border people-to-people social and economic ties, to complement the state level embargo. The personal embargo was to limit Cuba's access to hard currency that it desperately needed since having to reintegrate into the global market economy

---

[33] *Congressional Quarterly* August 20, 1994, cited in Sartori, "The Cuban Migration Dilemma," p. 328.

[34] Faced with the economic crisis rooted in Soviet aid and trade ending, the Cuban government had to concern itself with developing new bases of trade and new sources of hard currency. It hoped to negotiate a new immigration accord with the United States under the condition that Cubans abroad could remit hard currency. Carlo Jose Tabrave, ""Emigracióny Sociedad en al Recomposición de la Nueva Cuba," Latin American Studies Association, Dallas March 2003.

following the Soviet Union's demise. Castro also wanted the Clinton administration to shutter federally funded Radio Martí, which, when first broadcasting anti-Castro programs in 1985, had fueled the breakdown of the bilateral migration agreement that the Reagan administration had negotiated.

Acquiescing to President Clinton's insistence on negotiating only terms of immigration, on September 9 the United States and Cuba signed the Joint Communique on Migration. With both governments concerned about risky departures, often in unseaworthy vessels, the Joint Communique specified that the Cuban government would do all it could to prevent unsafe, illegal departures, primarily by "persuasive methods," while the United States would refuse to admit Cubans rescued at sea. Instead, the United States would take Cubans to offshore safe haven facilities, as it had been doing, since mid-August.

Denial of Entry to Cubans Arriving in "Irregular Ways"

From the US vantage point, the Joint Communique included another exclusionary measure that broke with precedent. It denoted that the United States would discontinue the practice of granting parole to Cuban migrants who reached US territory in "irregular ways."[35] Instead, such Cubans were to be placed in exclusion proceedings, along with undocumented migrants from other countries.[36]

On several occasions the Clinton administration affirmed that Cubans arriving in "irregular ways" would not be welcome. For example, an internal National Security Council (NSC) memorandum, dated February 16, 1995, denoted that "Cuban migrants who arrive on U.S. territory by irregular means are (to be) placed in Immigration Naturalization Service

---

[35] Department of State Dispatch 603 (1994), "US–Cuban Joint Communique on Migration" (http://heinonline.org/HOL/LandingPage?handle=hein.journals/dsp).

[36] Peter Tarnoff, "U.S. Policy toward Cuba," U.S. Department of State Dispatch vol. 6 no. 22 (May 29, 1995), p. 452; William Jefferson Clinton Presidential Library (WJCPL), Clinton Presidential Records ARMS/email no. 13, Briefing by Attorney General Janet Reno May 2, 1995, OA/ID 590000, Box 2; U.S. House of Representatives (USHR), Hearing before the Subcommittee on the Western Hemisphere of the Committee on International Relations, "The Clinton Administration's Reversal of U.S. Immigration Policy toward Cuba," 104th Congress, 1st session (May 18, 1995), p. 92 (https://babel.hathitrust.org/cgi/pt?id=pst.000024727501;view=1up;seq=95).

detention facilities in Miami."[37] No longer would they be paroled into the United States, as they had been since Eisenhower's presidency.

The Joint Communique, indeed, contributed to an immediate drop-off in unauthorized immigration. As of April 1995, the Coast Guard interdicted only 189 rafters, in contrast to 726 during the same month the preceding year.[38] However, the Clinton administration worried that more Cubans would try to make their way to the United States once the winter storm season had ended. For this reason, it negotiated a companion agreement to the Joint Communique: the Joint Statement with the Republic of Cuba on Normalization of Migration. The Joint Statement went into effect on May 2, 1995.[39] Its purpose was to further ensure safe, legal, and orderly migration between the two countries, and address problems the earlier accord left unresolved.[40]

Repatriation

The Joint Statement included new exclusionary measures. Most notably, it specified that, going forward, Cuban migrants who the United States intercepted in international waters would be returned to Cuba. No longer would they either be admitted to the United States or detained offshore. Here, the Clinton administration built on the offshore interdiction model (a "remote control" model, in Aristide Zolberg's terminology)[41] that President Reagan initiated to block unauthorized Haitians from the United States. This Clinton policy became dubbed the "wet foot policy." In the case of Cubans who were likely to be persecuted if they were returned to Cuba, immigration authorities would arrange for their resettlement in a third country. The Joint Statement, in turn, specified

---

[37] WJCPL, NSC Cables, Emails, and Records Management Systems, NSC Emails, MSMail-Record (September 1994-September 1997), Immigration and Naturalization #12 (02/02/1995-04/10/1995 (OA/ID 590000, ARMS: emails of the Executive Office of the President, MS Mail, Box 2.
[38] Tarnoff, "U.S. Policy toward Cuba," p. 450.
[39] William J. Clinton, "Joint Statement with the Republic of Cuba on Normalization of Migration," *The American Presidency Project* (May 2, 1995) (www.presidency.ucsb.edu/ws/?pid=51305).
[40] Tarnoff, "U.S. Policy toward Cuba," p. 441.
[41] Aristide Zolberg "The Archaeology of 'Remote Control," in *Migration Control in the North Atlantic World: The Evolution of State Practices in Europe and the United States from the French Revolution to the Inter-War Period*, Andreas Fahrmeir, Olivier Faron, and Patrick Weil, eds. (New York: Berghahn Books, 2003), pp. 195–222. See also, FitzGerald, *Refuge beyond Reach*.

that the United States would inform repatriated rafters how they might apply from Cuba for lawful admission to the United States.[42]

President Clinton had turned to his Undersecretary of State, Peter Tarnoff, to address problems that the Joint Communique had left unresolved. Tarnoff, together with his advisors, considered four ways to prevent the new influx of rafters that was anticipated once the wintry storm season subsided: interdict Cubans and bring them to the United States, detain them offshore, return them to Cuba, or arrange for their admission to other countries.[43] In deliberating the options, they assessed likely domestic political ramifications.

The last option, of diverting Cubans to alternative countries, was not viable on any scale. President Carter had tried to do that in 1980, but found few governments willing to accept Cubans. If, instead, rafters were admitted to the United States, more unauthorized rafters could be expected. Cubans on the island would assume that they too would be admitted on arrival. Meanwhile, sending the Cubans to Guantanamo would exacerbate already existing problems there. The Cubans detained both in Guantanamo and in Panama, angry about their imprisonment, their uncertain future, and the deplorable conditions under which they were forced to live, had staged protests, rioted, and self-mutilated.[44]

Tarnoff thus concluded repatriation to be the best option: the most viable, as well as least likely to unleash nativist resentment that could cost President Clinton reelection. Tarnoff prioritized domestic political concerns, in contrast especially to the Eisenhower and Kennedy administrations. He felt President Clinton could count on more votes from anti-immigrationists pleased with a new exclusionary policy than he would lose from Cuban Americans angry about the retraction of Cuban immigration entitlements.

President Clinton agreed. He viewed Cuban migration through his own political lenses, such that his 1996 presidential reelection ambitions shaped his choice of immigration policy in 1994. In his memoir, written after he left office, he reflected on the Cuban migration crisis:

---

[42] In addition, the United States agreed to inform returned rafters about procedures to apply for legal admission, and the Cuban government agreed not to penalize returnees for having attempted to immigrate illegally.

[43] Morley and McGillian, *Unfinished Business*.

[44] Bill Frelick, "U.S. Refugee Policy in the Caribbean: No Bridge over Troubled Waters," *Fletcher Forum of World Affairs* vol. 20 (Summer/Fall 1996): 67–87; Sartori, "The Cuban Migration Dilemma."

"Castro ... cost me one election. He can't have two."[45] The Arkansas electorate, irate about the Mariel émigrés who Clinton, as governor, had agreed to have interned in the state at President Carter's request, voted not to reelect him in 1980.

Nonetheless, repatriation presented its own set of problems. Recognizing that it would not sit well with Cuban exiles, Tarnoff deliberately excluded Jorge Mas Canosa, by then unequivocally the most influential Cuban American, from his team of consultants.[46] Mas Canosa had already objected to the 1994 Guantanamo detention policy, and had pressed the White House to admit Cubans who were detained there. Tarnoff also excluded the chief officer of the State Department's Cuba Desk, Dennis Hays, from his team of consultants. Hays was a close ally of Mas Canosa's and a Cuba hardliner.[47]

Yet, President Clinton did not entirely turn his back on the Cuban Americans who felt betrayed by the new repatriation policy. Trying to appease them, he explained, in a speech, that he had no realistic alternative: The United States could not admit all aspiring Cuban immigrants; it could not let Cubans risk their lives in unseaworthy rafts; and it could not continue to sentence Cubans to live in limbo at the Guantanamo naval base with no long-term solution. He noted that "tens of thousands ... were becoming increasingly frustrated and desperate (in Guantanamo). Senior United States military officials warned me that unrest and violence this summer were likely." President Clinton added that regularizing Cuban migration would help "our efforts to promote a peaceful transition to democracy on the island." While Clinton here implied that foreign policy considerations influenced new exclusion of Cubans, he never elaborated how and why "regularizing" immigration would spur regime change in Cuba. And indeed it did not. It did, however, put an immediate plug on unauthorized immigration, which helped Clinton win reelection, with the Florida vote, which he did not win in 1992.[48]

In order to repatriate Cubans, President Clinton needed to recast Cuban émigrés who previous administrations had claimed to be refugees

---

[45] Bill Clinton, *My Life* (New York: Alfred Knopf, 2004), p. 615.
[46] Steven Greenhouse, "How the Clinton Administration Reversed U.S. Policy on Cuban Refugees," *New York Times* (May 21, 1995b) (www.nytimes.com/1995/05/21/world/how-the-clinton-administration-reversed-us-policy-on-cuban-refugees.html).
[47] In anger over his exclusion, Hays requested a new job assignment.
[48] Administration of William J. Clinton, "Remarks to the Cuban-American Community" (June 27, 1995): 1137–39 (www.govinfo.gov/content/pkg/WCPD-1995-07-03/pdf/WCPD-1995-07-03-Pg1137.pdf).

as illegal immigrants. Returning "refugees" would violate Article 33 of the 1951 U.N. Convention relating to the Status of Refugees that specifies "no contracting state shall expel or return (*refouler*) a refugee ... to the frontiers of territories where his life or freedom would be threatened." In contrast, he could justify repatriation of "illegal immigrants."[49] In the words of a senior White House official, in repatriating Cubans, US authorities were "doing what we do with anyone – return them to their country when they are trying to immigrate illegally."[50] And consistent with the view that the Cubans attempting to immigrate were not refugees, the Coast Guard found less than 1 percent of the Cubans they interdicted to demonstrate credible fear of persecution were they returned to Cuba.[51]

In turn, following the signing of the May 1995 accord, Attorney General Reno reiterated her stance that rafters were not welcome. With the signing of the 1995 agreement she made it known that Cubans who managed to reach the United States in "irregular" ways would, like other illegal immigrants, be placed in exclusion proceedings. They could apply for asylum,[52] but with no assurance that their request would be honored. Cubans no longer were to be near-automatically admitted without proof of having fled persecution, basis for asylum.

THE GRANTING OF NEW AND REINSTITUTING OF REVOKED ENTITLEMENTS

Although the new exclusionary policies appeared to signal an end to Cuban privileging, the Clinton administration continued to implement entitlements that had previously been granted to Cubans, and it never stopped admitting Cubans who arrived in "irregular" ways, despite claiming that it would. Moreover, it granted new entitlements to Cubans.

New Immigration Entitlements

While calling for the offshore detention and repatriation of unauthorized Cubans, the 1994 and 1995 bilateral agreements also extended new,

---

[49] Greenhill, *Weapons of Mass Migration*, p. 119.
[50] Greenhouse, "U.S. Will Return Refugees to Cuba in Policy Switch," *New York Times* (May 3, 1995) (www.nytimes.com/1995/05/03/world/us-will-return-refugees-to-cuba).
[51] Ruth Wasem, "Cuban Migration Policy and Issues," *Congressional Research Report* RS20468, January 2007.
[52] WJCPL, NSC Cables, Emails, and Records Management Systems, NSC Emails #13 OA/ID 590000, MS Mail-Record (September 1994–September 1997), Box 2.

unique rights to Cubans: as had the migration agreements that the Johnson and Reagan administrations negotiated. The Clinton administration thereby combined new inclusionary with new exclusionary policies.[53]

For one, the 1994 Joint Communique committed the United States to admit *no fewer than* 20,000 Cubans yearly (plus immediate relatives of US citizens), a commitment made to no other nationals. The Cuban government had insisted on the minimum as a quid pro quo for it agreeing to put a plug on unauthorized immigration and accept the return of Cubans that the United States deemed inadmissible. Although the 1984 migration accord had specified a 20,000 maximum, the Reagan, Bush, and Clinton administrations, combined, had admitted barely more than half the cap for one year over the course of a decade. The Cuban government wanted the 20,000 minimum because departures (and the prospect of emigration) would defuse political tensions amid the economic crisis and because Cubans who immigrated would likely send remittances to family they left behind, in hard currency essential for the economy.

Two, in the Joint Communique the Clinton administration broadened its conception of Cuban family who could qualify for preference system-based immigration. It agreed to entitle unmarried children and distant relatives who resided with a nuclear family economic unit to immigration visas. More Cubans thereby qualified for family-based immigration visas. This was another unique entitlement the Clinton Administration granted Cubans.

Three, in conjunction with the Joint Communique, the Clinton administration also instituted a unique Cuban lottery for immigration visas: the Special Cuban Migration Program (SCMP). The lottery, known as "El Bombo" in Spanish, further broadened the range of Cubans who could immigrate lawfully.[54] The only restrictions were that lottery applicants needed to be between 18 and 55 years of age and to meet two of five additional criteria, namely to have completed at least a secondary school education, to have three or more years of work experience, to have previously expressed interest in immigration, to have job skills that were in demand in the United States, and/or to have family in the United States. Because at the time not enough Cubans wishing to immigrate had family in the United States to petition for their admission, in accordance with the

---

[53] See Tarnoff, "U.S. Policy toward Cuba," p. 450.
[54] The United States offers a diversity lottery for other nationals, but only from countries from where few have emigrated. As they lacked close family ties in the United States, these nationals would be unlikely to attain immigration visas through the preference system.

preference system, the Clinton administration instituted the lottery. Without the lottery it could not meet its commitment to admit 20,000 Cubans a year. In contrast to the preference system-based admissions, which, in effect, privileged light-skinned relatives of the largely light-skinned diaspora, "El Bombo" provided non-Whites with a new opportunity to immigrate lawfully.

The INS held the first lottery between November 15 and December 31, 1994. It held additional lotteries in 1996 and in 1998, with over half a million Cubans applying to the latter. The lottery entitled nearly 8,000 Cubans to immigrate in 1996, and twice that number three years later.[55] As an added bonus, lottery winners were eligible for refugee benefits, even though they had not fled persecution.

In conjunction with the 1995 accord, the Clinton administration also agreed to admit all Cubans who at the time were on the immigration waitlist. In contrast, aspiring immigrants from other countries often waited years in a queue for visas. Attorney General Reno estimated that 4,000–6,000 Cubans were admitted from the waitlist.[56]

Nonetheless, the Clinton administration immediately reinterpreted the migration agreement to mean that it would cap Cuban admissions at 20,000 per year, even though the agreement set 20,000 as a minimum, not maximum. Attorney General Reno noted at a May 1995 press briefing that "Last September...the United States announced that it would increase Cuban migration to the United States to permit 20,000 legal entrants per year." Thus, the Clinton administration, de facto, set limits to a guaranteed immigration entitlement it granted Cubans.

New Unique Bases for Refugee Admissions

Working to Cubans' favor, the Clinton administration also reinterpreted criteria for Cuban refugee admissions so that more Cubans qualified. It set aside for Cubans one-third of the yearly visas it granted for refugees

---

[55] Max Castro, "The New Cuban Immigration in Context," *The North-South Agenda* October 2002: 8–9 (published by North-South Center, University of Miami).

[56] Stanley Meisler, "U.S., Cuba Sign Accord to End Migrant Exodus," *Los Angeles Times* (September 10, 1994) (articles.latimes.com/1994-09-10/news/mn-36874_1_united_-states); US Department of State (USDS), "Regular Briefing," Department of State, Office of the Spokesman, Statement by Christine Shelly, Acting Spokesman (October 12, 1994), p. 4 (http://balseros.miami.edu/pdf/Oct12StateDept.pdf); USGAO, Cuba: U.S. Response to the 1994 *Cuban Migration Crisis*, pp. 7, 30; Morley and McGillion, *Unfinished Business*, pp. 78–79.

and their families;[57] it broadened criteria for Cuban refugee admissions; and it eased Cubans' ability to apply for admission as refugees.

What refugee criteria did it use? While the Refugee Act of 1980 had broadened criteria for refugee admissions beyond communist escapees, to include persons who had fled their homeland because of well-founded fear of persecution based on their race, religion, nationality, membership in a particular social group, and their political views, the Clinton administration further expanded criteria for Cubans. It extended eligibility to members of persecuted religious minorities and to human rights activists (irrespective of whether they had personally experienced persecution); to persons who had been consigned to work camps between 1965 and 1968 (some thirty years in the past); and to persons who claimed they had experienced job discrimination because of their political beliefs. In the first year of deploying the more inclusive criteria refugee admissions doubled.[58] The Clinton administration thereby reinterpreted refugee status to Cubans' advantage. Cubans alone could qualify for refugee status without having to demonstrate that they had either fled persecution or had well-founded fear of persecution if they remained in their home country.

In turn, the Clinton administration made it easier for Cubans to apply for refugee admission by allowing them to apply *in* Cuba.[59] The only other nationals who could apply for refugee admissions in their homelands were Haitians, Vietnamese, and persons from the former Soviet Union. Other nationals needed to apply from outside their home country.

Re-honoring Officially Retracted Entitlements

The Clinton administration even reinstituted entitlements that it had officially retracted. In particular, it quickly brushed aside its vow never to allow rafters into the United States and not to parole Cubans who had arrived in "irregular ways" into the country.

---

[57] USGAO, *Cuba: U.S. Response to the 1994 Cuban Migration Crisis*, p. 4.
[58] US Department of State, Special Briefing: Implementation of the Cuban Migration Agreement, October 12, 1994, cited in Sonia Mikolic-Torriera, "The Cuban Migration Agreement: Implications of the Clinton–Castro Immigration Policy," *Georgetown Immigration Law Journal* vol. 8 (1994): 668.
[59] Frelick, "U.S. Refugee Policy in the Caribbean," p. 80. While the United States had introduced the in-country Cuba processing program already in 1987, the Reagan and Bush administrations admitted few Cubans through these (or other) channels.

Within nine months of signing the Joint Communique, the Clinton administration admitted all of the rafters that it had detained offshore, even though the president as well as his Attorney General and INS commissioner had adamantly insisted that the Cubans who were detained in Guantanamo would never be admitted into the United States. Between its signing of the 1994 and the 1995 migration agreements the Clinton administration admitted approximately 15,000 of the Cubans it had detained offshore, individuals who immigration authorities had considered to be particularly at risk.[60] Then, in conjunction with the May 1995 Joint Statement, the Clinton administration paroled the remaining 15,000 Guantanamo detainees into the United States. The president even noted that the admitted Cubans would go "beyond those eligible for parole under existing criteria." The Department of Justice arranged with Cuban American groups to assist in the resettlement.[61]

INS Commissioner Meissner justified paroling the Cubans in Guantanamo into the United States: those whom she had previously claimed stood no chance of admission. She asserted that the administration's goal of closing the door to illegal migration in order to keep open the door for legal migration would thereby be served.[62] However, her rationale was not convincing. How would the paroling of the Guantanamo detainees into the United States put a halt to illegal immigration and ensure legal immigration?

Meissner further claimed that there were "compelling circumstances" for paroling the Guantanamo detainees into the United States.[63] She did not acknowledge that the "compelling circumstances" were entirely of Clinton administration making. Guantanamo had become a tinderbox. Florida Senator Bob Graham, who had visited Guantanamo, warned the White House that there would likely be riots as the hot summer months approached. The Cuban detainees resented their internment, their in-limbo status, and the conditions under which they were detained. Already, scores of them had self-mutilated. They drank bleach, ingested glass, slashed their wrists, and, in a few instances, hung themselves.[64]

---

[60] Read Sawczyn,"The United States Immigration Policy toward Cuba Violates Established Maritime Policy, It Does not Curtail Illegal Immigration, and Thus Should Be Changed So That Cuban Immigrants Are Treated Similarly to Other Immigrants," *Florida Journal of International Law* vol. 13 (2000–2001).
[61] Ernesto Rodríguez Chavez, *Emigración Cubana Actual* (Havana: Editorial de Ciencias Sociales, 1997), p. 127.
[62] Morely and McGillion, *Unfinished Business*, p. 77.
[63] Sartori, "The Cuban Migration Dilemma, p. 328.
[64] Morely and McGillion, *Unfinished Business*.

The "compelling circumstances" were also economic. General John Sheehan, who oversaw the detention camps, complained that the facilities were exorbitantly expensive to maintain, and required deploying more than four thousand soldiers just to control the Cubans.[65] They cost American taxpayers approximately $1 million per day to operate. He considered this a large bill for the administration to foot in order to keep Cubans out of the United States. It would not need to absorb such costs if the rafters were either paroled into the United States or repatriated.

In essence, in diverting the rafters to Guantanamo the Clinton administration created new problems, which it addressed by granting to more Cubans unique immigration rights. President Clinton pushed aside the assertion he had made less than a year earlier, namely, that the CAA did not apply to persons that the Coast Guard interdicted off-shore. Once his administration paroled rafters it detained in Guantanamo into the United States, they were eligible for lawful permanent residency on the basis of the CAA.

The Clinton administration also unilaterally decided not to enforce its official commitment in the Joint Communique to stop paroling Cubans into the country who arrived in "irregular ways": if they reached the United States by land; this became known as the "dry foot policy." Once they were paroled, the land entrants could take advantage of the CAA to become lawful permanent residents. The Clinton administration did, however, continue to enforce its "wet foot" policy, of repatriating Cubans that the Coast Guard had interdicted at sea (unless they demonstrated that they had fled persecution). The only difference between the Cubans that the United States admitted and those who were repatriated was the location where US officials first encountered them.[66]

While the Clinton administration never explicitly renounced the Joint Communique commitment to deny admissions to Cubans who arrived in "irregular ways," on several occasions in 1999 members of the administration acknowledged legal rights of illegal Cuban entrants. In March of that year, the Coast Guard noted that the United States gave sanctuary to Cubans who made it ashore, and in April the INS released the important Meissner Memo, detailed later, which outlined the rights of Cubans who

---

[65] Rodríguez Chavez, *Emigración Cubana Actual*, p. 127.
[66] In a December 1999 memorandum, the White House confirmed the dual policy, that "under the U.S. 'wet-feet/dry-feet' policy, Cubans who reach U.S. shores after fleeing the communist-ruled island are usually allowed to stay but those intercepted by the Coast Guard at sea are mostly repatriated." WJCPL, Presidential Records: NSC Cables, emails and Records Management Systems, Exchange mail, #3, Folder: OA/ID 62000, Box 5.

arrived by "irregular means." Against the backdrop of legislation that Congress had passed to restrict and penalize illegal immigration, most notably the Illegal Immigration Reform and Immigration Responsibility Act (IIRIRA), INS Commissioner Meissner exempted Cubans. She determined that Cubans were the only visa-less immigrants who could stay, receive work permits, and apply for permanent residence without having to go through the courts to appeal for political asylum.[67] Then, two months later, a National Security Council communication noted a new INS policy: that Cuban refugees qualified for lawful permanent residence.[68] Accordingly, Cubans paroled into the country with "dry feet" were to be eligible for a string of benefits, including lawful permanent residence on the basis of the CAA.

As a result, by the time Clinton ended his eight-year presidency, he reprivileged unauthorized Cuban entrants: if they had managed to reach America by land. At the same time, stepped-up policing of the Florida Straits had led to a marked drop-off in visa-less Cubans testing their luck by immigrating by sea. The risk of Coast Guard interdiction and repatriation was high.

Creation of New Immigration Statuses to Admit Cubans

The Clinton administration proceeded to invent yet another immigration status, and to modify a preexisting immigration status, in order to admit more Cubans and entitle them to special benefits. It built on the precedent that President Carter had set when creating the "Entrant: Status Pending" basis for Mariel Cuban admissions.

First, when detaining the rafters offshore, the Clinton administration stretched the application of the new immigration status that Congress had incorporated into the Immigration Act of 1990, that of Temporary Protective Status (TPS).[69] It granted them TPS, which spared them possible deportation, even though the Immigration Act of 1990 officially only empowered the Attorney General to grant TPS to nationals of foreign countries who were *in* the United States, and only when their personal safety was seriously threatened and they agreed to return to their

---

[67] WJCPL, NSC emails, Exchange Mail, From Fulton Armstrong, To: Scott Busby, Subject: U.S.-Immigrant Detainees, January 31, 1999, Folder OA/ID630000, #23, Folder OA/ID 630000, Box 7.

[68] WJCPL, ARMS email system #21, Subject: Opposition to Crackdown on Alien-Smuggling, Folder: NSC, Folder: OA/ID 120000, Box 1.

[69] Sartori, "The Cuban Migration Dilemma," p. 333.

homeland once conditions there improved.[70] The Clinton administration bent its interpretation of the legislation to Cubans' advantage, in granting the rafters TPS outside the United States, and with no presumption that they would return to Cuba.

Then, less than a year after granting the detainees in Guantanamo TPS, the Clinton administration admitted them. It invented a new admission category to do so that circumvented legislated immigration regulations. It reimagined the rafters as Special Guantanamo Entrants,[71] thereby entitling them to parole entry, and lawful permanent residence a year later on the basis of the CAA.

The Clinton administration had the Guantanamo detainees count toward the minimum of 20,000 Cubans that it had committed to admit yearly. For each of three years it credited 5,000 Guantanamo detainees toward the 20,000 visas that it agreed to issue annually, regardless of when they were paroled into the United States. It accordingly bent terms of the migration accord, and did so despite Cuban government opposition to admission of the rafters as part of the quota.[72] Meanwhile, for each of the three years the Clinton administration withheld visas for 5,000 Cubans who applied in Cuba to enter the United States lawfully. Thus, in bending terms of the migration accord the Clinton administration privileged unauthorized immigrants over Cubans who sought to immigrate with authorization. The administration could have admitted the Guantanamo detainees in addition to the 20,000 Cubans that it agreed to accept yearly, but it risked thereby angering nativists.

The Clinton administration proceeded to exempt the newly imagined Guantanamo Entrants from requirements that were imposed on immigrants from other countries, in that the INS exempted them from immigration exam and application fees.[73] Here, the Clinton administration built on precedent that was set by the Johnson administration in waiving status adjustment fees for Cubans.

Then, in 1998 the INS extended the same entitlements that the Refugee Education Assistance Act (REAA) of 1980 had made available to Cuban

---

[70] Ibid., pp. 321–22.
[71] USHR, "The Clinton Administration's Reversal of U.S. Immigration Policy toward Cuba," p. 88.
[72] Jesus Arboleya, *Havana Miami: The US–Cuba Migration Conflict* (Melbourne: Ocean Press, 1996), p. 68.
[73] U.S. Department of Justice, Immigration and Naturalization Service (INS), "Proposed Rules, Adjustment of Certain Fees of the Immigration Examinations Fee Account," *Federal Register* vol. 63 no. 7 (January 12, 1998).

and Haitian Entrants to the Special Guantanamo Entrants, namely, rights to comparable benefits as refugees.[74] The Special Guantanamo Entrants were even eligible for refugee-equivalent benefits after they became lawful permanent residents, without ever having to prove that they fled persecution.

Thus, the Clinton administration extended a series of entitlements to unauthorized Cubans that it initially had blocked from US entry. It (re)imagined them in ways allowing for the special privileging.

CONGRESSIONAL RESISTANCE TO RETRACTION OF ENTITLEMENTS FOR CUBANS

Congress did not stay entirely on the sidelines when President Clinton used his discretionary power to extend entitlements to yet more Cubans. While on a number of occasions some legislators sought to put a stop to Cuban privileging, during the eight years of Clinton's presidency Congress passed legislation that affirmed previously granted entitlements; that increased the number of Cubans who qualified for unique entitlements; that expanded entitlements for Cubans; and that exempted Cubans from restrictions that were imposed on other nationals.

Sunset the CAA?

Clinton's repatriation policy limited the number of Cubans who were able to take advantage of the CAA, Cubans' most exceptional entitlement. However, Cubans who managed to make it to the United States without authorization continued to be able to draw on the CAA to become lawful permanent residents. Only Congress could repeal the legislation.

It would have been an uphill battle for the White House to convince Congress to sunset the CAA once Republicans won control of both chambers of Congress in the 1994 mid-term elections. Compounding the uphill battle, three vehemently anti-Castro Cuban Americans, who were committed to protecting and promoting entitlements for Cubans, served in Congress at the time.[75] They sought to establish themselves as gatekeepers of Cuba policy.

---

[74] United States Citizenship and Immigration Services (USCIS), 2010: Chapter 3: Cuban and Haitian Entrant, p. 3 (www.myflfamilies.com/service-programs/refugee-services/web guides/eg_chapters/3.pdf).

[75] They were South Florida Republicans Ileana Ros-Lehtinen and Lincoln Díaz-Balart, and New Jersey Democrat Robert Menendez.

Indeed, legislative initiatives to repeal the CAA fell on deaf ears. In February 1994, for example, Mike Kopetski, an Oregon Democrat, referred H.R. 3854, which called for repeal of the CAA, to the House Judiciary Committee. Kopetski argued: (1) that continuation of the CAA was indefensible and unfair to people throughout the world who were seeking political asylum in the United States, (2) that the CAA was an obsolete, Cold War relic that was patently discriminatory in its privileging of Cubans from a country no worse off than many Caribbean and Latin American countries, and (3) that the CAA unjustifiably entitled Cuba-born people who were living in countries such as Germany, Spain, and Canada, where they suffered no persecution, to immigrate to America and receive refugee benefits. Substantiating his claims, he noted that in 1991 and 1992 the United States had granted lawful permanent residency rights to more Cubans than persons from war-torn and impoverished Cambodia, El Salvador, Romania, Somalia, Haiti, and the former Yugoslavia, combined. The Cubans attained the rights on the basis of the CAA, as presumed refugees.[76] Kopetski also noted that the CAA unfairly rewarded Cubans with a path to citizenship when they immigrated illegally. In his view, the CAA remained on the books owing to Miami politics and Florida's importance in presidential elections, and was unrelated to US foreign policy concerns. Despite his compelling arguments, the legislation he proposed never gained traction, and the Clinton White House did not press members of Congress to support the bill. President Clinton had his own agenda, which did not include antagonizing Cuban Americans who might help him win reelection in 1996.[77]

Two months after Congressman Kopetski proposed to sunset the CAA, the Senate Judiciary Committee also called for repeal of the law. Yet, Congress never approved that initiative either.

Then, on August 19 of 1994, on the day President Clinton announced his diversion-to-Guantanamo policy, Congressman Romano Mazzoli of Kentucky, also a Democrat, argued that the CAA "need[ed] to be sunset" and "need[ed] a second look."[78] Already in 1986, in conjunction with IRCA, the Immigration Reform and Control Act, Mazzoli, who chaired the Immigration, International Law and Refugees Subcommittee of the

---

[76] Mike Kopetski, "Cosponsors Sought for Bill to Repeal the Cuban Adjustment Act," *Congressional Record* August 18, 1994 vol. 140, no. 117 (www.gpo.gov/fdsys/pkg/CREC-1994-08-18/html/CREC-1994-08).

[77] Interview with Mike Kopetski May 2015.

[78] *Congressional Record* vol. 140 issue 118 (www.gpo.gov/fdsys/pkg/CREC-1994-08-19/html/CREC-1994-0...) (August 19, 1994).

House Judiciary Committee, proposed repealing the CAA. However, as noted in the last chapter, Congress enacted IRCA without the proviso to sunset the CAA.[79]

In 1995, the Senate did take a "second look" at the CAA, in the context of new immigration control and enforcement legislation it deliberated (S. 269).[80] Critics of the CAA claimed the law to be obsolete and unnecessary in that the Refugee Act of 1980 addressed refugee matters. Yet, Congress did not agree to this effort to repeal the CAA either.

Instead, in March of 1996 Congress passed legislation that affirmed the CAA as the law of the land: the Cuban Liberty and Democratic Solidarity (Libertad) Act, popularly known as the Helms–Burton bill after the names of its two key sponsors. This law did specify that the CAA might be revoked, but only once Cuba had transitioned to democracy.

Notwithstanding passage of the Helms–Burton bill, one month after its enactment another Senate initiative, the Immigration Control and Financial Responsibility Act (ICFRA), called for repeal of the CAA. ICFRA was intended to (re)strengthen Congressional control over immigration, to limit the Attorney General's parole authority, and to reduce immigrant access to welfare.[81] It called for limiting the CAA only to Cubans who were admitted into the country on the basis of the 1995 US–Cuban migration agreement, that is, admitted lawfully. Unauthorized Cuban entrants were to be denied rights to adjust their status. However, President Clinton requested deletion of the restriction on Cuban eligibility for legal permanent residence from the proposed legislation. With the proviso deleted from the final version of the bill, Cubans survived another congressional effort to close their unique path to lawful permanent residency.

Later the same year, Congress passed the Illegal Immigration Reform and Immigrant Responsibility Act (IIRIRA, P.L. 104-208). Drawing on the Helms–Burton bill, IIRIRA affirmed that the CAA would be repealed when the president determined that a democratically elected government had assumed power in Cuba. Otherwise, IIRIRA did not specifically address the CAA or Cuban immigration. It focused instead on improved deterrence of illegal immigration in general, and denoted that "an alien

---

[79] IRCA, the 1986 immigration reform, also denied rights to unauthorized immigrants.
[80] Wasem, *Cuban Migration to the United States: Trends and Issues*, report for Congress (Washington, DC: Congressional Research Service (CRS), Library of Congress, May 25, 1995), p. 9.
[81] US Senate, Immigration Control and Financial Responsibility Act of 1996, Report 104-249, 104th Congress, 2nd session, pp. 1, 2.

present in the United States without being admitted or paroled or who arrives in the United States at any time or place other than as designated by the Attorney General is inadmissible." It specified that immigrants were admissible only at officially designated ports of entry. By implication, even though the CAA remained the law of the land, Cubans who arrived in "irregular ways" were to have no entry rights. Or, so it seemed.

Exemption of Cubans from Restricted Immigrant Rights

Against the backdrop of the anti-immigrant mood that swept the country in the 1990s, the Republican-controlled Congress also passed the Personal Responsibility and Work Opportunity Reconciliation Act (PRWORA). Passed one month before the IIRIRA, PRWORA, in Clinton's famous words, reformed the welfare system "as we knew it." It denied lawful immigrants the right to federally funded welfare for five years, and unauthorized immigrants' rights to welfare indefinitely.

By implication, Cubans who were admitted as lawful permanent residents lost rights to welfare during their first five years in the country. They had enjoyed such rights on entry into the country first through the Cuban Refugee Program, and, since 1972, on the basis of an amendment to legislation that then-Senator Lawton Chiles of Florida had convinced Congress to pass that ensured Cuban eligibility for SSI, Supplementary Security Income, the federal welfare program for poor and disabled lawful permanent residents.[82] Chiles had pushed for the special entitlement once Cuban immigrants became an increasingly important political constituency in his state, as they took advantage of the CAA path to citizenship. With the Nixon administration at the time winding down the Cuban Refugee Program, Senator Chiles sought to ensure that the federal government continued to provide social assistance to Cubans.

While PRWORA threatened Cuban immigrants' rights to welfare, the year after it went into effect Congress came to their rescue, when passing the Balanced Budget Act of 1997. The Balanced Budget Act was designed to reduce federal spending in order to balance the budget by 2002. Yet, in the context of the fiscal belt-tightening initiative, some Florida politicians successfully lobbied to have the Balanced Budget Act exempt Cubans from PRWORA restrictions on welfare rights. South Florida Cuban

---

[82] Megan O'Matz and Sally Kestin, "Easy Money: History of Assistance for Cuban Immigrants," *Sun Sentinel* (September 30, 2015) (www.sun-sentinel.com/sfl-easy-money-timeline-20150930-htm).

Americans Ileana Ros-Lehtinen and Lincoln Díaz-Balart, elected to the House of Representatives in 1989 and 1992, respectively, and Chiles, who by then had been elected governor of Florida, lobbied for the exemption for Cuban immigrants.[83] As a result, the 1997 legislation entitled Cubans to food stamps and Medicaid, as well as SSI,[84] irrespective of whether or not they had entered the country lawfully and irrespective of how recently they had arrived.[85] Cubans thereby could receive assistance on setting foot on American soil, similar to refugees, even if they had not fled persecution.

In his autobiography, President Clinton acknowledged that his welfare reform's "hit on legal immigrants was particularly hard."[86] "The hit," however, was hard for all immigrants *except* Cubans. The welfare reform did not even "hit hard" on unauthorized Cuban entrants.

New Unique Entitlements for Cubans

Congress also passed legislation that extended new entitlements to Cubans, in the context of extending rights, selectively, to other nationals. Specifically, the 1997 Nicaraguan Adjustment and Central American Relief Act (NACARA) extended rights to Cubans who previously had been passed over.

The main purpose of NACARA was to grant lawful permanent residency rights to Nicaraguans who had fled the leftist Sandinista government that took power in 1979. NACARA, however, also spared unauthorized Guatemalans and Salvadorans who had fled the repressive governments in their homelands (and persons from former Soviet bloc countries) from deportation, and it expanded the number of Cubans who qualified for lawful permanent residency. It granted to Cubans who had not been inspected, admitted, or paroled into the United States lawful permanent residency rights.[87] Prior to NACARA, EWIs, "entrants without inspection," had not qualified for parole, and thus had been ineligible for legal residence, work rights, refugee benefits, and citizenship. Only

---

[83] O'Matz and Kestin, "Easy Money."
[84] They qualified for seven years, and longer if they became citizens.
[85] PRWORA also exempted Amerasians, persons born in Asia to a US military father and an Asian mother, from immigrant welfare restrictions.
[86] Clinton, *My Life*, p. 710.
[87] Carl Shusterman, "Department of Justice Rules on Cuban and Nicaraguan Adjustments (5-21-98)," Law Offices of Carl Shusterman, (shusterman.com/nacaracubanandnicaraguans.html,1998).

unauthorized Cuban entrants who had been screened and processed by immigration authorities on their arrival had qualified for the entitlements.

Díaz-Balart, with many Nicaraguans as well as Cuban immigrants in his South Florida district, had proposed NACARA. Although the new perk was intended for Central Americans, he slipped into the bill new rights for unauthorized Cuban immigrants.

The Meissner Memo: Cuban Exemption from Legislated Restrictions on Rights of Unauthorized Immigrants

In restricting rights of unauthorized immigrants, the IIRIRA appeared to rein in all rights of unauthorized Cubans. However, in 1999 INS Commissioner Meissner explicitly interpreted the CAA to exempt Cubans from IIRIRA restrictions on unauthorized immigrants. She argued that the CAA provided a legal basis for exempting Cubans, even though she previously had argued that the Refugee Act of 1980 made the CAA anachronistic.[88]

In what came to be known as the Meissner Memo, the INS Commissioner noted that the CAA, not the IIRIRA, applied to Cubans. As a result, Cubans, and only Cubans, could be admitted wherever they touched US land and , in turn, be entitled to lawful permanent residence. In her words, "Nothing in the legislative history ... suggest(s) that Congress ... intended to make (Cuban) aliens who arrive in the United States away from ports of entry ineligible for CAA adjustment." She also noted in the Memo that "(T)he inadmissibility ground based on an alien's having arrived at a place other than a port of entry does not apply to CAA applicants ... because many CAA applicants ... arrive in the United States in an irregular manner." In essence, she reasoned that because many Cubans came to the United States without authorization and entered at other than official ports of entry, they should be entitled to lawful permanent residency. She did not apply the same logic to the millions of undocumented immigrants from other countries, whose numbers were on the rise. She thereby determined that for Cubans rights were not geographically bound (to officially designated places of entry), whereas for other nationals they were.

In affirming that the CAA entitled *incoming* Cubans who arrived without authorization to lawful permanent residence, Commissioner

---

[88] Interview with Commissioner Meissner March 2014.

Meissner ignored Congress' initial intent in passing the CAA, namely to enable Cubans who were already *in* the United States – not newcomers – to adjust their status. Cubans came to benefit from the CAA independently of its original intent.

The Memo even lifted exclusionary Cuban measures that were specified in the 1994 US–Cuban Joint Communique, without the Cuban government consenting to the change. Commissioner Meissner noted in the Memo that the United States would admit Cubans who reached the country in "irregular ways," with so-called dry feet,[89] while continuing to return to Cuba Cubans interdicted at sea, "with wet feet." The Joint Communique, as previously noted, had specified that Cubans who arrived in "irregular ways" were to be placed in exclusion proceedings and treated similarly to undocumented migrants from other countries.[90] Commissioner Meissner argued that the inadmissibility of these Cubans would be contrary to the legislative intent of the CAA, in that the CAA entitled Cubans who entered the United States in "irregular ways" to lawful permanent residency after one year in the country.

The Meissner Memo, moreover, called for liberal interpretation of Cuban immigrant qualification both for parole and for status adjustment. Even though Congress had intended the Refugee Act of 1980 to rein in presidential parole authority, in the Memo Commissioner Meissner noted, "(T)he availability of CAA adjustment should ordinarily weigh heavily in favor of a grant of parole." Here, she turned the initial rationale for the CAA on its head. Rather than the CAA granting residency rights to persons whose immigration status was in limbo, she argued that Cubans should be paroled into the country because they could adjust their status. The Meissner Memo added that "the admissibility requirement of ... the CAA must be construed generously, in order to give full effect to the purpose of the CAA."

Meissner offered an economic argument for the Cuban exceptionalism. If the Cubans were paroled into the United States, she noted in the Memo, the INS would be spared detention costs, which she considered a

---

[89] Arboleya Cervera, *Cuba y los cubanoamericanos: El fénomeno migratorio Cubano* (Havana: Fondo Editorial Casa de las Américas, 2013).

[90] In practice, Cubans were rarely placed in exclusion proceedings. Most Cuban rafters were sent to the Krome Detention Center on arrival, but then released. Ted Henken, "Balseros, Boteros, and El Bombo: Post-1994 Cuban Immigration to the United States and the Persistence of Special Treatment," *Latino Studies* November vol. 3 no. 3 (November 2005): 80; Lizettte Álvarez, "In quiet policy shift, INS frees rafters who make it to the U.S.," *Miami Herald* January 21, 1995.

"'significant public benefit." Yet, in the Memo she also pointed to costs that the United States incurred in admitting Cubans, which were linked to their eligibility for federally funded means-tested public benefits. She recognized that "many, and perhaps most, Cuban nationals were dependent on some forms of public assistance ... (and that) the public charge ground (of inadmissibility) does not apply to CAA applicants." In addition, she specified in the Memo that Cubans were to be considered "Cuban-Haitian entrants," which meant entitlement to the same federally funded refugee-equivalent benefits that Congress had authorized for the Mariel émigrés (and for the Haitians who also arrived in 1980), in the Refugee Education Assistance Act of 1980. Unique entitlements for Mariel émigrés thus became the bedrock for similar entitlements for subsequent Cuban immigrants.

In summary, while Congress passed the IIRIRA to restrict unauthorized immigration and unauthorized immigrant entitlements, the INS Commissioner spared Cuban immigrants from the exclusionary measures. She interpreted the new law not to apply to them.

Reasons for the Combined Rollback and Expansion of Cuban Entitlements

President Clinton boldly broke with precedent when preventing Cuban rafters from US entry. President Carter had attempted to block the Mariel boatpeople, but quickly proceeded to offer them unique entry rights and unique resettlement benefits.

President Clinton's exclusion of unauthorized Cuban boatpeople in 1994 was consistent with the shift in US foreign policy concerns with the Cold War's end. However, even while denying entry to unauthorized Cubans he left a number of unique Cuban prerogatives in place and granted new entitlements to Cubans. How to explain his mix of new inclusionary and new exclusionary policies?

The new global context made policy change possible, not inevitable. President Clinton took advantage of the new world order to prioritize his domestic political concerns, which called for contradictory policies. First and foremost, neither he nor his Attorney General wanted "another Mariel," this time under their watch. Attorney General Reno had experienced the nightmare of dealing with the Mariel crisis firsthand when she served as district attorney in Miami, prior to joining the Clinton administration. President Clinton, in turn, blamed his 1980 gubernatorial (re) election defeat – as noted in Chapter 3 – on the Mariel émigrés interned in

Arkansas. Concerned as he was about reelection as president, he wanted to demonstrate control over the country's borders in order to not alienate increasingly politicized "nativists," an important political constituency who opposed immigration, especially unauthorized immigration.

Nonetheless, he also faced pressure to make immigration policy fairer, particularly vis-à-vis Haitians: but amid pressure from Cuban Americans to continue to admit Cubans. Previous entitlements had transformed Cuban Americans into an important political force to contend with, especially in Florida with its growing population, and, in turn, increased number of electoral college votes.

Demands of these different constituencies shaped how President Clinton addressed the deluge of new, unauthorized Cuban rafters: in the new, post-Cold War context. They imposed conflicting demands.

Immigration Equity? Cubans vs. Haitians

President Clinton formulated his stance on the rafters amid public outcry over unjust treatment of Haitian immigrants, in general and in comparison to Cubans.[91] By the 1990s, Haitian rights advocates were more active than in 1980, when President Carter faced tens of thousands of unauthorized Haitians attempting to come ashore at the same time as Cubans. Human rights advocates were irate over Reagan and Bush administration abusive treatment of Haitians in the 1980s and early 1990s, and Reagan administration denial of the same entitlements to Haitian as extended to Cuban Entrants (described in the Chapter 4). Might President Clinton have been driven by concern with better equity in the treatment of Haitians and Cubans? If so, did his concern for equity center on extending comparable rights to Haitians as to Cubans, or on retracting Cuban entitlements, to make them similar to Haitians'?

When running for president in 1992, Clinton did express concern with the unfair treatment of Haitians. He chastised his opponent, incumbent President Bush, for cruelly "returning Haitian refugees to a brutal dictatorship without an asylum hearing."[92] Making President Bush's Haitian repatriation policy a campaign issue, Clinton claimed, "If I were President

---

[91] Heather Kolinsky, "A Fine Line, Redefined: Moving toward More Equitable Asylum Policies," *Baltimore Law Review* vol. 40 (2010–11).
[92] Elaine Sciolino, "Clinton Says U.S. Will Continue Ban on Haitian Exodus," *New York Times* (January 15, 1993) (www.nytimes.com/1993/01/15/world/clinton-says-us-will-continue-ban-on-haitian-exodus.html).

I would – in the absence of clear and compelling evidence that they weren't political refugees – give them temporary asylum until we restored the elected Government of Haiti."[93] Although Clinton did not commit to admitting Haitians as refugees, he claimed that he would assure their safety until he, as president, restored Aristide to power.

In light of the protection that Clinton promised, Haitians built an estimated 700–1,000 boats immediately after he won the presidential election in November 1992. They planned to head to America on Clinton's inauguration in January 1993.[94]

The prospects of a massive Haitian influx panicked Clinton's transition committee. As a result, already prior to taking office Clinton retracted his campaign promise to grant Haitians asylum. On January 14 he announced that he would continue Bush's practice of repatriating Haitians who the Coast Guard interdicted.[95] He claimed that it would be better for Haitians to stay in Haiti and participate peacefully in building a better future for their country.[96] He noted that repatriated Haitians could apply for admission as refugees, though he offered no assurance that their requests would be granted.[97]

Clinton's critique of Bush's repatriation of Haitians to a brutally repressive regime proved to be an electoral ploy, to win Haitian American votes, especially in Florida where many of them lived, as well as votes of African Americans and others committed to racial justice. For his first two years as president, Clinton repatriated Haitians, admitted few as refugees, and made no arrangements for Aristide's return to power. Between January 15, 1993, and November 26, 1994, his administration interdicted and diverted to Guantanamo more than 25,000 Haitians, the same number of Haitians that President Carter had admitted as Entrants.[98]

Exclusionary policies of the past served as bedrock for Clinton's discrimination against Haitians, just as past policies of privileging Cubans served as basis for new Cuban privileging: at a time of rising racism and xenophobic nativism. Indeed, the Clinton administration blocked Haitians from the United States while admitting Cubans, as illustrated

---

[93] Ibid.   [94] Ibid.   [95] Ibid.
[96] WJCPL, Haiti [4] [OA/ID3105], "Message to the Haitian People: Actual Remarks President-Elect Bill Clinton," January 14, 1993, Box 8.
[97] WJCPL, Office of Press Secretary, White House, "Statement and Press Conference by the President," May 8, 1994, Box 2.
[98] FitzGerald, *Refuge beyond Reach*, p. 84.

in the book's opening, the anti-immigrant mood of the time notwithstanding.

By 1994 members of Congress were divided in their views toward the Clinton administration's Haitian policy: on whether or not to grant Haitians comparable rights to Cubans. Some legislators thought President Clinton treated Haitians unfairly, while others thought he treated them too generously.[99] At one extreme were legislators who argued that President Clinton was too lenient toward Haitians. Senator Robert Byrd, a West Virginian Democrat who Chaired the Appropriations Committee, for example, complained that Haitians who received unemployment compensation and other social benefits were a fiscal drain on US resources. He also argued that Haitians competed with American citizens for jobs, and that the very admission of some Haitians encouraged others to come. Senator Byrd was indifferent to the abuses that Haitians suffered in their home country, and dismissive of the United States' far greater fiscal expenditure on Cubans.[100]

At the other extreme were liberal members of Congress, including the Congressional Black Caucus. They pressed for halting repatriation of Haitians, and advocated for sanctions against the junta that ousted Aristide in a bloody coup in September 1991, eight months into his presidency. Two-thirds of Haitians had voted for Aristide, in the country's historically most honest election.[101] In addition, disconcerted about the blatant discrimination against Haitians and the differential treatment of Haitians and Cubans, in April 1994 Congressman Barney Frank, a Massachusetts Democrat, proposed a legislated basis for Cuban–Haitian

---

[99] Eric Schwartz, "Practicing at Home What We Preach Abroad: Four Lessons on Refugee Policy from the Clinton Administration," *Georgetown Journal of International Affairs* vol. 3, no. 1 (Winter/Spring 2002): 15.

[100] WJCPL, White House Staff and Office Files, Folder 2: National Security Council, OA/IF 3105, Box 8.

[101] Greenhill, *Weapons of Mass Migration*, p. 203; Barbara Crosette, "U.S. to Close Refugee Camp at Guantanamo to Haitians," *New York Times* (May 29, 1992) (www.nytimes.com/1992/05/29/world/us-to-close-refugee-camp). At the same time, Haitian rights advocates pressed for a more just Haitian migration policy. In advocating for Haitians, for example, Randall Robinson, executive director of the Trans-Africa Lobby, published a scathing full-page letter in the *New York Times* in the form of an ad, signed by over one hundred prominent Americans. It accused the Clinton administration of pursuing a racist policy toward Haitian refugees and demanded Aristide's return to power (which the Clinton administration finally orchestrated in 1994). Robinson also went on a much-publicized hunger strike to pressure the administration to end its Haitian repatriation policy.

equity: H.R.4249, the Haitian Adjustment Equity Act of 1994.[102] The bill called for amending the Cuban Adjustment Act to make it also applicable to Haitians. His proposed bill stipulated that the Attorney General report annually to Congress any disparate treatment of the two immigrant groups. No hearings were held on the bill, and the bill never was enacted. Not enough members of Congress were concerned about Haitian equity to support H.R.4249. As a result, unauthorized Haitian immigrants who arrived after 1982 did not qualify for legal residence (based on IRCA), all the while that incoming Cubans continued to qualify for CAA-based status adjustment rights. The Haitians, but not the Cubans, were subject to detention and repatriation.

Ronald Dellums, an African American congressman from California who chaired the Committee on Armed Services, was another of the legislators who was concerned about US policy toward Haitians. He opted, also in April 1994 to plead President Clinton directly to stop the forcible repatriation of Haitians "to the most vicious military regime in our hemisphere." Dellums claimed that repatriation was "a racially explosive foreign policy." With Haitians being "bludgeoned to death," Congressman Dellums felt they should be treated like other refugees.[103]

On May 8 President Clinton responded to Congressman Dellums. He noted that because conditions in Haiti had deteriorated, asylum seekers would indeed be given the opportunity to apply for refugee status and not automatically be repatriated. Acting on his words, the president had his administration increase the number of Haitians admitted to the United States as refugees: from 54 in 1992, President Bush's last year in office, and 1,307 in 1993, to 3,716 in 1994. In the latter year (according to available data), the United States for the first time admitted more Haitians than Cubans as refugees.[104] Also, President Clinton ordered Haitians to be entitled to asylum screenings when interdicted by the Coast Guard. Along with Congressman Dellums, civil rights interest groups, other members of Congress, including the Black Caucus, and deposed President Aristide had decried as racist the policy of entitling Cubans but not Haitians to asylum screening.[105]

---

[102] Interview with Barney Frank, September 2014.
[103] WJCPL, WHORM [White House Staff and Office Files, Subject File Case #062710 National Security Council, "Haiti-Safe Haven 1994–1995" HR4114, Folder 1 FOIA 2011-1045-F, Box 10.
[104] U.S. Department of Justice (USDOJ), 1997 *Statistical Yearbook of the Immigration and Naturalization Service* (Washington, DC: INS, 1999).
[105] FitzGerald, *Refuge beyond Reach*, p. 86.

Amid the mounting concern about inequitable treatment, Haitians who had been sent to Guantanamo became increasingly resentful about their detention, and the conditions under which they were detained. Angrily, on August 16 and 17, hundreds of them rioted. Scores of them were injured.[106] The protests did not, however, stop President Clinton, who was determined to prevent "another Mariel," from also interning Cuban rafters in Guantanamo, beginning a few days later.[107] Haitian policy provided a precedent, a bad precedent. Yet, even at Guantanamo, US officials treated Haitians and Cubans differently, informally. Guards invited Cubans to exhibit handicrafts they made and join them in running races. In contrast, they treated Haitians condescendingly.[108]

Meanwhile, pressure built up for President Clinton to act on his campaign promise to return democratically elected Aristide to power, on the presumption that repression in Haiti would thereby subside. The United Nations Security Council called for his return. So too did Haitian Americans. Finally, in September 1994 President Clinton acted on his promise. He negotiated the departure of the Haitian military from power and Aristide's return.

While acknowledging that Aristide's return to power never resolved Haiti's problems,[109] President Clinton used the occasion to reinforce US Haitian policy of the past: namely, admit few Haitians, even when their lives in Haiti were at risk.[110] He ordered the Haitians detained in Guantanamo to be returned to Haiti, as he paroled the Cubans there into the United States. He also ordered the Coast Guard to repatriate Haitians they interdicted at sea.

When the Clinton administration proceeded to negotiate the Joint Statement with the Republic of Cuba on Normalization of Migration in May 1995, which called for repatriation of Cubans that the Coast Guard found at sea, treatment of aspiring immigrants from the two countries seemed newly in sync: again, by retracting rights for Cubans, not by extending rights that Cubans enjoyed to Haitians. One might even argue that, for the first time, the United States treated Haitians better than Cubans, in returning Haitians to a democratically elected government, under Aristide. Cubans, in contrast, had to settle for the promise that their

---

[106] Times Staff Wire Reports, *Art Pine* (August 16, August 17, 1994).
[107] Wasem, *Cuban Migration to the United States*, p. 5.
[108] I am grateful to Holly Ackerman for this insight. At the time, Holly was Duke University Librarian for Latin America, Iberian, and Latino Studies.
[109] Clinton, *My Life*, p. 649.   [110] Frelick, "U.S. Refugee Policy in the Caribbean," p. 67.

government would not penalize them for having tried to emigrate illegally and for the possibility that the US Interests Section might issue them immigration visas. Critics of Washington's new Cuban repatriation policy even held the administration's Haitian policy up as example. Representative Robert Torricelli, the New Jersey Democrat with close ties to the Cuban American community who sponsored the Cuban Democracy Act (described in Chapter 4), argued at a congressional hearing that if it had been wrong to repatriate Haitians to a dictatorship (before Aristide's return to office), it was unjustifiable to return Cubans to a dictatorship.[111]

Even when repatriating both Cubans and Haitians interdicted at sea, the Clinton administration treated the two groups of boat people differently. The protocols were more protective of Cuban than Haitian rights.[112] Cubans, but not Haitians, were advised of how to apply for asylum and lawful migration.[113] Also, repatriated Cubans stood a better chance of securing immigration visas than did repatriated Haitians. Whereas the September 1994 US–Cuban migration accord guaranteed at least 20,000 Cubans immigration visas a year, Haitians had no comparable admissions assurance. Indeed, the Clinton administration admitted fewer Haitians than Cubans in all years except 2000 (in 1997 admitting twice as many Cubans as Haitians).[114]

In turn, the Clinton administration treated the Cubans and Haitians who managed to reach the United States without authorization differently. Almost without exception, immigration authorities paroled the Cubans into the United States, even though the Joint Communique denoted that the United States would discontinue the practice of paroling Cubans who arrived in "irregular ways" into the country. Then, in 1999, the previously noted Meissner Memo affirmed Cubans entry rights when they arrived in "irregular ways."

Meanwhile, in 1997, the NACARA, the Nicaraguan Adjustment and Central American Relief Act, brought congressional racist biases against Haitians to the fore. Unsympathetic legislators, like Byrd, kept Haitians

---

[111] USHR, "The Clinton Administration's Reversal of U.S. Immigration Policy toward Cuba," pp. 22–23.
[112] Schwartz, "Practicing at Home What We Preach Abroad," p. 22.
[113] Kolinsky, "A Fine Line, Redefined," p. 675.
[114] U.S. Department of Homeland Security (DHS), 2002 *Yearbook of Immigration Statistics* (Washington, DC: DHS, Office of Immigration Statistics, 2003) (www.dhs.gov/sites/default/files/publications/Yearbook_Immigration_Statistics_2002.pdf).

excluded from the list of Western Hemisphere nationals entitled to immigration status adjustment rights under the new legislation.

Faced with blatant congressional discrimination against Haitians, in this instance President Clinton took the high ground. He immediately issued a Delayed Enforced Departure directive that protected Haitians who had been paroled into the United States or who had applied for asylum prior to December 31, 1995. The directive assured Haitians that they would not be deported for one year while the administration sought a long-term solution for them.[115] The following year, the White House managed to convince Congress to pass the Haitian Refugee Immigration Fairness Act (HRIFA), which entitled Haitians to status adjustment rights that the CAA and NACARA had granted Cubans and Central Americans, respectively.[116] Dark-skinned Haitians thereby gained some of the legislated entitlements that, in the main, lighter skinned Cubans and Central Americans enjoyed.

HRIFA, accordingly, contributed to greater Cuban–Haitian equity. However, it did not provide bedrock for equality in treatment. For one, the CAA entitled unauthorized Cuban entrants on an ongoing basis to lawful permanent residency, whereas HRIFA only extended rights to Haitians to adjust their status for a brief period of time. Haitians needed to have arrived in the United States before December 31, 1995, and to apply before April 1, 2000.[117] Also, HRIFA presumed Haitians not to be refugees, which meant they were ineligible for refugee benefits. In contrast, the CAA presumed all Cuban entrants to be refugees, without evidence that they were.

Meanwhile, there was little pan-ethnic solidarity. Few Cuban Americans advocated for Cuban–Haitian equity. Cuban American Miami mayor Manny Diaz was one of the few. He argued that Haitians

---

[115] WJCPL, NSC emails, Exchange Record September 1997–January 1,1998, Immigration and Naturalization, "Statement by the President" (on Certain Haitians), December 23, 1997, Folder 1, Box 6.

[116] In order to avoid a full Congressional debate, proponents of HRIFA proposed the bill as an amendment to the omnibus appropriations bill for 1999. As a result, thirty years after passage of the CAA the United States established a "piecemeal" legal basis (to borrow Reagan administration terminology) for unauthorized Haitians to become lawful permanent residents, but within a defined (confined) time period. In 1986 IRCA had entitled Cuban–Haitian Entrants rights to status adjustment, in conjunction with a general amnesty for unauthorized entrants from all countries residing in the United States as of January 1, 1982.

[117] NumbersUSA, "The Seven Amnesties Passed by Congress" (www.numberusa.com/content/learn/illegal-immigration).

deserved permanent residency rights. However, he did so more with Cuban than Haitian interests in mind. He admitted that the extension of rights to Haitians would temper criticism of Cubans' unique status adjustment rights.[118]

In sum, the Clinton administration treated Cubans and Haitians relatively equitably when retracting rights for Cubans, but also when extending status adjustment and refugee rights to Haitians. However, it did not consistently treat Cubans and Haitians similarly. Had equity been its main concern, it would not have repatriated Haitian boatpeople when admitting Cuban rafters to the United States. Equity was, at best, a secondary concern.[119] If the Cold War had justified differential treatment of Haitians and Cubans who fled repressive Caribbean regimes of different political persuasions, its end removed any political justification for differential treatment. The Cold War's end laid bare a longstanding racial bias in immigration policy, and the "stickiness" of Cold War Cuban privileging.

Anti-Immigrant Backlash

As it happened, both the Cuban and Haitian rafters came to America in large numbers at a time when anti-immigrant sentiment swept the country, including Florida, where most Cubans and Haitians settled. Nativism, which was already an issue in the 1980s when the Mariel émigrés arrived, intensified in the 1990s. Might President Clinton have been trying to appease nativists when dealing with the Cuban and Haitian boatpeople?

In principle, the Immigration Reform and Control Act of 1986, IRCA, had put the problem of unauthorized immigration to rest. While entitling millions of undocumented immigrants then in the country to lawful permanent residency, IRCA also included measures to rein in unauthorized immigration (described in Chapter 4).

IRCA notwithstanding, unauthorized immigration continued and fueled nativist sentiments. By 1994 resentment of immigrants grew to the point that native-born residents in California mobilized to place Proposition 187, the Save Our State initiative, on the November ballot as a referendum. Proposition 187, directed primarily at Mexicans and

---

[118] Manny Diaz, *Miami Transformed: Rebuilding America, One Neighborhood, One City at a Time* (Philadelphia: University of Pennsylvania Press, 2013), p. 51.
[119] Council on Hemispheric Affairs (COHA), "Disparities in U.S. Immigration Policy toward Haiti and Cuba: A Legacy to be Continued?," *COHA* (June 24, 2010), p.10.

Central Americans who were the main unauthorized immigrants in the state, called for denying illegal aliens access to public education, nonemergency health care, and welfare benefits. During the summer months of 1994 (when the number of Cuban rafters soared), polls pointed to widespread support for the anti-immigrant referendum among likely California voters.[120] Then-Governor Pete Wilson, a Republican, benefited from his enthusiastic support of the referendum when running for reelection in November of that year. The referendum won with a wide margin of support (though subsequent legal challenges led to its repeal).[121]

Like Californians, Floridians resented being taxed to provide unauthorized immigrants with services. Thus, with the arrival of the rafters, Governor Lawton Chiles sued the federal government for $1.5 billion, for coverage of health, welfare, and education expenditure on the newcomers.[122] The case was finally settled in 1998 when President Clinton was still in office, but after the rafter crisis subsided. In the settlement, the INS agreed to absorb costs when large numbers of unauthorized migrants arrived, without specifying what constituted "large numbers."

Given native-born resentment toward the new unauthorized Cubans,[123] including for reasons other than being taxed to cover costs of resettlement benefits, Florida Governor Chiles had tried to block rafters from coming ashore in the state. Early in the summer of 1994 he announced that all Cubans who landed in Florida would be detained, rather than processed and released. Then, on August 18 he declared a state of emergency in the state and announced that rafters would be arrested and quarantined.[124] His blocking of rafters influenced President Clinton's decision, announced the next day, to divert incoming rafters to Guantanamo. President Clinton had met with Governor Chiles, as well as with Florida Senator Bob Graham, before making his diversion-to-Guantanamo plan known. The two Florida politicians were the only elected officials invited to the meeting.

---

[120] Philip Martin, "Proposition 187 in California," *International Migration Review* 29 no. 1, special issue (Spring 1995): 257.
[121] Ibid.
[122] USHR, "Clinton Administration's Reversal of U.S. Immigration Policy toward Cuba."
[123] Greenhill, *Weapons of Mass Migration*, p. 112.
[124] In addition, he demanded the federal government stop asylum seekers. Sartori, "The Cuban Migration Dilemma," pp. 332–33; "Mass Migration from Cuba," 140 *Congressional Record* E 1717, August 12, 1994.

Governor Chiles had responded to the surge in unauthorized Cuban boatpeople with his own political ambitions in mind. He was running for reelection that year and was embroiled in a tough campaign against Jeb Bush, who, as detailed in Chapter 4, was well known locally from his work for the Republican Party in Miami-Dade County. Immigration was a hot political issue at the time, and anti-immigrationists accused the governor of failing to protect state and national borders.[125] After President Clinton diverted the rafters to Guantanamo, Governor Chiles won reelection. The election was the second closest gubernatorial election in the state's post-Reconstruction history. Most voters disapproved of Washington's decades-old open-door policy toward Cubans.[126]

President Clinton had his own, as well as Governor Chiles', political interests in mind when intervening to prevent "another Mariel." The CIA had warned of a slow-motion Mariel in the making.[127] Pressed to choose among political constituencies, immigrant-restrictionists were likely to garner him more votes in the upcoming election than Cuban Americans who wanted the welcome mat for rafters maintained.[128] Both Clinton and Chiles enhanced their electoral prospects by blocking rafters from entry.

In denying Cuban rafters entry, President Clinton addressed the anti-immigrant mood that had taken hold nationwide. A CBS/*New York Times* poll in September 1994, for example, found 80 percent of Americans disapproved of letting Cubans into the United States (and 77 percent disapproved of allowing Haitians entry).[129]

When President Clinton did admit the rafters after their detention in Guantanamo, he did so in a manner that kept anti-immigration rage at bay. He had the rafters screened before entry, and admitted in an orderly manner that avoided media attention, with the INS agreeing to settle them in Florida only if they had immediate family there.[130] In contrast, when the tens of thousands of rafters initially tried to come ashore, the media provoked fear of "another Mariel" in the making. Meanwhile, Attorney General Reno assured "nativists" that the detainees admitted from

---

[125] Frohock, "Brisas del Mar," p. 45.   [126] LeoGrande, "From Havana to Miami," p. 79.
[127] Morley and McGillion, *Unfinished Business*, p. 73.
[128] LeoGrande, "From Havana to Miami," p. 79.
[129] Drew Desilver, "U.S. Public Seldom Has Welcomed Refugees into Country," Pew Research Center (November 19, 2015).
[130] USHR, "Clinton Administration's Reversal of U.S. Immigration Policy toward Cuba," p. 20. In actuality, the INS only settled 14 percent of the Guantanamo parolees outside Miami (p. 98).

Guantanamo would not increase the overall number of Cubans allowed into the country. They would be included, as noted earlier, in the 20,000 Cubans that the United States had committed to admit yearly in the 1994 bilateral migration accord. Florida's Senator Graham, who the White House consulted, believed that in this manner President Clinton would not lose votes in his upcoming reelection bid.[131]

President Clinton further upped his anti-immigration credentials in signing both IIRIRA and PRWORA into law. The two laws cracked down on unauthorized immigration, and restricted rights of unauthorized immigrants. He signed IIRIRA and PRWORA two and three months before the 1996 election, respectively. At the national level, PRWORA accomplished what Proposition 187 had not in California. It denied unauthorized immigrants' rights to welfare. While NACARA and HRIFA, enacted in 1997 and 1998, respectively, did extend status adjustment rights to Central Americans and Haitians (and to Cubans not covered by other legislation), they did so for only a time-limited period and without granting rights to welfare. Moreover, Clinton signed the two bills into law after his reelection, when he had little to lose politically.

Thus, President Clinton appealed to nativist sentiments first by blocking unauthorized Cubans from US entry, and then by implementing legislation that clamped down on unauthorized immigration in general and on benefits for unauthorized immigrants. Meanwhile, he addressed the rafter crisis in a manner that tempered Cuban American as well as nativist opposition.

Pressures from Cuban Americans

Amid anti-immigration pressures on the one hand, and Haitian rights pressures on the other, President Clinton also faced pressure from Cuban Americans who wished the continued privileging of "their people." No group likes to have their entitlements rescinded, and Cuban Americans were no exception.

From the administration's vantage point, Cuban Americans had become a political force to contend with. Many Cubans who relocated to the United States in the 1960s and 1970s by the 1990s had put the skills, social ties, and financial assets with which they emigrated, plus the exceptionally generous refugee benefits they received, to good use.

[131] Greenhouse, "How the Clinton Administration Reversed U.S. Policy on Cuban Refugees."

By the 1990s, 29 percent of the 1960s and 21 percent of the 1970s émigrés ranked among the top tercile of American income-earners.[132] Through the PAC associated with the "Foundation," the Cuban American National Foundation (described in Chapter 4), they channeled some of their earnings to political candidates who promoted Cuba-related policies that they wanted, including policies affecting Cuban immigrants.

By the 1990s, Cuban Americans also had more votes than in the past to parlay, in the key state of Florida. When Clinton ran for reelection, his advisors estimated that Cuban Americans comprised about 12 percent of the Florida electorate,[133] a significant percentage in a "swing state." By then Florida had surged to have the fourth largest number of electoral college votes (25), up from the eighth largest number when President Carter faced the Mariel crisis. Taking advantage of the citizenship rights the CAA put them on the path to attain, Cuban immigrants voted in large numbers. Although most of them voted Republican, the more Cuban American votes Clinton could garner, the greater his prospects of winning the state, and the national election, in turn.

Already in 1992, during his first Presidential campaign, Clinton had strategized to win Cuban American votes. He announced in Miami – as noted in Chapter 4 – that he supported the controversial Cuban Democracy Act (CDA) that Congress was deliberating at the time.[134] The Foundation, which lobbied for the legislation, had contributed half of the $1 million dollars that the Clinton campaign raised in Florida that year.[135]

If, in 1994, Clinton was concerned about his reelection in 1996, why would he risk antagonizing Cuban Americans by blocking rafters from entry? Indeed, out of concern with appeasing Cuban Americans, President Clinton had invited Mas Canosa to the White House meeting that preceded his August 19 (1994) announcement of the diversion-to-Guantanamo policy. Mas Canosa, director of the Foundation, which claimed fifty thousand members, by then was the most influential Cuban American. In attending the White House meeting, he became a stakeholder in the new policy.

---

[132] Eckstein, *The Immigrant Divide*, p. 71.
[133] Taylor Branch, *The Clinton Tapes* (New York: Simon and Schuster, 2009), p. 597.
[134] See Chapter 4 for a description of provisions of the Cuban Democracy Act.
[135] Jonathan Smith, "Foreign Policy for Sale? Interest Group Influence on President Clinton's Cuba Policy," *Presidential Studies Quarterly* (Winter 1998) (www.questia.com/read/GI-20/91093/foreign-policy-for-sale).

Opposed to blocking aspiring Cuban immigrants from the United States, Mas Canosa made his support of offshore Cuban detention contingent on President Clinton arranging for new federal funds for both Radio and TV Martí, to broadcast anti-Castro programs to Cuba.[136] He also made his support contingent on the president retracting his recent extension of rights for Cuban Americans to travel and send remittances to Cuba. While Mariel and subsequent arrivals wanted to visit Cuba and help family that they had not long ago left behind, Mas Canosa and fellow exiles who immigrated soon after the revolution backed the previously noted people-to-people embargo, to complement the state level embargo on trade and investment. They believed that without dollars spent by émigrés on visits, and remittances they sent to family on the island, the Cuban economy – and therefore the regime – would collapse. Although President Clinton had claimed to have loosened the "personal embargo" to strengthen Cuban civil society, a goal of the Cuban Democracy Act, he conceded to Mas Canosa's demands in order to temper Cuban American opposition to the diversion-to-Guantanamo policy. Mas Canosa convinced Clinton to tie nonimmigration to immigration policy, which Castro unsuccessfully had tried to do over the years.

Nonetheless, Cuban Americans did not quietly acquiesce to the new exclusionary policy, even with Mas Canosa signing off on the president's plan. After learning on Miami radio that Cubans were being diverted to Guantanamo, 2,500 Cuban Americans demonstrated in Miami's Little Havana, the symbolic center of Cuba-America. Others demonstrated in front of the Department of Justice, which was in charge of immigration.[137] They protested against internment, in solidarity with rafters.

Proving himself unable to temper Cuban American rage about the Guantanamo detention policy, Mas Canosa reneged on his commitment to support the Clinton administration's new exclusion of Cubans. Instead, he lobbied via the Foundation for the Guantanamo detainees to be admitted to the United States.[138]

Other Cuban Americans turned to the legal system to get the Cubans detained in Guantanamo admitted to the United States. Most notably, the

---

[136] Walt Vanderbush and Patrick Haney, "Policy toward Cuba in the Clinton Administration," *Political Science Quarterly* vol. 114 no. 3 (Autumn 1999), p. 399. Radio Martí voiced Mas Canosa's opposition to Clinton's new Cuba immigration policy. Greenhouse, "Top Cuban-American Misuses U.S. Broadcasts," *New York Times* (July 23, 1995).

[137] Frohock, "Brisas del Mar," p. 49.

[138] Morley and McGillion, *Unfinished Business*, p. 80.

Cuban American Bar Association (CABA), comprised mainly of Cuba-born lawyers who had fled the revolution early on, filed a class action suit in South Florida: CABA v. Christopher.[139] The case became an instant sensation in the Miami media. CABA sued the US government on behalf of the Guantanamo detainees, who claimed that they had fled Cuba on the presumption that they would be admitted to the United States. While US immigration officials had given rafters the choice of remaining in Guantanamo or returning to Cuba, the plaintiffs framed the latter option as "coerced repatriation."[140] Claiming the Guantanamo naval base as US territory, CABA argued that the CAA applied there, thus entitling the Cuban detainees to be paroled into the United States.

Given that the case was filed in Miami, exiles influenced the jury. CABA won the case at the district level. However, the 11th Circuit Court overturned the lower court decision in an opinion issued on January 18, 1995. It ruled that the Cubans (along with Haitians) who were interned in Guantanamo were migrants who were temporarily placed in a safe haven outside US territory. As such, they did not hold legal rights that were cognizable in the United States. The court concluded that "(A)ll the U.S. government had done was act graciously ... moved by (a sense of) *noblesse oblige* ... "[141] The court reasoned that US-leased military bases abroad, under the sovereignty of foreign nations, were not the same as US land borders, ports of entry, and US territory.[142] Because the Guantanamo naval base was not on US territory, it argued that the Cubans who were detained there had no a priori legal claims to asylum.

The 11th Circuit Court added that detainees had the option to repatriate voluntarily to Cuba, where they could apply for asylum through the US Interests Section in Havana. Alternatively, they could settle in a third country.[143] In the 11th Circuit Court's assessment, Cubans had to be in the United States in order to qualify for CAA rights. Interdiction at sea did not trigger the Act.[144] Although CABA appealed the ruling, the Supreme Court refused to consider the case. Thus, in the final analysis the judicial system supported the Clinton administration's decision to deny rafters US entry rights.

---

[139] Warren Christopher was Secretary of State at the time.
[140] Frohock, "Brisas del Mar," pp. 52–54.   [141] Ibid., pp. 61–62.
[142] Joyce Hughes, "Flight from Cuba," *California Western Law Review* vol. 36 no. 1 (1999), p. 60.
[143] Frohock, "Brisas del Mar," pp. 61–62.
[144] Sawczyn, "The United States Immigration Policy ... "

However, in May of 1995 Cuban Americans achieved through political channels what they had failed to accomplish through the courts. The 1995 bilateral Joint Statement committed the United States to admit the Guantanamo detainees. Yet, to the consternation of Cuban Americans, the Joint Statement also committed the United States to repatriate future Cubans that the Coast Guard interdicted at sea.

The Clinton administration had not consulted Mas Canosa before signing off on the Joint Statement. President Clinton's advisors had every reason to believe that Mas Canosa would oppose repatriation since he had already lobbied against the detention of Cubans offshore. In anger, Mas Canosa joined several thousand Cuban Americans who protested in Lafayette Park, across from the White House.[145] He also criticized the new repatriation policy on federally funded Radio Martí.[146]

Mas Canosa accused the Administration of "betrayal." Along with the three Cuban Americans who by then had been elected to Congress, Mas Canosa opposed the repatriation policy, as well as the secrecy in which the administration negotiated the arrangement with Cuba. New Jersey Congressman Robert Menendez, who, at the time, was both the only Cuban American Democrat and the only Cuban American elected to Congress outside of South Florida, claimed the new exclusionary policy to signify that the administration prioritized nativists' over Cuban Americans' interests. He accused the president – the highest-ranking member of his own party – of moving America down "a slippery policy slope when domestic anti-immigration sentiments determine our foreign policy toward the most brutal regime in this hemisphere."[147] In testifying before Congress, Mas Canosa expressed similar views. He criticized the President of pitting Cuban Americans against other Americans, and of seeking "political cover behind the so-called anti-immigrant political mood in the country."[148]

Why would President Clinton agree to admit the Guantanamo detainees but exclude future unauthorized boat people if he was cognizant that

---

[145] Morley and McGillion, *Unfinished Business*, p. 89.
[146] Greenhouse, "Top Cuban-American Misuses U.S. Broadcasts"; WJCPL, White House Staff Office Files, Caryn Hollis, Inter-American Affairs, Cuba Martí [3] [OA/ID 2930], Box 2. President Clinton threatened to oust Mas Canosa as chair of the station's advisory board, but was worried about antagonizing the influential Cuban American leader as the presidential election year heated up.
[147] USHR, "The Clinton Administration's Reversal of U.S. Immigration Policy toward Cuba," p. 6.
[148] Ibid., p. 100.

Cubans Americans opposed repatriation? He wanted to avert "another Mariel" as the summer months approached and the Florida Straits would be easier for rafters to navigate. The Cuban economy remained depressed. "Another Mariel" would anger anti-immigrationists who had more votes to cast in the upcoming presidential election than did Cuban Americans. At the same time, long-term offshore detention was not an option. Senator Graham, the Democrat who had visited Cubans in Guantanamo in March 1995, had reported to the White House that conditions at the naval base were a tinderbox that was likely to implode as the hot summer months approached.[149]

Already, the first Cubans interned in Guantanamo had scaled barbed wire fences around their tent camps, staged hunger strikes, and demanded improved treatment, family visits, access to news and information, and more freedom of movement.[150] Civil disturbances occurred on a daily basis. Similarly, rafters detained in Panama organized escapes and violent protests,[151] and a two-day mutiny to demand US visas. One thousand detainees escaped the Panamanian camps, and even more of them staged a revolt. They tore down fences and burned down one of the camps. Scores of them jumped into the Panama Canal to try to escape. Two died in their attempt.[152] The detainees complained that they were prisoners living under conditions comparable to Cuba, devoid of rights.[153]

---

[149] Greenhouse, "How the Clinton Administration Reversed U.S. Policy on Cuban Refugees," *New York Times* (May 21, 1995) (www.nytimes.com/1995/05/21/world/how-the-clinton-administration-reversed-us-policy-on-cuban-refugees.html).

[150] Sartori, "The Cuban Migration Dilemma," p. 345.

[151] WJCPL, NSC Cable, Email, and Records Management Systems, NSC Cables 1/93-12/94, Operation Safe Haven (7/11/94-12/31/94) [OA/ID 505000], Manuel Alvarez Cedona, "Two More Rafters Escape; Captured by U.S. Soldiers," *La Prensa* (Panama City), November 12, 1994, p. A-1, Box 2.

[152] WJCPL, Cable CD010/December 94/MSG5/M1408810.html, "Two Bodies of Cuban Rafters Found in Waters of Canal," *La Prensa* (Panama) December 11, 1994: Records on Operation Safe Haven, 1994–1995, Folder 3, Box 2; Sartori, "The Cuban Migration Dilemma," pp. 341, 345; Frohock, "Brisas del Mar," pp. 55, 79; Laurie Goldstein, "Cuban Refugees at Guantanamo Protest Pact," *Washington Post* (September 11, 1994), p. 30; Bill Murphy, "Brutality of 1994 Panama Fight Still Resonates with U.S. Troops," *Stars and Stripes* December 2, 2011 (www.stripes.com/brutality-of-1994-panama-fight-still-resonates); Larry Nackerud et al., "The End of the Cuban Contradiction in U.S. Refugee Policy," *International Migration Review* vol. 33 no. 1 (Spring 1999): 179.

[153] WJCPL, NSC Cables, Lastenia Murillo Munoz, *La Prensa* (Panama), January 4, 1995, p. 4, Subject: Rafters Criticize Use of Drug-Sniffing Dogs in Camps, Operation Safe Haven (12/31/94-02/06/1995 OA/ID 510000, Box 2.

Fortunately for President Clinton, Cuban American anger about repatriation of aspiring Cuban immigrants subsided as the number of new rafters tapered off, but especially as Cuban American attention turned elsewhere, for reasons to be described. However, as late as 1999 there was a demonstration in Little Havana that called for repeal of the repatriation policy. Protestors included Jorge Mas Santos, who had assumed the directorship of the Foundation after his father died in 1997; the three Cuban Americans then serving in Congress; Joe Carollo, the mayor of Miami; representatives of forty Cuban exile organizations; and hundreds of other Cuban Americans.[154] When the media captured Coast Guard cadre blocking rafters from coming ashore, the Cuban Americans had taken to the streets. They argued that Cubans who had been intercepted at sea, with "wet feet," ought to be treated the same as Cubans who managed to come ashore, with "dry feet." They demanded that those with "wet feet" be paroled into the country. While President Clinton held firm to repatriating Cubans found at sea, in having his Attorney General issue the Meissner Memo he responded to pressure from Cuban Americans to admit Cubans who reached the United States by land, with "dry feet."[155]

Back to 1996, President Clinton had handled the rafter crisis sufficiently well to garner enough Cuban American support to win the Florida vote, and reelection. He was helped by a Cuban government shoot down of Cuban American-piloted planes in February 1996, to which the exile community turned its attention. It was one of two additional crises that Cuban Americans provoked before he left office.

UNINTENDED CONSEQUENCES OF CUBAN IMMIGRATION POLICY: TWO CRISES THE CLINTON ADMINISTRATION CONFRONTED

After resolution of the rafter crisis, the Clinton administration was consumed by two additional crises that were provoked by Cuban émigrés and were rooted in their past privileging, and the sense of entitlement the

---

[154] Fidel Castro, *Lo Esencial de lo que Dijo El Presidente del Consejo de Estado de la República de Cuba sobre la Emigración Ilegal Promovida durante 40 Años por Estados Unidos contra Cuba*, August 3, 1999, *Cuba vs Bloqueo* (www.cubavsbloqueo.cu/es/discursos-e-intervenciones/lo-esencial-de-lo-que-dijo-el-presidente-del-consejo-de-estado-de-la).

[155] Aja Díaz, "El proceso migratorio externo de Cuba," pp. 15–16; Arboleya Cervera, *Cuba y los cubanoamericanos*, El p. 193.

privileging fueled. The two incidents mobilized the Cuban American community as never before, and shaped how the Clinton administration responded. They even impacted presidential politics.

An Exile Group's Provocation of a Cuban Government Shoot Down

Exiles formed the group Brothers to the Rescue (BTTR) in 1991, initially to perform search and rescue missions to bring rafters to the United States. However, after the Clinton administration implemented the repatriation policy, BTTR members did not want to assist the Coast Guard in returning Cubans to a regime that they despised. Rather than disband, the group reinvented itself. Members instead focused on promoting regime change in Cuba, in a manner that caused a major confrontation between the US and Cuban governments, and that unleashed a chain of events leading President Clinton to support the Cuban American-backed Helms–Burton bill he had previously opposed. Exile pilots who the CIA had trained in the early years of Castro's rule provoked the chain of events that unfolded.

José Basulto founded the BTTR. Its twenty-five members were pilots who were dedicated to rescuing rafters. The pilots flew planes over the Florida Straits and informed the US Coast Guard of rafters they spotted. The Coast Guard proceeded to rescue the rafters and bring them ashore, whereupon they were paroled into the country and entitled to the string of benefits that their admission, and the CAA in turn, ensured. At the same time, the Coast Guard brought tens of thousands of Haitians that they interdicted to detention facilities in Guantanamo, as they had during Bush's presidency.

Basulto had dedicated his life in the United States to toppling the Castro-led government. Having emigrated soon after Castro assumed power, the CIA trained him in intelligence, sabotage, and subversion. He participated in the ill-fated Bay of Pigs invasion. The next year he fired a canon at a Cuban hotel from a boat, and then supported paramilitary activity.

Following decades of failed terrorist plots, but still committed to toppling the Cuban government, he shifted strategy: in favor of aggressive nonviolent activity.[156] He raised money for BTTR endeavors from fellow

---

[156] Mireya Navarro, "Nonviolence of Castro's Foes Still Wears a Very Tough Face." *New York Times* (February 28, 1996) (www.nytimes.com/1996/02/28/world/nonviolence-of-castro-s-foes-still-wears-a-very-tough-face.html). Some exiles remained committed to

exiles as well as from such corporations as American Airlines that were headquartered in Miami.[157]

When the Clinton administration first ruled, in 1994, that Cubans found at sea would be detained in Guantanamo and no longer admitted to the United States, the BTTR ignored Attorney General instructions to stop assisting rafters.[158] The group ended its search and rescue efforts only after the administration began, in 1995, to repatriate rafters, at which point it shifted to promoting civil disobedience in Cuba. BTTR members coordinated their activity with that of dissident groups on the island that they funded. One of their initiatives involved releasing anti-government leaflets from planes that they flew into Cuban airspace. They had initiated their first Cuba flyover in May 1994, before the signing of the first migration accord, but the Cuban foreign relations ministry claimed that they had flown planes into Cuban airspace twenty-six times by February 1996, in violation of international law.[159] Angered by the overflights, the Cuban government filed several complaints with the US Interests Section. Meanwhile, the BTTR won bragging points in Miami for their flyovers.[160]

US, as well as Cuban, authorities were irritated by the flights. On multiple occasions the Department of State warned BTTR pilots – who violated their own reported flight plans – about the risks of their intrusions into Cuban airspace.[161] Personnel from the Inter-American Bureau met personally with Basulto and had several phone conversations with him.[162] They worried that Castro might retaliate and allow "another Mariel."[163] Concerned about the possible retaliation, US authorities tried to revoke and suspend BTTR members' pilot licenses. Their efforts, however, became ensnarled in appeals.[164]

---

violent tactics. For example, in January 1996 US customs agents captured five anti-Castro activists in the Florida Keys with a boatload of weapons and explosives. See Mike Clary and Norman Kempster, "United States Rarely Prosecutes Castro Foes," *Los Angeles Times* (February 28, 1996).

[157] Navarro, "Nonviolence of Castro's Foes Still Wears a Very Tough Face."
[158] Morley and McGillion, *Unfinished Business*, p. 75.
[159] For details on the shootdown, see WJCPL, White House Staff and Office Files, especially Boxes 1 to 8; Juanita Darling, "Cuba Complained to U.S. about Flights, Havana Says," *Los Angeles Times* (February 29, 1996) (www.latimes.com/archives/la-xpm-1996-02-29-mn-41418-story.html).
[160] Branch, *The Clinton Tapes*, p. 346.
[161] WJCPL, WHSO Files, NSC Inter-American Affairs, Folder 22: Questions from the Western Hemisphere Hearing, Department of State, Box 3.
[162] Ibid.   [163] Szulc, "Castro's China Model."
[164] Branch, *The Clinton Tapes*, p. 346.

Despite the Cuban and US government warnings, on February 24 of 1996 the BTTR coordinated an air mission with Concilio Cubano, a short-lived Cuban umbrella group of organizations dedicated to a peaceful transition to democracy.[165] In solidarity with Concilio Cubano, the BTTR flew three planes near Cuban territory. Although BTTR pilots had previously entered Cuban airspace, on February 24 they did not – or at least they had not yet – when Cuban authorities shot down two of their planes. A third plane carrying Basulto escaped unscathed. Although President Clinton acknowledged that the BTTR had previously entered Cuban airspace, he argued that the Cuban government shoot down of civilians was a flagrant violation of international law.[166]

Miami's Cuban American community did not remain passive on the sidelines. Outraged about the shoot downs, they collectively grieved the deaths of the pilots in a manner that reaffirmed their shared opposition to the Cuban government. Together with fifteen other exile groups, the BTTR organized a memorial service at the Orange Bowl. During the service, BTTR pilots flew planes over the waters where the shoot down occurred. A flotilla of boats met them.[167] At the same time, BTTR sympathizers in Miami dressed in black and draped buildings with black banners.

Florida politicians proceeded to pressure the Clinton administration to retaliate against Cuba. Senator Graham, who had close ties to the Cuban American community (from whom he received PAC contributions),[168] together with Miami's Cuban American Congressman Lincoln Díaz-Balart, and Mas Canosa, called for a naval blockade or intervention.[169]

---

[165] Concilio Cubano chose to meet on the anniversary of the start of Cuba's 1898 War of Independence from Spain, a symbol of successful Cuban resistance to colonial rule.

[166] WJCPL, White House Office of the Press Secretary, "Statement by the President, The Briefing Room," February 26, 1996, Folder 16, Box 6. Juan Pablo Roque, a former major in the Cuban Air Force who fled Cuba in 1992, working as an FBI agent, collaborated with the BTTR. He proved to be a Cuban spy. He mysteriously disappeared the day before the planned air mission and reappeared in Cuba, from where he criticized the BTTR. Tracey Eaton, "Retired Spy in Brothers to the Rescue Case Lives in Obscurity in Havana," *Miami Herald* (October 2, 2012) (www.miamiherald.com/latest-news/article 1943250.html).

[167] WJCPL, WHSO Files, Andres Viglucci, Carol Rosenberg, and Martin Merzer, "Saluting 4 Fallen Brothers," *Herald* (February 26, 1996). Folder 34, Box 3.

[168] While he was not Cuban and was a Democrat, Senator Graham was the sixth largest recipient of Free Cuba PAC funds between 1979 and 2000. See Center for Responsive Politics (www.opensecrets.org).

[169] WJCPL, WHSO Files, Public Liaison Cuban Affairs, David Hancock and Jack Rejtman "Cuba Bound Charter Airlines Suddenly Don't Exist," *Miami Herald* (February 27, 1996), Folder 34: Shootdown February 1996, Box 5.

In his effort to appease Cuban Americans without ordering a naval blockade or invasion, President Clinton worked with Congress to enact the Helms–Burton bill for which the Foundation had lobbied. Versions of the legislation had passed the Republican-controlled House and Senate in the Fall of 1995, but they never came up for a final vote because of White House objections at the time. The White House had been worried about lawsuits, and about angering foreign allies who found two provisions of the bill particularly objectionable,[170] one that granted Cuban Americans rights to sue foreign-based companies "trafficking" in property they had owned before the revolution, and one that denied corporate officers of companies involved in the "trafficking" rights to visas to visit the United States. President Clinton also objected that the bill legislated the embargo which, until then, had been enforced at presidential discretion. Attorney General Reno recommended that President Clinton veto the bill because it undermined presidential foreign policy discretionary power.

Nonetheless, against the backdrop of Cuban American fury over the shoot down, Clinton put his reservations about the bill aside. He deferred to his political and campaign advisers, who urged him to sign the controversial bill.[171] They argued that it would win him Cuban American votes in the upcoming election. With his reelection interests in mind, President Clinton not only approved the legislation, but, very deliberately, signed it in Florida. He invited relatives of the BTTR pilots who had lost their lives in the shoot down to the signing ceremony.[172]

---

[170] Larry Rohter, "Cuba's 2 Steps Back," *New York Times* (February 29, 1996) (www.nytimes.com/1996/02/29/world/cuba-s-2-steps-back.html). The objective of the Helms–Burton Act was to hasten a democratic-market transition in Cuba, by further strangulating the Cuban economy. Congressional negotiators did give the president the power to waive, for unlimited six-month intervals, the most disputed component of the bill: the provision giving Cuban Americans and others the right to sue in US courts for compensation from companies involved in property they had owned that the Cuban government had expropriated. The legislation also specified that any mass migration that the Cuban government instigated would be considered an act of aggression and be met with an appropriate response to maintain US national security and the health and safety of the American people (Title 1, Sec. 101, PL 104-114) March 12, 1996).

[171] WJCPL, Carla Ann Robbins, "Clinton Backs Bill to Tighten Cuban Embargo," *Wall Street Journal* (February 29, 1996), cable, Box 6. See also Phili Brenner, Patrick Haney, and Walter Vanderbush, "U.S. Policy toward Cuba, 1998–2001," *International Studies Perspectives* vol. 3 (2002): 192–208.

[172] After the shootdown, President Clinton also suspended flights to Cuba. While he had suspended them in the summer of 1994 to get Mas Canosa's support for the diversion-to-Guantanamo policy, he subsequently had reinstated them.

Antagonizing allies and stripping presidents of discretionary power was bad policy. However, supporting the bill was good short-term politics. Clinton calculated that if he held onto most of the states that he had won in 1992 and also won Florida, which he had only narrowly lost in 1992, he could win reelection.[173] He considered Cuban American support to be critical to a Florida victory. With 75 percent of Cuban Americans in Miami supporting the Helms–Burton bill,[174] his approval of the legislation helped him garner about one-third of the Cuban American Florida vote. The vote was insufficient to break the lock that Republicans held on the Cuban American vote, but sufficient for President Clinton to win the state's electoral college votes and reelection in turn.[175]

Once reelected, President Clinton sought to appease allies by never enforcing the provisions of the legislation they found most objectionable (establishing precedent for his presidential successors, until President Trump). However, the very signing of the bill damaged his relations with other countries.[176] As Clinton himself acknowledged, the bill reinforced the viewpoint that the United States was a bully,[177] and undermined whatever chance he might have had in his second term of office to convince the Cuban government to promote political reform in exchange for lifting the embargo.[178]

Thus, the BTTR provocations had wide-ranging ramifications. From President Clinton's vantage point they were undesired, unintended consequences of earlier Cuban immigration and Cuban immigrant policies.

The Fight for Elián

Cuban Americans unleashed a second migration-linked crisis in November 1999, which built on past privileging of Cubans, when two

---

[173] Clinton, *My Life*, p. 727.
[174] Florida International University Institute for Public Opinion (FIU-IPOR), "FIU Cuba Policy Study V," 1997 (ipor.fiu.edu/IPORpastProjects.htm#Cuba).
[175] In a further nod to Cuban Americans, the Illegal Immigration Reform and Immigrant Responsibility Act of 1996 (IIRIRA), which President Clinton signed into law, specified that the Cuban Adjustment Act would only be repealed on determination that a democratically elected government assumed power in Cuba.
[176] After passage of the Helms–Burton bill, however, other countries, in anger, broke with the United States and withdrew their support of the US Cuba embargo. Although it was not binding, when the issue of the embargo came up annually for a vote at the United Nations, increasingly fewer countries supported it.
[177] Branch, *The Clinton Tapes*, p. 346.   [178] Clinton, *My Life*, pp. 701, 727.

fishermen rescued Elián González, who they found unconscious three miles off the coast of Fort Lauderdale a few weeks before his sixth birthday. His Cuban mother, along with ten others, died on a boat that capsized when they tried to emigrate without authorization. Their effort demonstrated that Clinton's repatriation policy did not entirely deter unauthorized immigration.

Had it not been for the CAA, Elián would have remained nameless and faceless in US history: a child that immigration authorities would have detained and possibly deported. However, in coming ashore, Elián innocently unleashed what President Clinton called a "politician's nightmare." Although immigration law favored the claims of the boy's father, Juan Miguel González Quintana, who had divorced his mother and remained in Cuba, Cuban Americans viewed Elián as a political trophy.[179] An international custody battle consequently ensued that preoccupied the Clinton administration for more than half a year. It too impacted presidential politics.

On the one side of the battle were the US and Cuban governments – in rare agreement – plus Elián's father and the Cuban population-at-large. They all supported the paternity rights of Elián's father and, accordingly, the boy's return to Cuba. On the other side was the Cuban American community, including Elian's US relatives, and Cuban American politicians, lawyers, and organizations. They fought for Elián to stay in the United States. They argued that the CAA entitled him to US residency rights, and that his mother sacrificed her life for him to grow up in America. The Cuban American National Foundation financed the Cuban American legal battle.

On his rescue, Elián had been taken to a hospital for medical treatment. Once released, the INS immediately complicated his case. Typically, unaccompanied minors are placed in special detention centers. However, the INS paroled him into the temporary custody of his great-uncle, Lázaro González, who lived in Miami.[180] INS officials treated Elián differently not merely because he was Cuban, but because he came ashore in Florida, the heartland of the Cuban community in America. When Elián's father asked that his son be returned to him in Cuba, the great-uncle, with community support, refused to turn him over.

Cuban Americans sought to "save" Elián from living under the Castro "dictatorship," even if he thereby would be separated from his sole

---

[179] Branch, *The Clinton Tapes*, p. 585.
[180] Berta Esperanza Hernandez-Truyol, "On Becoming the Other," p. 693.

surviving parent after the traumatic death of his mother. The Cuban American community, along with their media stars – singer Gloria Estefan and actor Andy Garcia – rallied to the cause. Cuban Americans showered Elián with toys galore, unobtainable in Cuba since the revolution, and took him to Disneyworld, to entice him to want to stay in America.

Cuban Americans pursued diverse strategies to keep Elián in the United States. For one, they tried the legislative route. With the backing of the three Cuban American legislators then serving in Congress,[181] Republicans introduced a bill in January 2000 to grant Elián immediate US citizenship.[182]

When the bill was not enacted, Cuban Americans turned to protest tactics. They took to the streets to "save Elián." They demonstrated daily outside the home of Elián's great uncle, in protest over returning the boy to his father in Cuba.

In bipartisan unity, local officials joined in. The Democratic county mayor, Alex Penelas, together with twenty-two other civic leaders, vowed not to help federal authorities in their efforts to return Elián to his father. Penelas made it known on March 29, 2000, that the municipality would not lend police or other assistance to take the boy from his Miami relatives.[183] Similarly, the long-term Cuban American Democrat mayor of the heavily Cuban American city of Hialeah in Miami-Dade County sided with the Miami relatives in the custody battle, as did Cuban American New Jersey Democrat Congressman Bob Menendez.[184] Exile concerns took priority over partisan loyalty. The Cuban American Democrats defied President Clinton, the highest-ranking member of their party.

---

[181] They were Republican Ileana Ros-Lehtinen and Lincoln Díaz-Balart of South Florida, and Democrat Robert Menendez of New Jersey. Menendez served in the House of Representatives between 1993 and 2006, and afterward in the Senate.

[182] Tim Padgett, "How the Battle over Elian Gonzalez Helped Change U.S. Cuba Policy" (www.npr.org/sections/parallels/2015/06/28/4177161/3/how, 2015).

[183] Geraldo Rivera, "Exclusive: INS Agent at Center of Elian Gonzalez Saga Would Like to Host Him in the U.S." May 29, 2015 (www.foxnews.com/world/exclusive-ins-agent-at-center-of-elian-gonzalez-saga-would-like-to-host-him-in-the-u-s).

[184] Cuban Americans in Union City, New Jersey, where Menendez once served as mayor, also staged protests to pressure the Clinton administration to keep Elian in America. Andrew Jacobs, "The Cuban-American Heartland, North Version," *New York Times* (April 11, 2000), p. 29 (www.nytimes.com/2000/04/11/nyregion/the-cuban–heartland-north). In the 1960s, Cuban immigrants comprised 80 percent of the city's population, with the city then home to the second largest concentration of arrivals from Cuba. June Erlick, "First Week in a New Land: A time of Worry and Hope," *Jersey Journal* (November 30, 1970), p. 1.

Miami Cubans also tried other legal means to keep Elián in America. Lázaro, with the backing of the Foundation, challenged the Clinton administration's claims that a father's paternity rights superseded a minor's rights to immigrate without parental approval.[185] In that he was not running for reelection, as he was in 1996 when confronted with the BTTR crisis, President Clinton focused on the father's paternity rights. Consequently, even though local Miami INS bureaucrats had initially released Elián to his great-uncle, President Clinton went on to have his INS Commissioner announce the father's rights to the boy's custody and plans for Elián's return to Cuba.[186] Gregory Craig, of a powerhouse Washington law firm, defended the father and worked with the Justice Department to have him come to the United States as the legal process played out.[187] Even though Commissioner Meissner had sided with Cuban Americans in the preceding year – in the Meissner Memo – to exempt Cuban immigrants from restrictive IIRIRA regulations, in the case of Elián she did not. Lázaro had argued that Elián should stay in the United States because he would suffer persecution if returned to Cuba, but Commissioner Meissner, following an investigation, determined that would not be the case.[188] Attorney General Reno proceeded to announce that the US government would work "with everybody concerned" to have the boy returned to Cuba in an "orderly, fair, and prompt manner."[189]

The courts concurred with the administration's legal interpretation. Following months of legal battle, the 11th Circuit Court of Appeals in Atlanta affirmed a district court ruling that only Elián's father, rather than more distant relatives, could petition for asylum of a young minor. When Lázaro, along with other Cuban Americans, defied the order to turn Elián over to his father, a family court judge revoked Lázaro's temporary

---

[185] USDOJ, Memorandum for Doris Meissner, from Bo Cooper, General Counsel, Office of the General Counsel, Immigration and Naturalization Service, "Elian Gonzalez" (January 3, 2000); Gonzalez Ex Rel. Gonzalez v. Reno, 86 F. Supp. 2d 1167 (S.D. Fla. 2000), *Justia* (https://law.justia.com/cases/federal/district-courts/FSupp2/86/1167/2399370/).

[186] WGBH, "A Chronology of the Elian Gonzalez Saga" (n.d.) (www.pbs.or/wgbh/pages/frontline/shows/elian/etc/eliancron.html).

[187] John Broder, "For Elian's Father, a Lawyer with Ties to Clinton," *New York Times* (April 4, 2000) (www.nytimes.com/2000/04/04/us/for-elian-s-father-a-lawyer-with-ties-to-clinton.html).

[188] USDOJ, Memorandum for Doris Meissner, "Elian Gonzalez."

[189] [no author] "National News Briefs: Reno Meets Lawyer for Cuban Boy's Father," *New York Times* (March 23, 2000) (www.nytimes.com/2000/03/23/us/national-news-briefs-reno-meets-lawyer-for-cuban-boy-s-father.html).

custody rights. The Attorney General then arranged for a pre-dawn, three-minute raid on April 22 to retrieve Elián from Láazaro's house. After no one in the house would let them in, federal officials entered by force and took Elián at gunpoint. Elián finally was reunited with his father. However, father and son needed to stay in the United States until June, when the Circuit Court of Appeals ruled definitively that only Elián's father, rather than more distant relatives, could file for the boy's asylum. His father did not want his son to have asylum in the United States. He wanted custody of him in Cuba.

Cuban Americans did not, however, quietly acquiesce to Elián's removal at gunpoint. With the raid captured in a highly publicized photo, Cuban American hysteria erupted over the "Gestapo tactics" that US officials had used.[190] Thousands of Cuban Americans immediately took to the streets. They blocked a main highway and set more than 200 trash and tire fires in protest. Members of the exile group Mothers against Repression held hands and prayed in front of the house where one of the fishermen who rescued Elián lived.[191] During the week following the raid, Cuban Americans also staged a one-day work stoppage. Some 10 percent of Miami-Dade workers, including about one-seventh of public school teachers, refused to report to work, while tens of thousands of Cuban Americans peacefully marched through Little Havana. They protested the raid, and denounced President Clinton and Attorney General Reno for supporting it. It was Cuban Americans' biggest protest, with Miami-Dade Mayor Panelas joining the protesters.[192] Police (mis)handling of the raid led the police chief to resign and Joe Carollo, mayor of the City of Miami, in turn, to oust the city manager.

During the months of battle over Elián, the Cuban government defended Elián's father's paternity rights, but so too did it use the custody controversy to its own political advantage. Cuban authorities blamed the battle over Elián on the CAA because it enticed Cubans to immigrate without authorization, knowing that if they reached US shores they could become lawful permanent residents.[193] Elián's mother's fate testified to the law's "murderous" effect. Unknown numbers of Cubans had perished over the years before she had, in failed efforts to reach the United States in

---

[190] Branch, *The Clinton Tapes*, p. 598.
[191] "Enraged Cuban-Americans take to Miami Streets," April 22, 2000 (CNN.com).
[192] Clary, "Tens of Thousands Protest Miami Raid," *Los Angeles Times* (April 30, 2000) (http://articles.latimes.com/2000/apr/30/news/mn-25056).
[193] [no author], "Cuba and U.S. Open Talks about Immigration," *New York Times* (December 12, 2000) (www.nytimes.com/2000/12/12/world/cuba-and-us-open-talks).

unseaworthy vessels. Cuban authorities blamed the CAA, rather than conditions in their own country, for Cubans risking their lives to immigrate.

In turn, Cuban officials transformed the custody battle into a nationalist cause. They orchestrated demonstrations of thousands of Cubans in front of the US Interests Section in Havana to demand Elián's return to Cuba. Amid Cuba's post-Soviet-era economic crisis, nothing rallied Cubans more than a father's right to his child. Revolutionary zeal had fallen by the wayside as Cubans focused on sheer survival.

Cuban authorities even refused to put the controversy to rest after Elián returned to Cuba. Elián's father, with no national prominence before the international custody battle, became a member of the National Assembly. In turn, father and son were invited to special Communist Party events, and both Fidel and his brother Raúl, second-in-command at the time, attended Elián's birthday parties, which were covered by the media. Father and son became cause celebre. Even a decade later, in an officially choreographed event, Elián, by then a teenager, publicly criticized the CAA for having denied him rights to be with his father, rights to his nationality, and rights to remain in his cultural context.[194]

While back in America the Clinton administration had won its seven-month battle with Cuban Americans over Elián, the victory came at considerable cost, including to the sanctity of the American presidency and the American electoral process. Cuban Americans in Florida helped Republican George W. Bush secure the state's electoral college votes in 2000. Florida proved decisive in determining the election outcome that year.

In his desire to win Florida with Cuban American support, Vice President Al Gore, the Democrat candidate, defied the president he served. Rather than side with President Clinton, Gore publicly defended the custody claims of Elián's Miami relatives. Even so, he was so tainted by his association with Clinton that he dared not campaign in Cuban American neighborhoods in Miami for fear he would be met with protests.[195] Gore paid dearly for his association with a president who defended parental custody rights.

---

[194] "Elian Gonzalez: My Time in the U.S. Marked Me for My Whole Life," *Fox News Latino* (November 19, 2013). (latino.foxnews.com/latino/politics/2013/11/18/elian-gonzalez-my-time-in-us-marked-me-for-my-whole-life).

[195] Juan Flores, Maria Ilcheva, and Dario Moreno, "Hispanic Vote in Florida 2004 Election," in Rudy de la Garza, David Leal, and Louis DeSipio (eds.), *Latinos in the 2004 Election* (Boulder, CO: Westview Press, 2008).

Officially, Bush won Florida by slightly more than five hundred votes, with 82 percent of the Cuban American vote. In near-unprecedented unity, Cuban Americans supported Bush: despite Gore having sided with Elián's Miami relatives.[196] Cuban Americans were irate over the White House's handling of Elián, and Gore was tainted by association.[197] Seventy-nine percent of Cuban Americans in Miami felt Elián should have been able to stay in the United States with relatives.[198]

So enraged were Cuban Americans about the raid that they defended Bush when his presidential victory was disputed. They intimidated officials in charge of a Florida recount, and blocked validation of the vote.[199] Siding with fellow Cuban Americans, Mayor Penelas refused to provide security for a recount, which the South Florida Cuban American Republican members of Congress opposed.[200] Although Gore conceded the election, an investigation subsequently concluded that more Floridians had gone to the polls to vote for him than for Bush.[201] President Clinton admitted that he had worked for eight years to strengthen support for Democrats in Florida, among Cuban Americans in particular, but that the controversy over Elián wiped out most gains.[202]

Meanwhile, the controversy over Elián transformed the Cuban American community. The battle contributed to declining support for the Foundation. The strength of the Foundation had partially rested on its ability to speak in one voice for the Cuban American community. US-born Jorge Mas Santos, who took over the Foundation helm when his father passed away in 1997, had tried to broker a deal to reunite Elián and his father that "hardline" Foundation members opposed.[203] "Hard-

---

[196] In 1980, 86 percent of Cuban Americans in Dade County had voted for Reagan. Edward Cody, " In Miami, It's 'Reagan, Si'," *Washington Post* (May 21, 1983) (www.washingtonpost.com/archive/politics/1983/05/21/in-miami-its-reagan-si).

[197] Alex Leary, "Marco Rubio's Close Encounter with Elian Gonzalez," *Tampa Bay Times* (May 19, 2015) (www.tampabay.com/blogs/the-buzz-florida-politics/marco-rubio...).

[198] FIU-IPOR, *FIU/Cuba Poll* 2000 (Miami: Florida International University (FIU), Institute for Public Opinion Research (IPOR), 2000).

[199] William Finnegan, "The Cuban Strategy," *New Yorker* (March 15, 2004), p. 70.

[200] Francisco Aruca ran two well-known more liberal radio programs, one in Spanish, and the other in English. However, he did not own the media station that aired the programs. The Committee for Cuban Democracy also briefly ran a centrist radio program.

[201] Ford Fessenden and John Broder, "Examining the Vote: The Overview," *New York Times* (November 12, 2001) (www.nytimes.com/2001/11/12/us/examining-vote-overview-study-disputed-florida-ballot).

[202] Clinton, *My Life*, pp. 904–5.

[203] Lizette Álvarez, "A Crusader Carves a Niche with Boy's Case," *New York Times* (April 19, 2000), p. 16.

liners" blamed Mas Santos for their defeat in the battle over Elián. They claimed he was an ineffective leader. Elián's father's paternity rights did not matter to them. Disillusioned, they broke off to form a new group, the Cuban Liberty Council, the CLC. In the process, the Foundation's active membership, its financial base, and its influence within the Cuban American community became a shadow of its former self.

The failed battle to keep Elián in America also became a transformative experience for some Cuban Americans. For example, prominent businessman Carlos Saladrigas, who had been so active in the campaign to keep Elián in America that he was in the house of the Miami relatives at the time of the government raid,[204] shifted from being a "hard-liner" to a US–Cuba cross-border bridge-builder after losing the battle to "save Elián." In an interview, he noted that the Elián affair changed the dynamics of the Miami community, and changed him. "We didn't realize how much damage we were doing to ourselves and to our image ... By refusing to hand Elián over, Cuban Americans had hoped to humiliate Castro. It backfired badly."[205] Saladrigas went on to form a nonpartisan not-for-profit group of businessmen and professionals, the Cuba Study Group, dedicated to developing civil society and small businesses in Cuba, and the cross-border reunification of Cuban peoples. His group, however, never captured the hearts and minds of the Cuban American community as had the Foundation in its heyday.

The battle over innocent Elián, in sum, had wide-ranging consequences. While rooted in US Cuban immigration policy, it unleashed divisions within the Cuban American community that had the unintended effect of weakening Cuban Americans' collective political clout.

CONCLUSION

Although Clinton assumed the presidency after the United States won the Cold War, he continued, in the main, to privilege Cuban immigrants. When faced with an immigration crisis, he retracted one Cuban entitlement. However, he maintained other entitlements of old and granted additional entitlements to Cubans.

By the time President Clinton faced the makings of "another Mariel," previous privileging had transformed earlier Cuban immigrants into an

---

[204] He was on the phone with the Attorney General trying to negotiate a solution to the Elián crisis when the raid occurred.
[205] Padgett, "How the Battle over Elian Gonzalez Helped Change U.S. Cuba Policy."

influential domestic political force that pressed for continued privileging of "their people." In social science terminology, Cuban beneficiaries of entitlements as a "dependent variable," the result of Cold War politics, became an "independent variable" in the post-Cold War, an independent force contributing to the continued privileging of Cuban immigrants. Like President Carter, President Clinton initially tried to block large numbers of unauthorized Cubans from coming ashore, only to reverse his stance when he was faced with exile opposition. Building on earlier precedent, with his own political ambitions in mind, he proceeded to admit tens of thousands of unauthorized Cubans and to grant new, unique entitlements to Cubans.

Clinton responded to pressure from earlier Cuban immigrants against countervailing pressures from politicized anti-immigrant native-born Americans. The "nativists" were hostile to the surge in unauthorized immigration, from other countries as well as from Cuba. Absent Cold War foreign policy concerns, Clinton dexterously responded to conflicting demands of anti-immigrationists and Cuban Americans, by appealing in different ways to each constituency.

Meanwhile, as Cuban Americans became a political force in their own right, they fueled domestic as well as bilateral tensions and ceased to be the unequivocal political asset that Eisenhower imagined when first singling them out for special entitlements. On two occasions under Clinton's presidency Cuban Americans strained US–Cuba relations. They even challenged the legitimacy of a presidential election. Earlier privileging accustomed them to press for policies that they wanted.

In turn, Cuban Americans' failed effort to block the return of six-year-old Elian to his father in Cuba after his mother had died at sea trying to immigrate without authorization had the unintended effect of unleashing a political divide within the Cuban American community that deepened after Clinton's presidency, as detailed in Chapter 6. Amid the divide, "hard-liners" managed to secure additional entitlements from President Clinton's successor, George W. Bush, but not from Bush's successor, Barack Obama. The next chapter details how, by the time of President Obama's second term in office, Clinton-era Cuban immigration policies had the unintended effect of unleashing yet another surge in illegal Cuban immigration. The surge deepened the divide within the Cuban American community, and created conditions that contributed to President Obama officially reining in over fifty years of Cuban privileging with little political pushback.

6

From Further Expansion to the Unraveling of Cuban Privileging amid Mainly Exclusion of Haitians

The George W. Bush and Barack Obama Administrations

After President Clinton signed the 1994 and 1995 bilateral migration accords, lawful Cuban immigration dramatically increased, while unauthorized immigration dramatically decreased: through the remainder of his administration. He achieved his goal of making Cuban immigration safe, legal, and orderly, a modest goal compared to that of previous presidents who sought to leverage immigration to bring the Castro-led regime to heel.

How effective, however, were the accords in regulating Cuban immigration after President Clinton left office? If Cold War concerns had been the driving force behind Cuban immigration policy, subsequent administrations should have further reined in Cuban entitlements. Indeed, Clinton's successor, Republican George W. Bush (Bush II), prioritized a "war on terrorism" over containing communism in the few remaining communist countries once he was faced with the World Trade Center attack on September 11, 2001, a half year into his presidency. Yet, as detailed in this chapter, vis á vis Cuba he prolonged the Cold War. His administration continued to privilege Cubans. So too did that of his Democrat successor, Barack Obama, even after reestablishing full diplomatic relations with Cuba: through the remainder of Fidel's, and most of his brother Raúl's rule, including after Fidel died in November 2016. Raúl assumed temporary control of the country in July 2006, when Fidel fell ill, and permanent control in 2008.

There remained a "stickiness" to Cuban privileging. Under the Bush administration, Cuban immigrant beneficiaries of entitlements in the past pressed for not only the continuation but also the expansion of entitlements for "their people." President Bush was responsive. He expanded Cubans' path of privilege and lifted certain of President Clinton's restrictions on Cuban immigrants. In turn, President Obama honored the entitlements that President Bush, and his predecessors, had instituted. However, he did not extend new entitlements to Cubans. Then, without public forewarning, in his last full week in office he reversed policy. He ended Cuban exceptionalism "as we knew it" for over half a century.

After describing the entitlements President Bush implemented and President Obama continued for his eight years in office, the focus of this chapter shifts to detailing how and why President Obama ended more than half a century of Cuban privileging as he left office. Then, the focus shifts to Haitian immigration policy. Both the Bush and Obama administrations denied Haitians entitlements that they extended to Cubans, even amid stepped-up violence, repression, poverty, and persecution in Haiti. After a devastating earthquake, President Obama did extend temporary entitlements to Haitian immigrants. Yet, even then, Haitians did not receive comparable entitlements to those offered to Cubans. The United States continued to treat Cubans and Haitians differently, even if less so than in years past.

NEW CUBAN ENTITLEMENTS UNDER THE BUSH II ADMINISTRATION

After the terrorist attack on the World Trade Center, President Bush focused on what became known as the Bush Doctrine. The United States began attacking countries that harbored and assisted terrorists: especially in the Middle East. Yet, he did not bury his hostility toward Cuba and a commitment to regime change there. Even after Fidel fell ill and officially relinquished power to his brother Raúl, who had been second in command for decades, President Bush did not take advantage of the opportunity to try to improve bilateral relations. Instead, he extended new entitlements to Cuban immigrants that were intended to enhance family reunification, encourage immigration through lawful channels, and destabilize the Cuban government. In turn, with his Secretary of State, Condoleeza Rice, he encouraged "the Cuban people to work at home for positive change" and not turn to "alien smuggling" to enter the United States.[1]

---

[1] "Cuba's Future Political Scenarios and U.S. Policy Approaches, August–September 2006" (www.everycrsreport.com/reports/RL33622.html#_Toc234038435). See Antonio Aja Díaz, *Al Cruzar las Fronteras* (Havana: Centro de Estudios Demográficos, Universidad de La Habana, 2009) for an excellent analysis of the Cuban perspective of anticipated changes in US immigration policy.

Globalization of Cuban Immigration Privileging

The month after Raúl temporarily took over the reins of government in August 2006, President Bush extended Cuban immigration entitlements globally. He implemented the Cuban Medical Professional Parole Program (CMPPP), which allowed Cubans on official medical missions overseas to defect to the United States. In transnationalizing Cuban entitlements, the program built on precedent set by President Johnson when he granted Cubans in third countries unique immigration rights, which Presidents Nixon and Reagan continued when they granted Cubans safely settled in Spain special rights to immigrate to the United States as refugees. However, President Bush's initiative was particularly mean-spirited: as if the Cold War had not ended. The CMPPP was premised on manipulating immigration policy anew to destabilize the Cuban government.

The CMPPP permitted (and tacitly encouraged) Cuban doctors, nurses, paramedics, physical therapists, labor technicians, and sports trainers who were serving on official Cuban overseas missions to abandon their assignments and immigrate to the United States. The CMPPP enabled a new group of Cubans to circumvent congressional-regulated immigration and the visa queue that other nationals faced. It entitled the Cuban healthcare professionals working abroad to be paroled into the United States on the basis of their country of origin, despite the Immigration and Naturalization Act stipulating that parole be granted only on a case-by-case basis and only for an "urgent humanitarian reason" or "significant public benefit" (see Chapter 1). After one year in the United States, CMPPP beneficiaries could become legal permanent residents, and qualify for associated rights.

Although the CMPPP brought limited humanitarian and public benefit to the United States, it jeopardized the health welfare of people in the countries where the medics had served. When Cuban health workers overseas took advantage of the CMPPP, they deprived poor people where they had worked of medical care. The Bush administration was indifferent to that. It focused, instead, on the effects the CMPPP might have on Cuba: on undermining the Cuban government's ability to conduct medical diplomacy and to generate hard currency revenue from overseas health service contracts.[2]

The 50,000 healthcare workers the Cuban government assigned to overseas missions reflected the importance that it assigned to its

---

[2] Julie Feinsilver, *Healing the Masses: Cuban Health Politics at Home and Abroad* (Berkeley: University of California Press, 1993).

international medical assistance programs. The medics were to earn $8 billion for the Cuban government, more, at the time, than any other single export either of goods or services. The government had creatively transformed its investment in human capital, in the training of healthcare professionals, into a hard currency-generating export, to offset loss of sugar earnings when Soviet bloc trade ground to a halt.[3] Cuba needed hard currency to finance imports and investments.

Cuban exiles had lobbied for the CMPPP. President Bush responded, indebted to them for their help in the 2000 presidential election, when they blocked the Florida recount that assured him the Florida electoral college vote, and the national election, in turn. Cuban Americans also helped him win reelection in 2004, though winning Florida was not as pivotal in that victory. The CMPPP was payback.

The exiles who lobbied for the CMPPP were associated with the group that split off from the Cuban American National Foundation after Mas Canosa died and the organization, under the leadership of his son, adopted a more conciliatory stance toward Cuba. More importantly, they organized a new PAC, the US–Cuba Democracy PAC. The PAC quickly became the main collective source of Cuban American campaign contributions (and associated influence). The Free Cuba PAC lost its financial base when the Cuban American National Foundation splintered.

A New Family Immigration Entitlement

In 2007 President Bush initiated the Cuban Family Reunification Parole Program (CFRPP) that enabled yet more Cubans to benefit from special immigration rights. Compared to the CMPPP, the CFRPP was less controversial, less politically ambitious, and less corrosive of US–Cuban relations. The CFRPP allowed island relatives of Cubans in the United States who were either US citizens or lawful permanent residents to be paroled into the country while waiting for one of the twenty thousand visas that the United States had agreed, in the 1994–1995 bilateral migration accords, to issue yearly.[4]

---

[3] Marc Frank, "Cuba Ups Healthcare Sector Pay, Says Medical Export Earnings to Rise," *Reuters* (March 21, 2014) (www.reuters.com/article/cuba-reform-healthcare/cuba-ups-healthcare-sector-pay-says-medical-export-earnings-to-rise-idUSL2N0MI0C92014032).

[4] As early as August 2006, the DHS had announced that the US Citizenship and Immigration Services Agency (USCIS) would use its discretionary parole authority to increase the number of Cubans with family in the United States that it would admit, without increasing the total number of Cuban migrants. It admitted approximately 21,000

Once they were in the United States, CFRPP beneficiaries enjoyed work rights, even when they were not official "green card" holders, lawful permanent residents. The CFRPP thereby became another means by which Cubans could circumvent immigration regulations that Washington applied to other nationals. Together with previously granted entitlements, particularly the CAA, the CFRPP, like the CMPPP, had a Cuban-privileging multiplier effect. It put Cuban immigrants on a path to citizenship, welfare, and other rights.

The CFRPP was family-friendly in that it enabled relatives to reunite in the United States faster than was possible through normal legal immigration processing. It did, however, give some Cubans an advantage over others: namely, those with relatives who had previously emigrated. The CFRPP thus reinforced racial biases of earlier Cuban immigration policies. In turn, it gave Cubans an advantage over other nationals who were subject to the United States' regional yearly admission cap, with no expedited means of entry.

Reinstitution of a Formerly Retracted Entitlement: Formal Admission of Cubans Entering the United States in "Irregular Ways"

President Bush never publicly challenged, but in practice defied, President Clinton's formal commitment, in the US–Cuba Joint Communique on Migration, to deny entry rights to Cubans who arrived in "irregular ways": a commitment that Clinton's INS commissioner tacitly nullified in her 1999 Meisner Memo, in specifying that Cubans could enter the United States anywhere, visa-less, and be admitted into the country. The Bush administration paroled into the United States Cubans who arrived by land in "irregular ways," with "dry feet," all the while that it enforced President Clinton's "wet foot" policy, of repatriating Cubans that the Coast Guard interdicted at sea.

While nearly all unauthorized Cubans had arrived by sea when the Clinton administration negotiated the 1994 and 1995 migration agreements, after the turn of the century that ceased to be the case, in part because the Cuban and US governments effectively policed the Florida Straits. Instead, during Bush's presidency, Cubans in stepped-up numbers found ways to enter the United States visa-less by land, via Mexico.

Cubans in this manner. Cubans who attempted to enter the United States illegally were ineligible for the CFRPP. Office of the Press Secretary, DHS, "DHS Announces Additional Measures to Combat Alien Smuggling of Cubans," August 11, 2006.

Immigration authorities admitted them, per Meisner Memo, entitling them, after a year with parole status, to become lawful permanent residents (LPRs). The number of Cubans attaining LPR status rose from 18,960 in 2000, the year before Bush took office, to 49,500 in 2008, his last year in office: an average of 30,222 a year.[5] Over 80 percent of them were admitted as "refugees and asylees," without proof that they had fled persecution and without having been screened and selected abroad, in compliance with Congress-mandated immigration regulations. The typical Cuban "refugee" or "asylee" entered the United States in an "irregular way" and then drew on the CAA to adjust his or her status.

Conceding to pressure from Cuban Americans with close ties to his administration, in 2007 President Bush even agreed to allow imprisoned Posada Carriles released on bail. Posada Carriles was the Cuban American terrorist known for having committed crimes against humanity, most notably for masterminding the 1976 shoot down of the Cuban airplane with seventy-three passengers aboard. In 2005, he illegally had (re)entered the United States. President Bush had permitted Posada Carriles' release from jail at the same time that he ordered *alleged* Muslim terrorists associated with 9/11 to be detained, without trial, under deplorable conditions at the US naval base in Guantanamo. Posada Carriles was a terrorist of a different sort: a relic of the Cold War, backed by politically well-connected Cuban Americans.

The Bush administration admitted the unauthorized Cubans while strategizing to foment regime change on the island, as if the Cold War had not ended, and by means other than the CMPPP. In a near five hundred-page report released in May 2004, and in a briefer, follow-up report released two years later, the Bush administration addressed ways to block Fidel's succession to his brother Raúl; greater restrictions on tourism, travel, and remittance-sending to Cuba, to deprive the Cuban government of hard currency revenue; and assistance to dissidents.[6]

When leaving the door ajar for unauthorized Cubans to come, President Bush pursued a combination of inclusionary and exclusionary

---

[5] Department of Homeland Security (DHS), *Yearbook of Immigration Statistics 2010* (through 2018) (www.dhs.gov/sites/default/files/publications/Yearbook_Immigration_Statistics_2010.pdf), Table 2 and "LPR_adjustment_by_year-of-entry-2000-2018."

[6] US Department of State, *Commission for Assistance to a Free Cuba*, Report to the President, May 2004 (US Department of State Archive, https://2001-2009.state.gov/p/wha/rt/cuba/index.htm). It released a follow-up report in July 2006 (*Second Report of the Commission for Assistance to a Free Cuba and the Compact with the Cuban People*, (https://2001-2009.state.gov/secretary/rm/2006/68776.htm).

measures toward unauthorized immigrants from other countries. In May 2006 he delivered the first prime-time presidential address on immigration, in which, building on IRCA, he called for improved border enforcement and improved verification of the legal status of workers, but also for granting the then-estimated 12 million unauthorized immigrants in the country a path to citizenship.[7] IRCA, enacted in 1986, had failed to stop illegal immigration.

In his 2007 State of the Union speech, President Bush repeated his call for immigration reform. Together with the Speaker of the House, Democrat Nancy Pelosi, he urged Congress to pass a bipartisan immigration bill. However, he faced opposition from members of his own party, who were averse to what they considered an amnesty rewarding illegal immigration. Consequently, his proposed reform never came to a vote, and the millions of immigrants from countries other than Cuba who had entered the United States in "irregular ways" remained unable to follow unauthorized Cubans' CAA-based path to lawful permanent presidency.

****

The eight-year Bush presidency thus ended with continued privileging of Cubans over other nationals. Bush's administration not only honored Cuban entitlements of the past but also extended new entitlements to new Cubans. While the privileging of Cubans became ever more detached from his primary foreign policy preoccupation after 9/11, his "war on terrorism," he never fully buried the Cold War concern with regime change in Cuba. Cuban Americans, who were important to his 2000 electoral victory, pressed for new immigrant entitlements, along with other policies, to foment regime change in Cuba to which they remained committed.

THE OBAMA ADMINISTRATION NO CHANGE TO MAJOR CHANGE IN CUBAN IMMIGRATION POLICY

Unlike his predecessors, President Obama extended no new entitlement(s) to Cubans. However, he enforced entitlements of the past. Even after he announced plans, in December 2014, to reestablish full diplomatic ties with Cuba and normalize US–Cuban relations, he explicitly noted that US

---

[7] "Bush's Speech on Immigration," *New York Times* (May 15, 2006) (www.nytimes.com/2006/05/15/washington/15text-bush.html).

immigration policy would not change: a commitment he maintained until eight days before leaving office. At the same time, he did reinstate routine bilateral migration meetings, which President Bush had discontinued in deference to the "hardline" Cuban Americans who considered them a conciliatory gesture toward the Cuban government.

Eight-Year Enforcement of Entitlements of the Past

Building on policies of the past, President Obama not only implemented but expanded the US commitment to President Bush's Cuban Medical Professional Parole Program, the CMPPP. By 2010, US consulates in sixty-five countries had issued approximately 1,600 CMPPP visas to overseas Cuban healthcare professionals,[8] and by the end of 2015 the United States had approved over 7,000 applicants.[9]

President Obama expanded the CMPPP even though the program was not problem-free. Cuban medics who were on overseas assignments, for example, very publicly rebelled when the United States did not admit them in a timely manner. This was true of Cuban healthcare professionals in Colombia who had planned to use the CMPPP to immigrate. They protested when they were not paroled into the United States. In 2015, hundreds of Cuban doctors, dentists, and nurses who had been assigned to medical missions in Venezuela fled to Colombia, with the expectation that the US Embassy there would admit them into the United States. When they were not admitted, they rallied in Bogota to raise awareness of their plight and to pressure the United States to admit them.[10] They believed that the CMPPP entitled them to admission to the United States, outside regular immigration channels.

Meanwhile, President Obama made no effort to end other unique entitlements that Cuban immigrants enjoyed. Like his presidential predecessors, he did not try to convince Congress to sunset the CAA, controversial as it was: not even when promoting a new comprehensive immigration reform in 2013. Also, as detailed later in this chapter, his

---

[8] Fox News, "Little Known Immigration Program Allows Cuban Doctors to Easily Defect to U.S." (January 16, 2011) (www.foxnews.com/us/2011/01/16/cuban-docs-defect-little-known).

[9] Cuba Journal, "US May End Cuban Medical Professional Parole Program," *Cuba Journal* (January 8, 2016) (http://cubajournal.co/us-may-end-cuban-medical-profesional-parole-program).

[10] Jim Wyss, "Fate of Fleeing Cuban Doctors Not Part of Negotiations with Island: U.S. State Department," *Cuba Verdad* (August 21, 2015) (www.cubaverdad.net/weblog/2015/08/fate-of-fleeing-cuban-doctors).

The George W. Bush and Barack Obama Administrations 249

administration paroled Cubans who arrived by land in "irregular ways" into the United States, and in stepped up numbers. The Mexican government was complicit. In that it considered Cuban migration to be primarily a US problem, it allowed Cubans to transit through Mexico to reach Texas and California.[11]

The Obama administration did invest in trying to transform Mexico into a buffer country to keep out unauthorized immigrants, Cubans included. It provided Mexico with financial resources, border infrastructure, and training. Building on programs that the Bush administration had introduced, such as the Merida Initiative, a security cooperation agreement to combat drug trafficking, transnational organized crime, and money laundering, the Obama administration helped improve Mexico's migration control capacity, to prevent unauthorized migrants from reaching the United States.[12] Its efforts to involve Mexico in blocking immigrants from the United States did not, however, keep Cubans who were determined to immigrate to the United States from coming.

The Build-Up of Bilateral Trust

Although Cuban authorities were angered by the expanded CMPPP, the migration talks that President Obama reinstituted helped to build bilateral trust. They provided an opportunity for the United States and Cuba to address their respective concerns. President Obama, for example, used the occasion of the talks to press for the release of Alan Gross, who the Cuban government had arrested in 2009 for intelligence-related activities associated with a Bush administration Agency for International Development "democracy promotion program."

In December 2014 bilateral trust built up to the point that the United States and Cuba agreed to reestablish full diplomatic ties and "normalize" relations. When it announced the plan, the Cuban government agreed to free Gross, and the United States simultaneously freed Cuban spies. These were the first steps in the official commitment of the two countries to improve bilateral relations.

In turn, in conjunction with "normalizing" relations, the Cuban government pressed for changes in US Cuba immigration policy.[13] It wanted

---

[11] David Scott FitzGerald, *Refuge beyond Reach* (New York: Oxford University Press), p. 119.
[12] Ibid., pp. 139–140.
[13] Reuters, "U.S. and Cuba Clash over Immigration at Start of Historic Talks" (January 22, 2015) (www.newsweek.com/us-cuba-clash-over-immigration-start-historic-talks/).

the United States to revoke both the CAA and the CMPPP. Josafina Vidal of the Cuban Ministry of Foreign Affairs (MINREX), Cuba's chief negotiator in the US–Cuban rapprochement, assailed the CMPPP as a "reprehensible brain drain practice," and the CAA as undermining the 1994 and 1995 bilateral migration agreements that were designed to promote safe, legal, and orderly immigration.[14] Cuban officials argued that the CAA encouraged Cubans to immigrate without authorization, knowing that on reaching US soil they would be admitted. Yet, when the two governments began to address trade, investment, travel, counter-narcotics, and environment matters of mutual concern, the Obama administration insisted that neither the CAA nor the CMPPP would be on the negotiating table. Immigration policy remained unchanged.

Retraction of Cuban Immigration Entitlements: Cubans' Reversal of Fortune

During his last full week in office, President Obama ended his no-change-in-Cuban-immigration-policy, without any prior public warning. On January 12, 2017 he announced, "Today the United States is taking important steps forward to normalize relations with Cuba to bring greater consistency to our immigration policy."[15] The United States would treat "Cuban migrants the same way we treat migrants from other countries." Effective immediately, "Cuban nationals who attempt to enter the United States illegally and do not qualify for humanitarian relief will be subject to removal."

President Obama used the occasion to portray most Cubans as immigrants, not refugees. He also noted that the new policy would enhance Cubans' ability to determine their own destiny. Over half a century after Castro took power in order to break Washington's imperialist yoke over Cuba, President Obama stated that "the future of Cuba should be in the hands of the Cuban people." President Obama implied that the United States had stood in Cuba's way, including with respect to immigration.

Most noteworthy, President Obama officially repealed the "dry foot" policy of paroling Cubans who arrived by land in "irregular ways" into the United States. If they were not officially admitted, "irregular entrants," in principle, could not adjust their status on the basis of the

---

[14] Ibid.
[15] "Statement by the President on Cuban Immigration Policy" (January 12, 2017) (https://obamawhitehouse.archives.gov/the-press-office/2017/01/12).

CAA. Instead, they would join the millions of unauthorized immigrants from other countries, and be subject to deportation. They also would not be entitled to work and other legal rights.

Jeh Johnson, Obama's Secretary of the Department of Homeland Security (DHS), noted that the policy of encouraging the parole of Cuban nationals, which enabled them to qualify for relief under the CAA, was outdated.[16] He added that, effective immediately, the DHS would consider Cuban requests for parole in the same manner as requests filed by nationals of other countries. Political asylum remained an option, but only for Cubans who successfully demonstrated well-founded evidence that they had fled actual or likely persecution.

At the same time, the Obama administration announced the retraction of two other Cuban entitlements.[17] Cubans would no longer be exempt from the expedited removal proceedings to which Clinton era legislation had subjected other unauthorized arrivals, in a nod to "anti-immigrationists." Going forward, visa-less Cubans would be subject to removal unless they qualified for asylum.[18] The Obama administration also terminated the CMPPP, after having expanded it, explaining that "The U.S. and Cuba are working together to combat diseases that endanger the health and lives of our people. By providing preferential treatment to Cuban medical personnel, the medical parole program contradicts those efforts, and risks harming the Cuban people."[19]

Meanwhile, the Obama administration negotiated with Havana authorities procedures for returning to Cuba Cubans who the United States deemed inadmissible. It convinced the Cuban government to accept not only the repatriation of Cubans that the US Coast Guard found at sea trying to immigrate without authorization, which had been common

---

[16] The DHS, formed in 2002, replaced (and expanded on) the INS.
[17] US Department of Homeland Security (DHS), "Fact Sheet: Changes to Parole and Expedited Removal Policies Affecting Cuban Nationals" (January 12, 2017) (www.dhs.gov/sites/default/files/publications/DHS%20Fact%20sheet%20FINAL.pdf).
[18] The Mexican government, in turn, signed an agreement with Cuba to deport unauthorized migrants who entered its territory. Nora Gámez Torres, "For Cubans Stranded in Third Countries, Few Options Remain," *Miami Herald* (February 4, 2017) (www.miamiherald.com/news/nation-world/americas/Cuba...).
[19] Mimi Whitefield, "Obama Ends Controversial Policy That Allowed Cubans to Enter U.S. without Visas," *Miami Herald* (January 12, 2017) (www.miamiherald.com/news/nation-world/americas/Cuba). In 2005 the Supreme Court had ruled that the US government could not indefinitely detain Mariel Cubans. They remained in America because the Cuban government blocked their return.

practice since implementation of the 1995 migration accord, but also the return of Mariel "excludables" that presidents since 1980 had failed to convince Cuban authorities to accept.[20] In addition, it convinced the Cuban government to consider, on a case by case basis, the return of tens of thousands of other Cubans who had received deportation orders since 1980 for crimes committed in the United States, and to accept, in the future, Cubans that the United States ordered to be removed.[21] Ironically, Cuba became the only country with which the United States negotiated both deportation and repatriation agreements, despite over a half century of bilateral tensions. The Cuban government thereby became an agent of US exclusion.

The two governments also committed to cooperate to prevent alien smuggling, as well as aircraft and boat hijackings. These were longstanding concerns of both governments. Previous efforts to rein in human smuggling had not succeeded.

Remaining Entitlements

While one administration after another had honored and expanded Cuban rights to special immigration entitlements for nearly sixty years, President Obama reined in the privileging. However, he did not end all Cuban entitlements.

Remaining entitlements included the Cuban Family Reunification Parole Program that allowed family-sponsored immigration applicants to move to the United States while they were in the immigration visa queue; the entitlement of minimally 20,000 Cubans to immigration visas yearly; the ability of Cubans to apply in-country for admission to the United States as refugees; the right to federally funded welfare on arrival in the United States; and eligibility for lawful permanent residence, on the basis of the CAA, should they enter the United States without authorization and escape detection for a year. The CAA remained in effect, despite President Obama diminishing its significance when he ended Cuban entitlement to parole entry. Obama made it known that he would welcome sunsetting the CAA, but with a Republican-controlled Congress, he

---

[20] President Obama's migration agreement allowed the United States to substitute new people for those on the original list of "inadmissibles" who had died.
[21] Frances Robles, "For Cubans, An Expulsion Long Delayed" *New York Times* (January 15, 2017), pp. 1, 9.

could not secure the necessary support (especially when revising Cuban immigration policy in his last full week in office).

With the CAA still on the books, Cubans could enter the United States without immigration visas and still qualify for CAA-based status adjustment rights.[22] If they were dual citizens of another country, such as Spain (a "visa waiver country"), and of Cuba, they could be inspected and admitted to the United States for three months. If they proceeded to stay in the United States for a year, they could draw on the CAA to become lawful permanent residents. During the interim nine months, however, they had no work or other rights, and they were subject to removal and deportation if caught..

Also, Cubans who entered as tourists might stay beyond the date on which their temporary entry visa expired and apply for asylum. However, they no longer benefited from the presumption that they fled persecution. Thus, they needed to prove that they fled persecution or that they would likely suffer persecution if they returned to Cuba. Should their case not be finalized within a year they could apply for CAA-based lawful permanent residency. During the course of the year, they, like dual citizens, would be ineligible for government benefits and work authorization, and could be subject to removal proceedings and have their residency status revoked. Furthermore, should they return to Cuba for any reason while waiting to have their status adjusted, they would unlikely win their asylum claims since return-visits demonstrated that persecution was not a problem.

Without a tourist visa, Cubans who arrived at a US border could request asylum. However, they, like other asylum seekers, needed to convince immigration judges that they warranted refuge.

In sum, President Obama reined in Cubans' path of privilege that one administration after another had honored and expanded on since Castro assumed power in 1959. Nonetheless, he left in place entitlements that were embedded in bilateral agreements, entitlements only Congress had the authority to revoke, and one entitlement President Bush (II) had implemented that drew on his discretionary authority.

WHY PRESIDENT OBAMA RETRACTED CUBAN ENTITLEMENTS

Why did President Obama break the more than fifty-year precedent of granting unique entitlements to Cubans? And why would he make the

---

[22] Whitefield, "Deciphering the New U.S. Policies That Affect Cuban Migrants," *Miami Herald* (January 13, 2017) (www.miamiherald.com/news/nation-world/americas/Cuba).

path-breaking decision in his last full week in office? A number of factors contributed to his decision.

First, President Obama was deeply committed to the normalization of relations with Cuba as part of his presidential legacy. As he noted, immigration reform marked one more step in the normalization process, one that had taken considerable time to negotiate.

President Obama stopped allowing Cubans to be paroled into the United States also to regain control over the country's borders. Under his presidency, unauthorized immigration had spun out of control, the antithesis of the driving principles of the 1994 and 1995 migration agreements. Immigration had once again become unsafe, illegal, and disorderly. In the years leading up to Obama's policy change, Cubans coming to the United States without authorization outnumbered those whose immigration was authorized. Only in 1980, the year of Mariel, had more visa-less Cubans entered the United States than in 2016: a time when Cubans lacked a legal migration option, which they had during Obama's presidency. In addition to the approximately 20,000 Cubans to whom the United States granted visas, in conjunction with the Clinton administration-negotiated migration agreement, in FY2016 nearly 57,000 visa-less migrants entered the United States by land: a "Land Mariel" of sorts. The number of unauthorized arrivals would have been even greater had the Coast Guard not apprehended more than 5,000 Cubans at sea (more than from any other country).[23]

When he was on the verge of leaving office, President Obama responded differently to the large influx of unauthorized Cubans under his watch than had Presidents Johnson, Carter, and Clinton, who, after attempting to block mass unauthorized migrations of Cubans, admitted them. President Obama responded differently because the underpinnings of Cuban privileging, first Cold War geopolitics and then political pressure from Cuban American beneficiaries of earlier entitlements, by 2014 were history. The "land Mariel" built up against the backdrop of President Obama's commitment to improve bilateral relations. Both he and Raúl Castro wanted to put a stop to a new surge in unauthorized migration, each for their own reasons: President Obama to regain control over America's borders and contain Cuban immigration to lawful channels, and Raúl Castro to halt the

---

[23] Congressional Research Service, "Cuba: U.S. Policy in the 116th Congress," May 14, 2020 (https://fas.org/sgp/crs/row/R45657.pdf); DHS, *Yearbook(s) of Immigration Statistics FY 2016–2018* (www.dhs.gov/immigration-statistics/yearbook/2016, 2017, 2018/table10; DHS, lpr_adjustments_by-year_of_entry_2000_2018; Jens Manuel Krogstad, "Surge in Cuban Immigration to US Continued through 2016," *PEW Research Center* (July 13, 2017) (www.pewresearch.org/).

"bleeding" of the island population, particularly the younger generation on which the country's future depended.

In addition, in his parting days in office President Obama had little to lose politically in revoking unique Cuban entitlements. He was not concerned with reelection. Also, he was not constrained by Cuban Americans who pressured for special Cuban immigrant entitlements. By January of 2017 the Cuban American community had changed in ways that created an opening for President Obama to retract Cuban entitlements with minimal political pushback.

For one, as is well known, "money speaks." By the time President Obama had announced his policy change, Cuban Americans were no longer the campaign finance powerhouse that they had been since the 1980s. After 2008, US–Cuba Democracy PAC campaign contributions declined. Although the main Cuban American PAC since 2004, in the 2014 and 2016 election cycle, the PAC contributed one-third as much money to political candidates as in 2008. With lower revenue intake, the PAC slashed the number of campaigns to which it contributed; it reduced the average size of contributions to campaigns; and it directed most of the diminished funds to Republicans. After allotting 59 percent of its campaign contributions to Democrats in 2008 and 2010, Democrats received only 36 and 17 percent of the PAC's diminished campaign contributions in 2014 and 2016, respectively. Moreover, while top Cuban American donors had given to presidential candidates of both political parties in the past, they did not contribute to President Obama's campaign. Obama thus was far less constrained in his policymaking by Cuban American financial contributors than other presidents since the 1980s.

In addition, in curtailing Cuban entitlements President Obama addressed a claimed concern of his: fairness in treatment of diverse immigrant groups. When he announced the retraction of Cuban parole rights, he noted that Cubans thereby would be treated the same as migrants from other countries. Immigrant rights groups had been critical of the United States admitting tens of thousands of unauthorized Cubans while deporting Haitians who had fled a country where conditions were far worse than in Cuba. Indeed, Haitian rights activists were pleased when President Obama's 2017 Executive Order leveled the playing field for Cuban and Haitian immigrants.[24] Mexican Americans, who complained that Mexicans were deported while Cubans received green

---

[24] Whitefield, "Deciphering the New U.S. Policies That Affect Cuban Migrants."

cards,[25] also were pleased with cutbacks in special Cuban entitlements. Yet, concern with equity cannot explain why President Obama waited until his last full week in office to rescind Cuban entitlements. Indeed, had he prioritized fair treatment among immigrant groups, he would have proposed the retraction of Cuban entitlements in 2013 when he tried to get Congress to pass an immigration reform bill (described later in the chapter).

The Obama administration offered another rationale, specifically for ending the "dry foot" policy. Deputy National Security Adviser Ben Rhodes stated: "It's important that Cuba continue to have a young, dynamic population that (sic) are clearly serving as agents of change."[26] Typically, Cuban immigrants were young adults, the most employable in the United States and the most willing to take on the risks of migration, including the treacherous trek through Central America and Mexico that Cubans, at the time, pursued to reach the United States by land. Rhodes' commentary marked the first time that the United States had presented a generational-based argument for immigration policy. Even so, his argument cannot account for the major policy shift, which President Obama announced only as he departed the White House.

In essence, multiple considerations contributed to President Obama reining in Cuban immigration entitlements. Above all, the continued privileging of Cubans was at odds with the US-Cuba bridge-building foreign policy to which he was committed. At the same time, domestic pressure for privileging Cubans dissipated, as detailed later in the chapter. President Obama took advantage of the changed conditions to change Cuban immigration policy.

WHY THE SURGE IN UNAUTHORIZED CUBAN IMMIGRATION?

If the Clinton administration had negotiated two complementary accords to make immigration safe, legal, and orderly, then why did the number of unauthorized Cuban arrivals balloon during President Obama's last two years in office? In turn, if President Obama's parting policies were

---

[25] Olivia Tallet, "Cubans React Negatively to the End of 'Wet Foot, Dry Foot' Policy," *Houston Chronicle* (January 12, 2017) (www.chron.com/lifestyle/calle-houston/article/Cubans-react).
[26] NBC, "Obama Ending 'Wet Foot, Dry Foot' Policy for Cubans." n.d. (www.nbcmiami.com/news/local/Obama-Ending-Wet-Foot-Dry-Foot).

intended to make Cuban immigration safe, legal, and orderly once again, he needed to address the root cause of the surge in unauthorized entrants.

Cuba's unresolved economic problems contributed to the surge. A quarter century after Soviet aid and trade ended, the Cuban economy still had not fully rebounded, which shattered Cubans' faith in the revolution. As a result, Cubans viewed immigration more positively than when the revolution had captured their hearts and minds. Increasingly, Cubans envisioned emigration as their best hope for the future.[27]

Nonmigration policies that both the United States and Cuban governments implemented, which facilitated bonding among Cubans living on the two sides of the Florida Straits, further fueled Cuban interest in moving to America. On the US side, in 2009 President Obama lifted restrictions that President Bush had imposed on homeland visits. The lifting of restrictions led trip taking to soar, from around 5,000 in 1990 to 350,000 in 2013, and to over 470,000 in 2014: followed by a slight dip in 2016 to 428,000.[28] In 2013, President Obama proceeded to make it easier for Cubans to visit the United States in issuing multiple-entry visas that were valid for five years. Since the revolution, the United States had only granted six month, single-entry visas. The new policy made Cuban visits to the United States easier and cheaper, with more Cubans, as a result, coming to the United States and visiting with greater frequency. The bonding ignited Cuban interest in immigration, as had the first Cuban émigré return visits, in 1979.

President Obama also removed restrictions on remittance sending that enabled more Cubans to finance moves to America. After the lifting of restrictions, remittances soared from an estimated $50 million in 1990 to over $2 billion in 2013 and to $3 billion in 2016.[29] Cubans used remittances mainly to cover their daily needs, but, if they so chose, to cover costs of migration as well. Immigration cost Cubans as much as $10,000 to $15,000, an unaffordable expense on official Cuban earnings, the equivalent of about $20 to $25 a month.

---

[27] I discuss these factors in detail In Susan Eckstein, *The Immigrant Divide: How Cuban Americans Changed the US and Their Homeland* (New York: Routledge, 2009).

[28] Ibid., p.133; Ben Piven, "How New U.S. Policy Will Change Relations with Cuba," *Aljazeera America* (December 17, 2014) (america.aljazeera.com/articles/ /2014/12/17/partial-lifting-cubaembargo.html); Whitefield, "Cuba Announces New Measures to Make Travel to the Island Easier for Cuban Americans," *Miami Herald* (October 28, 2017) (www.miamiherald.com/news/nation-world/world/americas/Cuba/article).

[29] Eckstein, *The Immigrant Divide*, p. 78; money.cnn.com/2014/12/17/news/.../cuba-remittances.

New Cuban government policies had the unintended effect of further fueling immigration. Complementing the Obama administration reforms, the Cuban government relaxed its restrictions on émigré return visits and on Cuban receipt of remittances, so as to infuse more, desperately needed, hard currency into the economy. In this context, the Cuban government reimagined Cuban émigrés it had portrayed in the Soviet era as traitors and worms as the "Cuban community abroad," in essence, as long-distance nationals.

As a result, Soviet era stigma toward Cubans who emigrated subsided, and Cubans who emigrated no longer needed to strain relations with friends and family in Cuba if they uprooted. In addition, in early 2013, the Cuban government eased restrictions on Cuban travel abroad. It even increased the length of time that Cubans could stay abroad without losing their Cuban residency rights, from less than a year to 24 months. If Cubans managed to get paroled into the United States while visiting, one year later they could have their immigration status adjusted on the basis of the CAA, and thereby get on a path to dual citizenship.

Human smugglers, in turn, contributed to the surge in unauthorized immigration. While Cubans would have preferred to come lawfully, in order to attain visas they would have needed to meet US preference system priorities and wait in a visa queue. Had more of them been able to emigrate with authorization, fewer would have come unauthorized. Human smugglers took advantage of the situation. In that they imposed no requirements on who they brought to the United States other than payment for their services, they became a key force behind the surge in illegal immigration during the last years of Obama's presidency. They were the reason why immigration became so costly.

Smugglers helped Cubans evade Coast Guard who policed the Florida Straits, by transporting them in hard-to-detect, low-lying and fast-moving cigarette boats. Following routes known from earlier drug-smuggling, they cruised at speeds faster than most Coast Guard vessels could intercept.

Even before President Clinton left office, human smugglers were helping Cubans to circumvent immigration barriers. In 1999, for example, an estimated 1,700 Cubans were smuggled into the United States.[30] Smuggling increased despite the punitive policies that were instituted with the Illegal Immigration Reform and Immigration

---

[30] Deborah Ramírez, "U.S., Cuba Pact Boosts Immigrant Smuggling," *Sun Sentinel* (February 1, 1999) (articles-sun-sentinel.com/1999-02-01/news/9902010060_1-illegals-cuban-immigrants-

Responsibility Act (IIRIRA) of 1996. The IIRIRA raised the terms of imprisonment for convicted smugglers, and, in cases when smuggled persons died, the human couriers could be subject to the death penalty. Yet, smugglers considered the gains from the lucrative, illicit business to outweigh the heightened penalties they faced if caught.

The stepped up policing of the Florida Straits with implementation of the 1994–1995 immigration accords led visa-less Cubans attempting to cross the Florida Straits often to be interdicted, even when they were guided by smugglers. Rather than give up on immigrating, smugglers mapped out a 7,000-mile trek through South and Central America that brought Cubans to the United States by land, with "dry feet," via the US–Mexican border.[31] Cubans would fly to Ecuador (and, subsequently, to Guyana), which did not require a visa.[32] From there, they met up with smugglers who guided the hazardous journey, mainly by land, to the United States. Thus, the migration accords that the Clinton administration had negotiated had the unintended effect of spurring illicit immigration over land, and fueling demand for smugglers to navigate the route.

The human smuggling became well-organized, across country borders, despite the US and Cuban governments committing, in the migration accords, to rein it in.[33] Networks of smugglers were involved. Then, when the smuggled Cubans arrived at the US–Mexican border with "dry feet," border patrol agents paroled them into the country. The Cubans typically were cleared for entry within hours, while Mexican, Central American, and other unauthorized immigrants were turned away.

Human smuggling became entrenched in informal Cuban networks on both sides of and across the Florida Straits. Smugglers to whom Cubans

---

varadero-boats). There were risks involved in relying on smugglers, who often overloaded their boats to maximize their per-trip profits, which contributed to boats sinking.

[31] One in twenty Cubans allegedly died in attempting the land route. Kelly Knaub, "The Cuban Adjustment Act 44 Years Later," *Havana Times* (May 15, 2010) (www.havanatimes.org/?p=24150).

[32] With the surge in Cubans flying to Ecuador to be smuggled to the United States, the South American government began requiring entry visas. Cubans subsequently were able to fly to a Central American country and begin their land trek there.

[33] Cuban and US government mutual interest in reining in human smuggling continued after the Clinton-negotiated migration agreements went into effect. They were of concern to the Obama administration when negotiating changes in immigration policy. Soraya Castro Marino, "The New Era of Cuba-U.S. Relations: Breaking Down Axioms and Establishing Lasting Legacies?," p. 56 in Margaret Crahan and Castro Marino (eds.), *Cuba–US Relations: Normalization and Its Challenges* (New York: Institute of Latin American Studies, Columbia University, 2016).

turned were of Cuban descent.³⁴ If they were arrested and brought to trial in South Florida, they often faced sympathetic jurors who sided with them because they brought friends and family to the United States. Jurors, if of Cuban descent, often were more concerned with having family members still in Cuba smuggled to the United States than in testifying against the illicit transporters.³⁵

Cubans turned to smugglers in stepped up numbers when President Obama announced plans in December 2014 to normalize US–Cuban relations. They feared that Washington would sunset the CAA, as part of the normalization process, and thereby end their unique path to legal permanent residence. While the Obama administration did retract the parole rights on which CAA-based adjustment of status had mainly rested, Congress left the CAA as the law of the land. Cubans thus were able to turn to a new path to take advantage of the CAA.

THE EMERGENT CUBAN AMERICAN DIVIDE AND THE POLITICAL OPPORTUNITY THEREBY CREATED FOR POLICY CHANGE

In light of the importance of Florida to the outcome of presidential elections, and the importance of Cuban American votes to the electoral outcome in the most important "swing" state, why would President Obama revoke entitlements that were exceedingly popular among Cuban Americans? Nearly all Cuban Americans supported the CAA, and most of them also favored the "wet foot/dry foot" policy: according to surveys of Cuban Americans in Miami.³⁶ True, President Obama revoked the entitlements as he left office and therefore he himself faced

---

³⁴ Rick Bragg, "Cubans Now Choosing Smugglers over Rafts," *New York Times* (July 21, 1999) (www.nytimes.com/1999/07/21/us/cubans-now-choosing-smugglers).

³⁵ Donald Brown, "Crooked Straits: Maritime Smuggling of Humans from Cuba to the United States," *University of Miami Inter-American Law Review* 33 no. 2/3 (Summer-Fall 2002): 273–93.

³⁶ A Florida International University poll reported that in 2014 86 percent of Cuban Americans supported the CAA and 63 percent favored continuation of the "wet foot/dry foot" policy, including, respectively, 92 and 66 percent of the most recent arrivals. See Florida International University (FIU), *2014 FIU Cuba Poll: How Cuban Americans in Miami View U.S. Policies toward Cuba* (Miami: FIU Cuban Research Institute, 2014) (cri.fiu.edu/research/cuba-poll/2014-fiu-cuba-poll.pdf); Patricia Mazzei, Lesley Clark, and Nora Torres, "Don't Expect Trump to Reinstate Special Immigration Status for Cubans," *Miami Herald* (January 14, 2017) www.google.com/search?client=firefox-b-1-d&q=patricia+mazzei+lesley+clark+nora+torres+Don%27t+Expect+Trump+to+reinstate+special+immigration+status+for+cubans.

no risk of losing an election. However, unpopular policies could cost other Democrats votes.

Despite the popularity of the entitlements, President Obama retracted them with minimal pushback from Cuban Americans. The very influential Cuban American Republican politicians who had defended and promoted entitlements for Cuban immigrants in the past, beginning in 2009 criticized their continuation. They did so in the context of changes within the Cuban American community that they disliked. The changes were socioeconomic, cultural, normative, and political.

The Socioeconomic, Cultural, and Political Transformation of the Cuban American Community

As Cuban immigration picked up in the post-Soviet era, first owing to US commitment in the Clinton-negotiated migration accords to formally admit no fewer than 20,000 Cubans yearly, and, after the turn of the century, owing to the surge in unauthorized entrants, differences between the immigrant waves took hold. A key divide erupted between the self-defined exiles who emigrated in the first years of the revolution and the post-Soviet era arrivals, whom I refer to as the New Cubans.[37]

The divide, in part, was class-based. According to a 2014 Miami survey by Florida International University, among the earlier émigrés 6 percent viewed themselves as upper class, 75 percent as middle or upper middle class, and 18 percent as lower middle class. In contrast, among those who emigrated after 1995 only 1 percent considered themselves upper class; 45 percent considered themselves middle or upper middle class, and 32 percent considered themselves lower middle class. About twenty times more of the recent than the earlier émigrés considered themselves lower class. Poor New Cubans were likely to draw on welfare, which became politicized.[38]

The differences in class identification reflected differences in census-reported earnings and job status between the more recent and earlier émigrés. In Miami, twice as many of the 1960s arrivals, in comparison to New Cubans, held high-status jobs. Furthermore, three times as many of the earlier arrivals ranked among the top tercile of US income earners,

---

[37] See Eckstein, *The Immigrant Divide*, especially chapter 1 (and references therein).
[38] The data on social class identity comes from the Florida International University 2014 poll cited in FN 37.

when compared to the more recent arrivals.[39] The economic differences were partly rooted in the longer period of time the earlier arrivals had to take advantage of economic opportunities in the United States. However, the differences also derived from the exceptionally generous benefits that exiles received through the Cuban Refugee Program; from exiles' astute use of opportunities that burgeoned as Miami transformed from a winter haven for northern "snowbirds" into a city with hemispheric reach; and from the greater human and social capital with which exiles immigrated.[40]

The divide was also rooted in differences among the émigré cohorts in their ties with Cuba and their stance toward such ties. Exiles opposed such ties; the New Cubans coveted them. In 2004 President Bush had mandated that Cuban immigrants could make homeland trips to see family no more than once every three years. Influential Cuban Americans from exile families, who, as staunch Republicans had helped him win the presidency in 2000, had pressed for tightened restrictions on homeland travel. In that they were morally opposed to relations with "Castro's Cuba," they favored a people-to-people level embargo to complement the state-level embargo.

With Republicans having had a near lock on exile votes for decades, President Obama reached out to the more recent arrivals who were committed to family still in Cuba when campaigning for the presidency in 2008. He promised them, if elected, to lift restrictions on homeland travel and remittance-sending: a promise he immediately acted on after assuming office. A 2011 Miami poll found three-fourths of the New Cubans to be supportive of the policy changes.

The immigrant cohorts, in turn, had conflicting views toward Washington's Cuban immigration policies. A 2014 survey found 76 percent of the New Cubans, but only 47 percent of the 1959–1964 émigrés, to strongly favor the CAA, and 66 and 52 percent of the respective cohorts to approve of the "wet foot/dry foot" policy.[41] New Cubans were more likely to have family in Cuba who might benefit from the policies.

---

[39] Eckstein, *The Immigrant Divide*, p. 71.
[40] I elaborate on economic differences among the immigrant waves in my book *The Immigrant Divide*, chapter 2; see also p. 16.
[41] FIU, *2011 Cuba Poll* (cri.fiu.edu/research/cuba-poll/2011-cuba-poll.pdf) and *2014 Cuba Poll*.

The divergent views of the immigrant cohorts derived from their different experiences in Cuba before uprooting. The self-defined exiles, who emigrated shortly after the transformation of Cuba, which they opposed, typically remained committed to their pre-revolutionary beliefs and ways and wanted nothing to do with the country transformed under Castro's rule. In contrast, New Cubans, who "lived the revolution" but became disillusioned with it on experiencing the crisis of the 1990s that the Soviet Union's collapse unleashed, perceived themselves as immigrants. Like immigrants from other countries, on moving to America they wanted to visit, and financially support, family they left behind.[42] Thus, when President Obama officially removed restrictions on travel to Cuba, the New Cubans ignored exiles' trip taking taboo and made homeland trips. Their family morality conflicted with exiles' political morality. Exiles, meanwhile, resented New Cuban defiance of their travel taboo.

The émigré cohorts came to differ also in their political involvements and partisan preferences. President Obama was successful in his outreach to New Cubans. In 2012, for example, more New Cubans voted for him than for his Republican opponent Mitt Romney; in contrast, over twice as many of the 1959–1966 émigrés voted for Romney than for him.[43] The New Cubans, accordingly, contributed to a partisan sea change that further divided the Cuban American community.[44]

Cuban American Politicians Defend Entitlements Only for "Authentic" Cuban Refugees

Beginning in 2009, South Florida Cuban American Republican legislators became selective in the Cuban immigrants for whom they defended benefits. Whereas in years past they had advocated for entitlements for all Cuban immigrants, they began to distinguish between Cubans who they considered worthy and unworthy of special rights. Although their changed stance was more a war on words than action, their statements

---

[42] I discuss, in detail, differences among Cubans who immigrated at different times with different lived experiences in my book *The Immigrant Divide*.

[43] FIU, *2014 Cuba Poll*; Bill Hoffman, "Cuban-Americans Voted for Obama in Record Numbers," *Newsmax* (www.newsmax.com/Newsfront/cubans-voted-obama-record/2012/11/09/id/463529/).

[44] See https://cri.fiu.edu/research/cuba-poll/2018-fiu-cuba-poll.pdf; Brookings Institute "Cuban American Opinions Concerning U.S. Policy toward Cuba and the U.S. Election" (www.brookings.edu/wp-content/uploads/2012/04/1202_cuba_poll.pdf).

signaled that their opposition to entitlement cutbacks would be more muted than would have been the case in the past. They were not likely to defend entitlements for Cubans who they felt to be unworthy.

The legislators launched their critique in Miami. Later, they took their case to Congress, where they proposed legislation to limit unique entitlements for incoming Cubans. The legislators identified with the Soviet era émigrés – the self-defined exiles – who formed the core of their political (and financial) base, the Cuban Americans behind the people-to-people embargo.[45]

The South Florida Cuban American Republican Mario Díaz-Balart, who was initially elected to the House of Representatives in 2003, was the first to challenge Cuban American solidarity publicly. In 2009 he complained that a significant number of Cuban immigrants had abused the CAA. The US-born son of the Batista government Cabinet member who fled Cuba soon after Castro assumed power, and brother of Lincoln, who served in Congress between 1993 and 2011, did not forget where his family came from and why. In a TV interview in Florida he went so far as to compare Cuban Americans who traveled to see relatives in Cuba with unscrupulous businessmen who dealt with German Nazis.[46] He argued that in visiting Cuba émigrés invalidated their refugee status. Subsequently, he clarified that he did not favor repealing the CAA but rather he wished to clamp down on its abuse. Visits to Cuba, he argued, were one such abuse. He also argued that the CAA should only be applied to Cubans who had suffered political persecution before emigrating,[47] a prerequisite the legislation did not specify and was never applied in the past. In making his claims, he called for compliance with the personal embargo: to not step foot in Cuba under Castro.

In 2011 another Cuban American Republican member of Congress from South Florida, US-born David Rivera, built on Díaz-Balart's critique. Rivera went a step further and proposed legislation to modify the CAA. He proposed to make rights to lawful permanent residency and citizenship more difficult, and contingent on no return trips to Cuba. The

---

[45] Rubio's and Menendez's families immigrated shortly before the revolution. However, the two senators received campaign financing from exiles, depended on exile votes, promoted exile interests, and identified themselves as exiles.

[46] Arturo López Levy, "Now It Is Not the Time to Change the 1966 Cuban Adjustment Act," *Huffington Post* (July 2013) (www.huffingpost.com/arturo-lopez-levy/now-it-is-not-the-time-to_b_3518237.html).

[47] Juan Tamayo, "Politicians Call for Revision of Cuban Adjustment Act," *Miami Herald* (February 12, 2013).

legislation called for an increase in the period of time that paroled Cubans needed to live in the United States before they qualified for lawful permanent residence: from 1 to 5 years. Eligibility for citizenship, in turn, thereby would be prolonged. Cuban immigrants who wanted to become citizens would be unable to take homeland trips for ten years, even, for example, to see a dying family member. The proposed legislation also empowered the Department of Homeland Security to revoke the residency status of any Cuban national who returned to Cuba before becoming a citizen.[48]

Under Congressman Rivera's proposed legislation, only "authentic refugees" were to qualify for lawful permanent residence under the CAA. Rivera defined "authentic refugees" as persons who honored the personal embargo, and neither traveled to Cuba nor sent remittances there: a new definition of refugee. He brushed aside the official near universally accepted definition of refugee that Congress embedded in the Refugee Act of 1980: as previously noted, someone who fled actual or likely persecution. While having no legal standing, the personal embargo on which Congressman Rivera's conception of refugee rested had deep moral significance to the anti-Castro exiles with whom he identified. In combination with the state level embargo, the personal embargo was to strangulate the Cuban economy to the point of collapse.

Congressman Rivera's proposed legislation was the first to differentiate "authentic refugees" from other Cuban émigrés and to limit entitlements to the "authentics." However, the session of Congress ended without approval of his proposed legislation, and in 2012 he lost his reelection bid. His alleged involvement in a scandal turned voters against him. He was considered one of the most corrupt members of Congress.

Other Cuban American members of Congress were not discouraged by Rivera's electoral defeat. They too advocated for limiting Cuban immigrant entitlements. In 2013, Marco Rubio, who had been a Florida Senator since 2011, argued at a Miami meeting of the US–Cuba Democracy PAC that President Obama's removal of restrictions on Cuban American travel to Cuba in 2009 was inconsistent with the Cuban Adjustment Act and thereby undermined its justification.[49] In

---

[48] "Rivera's Cuban Readjustment Act Reforms Get a Hearing/Naked Politics" (May 2012) (n.d.), *Miami Herald* (http://miamiherald.typepad.com/nakedpolitics/2012/05/Cuban-readjustment-act).

[49] The Free Cuba PAC, which was associated with the Cuban American National Foundation, had been the most influential and best-funded Cuban American PAC before Mas Canosa died. Afterwards, hardliners broke with the Foundation and formed the

the same year he also told the *Tampa Bay Times*, "it gets very difficult to justify someone's status as an exile and refugee" if they return home soon after arriving.[50]

Senator Rubio lashed out at Cuban trip takers. He accused them of hypocrisy, given that they claimed to be refugees.[51] He also called it a "travesty" to grant CAA rights to people who traveled to the island.[52] Genuine refugees, he argued, would not visit Cuba, for fear of persecution. Rubio was disingenuous in this critique in that Cuban émigrés had never needed to demonstrate that they were refugees to qualify for CAA-based adjustment of status and the path to citizenship that it provided.

In 2013, when Congress deliberated a new comprehensive immigration reform that President Obama hoped to implement, Senator Rubio served on the so-called Gang of Eight, a bipartisan Senate group formed to draft changes in immigration policy. In principle, he could have used the opportunity to propose sunsetting the CAA, which he claimed was no longer justifiable. Bob Menendez, the Cuban American Democrat from New Jersey who always sided with Cuban American Republicans on Cuba policy issues, was another member of the Gang of Eight who could similarly have proposed sunsetting the CAA.[53] However, neither of them did. In turn, Díaz-Balart, who served on the House of Representatives immigration reform committee, was equally silent on the matter. In silence, they tacitly supported the CAA remaining the law of the land.

South Florida's only Cuban American Democrat in Congress at the time, US–born Joe García, confirmed the silence of the Cuban American members of the Gang of Eight on the matter of Cuban entitlements. He reported having met with immigration reform negotiators in the White House, as well as in the House of Representatives and Senate, and the

---

US–Cuba Democracy PAC, which became the main Cuban American PAC. However, during Trump's presidency, the new PAC's financial base dwindled, as subsequently described.

[50] "Rubio Moves to Curb Benefits for Cuban Immigrants over 'Outrageous Abuse'," *The Guardian* (January 12, 2016) (www.theguardian.com).

[51] Wilfredo Cancio, "Record de visas a cubanos para visitar EEUU en 2014: 36,500," *Cafefuerte* (November 2014) (Cafefuerte.com/cuba/19321-record-de-visas-a-cubanos-para).

[52] Guillermo Martínez, "Cuban Adjustment Act Has Become a True Travesty," *Sun Sentinel* (March 27, 2014) (articles.sun-sentinel.com/2014-03-27/news/fl-gmcol-opedo327).

[53] Menendez began his political career as mayor of Union City, New Jersey, home to the second largest Cuban enclave in the United States in the 1960s. He chaired the Senate Committee on Foreign Relations from January 2013 until indicted on federal corruption charges two years later.

words "Cuban Adjustment Act" never came up in the meetings.[54] Had the Cuban American legislators genuinely been committed to revising or revoking the CAA, they were well positioned to advocate for the change on their respective immigration reform committees.

In a statement that was indicative of Senator Rubio's hypocrisy, in 2013 he claimed that he was "not sure we're going to be able to avoid, as part of any comprehensive approach to immigration, a conversation about the Cuban Adjustment Act." He dismissively brushed off the possibility when he noted that the CAA "just hasn't come up" in immigration reform conversations.[55] It did not come up because he, and the other Cuban Americans on the immigration reform committees, chose not to broach the subject.

While Congress never enacted the immigration reform, influential Cuban Americans continued their critique of Cuban immigrant "abuse" of entitlements. They called for limiting the CAA to Cubans who met their newly conceived definition of refugees: Cuban émigrés who made no homeland trips. For example, in 2014 the Miami-Dade County Commission – with no foreign policy authority – unanimously recommended that Congress revise the CAA so that it applied only to Cubans who had fled persecution, not to economic immigrants, who they defined as persons making return trips to Cuba as soon as they could.[56] Like the Cuban Americans in Congress, the Cuban Americans on the commission came from families that immigrated soon after the revolution and identified with them. In turn, the executive director of the US–Cuba Democracy PAC at the time, Mauricio Claver-Carone, argued that the CAA should be amended to deny asylum to Cubans who returned to Cuba before becoming citizens. Contributors to the PAC were mainly from families who emigrated shortly after the revolution.

Before 2009 Cuban American politicians never publicly questioned whether Cuban émigrés were refugees. Whatever private beliefs they held, in public they defended and promoted entitlements for the presumed refugees. They changed their stance when Cuban émigrés began to make

---

[54] Juan Tamayo, "Politicians Call for Revision of Cuban Adjustment Act."
[55] Alex Leary, "Senator Marco Rubio Says He Wants to Re-examine Cubans' Fast-Track Status but Immigration Bill Doesn't," *Tampa Bay Times* (June 25, 2013) (www.tampabay.com/news/politics/national/sen-marco-rubio-says-he-wants-to-re-examine-cubans-fast-track-status).
[56] Nick Miroff, "Fear of Immigration Policy Change Triggers New Wave of Cuban Migrants," *Washington Post* (January 27, 2014) (www.washingtonpost.com/world/the_americas/fears-of-immigration/).

homeland trips in substantial numbers, in defiance of the personal embargo to which they were committed.

Trip taking surged – especially among New Cubans – after President Obama lifted travel restrictions in 2009. In lifting the restrictions, he fueled the festering divide among the different Cuban immigrant waves. However, the New Cubans had no political organizations or political leadership of their own, and they did not make political contributions that might convince politicians to promote their interests. As a result, they did not openly challenge Cuban American politicians' critique of Cuban immigrant entitlements.

Media Revelations of Cuban Immigrant Abuse of Entitlements

In 2015 Cuban American Congressmen expanded their critique of what they considered abuse of entitlements. They pointed to media revelations, and implied that the illicit activity of some was reason to restrict entitlements for all Cuban arrivals.

At a swearing-in ceremony for members of the Miami Congressional delegation, Mario Díaz-Balart forewarned that some reform efforts would come from the "South Florida folks." In 2015, he lashed out. He bemoaned, "The level of fraud is frankly unsustainable. It's unacceptable."[57] He, along with other South Florida Republican members of Congress, accused fellow Cuban Americans of breaking the law in ways that were reported in a three-part series, "Easy Money," published in the South Florida newspaper *Sun Sentinel* in October 2015.

For one, the articles criticized recent Cuban arrivals for extensive use and abuse of social services and welfare. The newspaper reported that, in 2013, one in ten Cubans in Florida collected Supplemental Security Income (SSI), support for the disabled and elderly poor, in contrast to only one in twenty-five immigrants from other countries.[58] The newspaper also reported that federal expenditure on Cubans for welfare, food stamps, and Medicaid had ballooned from $1 million in 1960 to around $680 million in 2015, and that, in Florida, Cubans accounted for 90 percent of all recipients of refugee services.[59] These Cubans did not

---

[57] Megan O'Matz, "Cuban Adjustment Act Reform Planned," *Sun Sentinel* (February 6, 2015) (www.sun-sentinel.com/news/nationworld/fl-congress-cuban).

[58] O'Matz and Sally Kestin, "Easy Money: Florida Politicians Protect Special Status for Cubans," *Sun Sentinel* (October 1, 2015) (www.sun-sentinel.com/us-cuba-welfare-benefits/sfl-us-cuba).

[59] Ibid.

necessarily commit fraud, but they were portrayed as taking advantage of local taxpayers. Other lawful immigrants needed to live in the United States for five years before they were eligible for comparable benefits,[60] and unauthorized immigrants from other countries were never to be eligible, ever since President Clinton famously "ended welfare as we knew it."

The articles also noted ways that Cuban immigrants made illicit use of entitlements. They reported Cubans moving from the island to retire in Florida, where they drew on food stamps, Medicaid, and subsidized housing. The articles also reported Cuban immigrants selling their Medicare numbers to provide for family in Cuba,[61] and filing fraudulent claims for disability payments. Between 2000 and 2014, Cubans accounted for the majority of healthcare fraud arrests in Florida.[62] Some Cuban immigrants committed crimes to pay off their debts to the smugglers who had brought them to the United States. In such instances, illegal human smuggling spurred other illegal activity.

Some of the reported crime was highly organized. One of the articles described a forty-eight-person multi-state Cuban ring that stole $500 million in prescription drugs from Medicaid, another ring that stole $695 million from Medicare, and still another Miami-based criminal network that became national in reach, involving one hundred people. Cuban immigrants were also arrested for highly organized insurance fraud, cargo theft, marijuana production and trafficking, credit card fraud (including a $1 million credit card fraud ring), and drug dealing.

Some of the reported crime was transnational in reach. The *Sun Sentinel* attributed the formation of the highly organized Miami-based criminal networks to the ease with which visa-less Cubans gained US entry.[63] The articles revealed ringleaders of criminal networks who frequently traveled back and forth to Cuba, smuggling millions of dollars to the island, and who brought Cubans to the United States to work as foot soldiers in their criminal organizations. They brought persons from their

---

[60] O'Matz, Kestin, and John Maines, "Easy Money: Cubans Retire to Florida: With Help from U.S. Taxpayers," *Sun Sentinel* (October 1, 2015) (www.sun-sentinel.com/us-cuba-welfare-benefits/sfl-us-cuba-....).
[61] Lizette Álvarez, "Law Favoring Cuban Arrivals Is Challenged," *New York Times* (February 2, 2015) (www.nytimes.com/2015/02/02/.../law-favoring-cuba-arrivals-is-challenged.htm).
[62] Kestin, O'Matz, and William Gibson, "Plundering America: The Cuban Criminal Pipeline, Part III Congress Reacts," *Sun Sentinel* (January 8, 2015) (Interactive.sun-sentinel.com/plundering-america/three.htm).
[63] Álvarez, "Law Favoring Cuban Arrivals Is Challenged."

hometowns who they trained in Cuba. Cuban immigrants were reputed to travel back to Cuba with millions of dollars stolen from Medicare, auto insurance, and credit card scams.

The articles portrayed the CAA as part of the problem, in enabling Cubans to come to the United States without criminal background checks, and in allowing Cubans to visit Cuba soon after they arrived. However, the CAA does not account for the crime, much less for the immigration of criminals. Rather, it enabled Cubans who immigrated without authorization to become LPRs once they were in the United States. Furthermore, Cubans must be screened for admissibility before they can adjust their status on the basis of the CAA.

While the articles highlighted Cuban immigrant abuse of entitlements, they did not specify how many Cubans were involved in the reported crimes. Instead, the articles smeared the image of all Cuban immigrants, especially the most recent arrivals. The articles even became fodder for another critique by Cuban American Congressmen: that Cuban immigrants, recent Cuban immigrants above all, were "welfare chiselers."

Cuban American Politicians' Attack on "Welfare Chiselers"

In December 2015, two months after publication of the *Sun Sentinel* articles, Carlos Curbelo, who held the South Florida Congressional seat previously occupied by David Rivera and then Joe Garcia, proposed legislation about which Congressman Mario Díaz-Balart had hinted. Congressman Curbelo proposed the Cuban Immigrant Work Opportunity Act of 2015 (H.R. 4247), which he co-sponsored with Ileana Ros-Lehtinen, the then doyenne of the Cuban American Congressional delegation and former Chairwoman of the House Foreign Affairs Committee.[64] The bill called for ending Cuban immigrants' unique rights to welfare, despite Ros-Lehtinen, along with Lincoln Díaz-Balart (Mario's older brother who, as previously noted, served in Congress between 1993 and 2011) and Florida Governor Chiles, having craftily lobbied for inclusion of Cuban rights to welfare in the Balanced Budget Act of 1997. They did so after PRWORA had excluded unauthorized Cubans, and authorized Cuban immigrants during their first five years in the United States, from rights to welfare.[65]

---

[64] O'Matz and Kestin, "Easy Money: Florida Politicians Protect Special Status for Cubans."

[65] Lincoln Díaz-Balart also had opposed Clinton's "wet foot" policy. He felt all Cubans should be allowed to come to the United States. Ruth Wasem, *CRS Report for Congress:*

While the Balanced Budget Act did not require Cubans to be refugees or to comply with the personal embargo in order to qualify for welfare, H.R. 4247 called for Cubans to prove that they had suffered persecution in Cuba and that they therefore could not return "under the current totalitarian regime" in order to qualify for federal welfare assistance.[66] In essence, the Cuban American sponsors of H.R. 4247 distinguished between Cuban immigrants who were "deserving" and "undeserving" of welfare. Cuban trip takers, they argued, were not "deserving." In co-sponsoring H.R. 4247, Ros-Lehtinen reversed her stance of 1997, when she argued that all Cuban immigrants should be exempt from immigrant welfare restrictions.

In January of 2016, Senator Rubio proceeded to propose S. 441. It was companion legislation to Curbelo's in the House of Representatives.

Congressman Curbelo's critique of Cuban immigrant welfare recipients was two-fold. He suggested that some Cubans were collecting welfare who should not, and that others used the government handouts in inappropriate and illegal ways. He tied his critique of welfare abusers to homeland trip taking, and argued that trip takers abused refugee rights to welfare, as well as to food stamps, Medicaid, and SSI.

Echoing the conservative national critique of "welfare chiselers" before passage of President Clinton's 1996 welfare reform, Congressman Curbelo complained that Cubans in the United States had abused American generosity for too long. He highlighted the cases referenced in the *Sun Sentinel* articles involving Cubans returning to Cuba for months while collecting welfare benefits, and shuttling back and forth to Cuba illegally, carrying food and other goods to sell in Cuba.[67]

Democrat Joe García, who lost his Congressional seat to Curbelo, was the rare Cuban American politician to criticize Curbelo's proposed legislation. García argued that it unfairly discriminated against recent arrivals from Cuba.[68] They had the most family still living in Cuba, so they were most concerned about family visits. Also, as newcomers they were in need

---

Cuban Migration to the United States: Policy and Trends (Washington, DC: Congressional Research Service, June 2, 2009).

[66] O'Matz and Kestin, "Legislation Aims to Stop Welfare Abuse by Cuban Immigrants," *Sun Sentinel* (December 15, 2015) (www.sun-sentinel.com/local/broward/fl-curbelo-cuba-bill-2).

[67] Ibid.

[68] Patricia Mazzei, "Eliminating Automatic Refugee Benefits for Cubans Would Save U.S. Money, Report Says," *Miami Herald* (May 25, 201) (www.miamiherald.com/news/politics-government/article79792097.html#storylink=cpy).

of resettlement assistance. There were, as previously noted, far more poor people among recent arrivals than among earlier émigrés.

With Congress never passing the proposed Curbelo–Rubio legislation, in April of 2016 Rubio tried to convince the Senate to support an amendment tagged onto a bill that authorized funding for the Federal Aviation Administration (FAA). The amendment called for an end to Cubans' automatic rights to welfare and refugee status, and for prolonging the period until when Cubans qualified for welfare assistance. His reasoning was similar to Curbelo's. He chastised Cuban immigrants who traveled back to Cuba while collecting welfare checks.[69] In his words, "It is not fair to the American taxpayer."[70] Senator Rubio proposed restricting eligibility for both refugee status and welfare to Cubans who had fled persecution and who did not make homeland trips.[71] In the proposed amendment, he also specified that, with the exception of "real refugees," Cubans should be treated the same as immigrants from other countries: If they were authorized immigrants, they should not qualify for public assistance during their first five years in the United States; if they were unauthorized immigrants, they never should qualify. He reimagined as immigrants most Cubans that he and other Cuban American Republican politicians had imagined as refugees in the past.

The Cuban American legislators combined their critique of welfare "chiselers" with their stance on refugee rights. In an impassioned speech on the Senate floor when introducing the amendment to the FAA funding bill, Senator Rubio argued

> why should you automatically assume ... that anyone that comes from Cuba is a political refugee? The reason why that now is in doubt, is because many of the people that are coming from Cuba, supposedly as refugees seeking to flee oppression, are traveling back to Cuba 15, 20, 30 times a year ... You don't normally travel back to a place that you are fleeing from oppression, much less repeatedly ... (Cubans) are automatically assumed to be refugees without having to prove it ... (and are) immediately eligible for welfare.[72]

---

[69] O'Matz and Kestin, "Rubio to Propose Bill to Cut Aid to Cuban Migrants," *Sun Sentinel* (January 7, 2016) (www.sun-sentinel.com/local/broward/fl-rubio-bill-cuba-aid).

[70] Rubio, "In Floor Speech, Rubio Urges Senate to End Abuse of Cuban Refugee Benefits" (April 13, 2016) (/public/index.cfm/press-releases?ID=21453B0B-38FF-4F72-ABF6-62BF72634065).

[71] Ibid.

[72] Rubio, "Rubio: Resistance to Stopping Cuban Refugee Welfare Abuse Exactly Why People Hate Washington" (April 14, 2016) (/public/index.cfm/press-releases? ID-1D173258-183C-4A56-8373-A0B07F41399) (www.rubio.senate.gov/public/index.cfm/2016/4/rubio-resistance...).

He added that many Cubans "no longer deserved special treatment," and that their automatic welfare rights were "no longer justified."[73] Echoing Congressman Curbelo, Senator Rubio lashed out at Cuban immigrants who "stole" taxpayers' money in abusing welfare.[74] He did, however, acknowledge that there were genuine Cuban refugees and he did not oppose refugee benefits for them.

The other Cuban American members of Congress supported Senator Rubio's proposed amendment to the FAA funding bill. So too did key, non-Cuban American members of the Florida Congressional delegation, including Democrat Representative Debbie Wasserman Schultz and Democrat Bill Nelson, who, at the time, were, respectively, Democratic National Committee Chairwoman and Florida's senior senator. Like the Cuban American legislators, they received campaign contributions from the Cuban American PAC and from individual Cuban American exiles who were opposed to homeland visits.

Despite the support Senator Rubio rallied from the Florida delegation, the Senate blocked a vote on his proposed amendment. Congress thus continued to finance unique entitlements for Cubans that the Cuban American legislators argued were no longer justified.

Congressman Curbelo added that the CAA needed to be revised. He hoped to introduce legislation to modify the CAA, such that only Cubans who had fled persecution and who did not return to Cuba soon after settling in the United States qualified for lawful permanent residence. He claimed that he focused first on the Cuban Immigrant Work Opportunity Act because he believed it would attract more support since it called for welfare cutbacks. Yet, neither he nor Senator Rubio proposed legislation to revise or revoke the CAA. They and the other Cuban Americans in Congress did not even support legislation proposed in the House of Representatives by Republican Paul Gosar and nine other members of Congress in October 2015 to sunset the CAA.[75] In not supporting the legislation proposed by Gosar et al., the Cuban American legislators revealed that they were not really interested in repealing the CAA.

---

[73] James Rosen, "Sen. Marco Rubio Seeks End to Special Refugee Status for Cuban Immigrants" (April 13, 2016) (www.mcclatchydc.com/news/politics-government/congress/a...).
[74] Rubio, "Rubio: Resistance to Stopping Cuban Refugee Welfare Abuse Exactly Why People Hate Washington."
[75] Kestin and O'Matz, "Rubio Bill Would Curb Welfare Abuses by Cuban Immigrants," *Sun Sentinel* (January 12, 2016) (www.sun-sentinel.com/news/nationworld/fl-rubio-cuba-welfare-bill-filed-20160112-story.html).

Rather, they wished to threaten its repeal, in order to pressure Cuban immigrants to comply with the personal embargo.[76]

In sum, Cuban American politicians who for decades had defended and promoted entitlements for all Cuban immigrants, during the years of Obama's presidency became selective about those in whose interests they advocated. They argued for limiting entitlements to the Cubans that they defined as "deserving," "authentic refugees" who honored the personal embargo. Official refugee criteria did not matter to them.

Cuban American Politicians' Response to President Obama's Retraction of Cuban Immigrant Entitlements

In light of their critiques of continued Cuban entitlements, how did the Cuban American legislators respond to President Obama's retraction of Cuban entitlements? The four South Florida Republican members of Congress at the time were caught in a bind. The president, a Democrat, retracted entitlements that they sought to leverage for their own political agenda.

In the main, the Cuban American members of Congress criticized the Democratic administration for terminating the CMPPP. In Congresswoman Ileana Ros-Lehtinen's words, the elimination of the CMPPP was a "foolhardy concession to a regime that sends its doctors to foreign nations in modern-day indentured servitude."[77] Claiming that the CMPPP contributed to "undermining the Castro regime by providing an outlet for Cuban doctors to seek freedom from forced labor which only benefits an oppressive regime"[78] (an argument other Cuban American legislators also made), she felt the CMPPP should continue to be implemented.

Senator Rubio added that he was optimistic that the incoming Trump administration would reverse President Obama's executive order and allow doctors to seek asylum at US embassies or consulates in other

---

[76] Similarly, Rubio did not press for ending Cuban immigrant rights to welfare (www.miamiherald.com/news/politics-government/articles71886157.html; www.rubio.senate.gov/public/index.cfm/2016/4/rubio-resistance-to-stopping-Cuban-refugee-welfare-abuse-exactly-why-people-hate-Washington).

[77] NBC, "Obama Ending 'Wet Foot, Dry Foot' Policy for Cubans" (n.d.) (www.nbcmiami.com/news/local/Obama-Ending-Wet-Foot-Dry-Foot."

[78] Whitefield, "Obama Ends Controversial Policy That Allowed Cubans to Enter U.S. without Visas," *Miami Herald* (January 12, 2017) (www.google.com/search?client=firefox-b-1-e&q=Whitefield%2C+%E2%80%9CObama+ends+controversial+policy+that+allowed+Cubans+to+enter+U.S.+without+visas%E2%80%9D).

countries.⁷⁹ This was a disingenuous charge because, when ending the CMPPP, the Obama administration specified that Cuban medics could apply for asylum through foreign embassies. As with other asylum seekers, they would qualify if they demonstrated that they had either fled persecution or had well-founded fear of facing persecution if repatriated.⁸⁰

Cuban American legislators' responses to the retraction of parole rights were more complicated. Díaz-Balart, a top recipient of the diminished US–Cuba Democracy PAC campaign contributions, and of contributions from the key Cuban American individual campaign donors, expressed the most indignant reaction in Congress. His response to President Obama's executive order was, "Have you no shame, President Obama?" He accused President Obama of initiating yet another "way to frustrate the democratic aspirations of the Cuban people and provide ... (a) shameful concession to the Castro regime."⁸¹ He added that

> [the President's] policy has been a succession of betrayals of America's longstanding commitment to human rights and freedom, and a betrayal of the Cuban people who have suffered under oppression for far too long. This last act of diminishing lifelines to Cubans languishing in totalitarianism is one final despicable betrayal of a people who deserve better from an American president.

It is unclear what Díaz-Balart wanted beyond his war of words. He admitted that he would not necessarily ask incoming President Trump to reinstate the policy of admitting Cubans who arrived at the border without immigration visas, the main change that President Obama initiated. Moreover, his charge was disingenuous because President Obama continued to welcome asylum seekers with valid claims.

The other Cuban American legislators were more nuanced in their critiques. Congresswoman Ros-Lehtinen approved of ending the "dry foot" policy, but did not want President Obama to get credit for it. She

---

⁷⁹ Alex Leary, "Florida Reaction to Obama Scrapping 'Wet-Foot, Dry-Foot' Policy toward Cubans," *Tampa Bay Times* (January 12, 2017) (www.tampabay.com/blogs/the-buzz-florida-politics/florida-reaction. ...).
⁸⁰ Local Cuban American officials in Miami similarly called for reinstating the CMPPP. For example, Carlos Giménez, the Miami-Dade County mayor (who emigrated at age six with his family in 1960), announced that if Trump wanted to appease Cuban American Republicans he should reinstate the medical parole program. He considered its termination "a boon to the dictatorship."
⁸¹ https://mariodiazbalart.house.gov/media-center/press-releases/have-you-no-shame-president-obama; Alan Gómez, "Obama Ends 'Wet Foot, Dry Foot' Policy for Cubans," *USA Today* (January 12, 2017) (www.usatoday.com/story/news/world/2017/01/12/obama-ends-wet-foot-dry-foot-policy-cubans/96505172/).

noted that the policy was going to change "sooner or later: some reform, some change."[82] She complained, though, that President Obama had changed the policy without Congressional input, stating that "Congress would have done away with it." She too was disingenuous in that the "dry foot" policy rested on presidential, not congressional, discretion. Moreover, she did not acknowledge that she, as well as the other Cuban American members of Congress, had not supported the legislation to sunset the CAA that Republican Congressman Gosar had proposed two months prior to President Obama's announced changes. Without the CAA, Cubans admitted under the "dry foot" policy would not have been able to adjust their status.

Similarly, Congressman Curbelo claimed that Cubans' special treatment would "inevitably" end and that he was not unhappy to see it end.[83] Yet, he took the occasion to accuse President Obama of not following "through on humanitarian rights," and to complain that normalizing relations with Cuba legitimized "Castro's dictatorship."

Not surprisingly, Senator Rubio also offered faint praise for President Obama's changed policy. In his words,

While I have acknowledged the need to reform the Cuban Adjustment Act for some time now, the Obama Administration's characterization of this change as part of the ongoing normalization with the Castro regime is absurd ... The Cuban Adjustment Act has provided countless Cubans the opportunity to escape the Castro tyranny ... While some changes were needed, we must work to ensure that Cubans who arrive here to escape political persecution are not summarily returned to the regime, and they are given a fair opportunity to apply for and receive political asylum.

Even Senator Menendez critiqued Cuban immigration entitlements that President Obama, the preeminent leader of his political party, had revoked. Senator Menendez joined the Florida Cuban American Republican chorus in critiquing President Obama's revised Cuban immigration policy. He did so through Cold War lenses. In his words,

today's announcement will only serve to tighten the noose the Castro regime continues to have around the neck of its own people ... The Obama Administration seeks to pursue engagement with the Castro regime at the cost

---

[82] Mazzei, Clark, and Gamez Torres, "Don't Expect Trump to Reinstate Special Immigration Status for Cubans," *Miami Herald* (January 14, 2017) (www.miamiherald.com/news/politics/government/election).

[83] Ibid.

of ignoring the present state of torture and oppression, and its systemic curtailment of freedom.[84]

Senator Menendez also reprimanded the president for not consulting with Congress before changing Cuban immigration policy, even though all of the changes that President Obama initiated required no act of Congress. Senator Menendez applied different standards for himself and the President. It will be remembered that, in 2013, he had not consulted fellow members of the Senate immigration reform committee about whether Congress ought to revise or revoke the CAA, which required an act of Congress.

Local Miami Cuban American politicians and groups echoed Cuban American legislators' commentary. City of Miami Mayor Tomás Regalado, who had immigrated at age fourteen in 1962 as a "Peter Panner," noted "It was … inevitable that something would have to change because there had been so much abuse." Cuban entitlements "required adjustments."[85] Miami-based exile groups, in turn, took the opportunity to note that the CAA needed to be revised in order to rein in unauthorized immigration. Twelve groups, including the Bay of Pigs Veteran Group Brigade 2506, issued a declaration a few days after President Obama announced the new migration policy. They claimed that, unless the CAA was modified, the United States would face a mass inflow of Cubans: for reasons they never explained. These groups, like the Cuban American legislators, did not favor sunsetting the CAA but restricting its use to "deserving Cubans."[86]

US-born Jorge Mas Santos, who had taken over the directorship of the Cuban American National Foundation after his father died, was the rare Cuban American featured in the Miami media who praised President Obama's parting policy change. With the Foundation having become a voice of moderation after the more "hardline," and older, Cuba-born, members broke off to form the Cuban Liberty Council, Mas Santos argued that the new policy might prove more effective than the old policies that had been meant to bring change to Cuba. He claimed the changes would

---

[84] Tiffany Gabbay, "Cuban-American Lawmakers Blast Obama for Ending Wet-Foot-Dry-Foot Policy," *Truth Revolt* (January 13, 2017) (www.truthrevolt.org/news/cuban-american-lawmakers-blast…); Julie Hirschfeld Davis and Robles, "U.S. Ends Special Treatment for Cuban Migrants," *New York Times* (January 13, 2017): 1, 9.

[85] Marilia Brocchetto and Darran Simon, "Cuban-Americans React to End of 'Wet Foot, Dry Foot' Policy," *CNN* (January 13, 2017) (www.cnn.com/2017/01/13/us/wet-foot-dry-foot-reaction).

[86] Tamayo, "Politicians Call for Revision of Cuban Adjustment Act."

force Cuba's leaders to be more responsive to their citizens. "(U)ltimately, the solution for Cuba is people fighting for change in Cuba."

Irrespective of their arguments, Cuban American politicians quickly accepted President Obama's rollback of Cuban entitlements. Recent Cuban immigrants who wanted entitlements to be continued had no voice in the matter: and they had no advocates to promote their yearnings.

President Obama took advantage of the festering divide within the Cuban American community to end Cuban immigrant entitlements. His relaxation of Cuban homeland travel restrictions had triggered the divide.

CONTINUED DENIAL OF ENTITLEMENTS TO HAITIANS UNDER THE BUSH AND OBAMA ADMINISTRATIONS

The Obama as well as Bush administration followed past precedent and denied Haitians the same entitlements as Cubans. Most notably, the Bush administration expanded the Haitian path of disprivilege when it expanded Cubans' path of privilege. The Obama administration instituted a more conciliatory and inclusionary approach toward Haitians. However, it too offered Haitians fewer entitlements than Cubans, and the entitlements it offered were only of a temporary nature.

New Exclusionary Policies under the Bush Administration

Haiti remained the poorest country in the hemisphere. Yet, the Bush administration offered Haitians no relief when conditions there went from bad to worse. It lent no support to a bill that Florida Congressman Carrie Meek introduced in November 2002 to amend the Cuban Adjustment Act to apply also to citizens and nationals of Haiti (H.R. 5751), a bill that gained no more traction in Congress than the similar bill that Congressman Barney Frank had introduced eight years prior. Furthermore, the Bush administration offered no relief to Haitians after Haiti descended into tumult and violence following a coup in March 2004 that ousted Aristide, not even later in the year when Hurricane Jeanne destroyed most domestic crop production, took the lives of an estimated 3,000 people, and left a quarter million Haitians homeless. It offered no relief despite the US ambassador to Haiti declaring the hurricane-swept country a disaster.[87]

---

[87] Wasem, "U.S. Immigration Policy on Haitian Migrants," *CRS Report for Congress* (Washington, DC, Congressional Research Service, January 21, 2005).

Instead, the Bush administration focused on interdicting Haitians who were desperately attempting to flee the dire conditions in their homeland, and on detaining and deporting the unauthorized Haitians who managed to reach the United States. Drawing on the IIRIRA, Attorney General John Ashcroft ordered all unauthorized Haitians without immigration visas to be detained, in prison-like conditions, and placed in expedited removal. Haitians who claimed that they would face persecution were they to be returned to Haiti were kept in detention while their asylum claims were reviewed. If their claims were denied, they were deported. The Bush administration argued that were it to take a more permissive stance, and release Haitians whose cases were pending, other unauthorized Haitians would head for the United States.[88] Thus, for eight years it detained Haitians while paroling Cubans into the country who after a year the CAA entitled to lawful permanent residence.

In the context of 9/11, the Bush administration initiated additional discriminatory policies toward Haitians, but not Cubans. It used the pretext of security concerns to block Haitian asylum seekers from the United States. It claimed that Haitians were a national security threat because terrorists could pose as Haitian asylum seekers and because Haitian asylum seekers diverted the Coast Guard from homeland security duties.[89] Using this rationale, the INS issued new guidelines to fast-track Haitian asylum adjudications without due process, and the White House expanded INS detention authority vis à vis Haitians. Despite a Supreme Court ruling in 2001 that made it illegal to detain undocumented aliens beyond the time needed to secure their removal, the Bush administration allowed extended detention of Haitians, even if they had not been charged with a crime.[90]

Targeting unauthorized Haitians in particular, INS headquarters issued a directive to its Miami office: to not release any Haitian asylum seeker in expedited removal without its explicit approval.[91] Typically,

---

[88] Riva Verga, "U.S. Treatment of Haitian Refugees," CUNY [City University of New York], School of Law (www.cuny.edu/legal-writing/forum/immigration-law-essays/verga.html) (n.d.).
[89] Council on Hemispheric Affairs (COHA), "Disparities in U.S. Immigration Policy toward Haiti and Cuba: A Legacy to Be Continued?," *COHA* (June 24, 2010) (www.coha.org/disparities-in-u-s-immigration-policy-toward-haiti-and-cuba-a-legacy-t...).
[90] Carl Lindskoog, *Detain and Punish: Haitian Refugees and the Rise of the World's Largest Immigration Detention System* (Gainsville: University Press of Florida, 2018), p. 146.
[91] Lindskoog, *Detain and Punish*, p. 145.

local INS officers paroled into the country persons who were likely to be persecuted if they were repatriated without central INS headquarter approval. Making matters worse for Haitians, the INS granted few Haitians "credible fear" hearings and adequate legal representation. South Florida attorneys complained that immigration authorities restricted when and where they could meet with Haitian clients. In 2005, only nine hearings were held for the 1,850 Haitians who the Coast Guard had interdicted, and only one of the Haitians was granted refugee status and rights to refugee benefits. In the remaining years of Bush's presidency, a mere 5 percent of Haitians won asylum requests.[92]

The Bush administration policy was a throwback to the discredited Haitian Program of 1978 that President Carter terminated before leaving office.[93] While claiming that their Haitian policy was designed to address a national security threat, high-level INS officials admitted that the detention policy was designed to deter Haitians from seeking asylum in the United States.[94]

When they were pressured to halt discrimination against Haitians, immigration officials responded by extending the detention policy to other unauthorized entrants. They refused to improve their treatment of Haitians.[95]

Temporary Inclusionary Policies under the Obama Administration

President Obama continued President Bush's discriminatory policies toward Haitians, but less aggressively and with greater respect for due process. Moreover, when Haiti experienced yet another natural disaster, President Obama granted temporary residency and work rights to Haitians in the United States, and he helped Haitians on the island to reunify with their family in the United States. He also extended other entitlements to Haitians. However, Haitians were still left without a string of entitlements comparable to Cubans. Moreover, in his last year in office President Obama retracted Haitian rights. He resumed their detention and deportation.[96]

---

[92] Wasem, "U.S. Immigration Policy on Haitian Migrants."
[93] Lindskoog, *Detain and Punish*, p. 146.
[94] Wasem, "U.S. Immigration Policy on Haitian Migrants."
[95] Lindskoog, *Detain and Punish*, p. 146.
[96] Sally Kantar, "Haitians Alarmed by Renewed U.S. Deportations As Trump Era Looms" (www.newsdeeply.com/refugees/articles/2016/12/07/haitians-alarmed-by-renewed-u-s-deportations-as-trump-era-looms).

As if conditions in Haiti were not bad enough, on January 12, 2010, Haiti was devastated by a 7.0 magnitude earthquake that killed an estimated 46,000 to 316,000 people. In addition, it left one in seven Haitians homeless, and 75 percent of the population without work. In contrast to President Bush, who was unresponsive to the crisis conditions following Tropical Storm Jeanne, President Obama intervened on Haitians' behalf. Recognizing that deported Haitians would be returning to a country that offered even fewer economic opportunities than in normal times, the administration suspended deportations. It also offered Haitians who were in the United States at the time Temporary Protected Status (TPS). This was the same status that previous administrations had extended to Nicaraguans, Hondurans, and, especially, Salvadorans in the United States when their home countries were plagued by civil unrest, violence, and natural disasters. President Clinton had also extended TPS to the Cubans that his administration detained in Guantanamo.

As previously denoted, TPS is a humanitarian policy designed to spare unauthorized immigrants from deportation and to permit them work rights for up to eighteen months (a period that could be extended, at presidential discretion), when crisis conditions prevailed in their homelands. TPS does not, however, entitle unauthorized immigrants to public assistance or permanent residency rights. The Obama administration renewed Haitian TPS rights when they expired, for subsequent 18-month periods, and it also extended TPS rights to unauthorized Haitians who came to the United States up to one year after the earthquake. As of 2014, some 50,000–58,000 Haitians, about 8 percent of the Haitian population in the United States, had TPS.[97] While Cubans' parole status also only offered temporary residency rights, almost without exception they could draw on the CAA to become lawful permanent residents after one year: until President Obama's last full week in office when he ended Cubans' entitlement to parole entry. Moreover, paroled Cubans had rights to welfare and other social assistance whereas Haitians with TPS did not. Thus, Haitian entitlements did not compare to Cubans', even though Haitians, arguably, were more deserving.

In 2015, the Obama administration extended another entitlement to Haitians, to those with family in the United States who were willing to sponsor them: the Haitian Family Reunification Parole Program (HFRPP). Activists had fought a nearly five-year battle to mobilize

---

[97] Austin Dow, "Hurricane Matthew Further Complicates Haitian Immigration Policy," Council on Hemispheric Affairs (COHA) October 26, 2016.

bipartisan support for the program. Modeled after the Cuban Family Reunification Parole Program (CFRPP), the HFRPP allowed family members of US citizens and lawful permanent residents living in Haiti who were already approved for family-based immigration visas, to fast-track their reunification. As of September 2017, 6,864 Haitians had been approved for the program, and two years later nearly an additional two thousand were.[98] However, these Haitians did not enjoy a path to lawful permanent residence comparable to Cuban beneficiaries of the CFRPP, who could adjust their status after one year in the United States on the basis of the CAA. Moreover, even though one hundred thousand Haitians were, in principle, eligible for the program, many of them could not afford the costs involved, including with help from their family in the United States.

The Obama administration did grant HFRPP beneficiaries Entrant status, which was comparable to the immigration status that the Carter administration had extended to the Haitians who arrived alongside the Mariel Cubans. HFRPP beneficiaries thus were eligible for work and welfare benefits, per Title V of the Refugee Education Assistant Act (described in Chapter 3). In contrast, the Haitians who were granted TPS were entitled to work but not welfare.

Meanwhile, the Haitians who the Obama administration admitted as lawful permanent residents, in accordance with the immigration preference system, enjoyed work rights, plus a path to citizenship, but no right to welfare on arrival, in that the Clinton administration's welfare reform, PRWORA, denied all lawful immigrants' rights to cash assistance during their first five years in the United States (while the Balanced Budget Act of 1997 exempted Cuban immigrants from the welfare restriction). However, as detailed in Table 8.1, the Obama administration limited the number of Haitians granted immigration visas. The Obama administration offered about two and one-half times as many Cubans as Haitians lawful permanent residency rights (see sources in Table 8.1).

In 2016, the Obama administration did make another temporary exception for Haitians. Between May and September it granted three-year humanitarian parole to 5,000 visa-less Haitians who arrived at the

---

[98] Institute for Justice and Democracy in Haiti (IJDH), "Haitian Family Reunification Approvals Up from Last Quarter" (Boston: IJDH.org, 2017); Kantar, "Haitians Alarmed by Renewed U.S. Deportations As Trump Era Looms"; Jacqueline Charles, "Trump to Haitians Awaiting Green Cards: You Can't Come to the U.S., Wait in Haiti," *Miami Herald* (August 2, 2019) (www.miamiherald.com/news/nation-world/world/americas/haiti/article233447842.html).

southern California border crossing. These Haitians came mainly via Brazil, where they had fled after the 2010 earthquake in order to take advantage of a labor shortage linked to an economic boom in the South American country.[99] Unfortunately, when Brazil experienced an economic downturn in 2016, many of the Haitians lost their jobs. Under the circumstances, they sought refuge in the United States, where the majority of Haitians in the diaspora lived. Fearful that Donald Trump would win the presidential election and carry out his campaign pledge to build a wall along the US–Mexican border, Haitians rushed to make the 7,000 mile land journey through eight nations in order to reach the United States before the November election. Fear of US exclusion contributed to an uptick in unauthorized Haitian immigration, just as fear that President Obama would terminate the CAA had contributed to the surge in unauthorized Cuban immigration in 2015 and 2016.

Nonetheless, the Obama administration only welcomed Haitians selectively and temporarily. For one, all Haitians who arrived in the United States without authorization after the cutoff in eligibility for TPS in 2011 were subject to detention and deportation. As of 2015, the Obama administration had deported 1,500 Haitians with criminal records, some accused merely of misdemeanors and minor felonies, such as failure to return a rental car on time and providing false information to police.[100] The Obama administration did slow down Haitian deportations and step up release of Haitians who were held in detention while waiting for their assigned date to appear in immigration court.[101] It did so to contain festering unrest. Conditions of confinement went from bad to worse with the ongoing outsourcing of management of detention centers (since the Reagan administration) to private prison companies. The companies prioritized their profit margin over the quality of life they provided to detainees. Resentful of the conditions of their confinement, some Haitians rioted and staged hunger strikes at detention centers in

---

[99] See Kirk Semple, "Haitians, after Perilous Journey, Find Door to U.S. Abruptly Shut," *New York Times* (September 24, 2016), for an excellent description of Haitian immigration via Brazil (www.nytimes.com/2016/09/24/world/americas/haitians-mexico-brazil-deport-united-states.html).

[100] University of Miami School of Law, *Aftershocks: The Human Impact of U.S. Deportations to Post-Earthquake Haiti* (2015) (https://media.law.miami.edu/clinics/pdf/2015/Haiti-report.pdf).

[101] Daniel Denvir, "Deportation to a Disaster Zone: Obama under Pressure to Stop Crackdown on Haitian Migrants as Hurricane Matthew Wreaks Havoc on Island" (www.salon.com/2016/10/07/deportation-to-a-disaster-zone-...).

Washington, Texas, and Pennsylvania. Anti-detention activists organized and coordinated the protests.

Meanwhile, in September 2016 the Obama administration resumed pre-earthquake exclusionary practices. On September 21, it closed the door to visa-less Haitian immigrants, and announced that Haitian TPS would end. The more than 50,000 Haitians with TPS status were to become subject to detention and deportation if they remained in the United States: contributing to President Obama's reputation as Deporter-in-Chief.[102] In the words of the DHS Secretary Jeh Johnson, conditions in Haiti "improved sufficiently to remove Haitian nationals on a more regular basis, consistent with the practices for nationals from other countries."[103] Whether indeed conditions had improved in Haiti to absorb the tens of thousands of Haitians who might return on losing their TPS was highly questionable.

The Obama administration had barely announced its resumption of Haitian exclusionary measures when Haiti experienced yet another natural disaster: this time, Hurricane Matthew, the country's worst hurricane in over half a century. It took the lives of an estimated 1,000 people, and crop destruction generated near-famine conditions. Responding to pressure from the Haitian American community and from influential non-Haitian politicians, following the disaster the Obama administration agreed to suspend deportation flights and extend TPS rights, anew, to Haitians.[104] Senator Bill Nelson of Florida was among the non-Haitian advocates for Haitians. In principle, Haitians with TPS work rights could contribute to Haiti's recovery from the hurricane with remittances they sent to family on the island.

In sum, by the end of the Obama administration, Haitian immigrant rights were only somewhat improved over the past and paled in comparison to Cubans'. Even though the Obama administration included an African American president, an African American Attorney General,

---

[102] See Douglas Massey, "The Bipartisan Origins of White Nationalism," *Daedalus* (Spring 2021), figure 4. While deporting record numbers of unauthorized immigrants, the Obama administration dramatically reduced the number forced to leave the country during its second term in office.

[103] DHS, Press Office, "Statement by Secretary Johnson Concerning His Directive to Resume Regular Removals to Haiti," (September 22, 2016) (www.dhs.gov/news/2016/09/22/statement-secretary-johnson-concerning-his-directive-resume-regular-removals-haiti).

[104] Dow, "Hurricane Matthew Further Complicates Haitian Immigration Policy;" "US-Haitian deportation on hold following hurricane (USHDOHFH)" (www.us-immigration.com/us-immigration-news/us-immigration...) (October 13, 2016).

and an African American Secretary of Homeland Security, and even though Haitians sought refuge from the poorest country in the Western Hemisphere, wracked by corruption, violence, and disrespect for civil and human rights,[105] Haitians were subject to detention and deportation that Cubans were spared. The Obama administration also admitted more Cubans than Haitians through regular immigration channels.

In his final full week in office, President Obama did make Haitian and Cuban immigration rights more comparable: when retracting rights for Cubans. He did not make them more comparable by expanding Haitian entitlements.

CONCLUSION

President Obama honored Cuban entitlements that successive administrations had initiated over the years, although he granted Cubans no new entitlements. Then, immediately before leaving office he reined in Cuban immigration privileging "as we knew it" for over half a century. The main entitlements he left in place required Congress to revoke.

He reined in Cubans' path of privilege when both the conditions that had given rise to the privileging and that subsequently had sustained it ended. While US foreign policy-based interests in privileging Cuban immigrants had already subsided with Washington's Cold War victory, Cuban immigrant beneficiaries of earlier privileging by then had become sufficiently influential to press for continued entitlements for people from their homeland. However, during President Obama's second term of office continued Cuban privileging conflicted with his commitment to cross-border bridge-building. At the same time, influential Cuban Americans, exiles and their US-born children, turned on the New Cubans. They aggressively opposed the homeland visits by recent arrivals who took advantage of the Obama administration lifting of travel restrictions.

Accordingly, President Obama's travel opening unleashed a divide between the different immigrant waves. The exile cohort and their US-born children opposed recent arrivals' cross-border bonding, which they viewed as defying the personal embargo to which they were committed. In their effort to put a halt to homeland trips, politically influential exiles,

---

[105] For a report of human rights conditions in Haiti, see U.S. Department of State, Bureau of Democracy, Human Rights, and Labor, "Haiti 2013 Human Rights Report, Country Reports on Human Rights Practices for 2013" (www.state.gov/documents/organization/220661.pdf).

and their children, publicly critiqued Cuban immigrant rights to welfare and other special benefits if they traveled to Cuba. Unfortunately for the New Cubans, they lacked the political clout to defend entitlements. .

In turn, Cuban American politicians unwittingly helped set the stage for the Obama administration's retraction of entitlements. In chastising new Cuban abuse of entitlements they created a political opening for President Obama to change policies with little pushback.

During the course of Obama's presidency, Cuba also underwent change. With Cuba struggling to adapt to the new post-Soviet era world order, Raúl, who succeeded Fidel as head of state and the Communist Party, envisioned the United States under Obama's presidency as a source of hope, not the imperialist adversary of the past. He shared a common interest with President Obama in stopping unauthorized immigration.

In retracting Cuban privileges, President Obama had hoped to reinstitute immigration by design, not default. In principle, in reining in rights of unauthorized Cuban entrants and reemphasizing safe, legal, and orderly Cuban immigration, he gifted his successor, Republican Donald Trump. Yet, as detailed in Chapter 7, President Trump shut the door to legal as well as illegal Cuban immigration, all the while that he abandoned President Obama's commitment to cross-border bridge-building. However, in instituting new measures to strangulate the Cuban economy, the Trump administration gave Cubans new reason to emigrate.

7

From Heaven to Hell under the Trump Administration

Walls for Cubans After All

Republican Donald Trump assumed the presidency just eight days after Obama announced the presidential order that terminated key Cuban immigration entitlements. How did Trump respond? Did he implement the Obama reforms, rein in entitlements Obama had left intact, or reverse Obama's reforms and restore entitlements of old? Given that by the time Trump assumed the presidency the conditions that had sustained Cuban privileging for over half a century no longer prevailed – first the Cold War concern with defeating global communism, and, then, political pressure from Cuban American beneficiaries of earlier entitlements – did he seize the opportunity to revoke remaining entitlements so that Cubans would be treated the same as other nationals? And what impact did the Obama reforms have on immigration? Did massive unauthorized Cuban immigration subside and Washington regain control over the Cubans it let in? This chapter addresses these issues, in the context of President Trump's stance on immigration more broadly. It will show how, in his efforts to preserve "America for Americans" Trump made no exception for Cubans. He even pressured other governments to assist in blocking Cubans, along with other immigrants and asylum seekers, from the United States.

THE TRUMP ADMINISTRATION WAR ON IMMIGRANTS: BRIEF OVERVIEW

While nativist hostility toward immigrants waxed and waned over the years, President Trump oversaw the most fervent attack on immigrants and refugees. He aggressively sought to keep foreigners out of the country, allegedly to "Make America Great Again," code words for "Make America White Again."

Beginning with the announcement of his presidential campaign in 2015, Trump resurrected and expanded on earlier "wars on immigrants." He claimed he would build an impermeable physical wall across the two thousand mile US–Mexican border to keep out immigrants. Mexico would pay for the wall, he said, even though it never agreed to do so. He also promised to "lock them up," meaning immigrants who managed to enter the United States unauthorized. He branded Mexicans as rapists and criminals, and persons from predominately Muslim countries, categorically, as "terrorists." He even questioned whether President Obama was born in America, to discredit him.

On assuming the presidency, Trump continued to rail against immigrants, now with the power of the office. He immediately ordered the Department of Homeland Security (DHS) to construct new detention facilities at or near the southern border, to expedite removals, and to deport the millions of immigrants who were in the country without authorization. His mass deportation campaign was highly racialized. He targeted brown-skinned people crossing the border without authorization, not white-skinned people who overstayed temporary entry visas.[1] His administration even separated children at the border from their asylum-seeking parents, tried to end legal protections of the so-called Dreamers, who came to the United States as children with parents who immigrated unauthorized, and proposed a ban on admission of persons from predominantly Muslim countries.

President Trump did not publicly target Cubans for exclusion, and some of his anti-immigrant initiatives did not apply to them. Yet, other initiatives did affect them. Moreover, as he geared up for his 2020 reelection campaign, he intensified his nativist project. Even though he had denigrated Mexicans during his first campaign, he turned to the Mexican government, as well as to Central American governments, for assistance.

President Trump crafted his restrictionist policies to appeal to the same white working class voters as had President Reagan: who perceived immigrants as "taking their jobs," willing to work for lower wages, and enjoying welfare and other benefits on their tax dollars. However,

---

[1] Robert Warren, "US Undocumented Population Continued to Fall from 2016 to 2017 and Visa Overstays Significantly Exceeded Illegal Crossings for the Seventh Consecutive Year," Center for Migration Studies (2019) (https://cmsny.org/publications/jmhs-2019-warren-2017-undocumented).

From Heaven to Hell under the Trump Administration

President Reagan launched his attack on immigrants at a time when the unemployment rate reached a record post-World War Two high (nearly 11 percent, in November 1982), a situation that was conducive to nativism. Also, he went on to sign legislation, as noted in Chapter 4, that granted several million unauthorized immigrants the opportunity to become lawful permanent residents. President Trump, in contrast, pursued his attack of immigrants when the unemployment rate was low, including in 2019 when it reached its lowest level in three decades (3.5 percent),[2] and he offered the estimated 11–12 million unauthorized immigrants then in the country no comparable path to legal residence as had President Reagan.[3] When President Trump, in 2020, geared up his campaign for reelection, he beefed up his "war on immigrants," although by then amid a surge in unemployment, greater than in the early 1980s, owing to the impact that the COVID-19 pandemic had on the economy.

When the unemployment rate was low, President Trump focused on the inequality in the distribution of the nation's wealth. While the country prospered, the White working class (and African Americans) felt left out. Rather than blame the inequity on corporate greed and his tax policies favoring the rich, President Trump blamed immigrants who were willing to work for less pay than native-born workers. He also did not acknowledge that immigrants at times created jobs and took jobs that native-born Americans shunned. Nor did he acknowledge that businesses in the neoliberal era increasingly located their operations overseas where labor costs were lower, leaving fewer jobs for Americans, and that unions, weakened by global competition and declining membership, lost the bargaining power they formerly had to defend and promote worker interests, including worker earnings.[4] As jobs moved abroad, even the historically pro-immigrant business faction of the Republican Party ceased to be a counterveiling force to the party's nativist political base that President Trump courted politically.

---

[2] "United States Unemployment Rate" (https://tradingeconomics.com/united-states/unemployment-rate); Erin Duffin, "Unemployment Rate in the U.S: 1990–2019" (February 2, 2020) (www.statista.com/statistics/193290/unemployment-rate-in-the-usa-since-1990/).

[3] Elaine Kamarck and Christine Stenglein, "How Many Undocumented Immigrants Are in the United States and Who Are They?," *Policy 2020 Brookings* (November 12, 2019) (www.brookings.edu/policy2020/votervital/how-many-undocumented-immigrants-are-in-the-united-states-and-who-are-they/).

[4] For an excellent analysis of the build-up to Trump's restrictionist policies, see Jason DeParle, "How Stephen Miller Seized the Moment to Battle Immigration," *New York Times* (August 17, 2019) (www.nytimes.com/2019/08/17/us/politics/stephen-miller.html).

Having reined in unauthorized arrivals, President Obama's parting Cuban immigration reforms appealed to President Trump's political base. On taking office, President Trump will be shown to have further restricted Cuban immigrant entitlements: though de facto more than de jura. Meanwhile, Cubans will be shown to have tried to circumvent the new restrictions. In so doing they became victims of President Trump's general "war on immigrants."

DE FACTO RETRACTION OF CUBAN ENTITLEMENTS THE OBAMA ADMINISTRATION LEFT INTACT

On taking office, President Trump formally honored both the entitlements President Obama had revoked and those he had left intact. He did not reinstate the Cuban Medical Professional Parole Program (CMPPP) or the "dry foot" practice of paroling unauthorized Cuban arrivals into the United States. At the same time, he remained officially committed to the Clinton-negotiated migration agreement that guaranteed immigration visas to minimally 20,000 Cubans a year, to the Cuban Family Reunification Parole Program (CFRPP) that President Bush initiated, and to the admission of Cuban refugees in accordance with the Refugee Act of 1980: policies implemented in years past that President Obama had left intact.

In practice, though, President Trump retracted entitlements that President Obama had left in force. Cuban privileging, as a result, became ever more a matter of history. For one, the Trump administration ceased to issue 20,000 immigration visas to Cubans yearly. Indeed, beginning in February 2018, the US embassy in Havana suspended visa-processing, other than for Cuban officials and medical emergencies.[5] Instead, the Trump administration began requiring Cubans to apply for visas in third countries if they wished to immigrate lawfully: initially requiring them to seek visas at the US Embassy in Colombia, and, subsequently, in Guyana, with no guarantee that they would actually be awarded visas, or in a timely manner. Aspiring immigrants needed to absorb the costs of the offshoring of visa granting, nearly impossible on their official salaries, the equivalent of $20 to $25 a month.

---

[5] Nora Gámez Torres, "U.S. Promise to Issue 20,000 visas to Cubans Is Jeopardized by Cuts at Embassy in Havana," *Miami Herald* (February 9, 2018) (www.miamiherald.com/news/nation-world/world/americas/cuba/article199297749.html).

The Trump administration claimed it stopped visa processing, along with other consular services, in Havana because of the mysterious "sonic attacks" that US personnel suffered at the embassy shortly before President Obama left office. Whatever the cause of the "attacks," the Trump administration made no effort to reestablish consular services at the embassy when the "attacks" subsided. It reduced personnel at the embassy to a minimum.[6]

As a result, the United States admitted only 6,626–9,480 Cubans annually through lawful channels between FY2016 and FY2018, in no year more than half the minimum specified in the 1994 bilateral migration accord.[7] With respect to lawful admissions, the Trump administration subjected Cubans to its closing of the border to all immigrants. Between FY2016 and FY2019 it slashed the number of immigration visas issued worldwide by 25 percent.[8]

However, in a nod to continued commitment to the migration accord, the Trump administration did announce a range of Cubans who were eligible for visa slots. In February 2018, the State Department noted that Cubans who were admitted to the United States through the Cuban Family Reunification Parole Program (CFRPP), or who were otherwise paroled into the country, would be granted visas; so too would Cubans who were officially admitted as refugees (along with their families), visa lottery winners, spouses of US citizens, and relatives of Cuban doctors admitted through the CMPPP before President Obama terminated the program.[9]

Yet, with respect to the CFRPP, the Trump administration imposed new bureaucratic hurdles. It required family members in the United States

---

[6] Reflecting President Trump's effort to make Cuban migration especially difficult, his administration did not withdraw staff from the US Embassy in China after similar incidents occurred in China. "U.S.-Cuba News Brief," Center for Democracy in the Americas (October 23, 2020).

[7] Department of Homeland Security (DHS), *Yearbooks of Immigration Statistics FY 2016–2018* (www.dhs.gov/immigration-statistics/yearbook/2016, 2017, 2018/table10). The Congressional Research Service (CRS) reports that while the United States met its commitment under the 1994 bilateral migration accord to grant 20,000 immigration visas (mostly via the CFRPP) in FY2017, the State Department issued travel documents for only 4,060 Cubans in FY2018 and for only 3,480 Cubans in FY2019 (through June) (CRS, *Cuba: US Policy in the 116th Congress* (May 14, 2020) (https://fas.org/sgp/crs/row/R45657.pdf).

[8] Zolan Kanno-Youngs, "Legal Immigration Starts to Plunge, Blocked by Policy, Not a Wall," *New York Times* (February 25, 2020), pp. 1, 13.

[9] Gámez Torres, "U.S. Promise to Issue 20,000 Visas to Cubans Is Jeopardized by Cuts at Embassy in Havana."

to arrange interviews for their relatives in Havana through the US National Visa Center, which added months to the application process. It also required Cubans who hoped to be admitted through the CFRPP to apply in person in third countries for the special entry visas, which meant they needed to bear the same costs and uncertainties as Cubans who applied for regular immigration visas.[10] Then, the State Department cancelled all CFRPP applicant interviews.[11] The new requirements resulted in US consular officers issuing only 134 family reunification documents in FY2018 (between October 1, 2017 and August 3, 2018), even though over 20,000 Cubans had filed applications.[12] In 2019 the Trump administration went a step further and officially suspended the program, such that by 2021, when Joe Biden took over the presidency, over 100,000 applications (including for immigration visas) were pending.[13]

With his clampdown on Cuban immigration, President Trump furthered the political divide within the Cuban American community, siding with the earlier émigrés. The recent arrivals wanted the CFRPP continued because they had more family in Cuba who wanted to emigrate. Indeed, when Ecuador-born Congresswoman Debbie Mucarsel-Powell, a Democrat, proposed legislation to restart the CFRPP, in an appeal to her New Cuban constituency, Miami-Dade County Commissioners, from exile families, refused to support her initiative. As a result, her proposed legislation never gained traction in Congress.[14]

The Trump administration treated Cubans only slightly better than Haitians. In August 2019, the US Citizenship and Immigration Services (USCIS) officially ended the Haitian Family Reunification Parole Program that President Obama had initiated, which had allowed thousands of Haitians to live with relatives in the United States while waiting to be awarded "green cards." The USCIS claimed it revoked the Haitian program to improve border security and immigration enforcement. Yet, it

---

[10] Paul Guzzo, "With End of Dry Foot Policy, Cuban Refugees Coming to Florida Dwindles," *Tampa Bay* (December 12, 2017) (www.tampabay.com/news/politics/With-end-of-dry-foot-policy-Cuban-refugees-coming-to-Florida-dwindles_163264917/).

[11] Gámez Torres, "U.S. Promise to Issue 20,000 Visas to Cubans Is Jeopardized by Cuts at Embassy in Havana."

[12] Mimi Whitefield, "New Report Shows Significant Drop in Agreed 20,000 Annual Immigrant Visas for Cubans," *Miami Herald* (October 16, 2018) (https://cubapeopletopeople.blogspot.com/2018/10/drastic-reduction-in-cuban-migrant-visas.html).

[13] "U.S.-Cuba News Brief" (Washington, DC: Center for Democracy in the Americas), March 19, 2021.

[14] "U.S.-Cuba New Brief," January 22, 2019.

espoused no comparable rationale for suspending (but not sunsetting) the Cuban program.[15] Termination of the Haitian program advanced President Trump's racist efforts to block immigration from what he called a "shithole" country.

In turn, President Trump officially continued to honor the Refugee Act of 1980, and to offer Cubans one of the United States' only in-country refugee processing programs. In practice, however, his administration admitted few Cuban as refugees. In 2018 it did not admit any. In 2019 it admitted two, but announced it would accept no new applications.[16] By contrast, in 2005 the Bush administration had officially admitted more than 6,000 Cubans as refugees, and in 2016, Obama, in his last year in office, admitted 354. President Trump showed no mercy for the Cubans who indeed were persecuted for their beliefs. The Cuban government had become neither less repressive nor more tolerant of its critics, even after Miguel Díaz-Canel, in 2019, became the first non-Castro head of state since the revolution.

At a time when the number of refugees fleeing violence and persecution worldwide swelled to 80 million, a post-World War Two high,[17] the Trump Administration turned on refugees from all countries, not merely from Cuba. In 2020, he ordered the United States to admit fewer refugees than in any year since enactment of the Refugee Act.[18] Total US refugee admissions plunged from 110,000 in Obama's last year as president to record lows of 18,000 in fiscal years 2019 and 2020, and to 15,000 in FY 2021. In 2020, the Trump administration admitted only three times more refugees from around the world as the Bush administration had admitted just from Cuba in 2005. Moreover, while it assigned 1,500 refugee slots to Salvadorans, Guatemalans, and Hondurans, it assigned none specifically to Cubans.[19] The next year it ended the practice under the Refugee

---

[15] "United States Ends 'Haitian Family Reunification Parole Programme'," *Caribbean National Weekly* (www.caribbeannational weekly.com/caribbean-breaking-news-featured/united-states-ends-haitian-family-reunification-parole-programme).

[16] Hatzel Vela, "Trump Administration Reduces Number of Refugee Admissions," *Local 10* (www.local10.com/news/cuba/cubas-refugee-admission-program-not-accepting-new-applications).

[17] Zolan Kanno-Youngs and Michael Shear, "Trump Virtually Cuts Off Refugees as He Unleashes a Tirade on Immigrants," *New York Times* (October 1, 2020) (www.nytimes.com/2020/10/01/us/politics/trump-refugees.html).

[18] Ibid.; Amanda Taub and Max Fisher, "Trump Refugee Cuts Threaten Cornerstone of Global Order," *New York Times* (September 12, 2019), p. 7.

[19] Presidential Memoranda, "Presidential Determination on Refugee Admission for Fiscal Year 2020," November 1, 2019.

Act of explicitly allotting admission slots to the different regions of the world. Instead, it prioritized Iraqis who had worked for the US military and people persecuted for their religion.[20] It also ended most refugee resettlement assistance. It claimed it retracted refugee entitlements because of the COVID-19 pandemic.

At the same time, the Trump administration enforced the one exclusionary Cuba immigration policy the Clinton administration initiated that the Obama administration had left intact: repatriation of Cubans attempting to immigrate without authorization who the Coast Guard interdicted. The Trump administration thereby reenforced a sea wall to keep out unauthorized Cuban boat people, to complement its land wall for "foot people." With the policing of the Florida Straits constricting illegal immigration by sea, fewer Cubans pressed their luck, such that interdictions declined: from 5,230 in FY2016 and 2,109 in FY2017 to 384 and 464 (through August) in fiscal years 2018 and 2019, respectively (but with interdictions picking up again in FY 2021).[21]

EXCLUSION OF UNAUTHORIZED LAND ENTRANTS: DETENTION AND DEPORTATION

The Trump administration wasted no time in subjecting Cubans to the same exclusionary policies as other unauthorized entrants when they entered by land as well as by sea. It detained and deported them.

The Trump administration did not spare Cubans from detention. Between President Obama's last year in office and the end of FY2018, US Immigration and Customs Enforcement (ICE) detentions of Cubans soared 700 percent, to 8,514.[22] As of July 2019, it had detained over 16,000 Cubans, more than any other nationals, including more than from Mexico and any single Central American country.[23] The Trump administration detained Cubans for as long as two years, in part because once released they could apply, under the Cuban Adjustment Act, for LPR.[24] Making matters worse for Cubans, ICE interned them in for-profit detention centers in the Deep South, where they were forced to live under such

---

[20] Taub and Fisher, "Trump Refugee Cuts Threaten Cornerstone of Global Order."
[21] CRS, *Cuba: US Policy in the 116th Congress* (https://fas.org/sgp/crs/row/R45657.pdf).
[22] Daniel Rivero, "Number of Cuban Nationals Detained by ICE Has Skyrocketed, New Data Shows," *WLRN-Miami* (June 18, 2019) (www.wlrn.org/post/number-cuban-nationals-detained-ice-has-skyrocketed-new-data-shows#stream/0).
[23] TRACImmigration (https://trac.syr.edu/phptools/immigration/detention/) (citizenship data).
[24] "U.S.-Cuba News Brief," October 30, 2020.

deplorable conditions that they staged protests on numerous occasions. For example, in August 2019 150 of the Cubans who were detained in a Louisiana corrections center rebelled. One Cuban took his life.[25]

If they were detained, Cubans needed to fight for asylum in the courts. Those Cubans whose claims were rejected were subject to deportation. During Trump's presidency, deportations of Cubans increased, from 64 to 463 between FY2016 and FY2018, and to 1,179 the following year: an eighteen-fold increase in three years.[26] In FY2019 some 3,700 new Cuban deportation proceedings were filed in immigration courts. This marked a record number for Cubans, although far fewer than the 21,300 and 15,600 Guatemalan and Honduran cases that were, respectively, filed.[27]

RESTRICTION OF CROSS-BORDER FAMILY VISITS

The Trump administration also made it more difficult for Cubans to visit family in the United States. In this case, it officially changed policy. In 2019 it revoked the multiple entry visas instituted by President Obama that allowed for bureaucratically easier and less costly get-togethers among relatives living on the two sides of the Florida Straits. In its place,

---

[25] Noah Lanard, "Trump Panders to Cubans, Nicaraguans, and Venezuelans While He Deports and Detains Them," *Mother Jones* (February 5, 2020) (www.motherjones.com/politics/2020/02/trump-panders-to-cubans-nicaraguans-and-venezuelans-while-he-deports-and-detains-them/), cited in *U.S.-Cuba News* (February 7, 2020).

[26] Daniel Rivero, "Cuban Immigrants Were Given a Haven in the U.S.: Now They're Being Deported," *NPR* (May 11, 2019) (www.npr.org/2019/05/11/722201692/cuban-immigrants-were-given-a-haven-in-the-u-s-now-theyre-being-deported). Other sources cite different figures. See Department of Homeland Security (DHS), *2018 Yearbook of Immigration Statistics* (www.dhs.gov/immigration-statistics/yearbook/2018); Mario Penton, Havana/Miami, "Number of Cubans Seeking Asylum at US Southern Border Triples," *Translating Cuba* (October 12, 2019) (https://translatingcuba.com/number-of-cubans-seeking-asylum-at-us-southern-border-triples/); https://trac.syr.edu/phptools/immigration/charges/deport_filing_charge.php. Gaby del Vale, "ICE Put 120 Cubans on a Flight to Havana in Major Deportation Ramp-Up," *Vice News* (www.vice.com/en_us/article/d3a3gw/ice-put-120-cubans-on-a-flight...). In the first few months of FY2020 the United States ordered 2,000 Cubans to be deported (https://trac.syr.edu/phptools/immigration/court_backlog/deport_outcome_charge.php; https://trac.syr.edu/phptools/immigration/remove/). In FY2019 there also were 25,000 Cuban deportation proceedings in the pipeline, and more than 37,000 Cubans with deportation orders.

[27] Lomi Kriel, "At the Crowded Texas Border, A Crush of Cubans Hope for Their Lucky Number," *Houston Chronicle* (April 19, 2019) (www.houstonchronicle.com/news/houston-texas/houston/article/At-the-crowded-Texas-border-a-crush-of-Cubans-13781607.php).

the Trump administration reinstituted single entry visas that were valid for two-month stays (extendable for thirty days).[28]

More significantly, the Trump administration required Cubans to go to embassies outside Cuba to attain visas for visits as well as immigration. Cubans thus were forced to absorb the costs and inconveniences involved in this visa process as well, without assurance that when arriving at a third country a US consulate would grant them the requisite documentation to travel.

For Cubans, the Trump administration made extreme use of the visa system that governments around the world had implemented since the early twentieth century to restrict and regulate entry of foreigners. While the United States had a Visa Waiver Program that allowed nationals of thirty-eight countries to enter for up to three months without a visa, only people from countries with low levels of visa overstayers were eligible.[29] Cuba was not a visa-exempted country.

Thus, while not formally revoking Cuban rights to visit, the Trump administration made US get-togethers near impossible. This was quite a contrast from the days when the Eisenhower and Kennedy administrations generously issued Cubans travel visas and visa-waivers, and when the Obama administration lifted visitation restrictions that the Bush (II) administration had imposed.

In clamping down on visits, the Trump administration introduced yet another barrier to immigration. Fewer Cubans could thereby make use of the common informal immigration strategy, of overstaying travel visas, which Cubans could readily draw on to become lawful permanent residents after one year in the United States, on the basis of the CAA. Here too the Trump administration was indifferent to the wants of recent Cuban immigrants The barriers to visits that the Trump administration imposed were very unpopular among recent immigrants.[30]

RESURGENCE OF UNAUTHORIZED IMMIGRATION UNDER A NEW GUISE: ASYLUM SEEKERS

Determined Cubans, nonetheless, did not give up on trying to immigrate. They continued to seek entry by land, but with less assurance that they

---

[28] US Embassy in Cuba, "Decreasing B2 Visa Validity for Cuban Nationals," Media Note, March 15, 2019; CRS, *Cuba: US Policy in the 116th Congress.*

[29] David FitzGerald, *Refuge beyond Reach* (New York: Oxford University Press, 2019). Cubans did require visas.

[30] *2020 FIU Cuba Poll*, p. 20.

would get into the United States and secure rights to stay than during Bush's and Obama's presidencies. They turned to a new strategy, asylum seeking.

President Obama's retraction of Cuban entitlement to parole entry did lead to a drop-off in unauthorized arrivals, although not markedly, and not for long. After the number of visa-less arrivals granted lawful permanent residency declined slightly, from 66,000 in FY2016, before the Obama policy change, to about 64,700 in FY2017,[31] in 2018 the number soared to a post-Mariel high of over 75,000 (see sources in Table 8.1). At the southwest border, the Customs and Border Protection (CBP) agency reported a three-fold increase in visa-less Cuban arrivals between FY 2018 and 2019.[32] The spike reflected Cuban resolve to move to the United States when faced with the thicket of new Trump administration barriers to legal immigration.

In FY 2019 the Trump administration finally succeeded in dramatically reining in unauthorized Cuban immigration, when implementing a series of highly restrictive policies described later in this chapter. The number of persons born in Cuba who were granted lawful permanent residency plunged to 41,641, down from 76,486 the preceding year. Seventy-nine percent of those who became LPRs in FY 2019 were "refugees and asylees,"[33] though not, as in years past, because they were paroled into the country and then had their status adjusted. Instead, the Cubans had turned to the one lawful entry path that, in principle, remained open to them until 2020: asylum. On requesting asylum, they were transferred to ICE for a court hearing.[34] In 2018, Cubans accounted for 14 percent of asylum claimants, the third largest group.[35]

---

[31] See sources in Figure 8.1.

[32] DHS, *Yearbooks of Immigration Statistics FY 2016–2018*, Table 10; "U.S.-Cuba News Brief," February 21, 2020.

[33] DHS, *Yearbook of Immigration Statistics 2019*, Tables 3 and 10 (www.dhs.gov/immigration-statistics/yearbook/2019/table3 and table 10).

[34] Anna Giaritelli, "Some 700 Cuban Migrants Join Central American Caravan Traveling on Foot to US-Mexico Border," *Washington Examiner* (March 25, 2019) (www.washingtonexaminer.com/news/some-700-cuban-migrants-join-central-american-caravan-traveling-on-foot-to-us-mexico-border).

[35] David Bier, "Cuban Credible Fear Asylum Claims Surge after Ending Wet Foot, Dry Foot," *Cato at Liberty*, Cato Institute (March 20, 2019) (www.cato.org/blog/cuban-credible-fear-asylum-claims-surge-after-ending-wet-foot-dry-foot). Although Cubans had valid reasons for leaving the island, including to escape politically motivated harassment and economic hardship, they did not face the same threats to their lives as did many Central Americans.

Cubans could not assume that they would be granted asylum. For the first time they needed to prove that they had fled persecution or probable persecution and contend with a lengthy petitioning process. Moreover, they had to "compete" with others from around the world for hearings. For example, in 2020 Cubans faced a backlog of over 1 million asylum applications, up from half a million three years earlier.[36] The Trump administration's "zero tolerance" of unauthorized border crossers, including unauthorized Cubans, fueled the backlog. The number of Cuban asylum applicants rose 374 percent between September 2018 and December 2019. Compounding problems for Cubans, immigration judges did not routinely accept their asylum claims. In FY2019 judges rejected more than half of the claims Cubans filed,[37] in part because President Trump's first Attorney General, Jeff Sessions, sharply restricted legal grounds for asylum.[38] Also, the Trump administration initiated "performance quotas," requiring immigration judges to hear scores of cases, such that claimants had difficulty defending their cases. Cubans, among others, faced "assembly-line" hearings.

Making matters worse, in the spring of 2020, amid the COVID-19 pandemic, the Trump administration suspended immigration court proceedings. Cubans, along with other asylum seekers, were left unable to argue their cases.

Yet, as in years past, Cubans faced fewer barriers than Haitians. President Trump spared Cubans some of the indignity with which he treated Haitians. Several examples are illuminating. In December 2017 the *New York Times* reported that when a White House official reported that 15,000 immigration visas had been awarded to Haitians that year, the president responded by saying, "They all have AIDs," a fallacy discredited a quarter century in the past,[39] and thus a racist smear. Then, in January 2018, President Trump held a White House meeting with Democratic and Republican members of Congress to discuss

---

[36] Nolan Rappaport, "Trump's Latest Gambit: Send Asylum Seekers to 'Safe Third Countries' That Are Less than Safe," *The Hill* (November 24, 2019) (https://thehill.com/opinion/immigration/471820-trumps-latest-gambit-send-asylum-seekers-to-safe-third-countries-that-are).

[37] "U.S.-Cuba News Brief" (Washington, DC: Center for Democracy in the Americas), January 17, 2020. TRAC reports slightly different figures: that 2,342 of 5,228 Cuban asylum cases were denied in FY2019 (https://trac.syr.edu/phptools/immigration/asylum/).

[38] For example, victims of domestic, gender, or gang violence ceased to be considered valid claims for asylum.

[39] Nathalie Baptiste, "Trump Is Trying to Deport Haitian Immigrants. They're Fighting Back" (www.motherjones.com/politics/2018/12/haitian-immigrants-temporary-protected-status-trump/).

codifying rights for immigrants whose parents had brought them illegally to the United States as children. In the meeting, he asked whether Haitians could be excluded from consideration.[40] A year later, President Trump notoriously railed against Haitians, along with Salvadorans and some Africans, as coming from "shithole" countries, and therefore being unsuited for the United States. Matching deeds to his words, President Trump announced that Haitian entitlement to TPS, which President Obama had granted after the 2010 earthquake, would end in July 2019. Haitians who were not lawful permanent residents thus would (re)join the ranks of illegal immigrants and be subject to deportation, and also be ineligible for rights to work and welfare. Fortunately for Haitians, legal challenges led the Trump administration to extend Haitian TPS until January 2021.

Cubans had persisted in their efforts to circumvent the barriers that the Trump administration had imposed for a combination of what might be called "push" and "pull" reasons. On the "push" side, economic opportunities in Cuba remained depressed, exacerbated by President Trump's aggressive rollback of President Obama's "normalization" initiatives. Trump interventions were reminiscent of the Cold War, and were intended to strangulate the Cuban economy. He introduced new restrictions on Cuba tourism and on the money that Cuban Americans could remit to family on the island, to limit Cuban government access to direly needed hard currency. In addition, his efforts to strangulate the Venezuelan economy, to force its Left-leaning autocratic president, Nicolas Maduro, from power, indirectly hurt the Cuban economy. Venezuela, as a result, had less oil to export, which it had been selling to Cuba at a subsidized price. Cuba thus needed to purchase higher priced oil on the world market, which added to the country's economic woes. Had President Trump wanted to discourage Cuban emigration, he would have done better by improving, rather than constricting, opportunities on the island.

Meanwhile, "pull" factors contributed to stepped up Cuban interest in immigration. For one, in 2018 the Panamanian and Nicaraguan governments had begun to offer inexpensive tourist visas that made Cubans' trek by land to the United States faster, cheaper, and less risky. Until then, as noted in Chapter 6, Cubans had needed to begin their trek in Ecuador or

---

[40] Julie Hirschfeld Davis, Sheryl Gay Stolberg, and Thomas Kaplan, "Trump Alarms Lawmakers with Disparaging Words for Haiti and Africa," *New York Times* (January 11, 2018) (www.nytimes.com/by/julie-hirschfeld-davis).

Guyana, the countries closest to the United States that did not require entry visas.[41] Also, increasing numbers of Cubans came to have relatives in the United States who were willing to help finance their move and help them adapt on arrival. Anticipating that President Trump would crack down on immigration as he stepped up his reelection campaign, many Cubans did not risk waiting.

TRANSFORMATION OF MEXICO AND CENTRAL AMERICAN COUNTRIES INTO AGENTS OF CUBAN EXCLUSION

Beginning in 2014, the number of Central Americans seeking asylum in the United States soared, as El Salvador, Honduras, and Guatemala experienced widespread cartel and other gang violence, horrific levels of violence against women (the highest female homicide rates in the world), kidnappings, and murders. The dire conditions were exacerbated by economic downturns in the three countries, severe drought attributed to climate change, and unresolved tensions dating back to the civil wars in the region in the 1980s.

In his determination to block the tens of thousands of unauthorized Central Americans, as well as Cubans, seeking asylum in the United States, President Trump turned to foreign governments for assistance. He offered the governments little choice in the matter, threatening economic reprisal if they refused to cooperate. He turned to them to do what he was unable to achieve on his own.

Transforming Mexico into a Collaborator in US Immigrant and Refugee Exclusion

Faced with the threat of what could be viewed as a "Land Mariel Type Influx,"[42] President Trump went beyond previously described Bush and

---

[41] Kriel, "At the Crowded Texas Border, A Crush of Cubans Hope for Their Lucky Number."

[42] As early as 1989, an Immigration and Naturalization Service report on immigration issues to the Attorney General and the National Security Council under the Bush administration made reference to a "Land Mariel Type Influx" that should be avoided. The increase in Central American illegal immigration at the time was seen as possibly the beginning of such a land influx. George W. Bush Presidential Library, Nicholas Rostow Files, Subject Files, Presidential Record National Security Council, "Report to the Attorney General and the National Security Council on Immigration Issues," January 12, 1989.

Obama administration initiatives to pressure the Mexican government to assist in immigration control.[43] The fact that he had previously slandered Mexicans, claiming them to be rapists and criminals, did not inhibit him. Meanwhile, the Mexican government was left to deal with problems that Trump-initiated policies generated.

As a starter, in May 2018, the Trump administration introduced so-called metering, a new obstacle for asylum seekers. Metering involved restrictions on the number of persons admitted daily into the United States at ports of entry along the southwest border to make asylum claims. With the metering program, President Trump turned Mexico into America's waiting room. While affecting all prospective migrants seeking refuge in the United States at the southern border, Cubans, who used to walk across the border and immediately be paroled into the country, were forced to wait with others in Mexico.

Under the metering system different US ports of entry set different, seemingly arbitrary, caps on the number of "credible fear" claimants they allowed in daily. All caps were low, varying from zero to a few dozen.[44] Cubans would gravitate to Mexican border cities where they believed their entry prospects to be best and quickest, sharing information among themselves by social media and WhatsApp.[45]

The metering system required Mexican government cooperation since asylum seekers needed to stay in Mexico until the United States admitted them to make their claims for refuge. President Trump threatened Mexico's incoming president, Andrés Manuel López Obrador, with new tariffs on Mexican imports if he did not cooperate with the metering policy. Tariffs would reduce the competitiveness of Mexican exports in the US market. President Trump did not let multilateral accords dedicated to reducing trade barriers between the United States and Mexico stand in his way: neither the North American Free Trade Agreement (NAFTA),

---

[43] James Fredrick, "How Mexico Beefs Up Immigration Enforcement to Meet Trump's Terms," *NPR* (July 13, 2019) (www.npr.org/2019/07/13/740009105/how-mexico-beefs-up-immigration-enforcement-to-meet-trumps-terms).

[44] Kirk Semple, "Migration Surge from Central America Was Spurred, in Part, by Mexican Policies," *New York Times* (April 1, 2019) (www.nytimes.com/2019/04/01/world/americas/mexico-migration-border.html).

[45] For example, before President Trump imposed the metering policy, Cubans entering the United States by land typically did so via the Mexican city of Nuevo Laredo, across the border from Laredo, Texas. After the metering was instituted, Cubans began to gravitate to other border cities as well, such as to Ciudad Juarez, across the Rio Grande from El Paso. Bier, "Cuban Credible Fear Asylum Claims Surge after Ending Wet Foot, Dry Foot."

nor its successor, the United States–Mexico–Canadian Agreement (USMCA), which his administration was negotiating at the time. Faced with the threat of economic reprisals, López Obrador backtracked on his campaign promise to defend and promote migrant rights. The Trump administration pressured him to concede control over his country's immigration policies.

As a further discouragement to potential asylum seekers, in January 2019 the Trump administration introduced the highly contentious program, Remain in Mexico, which was also dependent on Mexican government collaboration. Officially known as the Migrant Protection Protocols (MPP), it left asylum seekers anything but protected in Mexico.[46] Remain in Mexico was designed to further transform Mexico into the waiting room for US asylum seekers, in requiring them to stay in Mexico not only until they were "metered" into the United States to register their asylum claims but also afterward, while waiting for their court hearings in the United States.[47] Cubans comprised the third largest group of asylum seekers that the Trump administration forced to wait in Mexico.

While López Obrador initially opposed the MPP, he ultimately acquiesced to it in order to avoid additional tariffs, as high as 25 percent on Mexican products, which President Trump threatened to impose.[48] As of May 2020, 8,438 Cubans, out of a total of 65,246 asylum-seekers, were forced to wait for their asylum hearings in Mexico.[49] Many waited in Mexico eight months, without work and legal protections, under substandard, unsanitary, dangerous living conditions, in tent encampments. They faced the backlog of cases in immigration courts that had come to exceed a million.

While they waited in Mexican border cities, the Cubans, along with other asylum seekers, were at the mercy of criminal gangs that vied for control of drug trafficking routes; murderers; armed robbers; kidnappers; and persons who extorted and sexually assaulted them (including police,

---

[46] Jay Root, "In a Mexican Border City, Trump's Plan to Discourage Migrants Appears to Be Working As Some Give Up on Asylum," *Texas Tribune* (July 26, 2019) (www.texastribune.org/2019/07/26/migrants-giving-asylum-after-trump-policies-slow-them-down/).

[47] "U.S.-Cuba News Brief," February 7, 2020; TRACImmigration, "Details on MPP (Remain in Mexico) Deportation Proceedings" (trac.syr.edu/phptools/immigration/mpp/).

[48] Azan Ahmed and Paulina Villegas, "Mexico Has Two Options in Dealing with Trump Demands on Migration. Both Could Hurt," *New York Times* (June 7, 2019) (www.nytimes.com/2019/06/07/world/americas/mexico-tariffs-amlo.html).

[49] TRACImmigration, "Details on MPP (Remain in Mexico) Deportation Proceedings." (https://trac.syr.edu/phptools/immigration/mpp).

immigration officers, and customs officials).[50] The Trump administration was indifferent to their suffering.

Indicative of the suffering to which asylum seekers were subjected, a lawyer in Laredo, Texas found half of the migrants she interviewed to have had someone in their family kidnapped, extorted, or assaulted by narco cartels while waiting across the border in Nuevo Laredo, one of the border Mexican cities where Cuban asylum seekers were forced to wait. The US State Department compared the risk level in Nuevo Laredo to that of Syria, North Korea, and Yemen. In turn, the homicide rate in Ciudad Juarez, across the border from El Paso, where many Cubans also waited for their US court hearings, was four times that of New York, with six times the population.[51]

So horrific were the conditions in Mexico where asylum seekers were forced to wait that one asylum officer resigned, in protest that the officers were having to "literally send(ing) people back (to Mexico) to be raped and killed."[52] The metering and the Remain in Mexico policies compounded risks that asylum seekers confronted above and beyond the dangers they experienced on their treks through Central America to the US–Mexican border.

Cubans' problems were further compounded by the gangs and other criminals who targeted them more than other migrants. In that Cubans were believed to have family networks in the United States with greater economic means than other asylum-seekers, they were held for greater ransom.

Making matters worse, in Mexico few asylum seekers had access to legal counsel.[53] Because US-based lawyers were reluctant to work in the high-crime Mexican border cities, asylum seekers had difficulty attaining legal representation. In 2019, only 4 percent of the asylum seekers waiting in Mexico for their court hearings in the United States had attorneys, compared to nearly one-third of asylum seekers living in the United States.[54] Yet, immigrants with legal counsel were five times more likely than those without it to win their cases.[55] Furthermore, Cuban asylum

---

[50] Cedar Attanasio, "Migrants Face Violence As US Makes Them Wait in Mexico," *AP News* (June 27, 2019) (https://apnews.com/od4a28d1153547a7a777e29489e7fb85).
[51] Ibid.
[52] Sonia Nazario, "'What Part of Illegal Don't You Understand'," *New York Times* (February 23, 2020), Opinion Section, pp. 4–5.
[53] Kino Border Initiative, "Remain in Mexico: An Assault on Asylum" (June 23, 2019) (www.kinoborderinitiative.org/remain-in-mexico/).
[54] Alejandro Lazo, "Fewer Asylum Seekers Get Lawyers," *Wall Street Journal* (February 1–2, 2020), p. A3.
[55] Ibid.

seekers complained that US immigration authorities required a lot of proof, with little time to present their claims.[56] Thus, even though the Trump administration referred to Cuba as part of a "troika of tyranny" – Cuba, Venezuela, and Nicaragua – it impeded Cubans' ability to attain asylum in the United States.

Confronted with the dangerous and tumultuous conditions in the Mexican border cities and without assurance that they would be granted asylum once they were allowed to present their claims to US immigration judges, Cubans in stepped up, but unknown, numbers gave up on waiting in Mexico and tried to enter the United States illegally, between ports of entry, often with the assistance of people smugglers they hired.[57] They climbed over the fence, traversed the desert, and crossed the Rio Grande. While asylum seekers were better protected in the United States than in Mexico, Border Patrol data show that many of the Cubans who tried to enter the United States without authorization during Trump's presidency did not succeed. The number of Cubans who Border Patrol apprehended soared from 194 in FY 2018 to nearly 12,000 the following year.[58] President Obama's retraction of Cubans' near-automatic rights to parole had not convinced them to give up on trying to immigrate.

President Trump's contentious, cruel interventions that embroiled Mexico in his efforts to keep asylum seekers out of the United States did spur litigation on asylum seekers' behalf. An appeals court, for example, blocked implementation of the Remain in Mexico program. It contended that the program was at odds both with federal law and international treaties, and that it caused "extreme and irreversible harm" to asylum seekers. However, on March 11, 2020 the Supreme Court ruled that the Trump administration could continue the program while the lower courts continued deliberations. The ruling applied to people from a third country who traveled through Mexico to reach the US border. Remarkably, the Supreme Court permitted continuation of the Remain in Mexico program, despite the State Department issuing a human rights report

---

[56] Mario Penton, Havana/Miami, "Number of Cubans Seeking Asylum at US Southern Border Triples," *Translating Cuba* (October 12, 2019) (https://translatingcuba.com/number-of-cubans-seeking-asylum-at-us-southern-border-triples/).

[57] U.S. Border Patrol, "U.S. Border Patrol Nationwide Apprehensions by Citizenship and Sector" (2018, 2019) (www.cbp.gov/sites/default/files/assets/documents/2020-Jan/U.S.%20Border%20Patrol%20Nationwide%20Apprehensions%20by%20Citizenship%20and%20Sector%20%28FY2007%20-%20FY%202019%29_1.pdf).

[58] U.S. Border Patrol, "U.S. Border Patrol Nationwide Apprehensions by Citizenship and Sector in FY2007" (www.cbp.gov/sites/default/files/assets/documents/2018-Jul/usbp-nationwide-apps-sector-citizenship-fy07-fy17.pdf).

warning of "arbitrary killings, forced disappearance and torture" of migrants by armed groups in Mexico.[59]

Outsourcing Immigrant Control to Mexico

The Trump administration proceeded to pressure the Mexican government to implement its own policies to block Cubans and other nationals seeking asylum in the United States. It thereby turned Mexico into a formally independent agent of US exclusion.

In this vein, in early 2019, Mexico stopped issuing "exit passes," a type of humanitarian visa it had been offering to undocumented migrants. "Exit passes" had enabled asylum seekers to traverse Mexico legally, from the country's southern border with Guatemala to its northern border with the United States. Without such a pass, visa-less migrants did not have legal protections in Mexico. The Mexican government stopped issuing the passes at Trump administration insistence, when threatened again with tariffs on Mexican imports.

Mexican authorities proceeded to detain US asylum seekers who were without "exit passes," including Cubans. Between 2018 and 2019, the number of Cubans who Mexico detained increased nearly fifteen-fold, from approximately 500 to 7,428.[60] Aside from having to absorb the costs of detaining the Cubans, Mexico had to contend with Cuban resistance to their detention and to the abysmal conditions of their detention: having been accustomed to being paroled into the United States for more than half a century. In April of 2019 some 1,300 angry Cubans staged a mass escape from a detention center in Tapachula, in the southern Mexican state of Chiapas, after detention officers ignored earlier protests.[61] Mexico operated the facilities at roughly double capacity, with insufficient food for detainees.[62]

---

[59] Adam Liftak and Kanno-Youngs, "Justices Revive Trump's Migrant Program," *New York Times* (March 12, 2020), p. 21.
[60] Cuadro 3.1.1 "Eventos de extranjeros presentados ante la autoridad migratoria, según continente y país de nacionalidad," 2017, 2018, 2019, *Boletín Mensual de Estadísticas Migratorias* (http://portales.segob.gob.mx/es/PoliticaMigratoria/CuadrosBOLETIN?Anual=2017, 2018, 2019).
[61] Associated Press, "Mass Breakout: 1,300 Cubans Escape from Immigration Centre in Mexico," *South China Morning Post* (April 26, 2019) (www.scmp.com/news/world/americas/article/3007776/mass-breakout-1300-cubans-escape-immigration-centre-mexico).
[62] Greg Norman, "More than 1,000 Cuban Migrants Break Out of Mexican Immigration Facility," *South China Morning Post* (April 26, 2019) (www.foxnews.com/world/cuban-migrants-escape-in-mexico).

Under US pressure, Mexico also increased deportations of the unauthorized immigrants without "exit passes," sparing the United States from deporting them. As of 2019 Mexico deported more Cubans than did the United States, even though most of the Cubans that Mexico deported were seeking refuge in the United States, not in Mexico.[63] Mexican deportations of Cubans rose more than eight-fold between 2018 and 2019, from 179 to 1,503, while the United States deported around 500 Cubans.[64]

Faced with the new obstacles that the Mexican government, as well as US border patrol, imposed, some Cubans joined Central Americans in what came to be known as caravans. Caravans included as many as one thousand, and sometimes even more, asylum seekers, who, en masse, better shielded themselves from gangs, criminals, and extortion by Mexican officials along their trek to the United States than when traveling on their own. For example, in 2019 about 700 Cubans joined a Central American caravan of about the same size.[65] They joined the caravan after Mexican authorities closed the National Institute of Migration office in the southern state of Chiapas, abutting Guatemala, which left approximately 2,000 Cubans stranded without legal rights in Mexico. The Mexican government shut the office when firing 500 immigration agents who were illegally charging migrants as much as the equivalent of $700 to $800 dollars to expedite their admission to Mexico.[66]

Nonetheless, the caravans did not escape President Trump's aggressive effort to block US asylum seekers. He pressured the Mexican government to break up the caravans and set up road barriers to block their route to the United States: in this case, threatening not only to impose tariffs on

---

[63] Rui Ferreira, "United States Has Deported 1,179 Cubans in 2019," *On Cuba News* (December 20, 2019) (https://oncubanews.com/en/cuba-usa/united-states-has-deported-1179-cubans-in-2019); Associated Press, "More Cubans Are Being Deported under the Trump Administration," *News* (October 11, 2019) (www.nbcnews.com/news/latino/more-cubans-are-being-deported-under-trump-administration-n1065041); Cuadro 3.2.1, "Eventos de extranjeros devueltos por la autoridad migratoria mexicana, según continente y país de nacionalidad," 2017, 2018, 2019, *Boletín Mensual de Estadísticas Migratorias*.

[64] TRAC Cuba Detention (www.google.com/search?q=TRAC+Cuba+detention&tbm=isch&ved=2ahUKEwjT8KbaosvsAhUDPd8KHW8fByAQ2-cCegQIABAA&oq=TRAC+Cuba+detention&gs_lcp=CgNpbWcQDFAAWABg-8MGaABwAHgAgAEAiAEAkgEAmAEAqgELZ3dzLXdpei1pbWc&sclient=img&ei=bomTX5P9HoP6_AbvvpyAAg&client=firefox-b-1-d).

[65] Anna Giaritelli, "Some 700 Cuban Migrants Join Central American Caravan Traveling on Foot to US-Mexico Border."

[66] Fredrick, "How Mexico Beefs Up Immigration Enforcement to Meet Trump's Terms."

Mexican exports but also to close part of the border that was an essential lifeline for the Mexican economy if the Mexican government did not comply.[67] Until then, Mexican authorities had let caravans freely transit the country.

Then, in June 2019 the Trump administration convinced Mexico to sign a Joint Declaration that formally committed Mexico to serve as Washington's foreign "police force." The Joint Declaration called for militarizing Mexico's immigration control, to block asylum seekers from the United States. In the context of the agreement, López Obrador ordered Mexican soldiers and National Guard to police the country to stop so-called irregular migration. Within a month after signing the agreement he commissioned 6,500 National Guard to serve near the country's southern border, to block "irregular migrants" from entering. In addition, he ordered 15,000 National Guard to serve in the country's north, to prevent those who managed to enter the country from reaching the United States. The build-up of the National Guard broke Mexico's commitment since the revolution of the early twentieth century to restrict military and paramilitary involvement in civil society. Mexico's National Guard came to serve as a human wall, to supplement the physical wall across the US–Mexican border that remained only partially constructed.

In the Joint Declaration, Mexico also committed to take "decisive action" to dismantle human smuggling and trafficking organizations, and to disrupt the illicit financial and transportation networks on which much of the "irregular migration" rested.[68] The earlier efforts by the Obama and Clinton administrations to stop human smuggling of Cubans (and others) never succeeded: undermined by the economic interests of the smugglers, and continued interest in immigration to the United States, without authorization if not possible with authorization. Arguably, the demand for smugglers increased with the Trump administration's clampdown on legal immigration despite Mexico's official commitment to take "decisive action."

By late 2019 President Trump made transparent his effort to transform Mexico into a buffer country for the United States: "I'm using Mexico to

---

[67] Julia Love, "Inspired by Migrant Caravans, New Wave of Cubans Seek U.S. Asylum," *Reuters* (April 8, 2019) (www.reuters.com/article/us-usa-immigration-mexico-cuba/inspired-by-migrant-caravans-new-wave-of-cubans-seek-us-asylum-idUSKCN1RK2KI).

[68] US-Mexican Joint Declaration, Department of State, Office of the Spokesperson, Washington, DC (www.state.gov/u-s-mexico-joint-declaration/).

protect our border,"⁶⁹ he announced. The Mexican government, indeed, kept many, though far from all, asylum seekers from the United States.

Offshoring US Exclusion to Central America

The outsourcing of immigration control to Mexico was only partially effective in that in FY2019 US Border Patrol arrested nearly a million migrants at the southwest border who managed to get past Mexican government barriers.⁷⁰ The Trump administration responded in the summer and fall of 2019 by offshoring US immigration control also to the governments of Guatemala, El Salvador, and Honduras, the so-called Northern Triangle countries. It did so on the basis of so-called Asylum Cooperation Agreements, also referred to as Safe Third Country Agreements, on terms that the United States largely dictated.

The Asylum Cooperation Agreements required migrants to seek asylum in countries through which they passed. For the first time, if migrants passed through a country (other than their own) before reaching the United States, their intended destination, the Trump administration deemed them ineligible for asylum in the United States: a ruling that went on to be challenged in the courts.⁷¹ Only if they were denied asylum in another country or were a victim of severe human trafficking abuse were they to be eligible to apply for asylum in the United States.

The Asylum Cooperation Agreements also called for deporting asylum seekers who managed to reach the United States to Central American countries that were party to such agreements. Asylum seekers thereby would be sent to countries that were consumed with their own domestic economic, political, and social problems, to countries that were unsafe and ill-equipped to absorb asylum seekers, and to countries in such bad straits that they fueled the very massive uptick in US asylum seeking that President Trump sought to contain. Cubans were among the asylum

---

⁶⁹ Cited in Jorge Ramos, "Mexico Is the Wall," *New York Times* (October 8, 2019), p. 23.
⁷⁰ U.S. Customs and Border Patrol, DHS, "Southwest Border Migration FY2019" (www.cbp.gov/newsroom/stats/sw-border-migration/fy-2019).
⁷¹ Nicole Narea, "Trump's Agreements in Central America Are Dismantling the Asylum System As We Know It," *Vox* (November 20, 2019) (www.vox.com/2019/9/26/20870768/trump-agreement-honduras-guatemala-el-salvador-explained); "Trump Administration's Third-Country Transit Bar Is an Asylum Ban That Will Return Refugees to Danger," *Human Rights First* (September 13, 2019) (www.humanrightsfirst.org/resource/trump-administration-s-third-country-transit-bar-asylum-ban-will-return-refugees-danger); Adam Liptak, "Justices Permit U.S. to Exclude More Asylum Seekers," *New York Times* (September 12, 2019), p. 29.

seekers subject to forced resettlement in Central America. Although the asylum seekers were not, by any stretch of the imagination, sent to "safe third countries," the Trump Administration intended the new program to replace the Remain in Mexico and metering programs, in which asylum seekers stood some chance of refuge in the United States.

The new program called for the most monumental change in US asylum policy since enactment of the Refugee Act of 1980. It was designed to shut down the United States almost entirely to asylum seekers. In formulating the program the Trump administration exploited a loophole in the 1951 United Nations Refugee Convention specifying that while refugees could not be forcibly returned to countries where they might be persecuted, they could be sent to a third country where they would be safe.[72] The Trump Administration would not return asylum seekers to their home country, but to a different country. However, the countries with which it had agreements, namely, El Salvador, Honduras, and Guatemala, had the highest, fifth highest, and sixteenth highest homicide rates in the world, respectively.[73]

The Trump administration pressured Central American governments to sign "Asylum Cooperation Agreements." It focused first on Guatemala. It threatened the Guatemalan president that if he did not sign one such agreement then Guatemalans would be banned from the United States, heavy tariffs would be imposed on Guatemalan exports to the United States, and charges would be increased for Guatemalans in the United States who sent money to family back home.[74] Faced with the threats, the Guatemalan president conceded, but did so amid strong opposition from Guatemalans who believed that their country's agreement would make Guatemala even more unsafe than it already was, as well as from the country's Constitutional Court, which raised technical issues.

Despite the protests, in November 2019 the Trump administration began to deport Honduran and Salvadoran asylum-seekers to Guatemala, facing immediate resistance from those deported. Rather than be forced to resettle in Guatemala, some deportees opted to return to their

---

[72] Christopher Sherman, "AP Explains: US Sending Asylum Seekers to Central America," *Washington Times* (January 15, 2020) (www.washingtontimes.com/news/2020/jan/15/ap-explains-us-sending-asylum-seekers-to-central-a/).
[73] Rappaport, "Trump's Latest Gambit."
[74] Narea, "Trump's Agreements in Central America Are Dismantling the Asylum System as We Know It."

home country, from which they, in desperation, had fled.⁷⁵ The Trump administration even faced resistance from immigration bureaucrats who were in charge of the deportations. Particularly notably, in March 2020, after more than 800 Hondurans and Salvadorans were sent to Guatemala, the union representing the federal asylum and refugee officers commissioned to implement the Safe Third Country agreement protested. In a brief that the union filed in support of a lawsuit challenging the Safe Third Country policy, it claimed that deporting migrants to a country where they were likely to face persecution violated international treaty obligations; that the officers were being forced to enforce a policy that ran contrary to the laws they were trained to implement and that violated their oath of office; and that refugees from the Northern Triangle countries were being sent to other Northern Triangle countries, some of the most dangerous countries in the world. One spokesperson for the union referred to Trump's Safe Third Country policy as a "refugee deterrence system."⁷⁶

While deporting asylum seekers to Guatemala amid resistance, the Trump administration negotiated similar agreements with the Salvadoran and Honduran governments. In order to convince the Salvadoran government to sign an "asylum cooperation agreement" after denigrating Salvadorans, like Haitians, as coming from a "shithole" country, the Trump administration offered, as a quid pro quo, to invest in El Salvador and arrange for the approximately 200,000 Salvadorans with TPS to be given rights to permanent residency in the United States. President Trump left office without acting on his promises.⁷⁷

The Honduran accord mainly targeted Cubans and Nicaraguans, the main asylum seekers who transited through Honduras. The Honduran government claimed that sixteen thousand Cubans arrived during FY 2019.⁷⁸ They were to be diverted to a country far more dangerous than Cuba, and even more dangerous than Mexico, where the Trump administration forced Cuban, along with other, asylum seekers to live while

---

⁷⁵ Nick Miroff, Mary Beth Sheridan, and Kevin Sieff, "Surge of Mexican Migrants Is New Challenge for Trump Border Crackdown," *Washington Post* (October 18, 2019) (www.washingtonpost.com/national/surge-of-mexican-migrants-is-new-challenge-for-trump-border-crackdown/2019/10/18/c40f6e72-f029-11e9-b648-76bcf86eb67e_story.html).

⁷⁶ Kanno-Youngs, "Immigration Officers Condemn Guatemala Deal," *New York Times* (March 7, 2020), p, 13.

⁷⁷ Narea, "Trump's Agreements in Central America Are Dismantling the Asylum System as We Know It."

⁷⁸ "U.S.-Cuba News Brief," September 13, 2019.

waiting for asylum hearings in the United States under the "metering" and Remain in Mexico programs. The Honduran agreement notwithstanding, the State Department warned against going to Honduras, where homicide, armed robbery, extortion, violent street crime, rape, narcotics, and human trafficking were widespread.[79]

The Salvadoran and Honduran governments signed the agreements after Secretary of State Mike Pompeo withheld aid, per request of President Trump. President Trump insisted that aid to the impoverished countries be conditional on the governments serving as offshore agents of US migration control.[80] However, neither of the agreements were ever implemented, unlike the agreement with Guatemala (and, fortunately for asylum-seekers, the Biden administration immediately withdrew from all three of the highly contentious accords).

The Mexican government, meanwhile, resisted US pressure to sign a Safe Third Country style agreement: after having acquiesced to the "metering" and the Remain in Mexico programs. Had López Obrador agreed, tens of thousands of Guatemalans would have been diverted to Mexico. Mexico is the only country through which Guatemalans pass en route to the United States. With the Mexican government itself expelling asylum seekers, it opposed accepting persons that the United States had rejected.

To address the flood of asylum seekers, López Obrador recommended that the Trump administration invest heavily in Central America, to deter interest in immigration at its origin: the antithesis of Secretary of State Pompeo's punitive approach. In October 2019, the Trump administration did agree to restore some "targeted assistance" to countries in the region, although not enough to put a halt to the mass migration from the region. In extending assistance, President Trump claimed he was rewarding governments for having agreed to Safe Third Country accords, as well as for working to end the scourge of human smuggling (albeit without success).[81]

---

[79] Priscilla Álvarez and Geneva Sands, "US Signs Asylum Deal with Honduras, the Latest in A String of Agreements with Central America," *CNN Politics*, September 25, 2019.

[80] Daniel Trotta, "U.S. Restores Aid to Central America after Reaching Migration Deals," *Reuters* (October 16, 2019) (www.reuters.com/article/us-usa-immigration-aid/us-restores-aid-to-central-america-after-reaching-migration-deals-idUSKBN1WV2T8).

[81] Alan Gómez, "U.S. Aid to Central America: What It Does, Why Trump Cut It and Why That May Not End the Migration Crisis," *USA Today* (April 4, 2019) www.usatoday/news/politics/2019/04/04.

In an off-the-record conversation at Boston University in January 2020, a high-ranking Mexican foreign service official acknowledged that the limited assistance the Trump administration offered would not suffice. She opined that the United States needed a Central American "Marshall Plan." Such a plan would offer massive aid to foster social and economic development, to address problems caused by climate change, to rein in corruption, and to improve security. Moreover, because the limited aid that the United States provided mainly went to law enforcement and security, the Trump administration left the conditions causing Central Americans to flee their homelands unaddressed.

The offshoring of asylum had a precedent in the European Union. However, in not addressing problems that Europe incurred – the failure to deter asylum seekers, the failure to rein in smuggling networks that helped migrants escape overseas detention, and the failure to effectively enforce migration policy[82] – the Trump administration faced comparable problems.

The Trump administration, in essence, turned to the Mexican and then the Guatemalan government not only to serve as agents of US border control but also to accommodate Cuban and other asylum seekers. The Honduran and Salvadoran governments were to do the same. The governments cooperated not under conditions of their choosing, but under threats of economic reprisal if they refused. Finding themselves between a rock and a hard place, they prioritized their countries' economic interests over protecting and advancing the human rights and yearnings of asylum seekers. Meanwhile, President Trump was indifferent to the adverse consequences his outsourcing and offshoring of immigration control had both on the asylum seekers and the countries involved. His policies exacerbated the very dire conditions that fueled immigration. With regard specifically to Cubans, the Trump administration outsourced and offshored immigration control while officially remaining committed to admitting at least twenty thousand of them yearly, lawfully.

Faced with the Mexican and Central American governments collaborating with the Trump administration to make US asylum more difficult, Cubans in stepped up numbers directly sought asylum in Mexico. With the closing of the US option, the number of Cubans who sought asylum in

---

[82] Susan Fratzke, "International Experience Suggests Safe Third-Country Agreement Would Not Solve the U.S.-Mexico Border Crisis," *Migration Policy Institute* (June 2019) (www.migrationpolicy.org/news/safe-third-country-agreement-would-not-solve-us-mexico-border-crisis). FIU, *2016 FIU CubaPoll* (https://cri.fiu.edu/research/cuba-poll/2016-cuba-poll.pdf).

Mexico soared, from 214 in 2018 to over 8,700 the following year.[83] Cubans became the main asylum seekers in Mexico.

WHY THE TRUMP ADMINISTRATION DEEPENED CUBAN IMMIGRANTS' REVERSAL OF FORTUNE

As noted in Chapter 6, President Obama revoked Cuban entitlements that fueled unauthorized immigration, that conflicted with his commitment to improve US–Cuban relations, that influential Cuban Americans no longer defended, and that other immigrant groups resented. On assuming the presidency, Trump had no interest in reinstating the entitlements, even though he revamped a Cold War-style hostile foreign policy toward Cuba, on which initial privileging of Cubans had rested. For his own reasons, President Trump not only left in place the entitlements President Obama retracted but expanded entitlement cutbacks.

Given his hostility to the Cuban government, President Trump, for one, had little reason to reinstate unique Cuban immigration entitlements that could serve as an "escape valve" for disgruntled Cubans. Also, admission of Cubans provided little gain to him on the propaganda front. The United States had full-fledged economic and diplomatic relations with other communist countries, namely with China and Vietnam.

Furthermore, Senator Marco Rubio and Mauricio Claver-Carone, to whom President Trump turned for Cuba policy advice, opposed resumption of entitlements of old. Under the Trump administration, Claver-Carone served as chief Cuba (and general Latin American) policy advisor on the National Security Council (NSC) until he resigned in October 2020 to become president of the Inter-American Development Bank. In turn, Senator Rubio, along with the other Cuban American members of Congress, since 2009 had criticized Cuban entitlements that they previously had defended and promoted, as detailed in Chapter 6.

Even if Cuban American politicians had wanted to reinstate Cuban immigrant entitlements that President Obama had withdrawn, they had diminished resources to press their case. Cuban American PAC contributions became a fraction of what they previously had been. The US–Cuba Democracy PAC, the main Cuban American PAC, which Claver-Carone had directed before he joined the NSC, had become a skeleton of its

---

[83] "Solicitantes x nacionalidad 2018, 2019, a marzo 2020 (personas)" (www.gob.mx/cms/uploads/attachment/file/544676/CIERRE_DE_MARZO_2020__1-abril-2020_-2__1_.pdf).

former self. Its political contributions to candidates plunged from $524,500 to $156,400 to $48,000 in the 2016, 2018, and 2020 electoral cycles, respectively.[84] While the PAC thereby lost its muscle to leverage campaign contributions for policy favors, it would not likely have lobbied to reinstitute Cuban entitlements even had it been better funded, in that its main contributors, exile families, were unsympathetic to the more recent Cuban immigrants who would benefit from continued entitlements.

Another PAC, the New Cuba PAC, was committed to supporting elected officials and candidates favoring a new course on Cuba, consistent with the policies that President Obama promoted: pro travel and trade.[85] Formed during the 2016 electoral cycle, by 2018 the PAC, however, took in almost no contributions.[86] It thus did not influence Trump's decision-making.

Under Trump, even the influence of Cuban American gatekeepers of US Cuba policy in Congress diminished. In 2018, Cuban Americans lost two of the four South Florida seats they had held in the House of Representatives: the seat held by Ros-Lehtinen until she retired, which the Democrat Donna Shalala won against Maria Elvina Salazar, a daughter of Cuban exiles, and the seat held by Carlos Curbelo, who lost his reelection bid to an Ecuadoran-born Democrat (two years later, though, Cuban Americans reclaimed the two districts they had lost in the preceding electoral cycle).[87]

The Cuban Americans from South Florida and New Jersey who continued, uninterrupted, in office, Senators Rubio and Robert Menendez, and Congressmen Mario Díaz-Balart and Albio Sires, remained vocal voices for further strangulating the Cuban economy and delegitimizing the Cuban government. However, they did not advocate for reinstating Cuban immigrant entitlements. Although as of 2020 the post-Soviet era New Cuban immigrants, who by then accounted for nearly half of Miami's Cuban American population,[88] disapproved of Trump

---

[84] Center for Responsive Politics, "US-Cuba Democracy PAC PAC Profile" (www.opensecrets.org/pacs/lookup2.php?strID=C00387720&cycle=2016 (and cycle=2018, 2020).
[85] *New Cuba PAC* (www.newcubapac.com/about).
[86] *New Cuba PAC: Spending by Cycle* (www.opensecrets.org/pacs/lookup2.php?cycle=2018&strID=C00572628).
[87] Salazar won the congressional seat she had lost to Shalala in 2018, and Carlos Gimenez, who immigrated from Cuba in 1960 at age six, won the seat Ecuadoran-born Mucarsel-Powell had held for two years.
[88] FIU, *2020 FIU Cuba Poll: How Cuban Americans in Miami View U.S. Policies toward Cuba*, p. 7.

entitlement cutbacks, they were a growing silent majority. They lacked the organization and money to sway policy, and had no presence among Cuban Americans in top political positions. Moreover, at least in Miami, after voting in large numbers for Obama and Hillary Clinton, 56 percent of them favored Trump (versus 71 percent of the earlier émigrés).[89]

They were won over by new right-wing media personalities who promoted Trump: especially by Alex Otaola, a YouTube star with legions of Cuban American fans (a Hillary Clinton supporter turned Trump zealot).[90] Joe Biden, the Democrat candidate, was smeared as a socialist, to scare Cuban immigrants (along with Venezuelans who fled the Maduro government) from voting for him.

Against this backdrop, President Trump advanced his nativist antiimmigrant agenda to appeal to White workers in "swing states" that were important to the 2020 electoral outcome. With farmers permitted to hire foreign laborers on temporary contracts, and industrialists who historically had relied on unskilled immigrant labor having relocated their factories overseas where labor was cheaper, the Trump administration faced little pressure from the business community to be welcoming of immigrants, including from Cuba.[91]

Thus, even though Cubans had pursued a revolution partly to repel domination by the "Colossus of the North," more than half a century later many of them were as lured by opportunities that the United States offered as were other Latin Americans. When they were blocked from the United States by barriers imposed by the Trump administration, they

---

[89] Ibid., p. 43.
[90] Noah Lanard, "Meet the YouTube Star Who's Pushing a Generation of Florida Cuban Voters to Trump," *Mother Jones* (October 7, 2020) (www.motherjones.com/politics/2020/10/meet-the-youtube-star-whos-pushing-a-generation-of-floridas-cuban-voters-to-trump/. In revamping a culture Cold War, Otaola organized boycotts to ban Cuban musicians with alleged ties to the Cuban government from performing in Miami ("U.S.-Cuba News Brief" [Washington, DC: Center for Democracy in the Americas, February 7, 2020]).
[91] There were some high-ranking members of the Trump administration who argued in favor of the United States accepting more immigrants, especially high-skilled immigrants. In 2020 Acting White House Chief of Staff Mick Mulvaney noted at a meeting that the United States was "desperate" for more immigrants in order that the economy continue to grow. He was fired from the job not long thereafter. Nick Miroff and Josh Dawsey, "Mulvaney Says U.S. Is 'Desperate' for More Legal Immigrants," *Washington Post* (February 20, 2020) (www.washingtonpost.com/politics/mulvaney-says-us-is-desperate-for-more-legal-immigrants/2020/02/20/946292b2-5401-11ea-87b2-101dc5477dd7_story.html).

found themselves forced to take refuge in Mexico and Central America, in countries where conditions were worse than those from which they fled. Cuban privileging ended, and brutally, although Cubans did not give up on trying to find ways to leverage the US immigration system to their advantage.

8

Exceptionalism in Practice?

Actual Immigration, Lessons Learned

Policies are one matter, outcomes another. What effect did the special entitlements granted Cubans have on inducing Cubans to immigrate? Did more Cubans come to America than nationals of other countries that were offered no comparable entitlements? In this chapter, after briefly summarizing many of the Cuban entitlements detailed in earlier chapters, their impact on immigration is addressed. In order to "tease out" how distinctive the cumulative effect of Cuban entitlements has been, rates of immigration from Cuba are compared not only with those from Haiti but also from the Dominican Republic, despite the book having only minimally addressed US Dominican policies. The three countries, all located in the Caribbean, are of approximately the same size. While the United States, as shown in earlier chapters, subjected Haitians to uniquely exclusionary and discriminatory practices, it typically treated Dominicans similarly to other immigrants: neither offering them special entry rights and benefits nor targeting them specifically for exclusion. Yet, in many years more Dominicans than Cubans, and in some years even more Haitians than Cubans, became lawful permanent residents, a paradox to be explained.

This chapter also addresses "lessons learned" about US immigration policy that has privileged certain immigrant groups over others, about use and abuse of presidential discretionary power to favor certain immigrants and disfavor others, and about how and why immigration and immigrant-related policies and practices may persist after their initial rationale ceased to justify their continuation. "Lessons learned" also include an explanation of how and why a country as powerful as the United States has been limited in its control over immigration. The Cuban government, with far fewer resources than the United States, as well as ordinary Cubans, in the United States and in Cuba, have also shaped policies and how effective they have been.

BRIEF SUMMARY OF UNIQUE CUBAN ENTITLEMENTS

The book described unique entitlements that the United States granted to Cubans from the time Fidel Castro assumed power in 1959 through January 2021, after he died, his brother Raúl, who succeeded him as president, retired, and Cuba transitioned to its first post-Castro head of state: under twelve US presidents. During these years, Congress enacted laws that singled Cubans out for special entitlements, while presidents used and abused their discretionary power to grant them entitlements not offered to other nationals.

Analytically, entitlements were of two sorts: "horizontal" and "vertical." The "vertical" refer to new entitlements that Congress and successive administrations piled on to earlier entitlements granted to Cubans; the "horizontal" refer to the expansion of beneficiaries. New "vertical" entitlements often came with an expansion of beneficiaries.

Key entitlements that were extended to Cubans over the years included:

1. Transporting nearly a third of a million Cubans to the United States, most of whose lives were not at risk, at US taxpayers' expense: during the Kennedy, Johnson, and Nixon administrations.
2. The Coast Guard bringing visa-less Cubans that they interdicted at sea to the United States (until 1994): at the same time that they repatriated other unauthorized immigrants.
3. The granting to Cubans of various temporary entry rights, including admission as tourists when known not to be, which served as stepping stones for attaining permanent residency rights.
4. The paroling of unauthorized Cuban entrants into the United States, regardless of where they entered, on the basis of their nationality, and entitling them to LPR status (until 2017), despite US law specifying that immigrants could only be granted parole entry on a case-by-case basis and at official ports of admission.
5. The inventing, by presidents, of new, unique immigration statuses for Cubans, in order to circumvent regulations set by Congress, such as the "Entrant" status that President Carter created for

Cubans arriving from Mariel, so as to entitle them to temporary entry rights and unique resettlement benefits; President Reagan's reimagining of the Entrants as refugees, in the absence of evidence that they had fled persecution, to allow them to become LPRs, and then citizens; and President Clinton's "Special Guantanamo Entrant" status, to admit unauthorized Cuban boatpeople into the United States in 1994 and entitle them to the same rights as lawful immigrants. In turn, the Bush II administration circumvented Congress-regulated immigration admissions by creating special parole programs, one to admit Cuban medics working on Cuban government overseas missions and another to allow relatives of Cubans in the United States to immigrate before receiving preference system visas.

6. Access initially to the most expansive set of federal government-funded refugee benefits in US history, then to the same benefits as refugees, irrespective of whether they met criteria for refugee status applied to all other nationals.
7. The right to immigrate between 1988 and 1993 through one of the only privately run programs in US history, and to be admitted as refugees when not fleeing persecution.
8. The right to full federally funded welfare benefits on arrival in the United States, whether or not they had entered lawfully, when unauthorized immigrants from other countries were ineligible for welfare and authorized immigrants from other countries were ineligible during their first five years in the United States. Since 1997 Cubans have been the only foreign-born people entitled to welfare on the basis of their nationality.
9. The unique right, since 1966, to become lawful permanent residents if they were a public charge.
10. An official guarantee, since 1994, that no fewer than 20,000 Cubans would be awarded immigration visas yearly, on a country-of-origin basis, a guarantee offered to no other nationals: a guarantee the Trump administration ceased to honor, all the while that the entitlement remained formally in effect.
11. The unique right to work, and qualify for social security, Medicare, and Medicaid, when not a lawful permanent resident or citizen.

The privileging of Cubans spanned Democrat and Republican administrations. It was not partisan-based. Between January 1959 and January 2017, Nixon, Clinton, and Obama were the only presidents to revoke

Cuban entitlements,[1] with Obama being the only president during these years to revoke without also extending one or more new entitlements to Cubans. Although President Obama officially ended Cuban exceptionalism "as we knew it" for over half a century as he left office, entitlements remained in effect that only Congress could retract. President Trump further retracted Cuban entitlements as he aggressively restricted rights of all immigrants, refugees, and asylum seekers, but de facto, without formally changing Cuban immigration policy.

While Congress collaborated with presidents to single Cubans out for unique prerogatives over the years, the only entitlements it rescinded were of a budgetary nature. On numerous occasions Congress considered revising or revoking Cubans' most exceptional of entitlements, the Cuban Adjustment Act (CAA), but modified it only once, in 1980, and in Cubans' favor. In that year it reduced from two years to one year the period that Cubans who were paroled into the country needed to wait before they could become lawful permanent residents. Legislated entitlements remained resilient to change, including after Cuba passed the presidential torch from the Castro brothers to a new generation of leadership.

Thus, together, presidents and Congress made Cuban privileging possible. At times they privileged Cubans at the expense of other immigrants, and at times at the expense of native-born people. They piled new entitlements on to old, and extended entitlements to ever more Cubans.

CUBAN IMMIGRATION IN COMPARATIVE PERSPECTIVE

What impact did the array of entitlements granted to Cubans have on actual immigration from Cuba? A comparison of rates of immigration from Cuba, Haiti, and the Dominican Republic highlights the "entitlement effect."[2]

---

[1] The Reagan and Bush I administrations issued few immigration visas to Cubans without formally changing immigration policy.

[2] Mexico provides a less appropriate comparison in that its population is much larger and the country shares a near-2,000 mile land border with the United States. In addition, Mexicans enjoyed the *bracero* program, which set the stage for Mexican migration. For these reasons, I do not compare the Cuban with Mexican experiences. I also do not compare the Cuban with Central American experiences. Though worthy of study, large-scale immigration from Central America began approximately two decades after that from Cuba, Haiti, and the Dominican Republic, and under different historical conditions. The differences notwithstanding, in Chapter 5 I briefly address specific immigration legislation that is relevant to Central Americans, in relation to US Cuban immigration policy, and in

Dominicans, who neither received entitlements comparable to Cubans nor were subjected to exclusionary policies comparable to Haitians, offer the best "control case" of what Cuban immigration would likely have been had the revolution not led the United States to single Cubans out for special entitlements. In contrast, as detailed in earlier chapters, the United States only occasionally extended special immigration entitlements to Haitians. It did so on a temporary basis in time of crisis under Obama's presidency and on a permanent basis when extending entitlements also to Cubans (in 1980). In addition, in 1998 Congress corrected the blatant racist exclusion of Haitians from status adjustment entitlements that had been extended to others in the region (with the Haitian Refugee Immigration Fairness Act [HRIFA]). Such exceptions aside, typically Haitians were subject to exclusion: to repatriation, detention, and deportation. Thus, while the Cuban–Dominican comparison, in the main, points to the different impact that unique versus general, noncountry-specific immigration policies have had on actual immigration, the Cuban–Haitian comparison sheds light on the impact that inclusionary versus exclusionary policies have had on immigration.

The Cold War Era

Figure 8.1 shows that until the 1980s the United States granted more Cubans than Dominicans or Haitians lawful permanent residency (LPR) rights, which is hardly surprising in view of the unique entitlements that successive Presidents awarded Cubans. In the 1960s, the United States granted LPR rights to about two and a half times as many Cubans as Dominicans and to about seven times as many Cubans as Haitians.

While privileging Cubans with the Freedom Flights program and with the Cuban Adjustment Act, the Johnson administration adopted a laissez-faire stance toward Dominican immigration. Following the assassination in 1961 of the unpopular, corrupt, and repressive dictator Rafael Leonidas Trujillo Molina, who had ruled the country for thirty years, the Dominican Republic experienced coups and counter-coups and the

---

Chapter 7 I describe how the Trump administration subjected Cubans to the same exclusionary treatment as Central Americans.

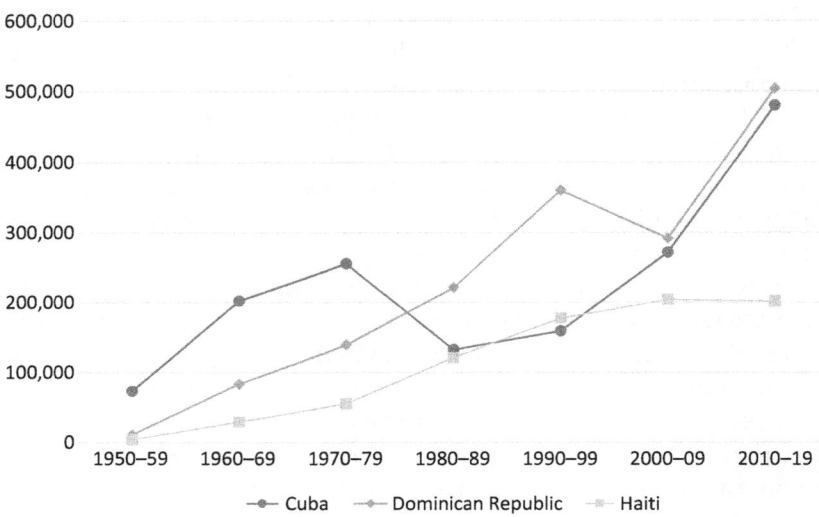

FIGURE 8.1 Persons obtaining LPR status by country of last residence: Cuba, Dominican Republic, and Haiti, FY1950–2019
Source: Department of Homeland Security, *Yearbook of Immigration Statistics*, Table 2 (dhs.gov/immigration-statistics/yearbook/2005 (2010, 2015, 2019).

election of the populist, reformist Juan Bosch to the presidency in 1962. With the Johnson administration concerned that the Dominican Republic might turn into "another Cuba" in America's backyard, it ordered a military invasion that backed an anti-Bosch faction of the Dominican armed forces;[3] it extended foreign aid to the new government; and it adopted a permissive stance toward Dominican immigration. The United States liberally issued temporary visitors' visas to Dominicans, despite common knowledge that many of them would overstay the expiration of their visas.[4] Against this backdrop, in the course of the 1960s support for the Left dissipated while Dominican immigration picked up, though less than from Cuba.

---

[3] Christopher Mitchell, "Introduction: Immigration and U.S. Foreign Policy toward the Caribbean, Central America, and Mexico," in Christopher Mitchell (ed.) *Western Hemisphere Immigration and United States Foreign Policy* (University Park: Pennsylvania State University Press, 1992), pp. 1–30. I am also grateful to Chris for informative discussions about US Dominican immigration policy.

[4] See Aristide Zolberg, *A Nation by Design: Immigration Policy in the Fashioning of America* (New York and Cambridge, MA: Russell Sage Foundation and Harvard University Press, 2006), p. 351.

With the "seeds" of immigration planted, in subsequent decades Dominicans moved to the United States in ever larger numbers: and in excess of the 20,000 a year cap that the 1976 INA Amendments established for preference-system admissions from countries in the Americas (excluding immediate kin). Immigrating without, as well as with, authorization, Dominicans relied heavily on family networks to relocate. The Dominican government, in turn, tacitly encouraged Dominican transnational ties on which family networks conducive to immigration were embedded. It sought thereby to encourage Dominicans abroad to send remittances, an important source of hard currency for the Dominican government. It also permitted dual citizenship and extended voting rights to Dominicans in the diaspora. Dominican politicians even campaigned and fundraised in the United States.

As a result, in a remarkable turn, since the 1980s more Dominicans than Cubans have become lawful permanent residents: despite the unique immigration entitlements offered Cubans. How could that be? For one, as detailed in Chapter 4, the Reagan, followed by the Bush I, administration deliberately restricted Cuban immigration, in the hope that without entry rights Cubans dissatisfied with life in their revolution-transformed country would press, instead, for change at home: in Hirschman's words, that they would turn to "voice" over "exit."[5] At the same time, Castro put a lid on emigration, to prevent "another Mariel," another mass exodus of the populace. Cuban immigration consequently declined markedly: though without unleashing the political change in Cuba the Reagan and Bush I administrations aspired. Meanwhile, faced with no comparable restrictions, Dominican immigration soared. Then, those who had come without authorization benefited in 1986 from the Immigration Reform and Control Act (IRCA), which permitted nearly all undocumented immigrants who came to the United States before 1982 to have their immigration status adjusted. Undocumented Dominicans came "out of the woodwork" when IRCA offered rights to lawful residence.

In turn, with IRCA the number of Haitians granted lawful permanent residence also picked up.[6] However, their numbers would have been far greater had the Haitian Program in the 1970s, and the interdiction,

---

[5] The Mariel Cubans to whom the Reagan administration granted refugee status account for most Cubans granted LPR rights in the 1980s.

[6] Section 202 of IRCA permitted Cuban–Haitian Entrants both to apply for adjustment to legal permanent residency status and to qualify for benefits once adjusting their status. In contrast, Lawful Temporary Residents (LTRs) were ineligible for financial assistance during their first five years in the United States.

repatriation, and deportation policies of the Reagan administration in the 1980s, not blocked tens of thousands of Haitians from immigrating. The exclusionary policies meant there were far fewer unauthorized Haitians in the United States when IRCA went into effect.

The Post-Cold War Build-Up of Safe, Legal, and Orderly Cuban Immigration under the Clinton Administration

How did the post-Cold War geopolitical context impact Cuban immigration? Did the United States reduce its privileging of Cubans once its battle against communism ground to a halt, with the collapse of the Soviet bloc and the Soviet Union, and its foreign policy concerns, as a result, shifted?

Midway through his first term, Clinton, the first president to serve entirely in the post-Cold War era, actually expanded, rather than retracted, Cuban immigration entitlements: against the backdrop of over 30,000 Cubans seeking US entry without authorization. Focusing, in the new global context, on domestic politics, namely, on averting an anti-immigration backlash that could jeopardize his reelection prospects, President Clinton negotiated the bilateral 1994 and 1995 accords that combined unique inclusionary, along with exclusionary, immigration provisions. For the remainder of his presidency, the accords contributed to authorized immigration from Cuba increasing while unauthorized immigration tapered off.

Yet, comparisons with Dominican immigration reveal that the bilateral agreements did not uniquely privilege Cubans in the 1990s: The United States granted more than twice as many Dominicans as Cubans lawful permanent residence, the mirror opposite of the 1960s when the United States granted LPR rights to more than twice as many Cubans as Dominicans. How to explain why more Dominicans than Cubans attained LPR rights in the 1990s? For one, the Clinton administration quickly (re)interpreted as a maximum the 20,000 minimum number of visas that it had committed the United States to issue annually to Cubans. As a result, the Clinton migration accord, in effect though not stated intent, limited authorized immigration from Cuba. Meanwhile, transnational family dynamics worked to Dominicans' advantage. Earlier Dominican immigration set in motion kinship networks that, after IRCA legalized the status of nearly all Dominicans who had immigrated before 1982, broadened the base of Dominicans who could immigrate lawfully. Almost all Dominicans lawfully admitted in the 1990s had family sponsors.

In the 1990s, Cubans lacked comparable cross-border family networks, such that informal transnationally embedded social dynamics disadvantaged them. At the time, few Cubans had kin in the United States to claim them; for this reason the 1994 migration accord included a lottery, to ensure that at least 20,000 Cubans could immigrate lawfully yearly. Most Soviet-era families already had reunified in the United States, and ties between Cubans in the United States and on the island had been strained by their opposing views toward the revolution.

Briefly in the 1990s, and only in the 1990s, the United States even granted more Haitians than Cubans lawful permanent residence. The Haitian "exceptionalism" followed enactment of HRIFA, which granted unauthorized Haitian entrants a temporary window to have their status adjusted.

THE BREAKDOWN OF SAFE, LEGAL, AND ORDERLY CUBAN IMMIGRATION UNDER THE BUSH II AND OBAMA ADMINISTRATIONS

After President Clinton left office in January 2001, Cuban LPR admissions first rebounded to pre-1980 levels and then soared, nearly doubling in the 2010s: during Bush II's, and especially Obama's, presidencies. It would appear that both presidents reinterpreted the 1994 Clinton-negotiated accord to honor the initial specification that the United States would offer no fewer than, as opposed to a maximum of, 20,000 immigration visas to Cubans yearly. In Obama's last year in office, his administration granted nearly three times as many Cubans lawful permanent residence as the minimum specified in the accord, such that the differential in the number of Cubans and Dominicans who were awarded lawful permanent residency nearly closed.

However, Cuban admissions did not soar by design. Rather, it soared once again because Washington had lost control over Cuban immigration. The Clinton accords reined in unauthorized immigration only in the short, not the long, run. They were effective until Cubans found illicit ways to evade the Coast Guard policing of the Florida Straits, with the help of human smugglers, after which more Cubans entered the United States without authorization than with it.

In 2019, during Trump's presidency, the number of Cubans awarded LPR status did plunge, to barely more than half the preceding year. While still exceeding the 20,000 minimum number of LPR admissions specified

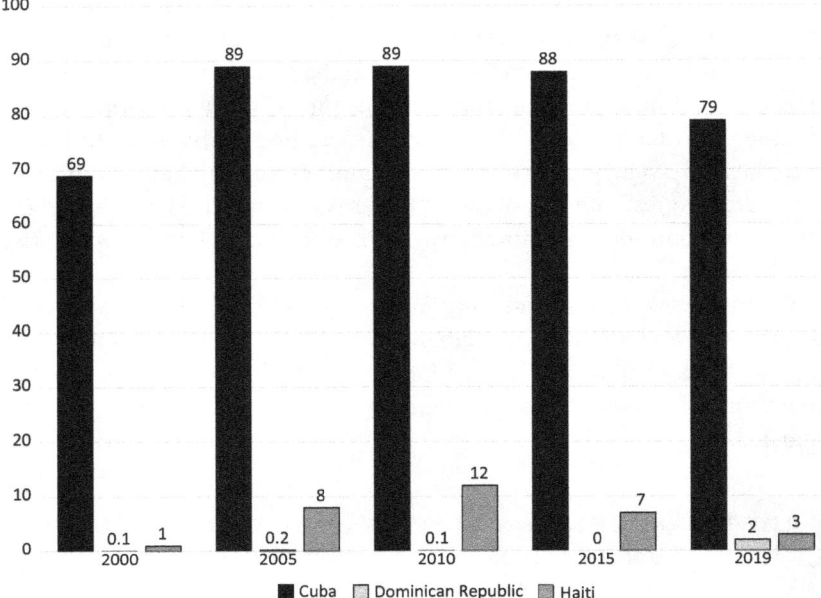

FIGURE 8.2 Percentage of persons born in Cuba, the Dominican Republic, and Haiti granted LPR status as refugee and asylee adjustments, 2000–2019
Source: Same as Figure 8.1.

in the 1994 migration accord, the United States granted more Dominicans than Cubans lawful permanent residence. And US counselor services in Havana did not screen most of the Cubans admitted.

The rise and then fall in Cuban LPR admissions, in absolute numbers and relative to Dominicans, reflects the different entry paths that people from the two countries had. Figure 8.2 reveals that US authorities only screened a small percentage of Cubans before their arrival, through the Interests Section-turned-Embassy in 2015 (following the United States and Cuba reestablishing full diplomatic relations in December 2014), despite immigration law specifying that foreign-born people were to be screened abroad for entry. Of the Cubans granted lawful permanent residence in 2000, 69 percent were "refugee and asylee adjustments" – unauthorized entrants paroled into the country by immigration authorities – who, after a year, drew on the CAA to become LPRs. Only a minority of the Cubans had been admitted on the basis of the preference system, which, in principle, governed immigration. Moreover, after 2000, the percentage of Cuban LPR admissions that were "refugee and asylee" adjustments increased, to a high of 89 percent.[7]

In a break with the past, the Trump administration made asylum seeking as well as lawful immigration difficult for Cubans. Cuban, along with other unauthorized immigrants who managed to circumvent entry barriers, were slated to join the estimated eleven million unauthorized immigrants who were in the United States at the time. Research shows legal status to be a major determinant of immigrant disadvantage.[8]

Fortunately for Cubans, if they filed asylum claims, they still had a path to lawful permanent residence. In view of the backup in immigration court hearings, after one year Cubans could draw on the CAA, which remained in effect, to adjust their status. They thereby circumvented President Obama's effort to rein in unauthorized Cuban immigration.

In contrast, Figure 8.2 reveals that almost all Dominicans who were granted LPR status since the turn of this century were admitted in accordance with the legislated preference system, on the basis of family ties to earlier immigrants. In the years recorded in Figure 8.2, less than 1 percent of Dominicans were admitted as "refugee and asylee adjustments." Authorized Dominican immigration soared after the turn of the century (see Figure 8.1), against the backdrop of the Bush II administrating having negotiated an agreement with the Caribbean country, which was modeled after the United States' Haitian and Cuban maritime interdiction agreements, to contain unauthorized Dominican migration.[9]

At the same time, Haitian LPR admissions leveled off. As summarized in Figure 8.1, in every decade except the 1990s the United States granted far fewer Haitians than either Cubans or Dominicans LPR rights: in some years, one-third to one-half as many. Haitian LPR admissions peaked in 2016 during Obama's presidency, at 23,200, after which they declined, to 17,100 in 2019, under Trump's presidency. Meanwhile, the number of unauthorized Haitians who adjusted their status under HRIFA, and thereby became LPRs, dropped from 2,500-to-3,375 yearly between 2005 and 2008

---

[7] Calculated from sources cited in Figures 8.1 and 8.2.
[8] Mary Waters and Marisa Gerstein Pineau (eds.), *The Integration of Immigrants into American Society* (Washington, DC: National Academies Press, August 2010) (www.nap.edu); Mary Waters and Philip Kasinitz, "Race, Legal Status & Social Mobility" *Daedalus* (Spring 2021).
[9] Katherine Tennis, "Offshoring the Border: The 1981 United States–Haiti Agreement and the Origins of Extraterritorial Maritime Interdiction," *Journal of Refugee Studies* (February 2019) (https://doi.org/10.1093/jrs/fez005).

when Bush was president, to 22 in 2014, during Obama's presidency.[10] HRIFA ceased to offer Haitians a path to lawful permanent residence.

Neither Figures 8.1 nor 8.2 capture immigrants living in the United States without authorization, of which there were far more Haitians and Dominicans than Cubans. Until 2017 few Cubans lived in the United States for more than a year without drawing on the CAA to become LPRs (and during that one year they enjoyed authorized parole status). In contrast, as of 2014 there were an estimated 100,000 Haitians and an estimated 170,000 Dominicans in the United States without authorization.[11] They had moved to the United States since the cutoff dates of legislation entitling unauthorized entrants from the two countries to legalize their status.[12] Following the devastating 2010 earthquake in Haiti, the Obama administration did grant about 42 percent of the unauthorized Haitians in the United States Temporary Protective Status (TPS), which entitled them to rights to work and a stay on deportation, but no path to lawful permanent residency. For renewable eighteen month periods, the Trump administration extended Haitians' TPS (despite threatening to withdraw it) until January 2021, at which point they were scheduled to rejoin the ranks of unauthorized immigrants and lose the temporary rights they had enjoyed. Fortunately for them, the incoming Biden administration immediately extended their TPS until October of 2021, and then extended it again until November 2022.[13]

REFUGEE ADMISSIONS

The Cubans who were granted "refugee and asylee status adjustments" convey the impression that Cubans flocked to the United States for

---

[10] U.S. Department of Homeland Security (USDHS), *2013 Yearbook of Immigration Statistics* (Washington, DC: Office of Immigration Statistics, DHS, August 2014).

[11] Statista, the Statistics Portal, "Unauthorized Haitian immigrants in the United States from 1990 to 2014 (in 1,000)" (www.statista.com/statistics/646419/unauthorized-haitian-immigrants-in-the-united-states/) and "Unauthorized Dominican Immigrants in the United States from 1990 to 2014 (in 1,000)" (www.statista.com/statistics/646406/unauthorized-dominican-immigrants-in-the-united-states/). See also Marc Rosenblum and Ariel Ruiz Soto, "An Analysis of Unauthorized Immigration in the United States by Country and Region of Birth," *Migration Policy Institute* (August 2015), p. 15.

[12] Legislation included IRCA in 1986, and, in the case of Haitians, HRIFA.

[13] Mary Waters and Marisa Gerstein Pineau (eds.), *The Integration of Immigrants into American Society* (Washington, DC: National Academies Press, August 2010) (www.nap.edu); Mary Waters and Philip Kasinitz, "Race, Legal Status & Social Mobility" *Daedalus* (Spring 2021).

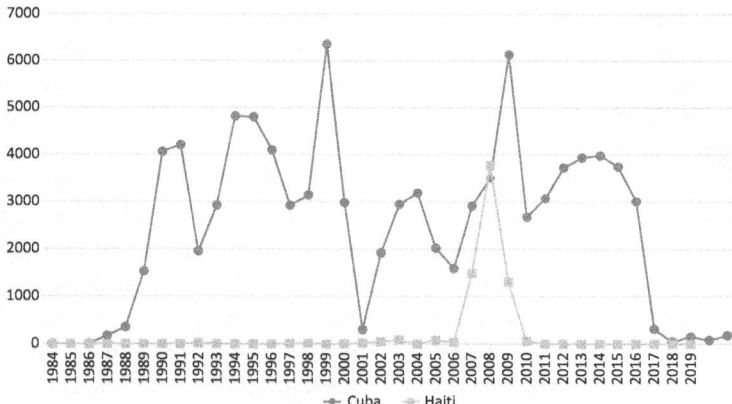

FIGURE 8.3 Refugee admissions from Cuba and Haiti, 1984–2019
Sources: U.S Department of Justice, 1997 *Statistical Yearbook of the Immigration and Naturalization Service* (INS) and *1990 Statistical Yearbook of the INS* (Washington D.C.: INS 1997, 1990); US Department of Homeland Security (DHS), *Yearbook of Immigration Statistics*, for years 2003, 2005, 2006, 2013, 2015, 2018 (Washington D.C.: DHS) (https:// www. dhs.gov/immigration-statistics/yearbook/table 14); US Department of State, Refugee Admissions Statistics (https:// 2009-2017.state.gov/j/prm/releases/statistics/index.htm) Daniel Martin and James Yankey, "Refugee and Asylees 2011" (USDHS, Office of Immigration Statistics, May 2012), p.3; Ruth Wasem, *Cuban Migrants to the US: Policy and Trends* (Washington D.C.: Congressional Research Service, Report to Congress, June 2, 2009).

political reasons, to escape persecution. However, the United States admitted far more Cubans as "refugee and asylee adjustments" than as refugees in accordance with the Refugee Act of 1980, which officially regulates refugee admissions (see Figures 8.2 and 8.3).

Cubans who were officially admitted as refugees, and screened by Washington outside the United States in accordance with legislated refugee admission criteria, need not have their status adjusted once in the United States, in that they were admitted with rights to permanent residency. In contrast, "refugee and asylee adjustments" mainly involve what I refer to as "imagined refugees," persons to whom US immigration authorities granted lawful permanent residency rights once they were living in the United States, whether or not they fled persecution. These Cubans were paroled into the country and then had their status adjusted on the basis of the Cuban Adjustment Act, as presumed refugees. Between 2000 and 2016, under the Bush II and Obama administrations, LPR "refugee and asylee adjustments" soared, from approximately 14,400 to

57,000; these were years during which Cubans who were officially admitted as refugees, vetted before arrival, declined from about 3,200 to 354. Thus, the number of "imagined refugees" soared while the number of what I call, in contrast, "real refugees," admitted on the basis of US refugee law, decreased. Remarkably, "refugee and asylee" admissions rose even more after President Obama officially ended Cuban near-automatic rights to parole, to a record of 69,860 in 2018. The number dramatically declined only in 2019, when President Trump revved up his anti-immigrant reelection campaign. In 2019 such admissions dipped to 32,900 (and total LPR admissions to slightly over 41,600).[14]

The contrast with Haitians' experience is striking. In most years the United States admitted thousands more Cubans than Haitians, both as "real refugees" and as "imagined refugees" (see Figures 8.2 and 8.3, and sources therein). In only one year between 1984 and 2018 (for which information is available) did the United States admit more Haitians than Cubans as "real refugees;" in only eleven years did the United States admit more than ten Haitians as "real refugees"; and between 2015 and 2019 it admitted no Haitians as refugees, despite the state violence and repression that plagued the country. Meanwhile, "refugee and asylee" adjustments accounted for a mere 1 percent of Haitian LPR admissions in 2000 and, until 2019, for never more than 12 percent; the percent increased only in 2019, as other bases of immigration closed down.

Even fewer Dominicans than Haitians became lawful permanent residents as "asylum and refugee adjustments" or were admitted officially as refugees, while more of them were admitted as lawful permanent residents on the basis of preference system family ties. Only during Trump's presidency did the number of Dominican "refugee and asylee" admissions increase: when his administration made preference system immigration difficult.

LESSONS LEARNED

Extrapolating from US immigration policy from the time Fidel took power through the transition to a non-Castro head of state, certain patterns come to the fore. The patterns are both substantive and analytic in nature. For Cubans, initial privileging became the bedrock for

---

[14] See USDHS, *Yearbooks of Immigration Statistics 2014–2019.*

subsequent privileging until Obama left office and Trump unleashed his aggressive nativist attack on all immigrants, Cubans included.

Inequitable Treatment of Immigrant Groups

First and foremost, the Cuban experience reveals that neither presidents on the basis of their discretionary authority nor Congress on the basis of its legislative power treat immigrants, and aspiring immigrants, from all countries equally and equitably. Fortunately for Cubans, for over half a century both presidents and Congress singled them out for special entitlements.

President Eisenhower, the first to privilege Cubans, did so to leverage immigration for foreign policy geopolitical gain. He set a precedent that subsequent presidents, and Congress, elaborated on, even after it became apparent that the privileging of Cubans did not accomplish the foreign policy goal for which it was intended, and, arguably, strengthened Castro's hold on power by ridding Cuba of regime opponents.

Once they were accustomed to entitlements, Cuban émigrés became agents of their own continued privileging. They pressed for more. They came to lobby, make campaign contributions, leverage their vote, and mobilize in the streets of Miami and Washington to defend and promote their interests and concerns, on immigration-related, along with other, matters. Settling mainly in Florida, which acquired a mounting number of electoral college votes as ever more of the country's population settled in the state, they attained outsized political influence, despite comprising less than 1 percent of the total population. In the process, domestic politics replaced foreign policy as the driving force behind Cuban immigrant privileging.

For a period, Cubans were admitted at the *expense of* other aspiring immigrants, in that they received "first dibs" at the Western Hemisphere annual immigration quota, when it was instituted. The more Cubans that were admitted, the fewer immigrant slots were available for others from the region. In 1976 Congress amended the Immigration and Nationality Act to admit Cubans independently of the regional quota, at which point Cubans became the only nationals to have their own, uncapped entry track. Once in the United States, Cubans were also privileged over other immigrants as well as native-born people, when offered unique education, training, job placement, and other benefits.

Had US immigration policy been premised on fairness, then Haitians would have been better treated. They sought refuge from worse poverty, worse violence, and, in the main, worse persecution than Cubans, although there certainly were Cubans who suffered persecution. Numerous administrations interdicted Haitians at sea and repatriated them. They also detained those who managed to come ashore under deplorable conditions, both within the United States and offshore, and then deported many of them. Haitians had the bad luck of coming from a country allied with the United States during the Cold War, so that US presidents saw no geopolitical advantage in singling them out for special entitlements. To the contrary, in exchange for Haiti siding with the United States in the Cold War, presidents tolerated Haitian government persecution and abuse of its people. Haitians had the added misfortune of race-based biases against them: both during and after the Cold War.

The US privileging of Cubans and disprivileging of Haitians point to continued country-based racial biases in American immigration policy since the omnibus 1965 immigration reform officially ended such practices. The Haitian experience reveals persistent, pernicious racial discrimination in the United States' admissions system. Successive presidents (ab) used their discretionary authority to Haitians' disadvantage, with occasional exceptions: President Carter offered Haitians comparable entitlements to Cubans when they came ashore at the same time; Congress in 1986 extended lawful permanent residency rights to Haitian, along with other, unauthorized immigrants, in the context of implementing a comprehensive immigration reform, and in 1998 it passed legislation that entitled unauthorized Haitians who immigrated after the IRCA cutoff date to adjust their status, following their exclusion from earlier status adjustment-entitling legislation for immigrants from other countries in the region; and President Obama paroled Haitians into the United States who had fled Brazil in desperation, extended a family reunification parole program to Haitians after their exclusion from the family reunification program that the Bush II administration had initiated for Cubans, and granted unauthorized Haitians TPS following natural disasters in Haiti.

In turn, the Cuban experience points to continued preferential treatment of light-skinned foreigners, even if no longer from Europe, from where few people have emigrated since economic opportunities improved there following the formation of the European Union and the drop in the fertility rate, which alleviated demographic pressures to uproot. Cubans in the United States are exceptionally light-skinned, although a smaller percentage since the arrival of the Mariel Cubans. The first to take advantage of the US welcome mat were the light-skinned upper and middle classes, when the Castro-led government stripped them of their property and privilege and turned on opponents of the revolution's increasing radicalization. With the United States prioritizing immigration of relatives, the initial racial (and class) biases in who the United States admitted set in motion long-term biases in Cuban admissions. The Cuban immigration lottery, which was first instituted in 1994, somewhat diversified immigration through authorized channels. In turn, the large-scale unauthorized Cuban immigrations of 1980, 1994, and the first and especially second decade of this century further diversified the diaspora racially: though only moderately. As of 2020, 80 percent of Cuban Americans in Miami identified themselves as White.[15]

Time has shown no long-term "trickle down" or isomorphic effect of Cuban privileging on other immigrant groups. Only rarely have entitlements offered to Cubans been extended to other nationals, even though the Cuban experience has demonstrated positive payoff of the entitlements they received. Cuban immigrants have played a central role in transforming Miami into a dynamic city with global reach, and they have secured high-income, top level jobs.[16]

The immigration policy changes that President Obama introduced during his last days in office officially did level the playing field between Cuban and other immigrants, but they did so by subjecting unauthorized Cubans to the vulnerabilities and deprivations that other unauthorized entrants experienced, rather than by extending to other immigrants entitlements that Cubans enjoyed. President Trump further leveled the playing field, by sparing no foreigners, Cubans included, from his aggressive nativist attack on immigrants.

The Social Construction of Refugee Status[17]

The Cuban, together with the Haitian, experiences also point to how socially and politically constructed, and thereby biased, US refugee policy has been. Both presidents and legislators have considered Cubans to be

---

[15] The American Community Survey put the percentage of Whites among Miami Cuban Americans higher, at 95 percent. 2020 *FIU Cuba Poll: How Cuban Americans in Miami View U.S. Policies toward Cuba* (Miami: Florida International University, Steven J. Green School of International and Public Affairs, 2020), p. 7.
[16] Susan Eckstein, *The Immigrant Divide: How Cuban Americans Changed the US and Their Homeland* (New York: Routledge, 2009): pp. 75, 76.
[17] On an early discussion of the concept of social construction, see Peter Berger and Thomas Luckmann, *The Social Construction of Reality: A Treatise in the Sociology of Knowledge* (New York: Anchor, 1967). Also, see Preface, FN 5.

refugees in order to privilege them in ways they otherwise could not, and construed Haitians not to be refugees to exclude them from comparable entitlements. In the United States, a refugee has not necessarily been a refugee!

Indeed, in the case of Cubans the United States devised a dual refugee policy: one Cuban-specific and the other premised on more universalistic refugee criteria. Cubans benefited from being considered refugees, both real and imagined. Doors accordingly were opened to them that were closed to other nationals, including to persons who were more deserving of admission as refugees and more deserving of refugee benefits.

The United States was shown even to apply unique criteria for admitting Cubans as refugees, and to modify the criteria over the years. When Castro first came to power, any incoming Cuban was deemed a refugee, no questions asked. In more recent times, Cubans qualified for US admission as refugees if they were paroled into the country. In addition, they qualified as "real refugees," entitled to refugee benefits, if associated with a group that experienced persecution, whether or not they personally experienced persecution, and even if the persecution they experienced transpired decades in the past. The US Embassy in Havana admitted Cubans as "real refugees" on the basis of Refugee Act regional and country specific admission quotas, if they demonstrated that they belonged to a persecuted religious minority; if they were human rights activists, former political prisoners, or forced labor conscripts between 1965 and 1968; or if they experienced discrimination because of their political or religious beliefs.[18]

Meanwhile, Washington was shown to allow Cubans to become refugees *on* US entry, even though officially only persons screened (and vetted) abroad qualify for admission as refugees. Included among these "refugees" were persons who were safely settled in third countries and wished to relocate to America, despite US law specifying that persons who were firmly resettled in another country do not qualify for admission as refugees. Were the Cubans not conceived as refugees they would have been bound by the preference system-based immigration regulations set by Congress that were not country of origin-based. In turn, both the "real" and the imagined refugees qualified for refugee benefits, and for an extraordinary range of refugee benefits, through the Cuban Refugee Program before its termination.

---

[18] US Embassy in Cuba, "*Refugee Program n.d.*" (https://cu.usembassy.gov/embassy/refugee-program).

Cubans were even imagined as refugees after initially being determined not to be refugees, and in the absence of new evidence demonstrating that they had fled persecution. President Reagan was shown to have reimagined Mariel Cubans as refugees after President Carter determined them not to meet the criteria for refugee status. President Reagan reimagined them as refugees in order to enable them to become lawful permanent residents, and to woo them to become Republican Party stalwarts on attaining citizenship, with voting rights.

Meanwhile, when one basis of granting Cubans special entitlements as refugees ended, policymakers found new bases. By way of illustration, when Congress cut funding for the Cuban Refugee Program, Cubans were "refugee mainstreamed," that is, entitled to the benefits received by "real refugees," those officially admitted into the country on the basis of the Refugee Act.

Furthermore, Congress passed legislation to treat Cubans the same as refugees when a president, Carter, deemed them not to be refugees: to entitle them to full federally funded benefits for which they otherwise could not qualify. Florida members of Congress pressed for the enabling legislation, not because they believed Cubans to be refugees, but because they wanted them to qualify for refugee benefits, and not at Floridian taxpayers' expense. President Carter, in turn, signed the enabling legislation not because he had become convinced that the Mariel Cubans indeed were refugees and were accordingly entitled to refugee benefits, but because he hoped thereby to win Florida in the upcoming presidential election. Domestic politics shaped how Cuban émigrés were imagined, to their (and Florida taxpayers') advantage.

In essence, Congress and presidents, together with their administrations, considered Cubans to be refugees not merely or even mainly based on humanitarian considerations. They manipulated their conception of refugees to privilege Cubans first for Cold War advantage, and then for domestic political advantage, even before the Cold War's end.

Ordinary Cubans, in turn, (re)imagined themselves as asylum seekers when the Trump administration slashed both refugee and immigration admissions but left open the possibility to petition for asylum. However, the administration made asylum difficult, as it turned viciously on all immigrants, no matter where they came from.

"Path Dependent" Privileging

The book, in turn, shows the importance of historical analysis. A short-term focus on US Cuban immigration policy, under, for example, a single presidential administration, would not have captured how and why the causal factor shaping policy changed over the years, and how and why Cubans continued to be privileged after the basis for their initial privileging no longer existed. The very awarding of unique entitlements to Cubans even contributed to the build-up of a "culture of entitlements" that led to continued privileging. A path-dependent historically grounded analysis can explain these dynamics.[19]

Ongoing Cuban privileging was not inevitable. However, the first entitlements established a precedent, and created conditions that inclined one president and his administration after another, as well as Congress, to grant additional entitlements. New entitlements addressed problems that earlier entitlements created or left unresolved, as well as new problems that arose. In this vein, in granting Cubans temporary entry rights, the only admission authority they had, Presidents Eisenhower, Kennedy, and Johnson were shown to create the problem of what to do about the entrants' long-term residency rights. To address that problem, President Kennedy tried and President Johnson succeeded in convincing Congress to pass legislation entitling Cubans to their own unique path to lawful permanent residency. They also arranged for them to receive an extraordinary range of resettlement benefits. Alternatively, President Johnson might have kept Cuban immigrants' status in limbo or deported those without lawful permanent residency rights. He chose the option that expanded Cuban immigrant entitlements. Together with Congress, President Johnson extended Cubans' path of privilege both "vertically" and "horizontally."

Subsequent administrations interpreted the legislated status adjustment entitlement to mean that new, incoming unauthorized Cuban entrants could be paroled into the country and be assured a path to lawful permanent residence. They found themselves "locked into" the continued privileging of Cubans over other unauthorized immigrants. When they tried to retract entitlements for Cubans, they typically reversed their stance and extended new entitlements to Cubans, including to more Cubans. By way of illustration, when faced with large numbers of visa-less Cuban boatpeople, both the Carter and Clinton administrations were shown to have tried to block their entry, but then to grant them special entry rights and special benefits to help them adapt. They perceived it to be in their interests to do so, for reasons rooted in domestic politics, rather than foreign policy. Earlier privileged Cuban immigrants became a force

---

[19] See Chapter 1, FN 5, for discussions of path-dependent analyses.

for continued Cuban immigrant privileging. Moreover, when President Clinton indeed retracted an entitlement, he tempered émigré opposition by simultaneously extending new entitlements to additional Cuban immigrants.

As to legislated entitlements, when members of Congress tried to revise or revoke special Cuban prerogatives, they failed. Such was the case with the CAA, which legislators, on numerous occasions, tried to sunset.

A path-dependent analysis, in turn, helps explain entitlements that are otherwise inexplicable. In principle, if policymakers had privileged Cubans to advance their Cold War concern with defeating global communism, the privileging should have ground to a halt with the Soviet Union's collapse, especially in that Cuba, much weakened as a consequence, no longer posed a threat to the United States. Cuban immigrant privileging nonetheless continued. It continued because the initial policy, which was driven by foreign policy concerns, by then had built up a domestic political constituency for continued Cuban immigrant privileging. Cuban Americans not only had votes to leverage, thanks to the CAA, but they also were economically successful, and thus had campaign contributions to parlay for policies that they wanted, including immigration-related ones. Furthermore, beginning in 1989, Cubans successfully elected "their own" to political office: politicians who protected and advanced their concerns.

President Obama officially closed Cuba's path-dependent privileging only after it unleashed unintended and unwanted unauthorized Cuban immigration, at near-record levels, that undermined his new foreign policy commitment to cross-border bridge-building. Also, an emergent social, economic, and political divide by then had taken hold within the Cuban American community that created an opening for him to retract Cuban entitlements with minimal political pushback. In the terminology of path-dependent analysts, new contingent conditions arose that were conducive to shutting the path of privilege. On assuming the presidency, Trump took advantage of the situation to further rein in Cuban privileging, when closing the US border almost entirely to immigrants, refugees, and asylum seekers.

All along, Haitians faced a different path: of disprivilege. They faced discrimination and exclusion, as immigrants and refugees. One president after another, across partisan lines, drew on the discriminatory precedent that their predecessors had set, and detained, deported, and repatriated Haitians. Only occasionally and on a temporary basis did presidents respond to political pressure and put a stop to Haitian discriminatory practices.

Returning to Cubans, had Eisenhower not set in motion Cuban immigrant privileging, the half-century of successive implementation of entitlements might never have transpired. And without immigration being made so attractive to Cubans, history might have taken a different turn. Cubans who were opposed to, and disillusioned with, the Cuban revolution might instead have opted for "voice" over "exit," for change at home. We will never know.

Limits to State Policy

The Cuban immigration experience demonstrates the limits as well as possibilities of state regulation of immigration. Scholars have pointed to an expansion of the role of the state within the international arena beyond its monopoly of the legitimate use of force and regulation of trade to include also a monopoly on the legitimate movement of people to, from, and through its sovereign territory, as well as how migration effects how states conduct diplomacy.[20] So too has domestic politics been shown to shape migration policy.[21] Yet, the analysis of US Cuban immigration has revealed how at times different divisions of the state implemented conflicting policies that impacted immigration, how different administrations did not always implement policies of their choosing, and how implemented policies did not always generate their intended outcomes, and even unleashed unintended and undesired consequences.

In principle, Congress sets immigration policy. In practice, the Cuban experience demonstrates that presidents and their administrations have exercised considerable discretionary power over immigration. On occasion they circumvented legislated immigration regulations, and influenced legislation that Congress had enacted.

Immigration policymaking and implementation were shown, in turn, to rest on more than state and intrastate dynamics. They did not transpire in a political vacuum. At different times, and in different

---

[20] On these issues, see John Torpey, "Coming and Going: On the State Monopolization of the Legitimate 'Means of Movement'," *Sociological Theory* vol. 16 no. 3 (December 2002): 239–59; Fiona Adamson, "Crossing Borders: International Migration and National Security," *International Security* vol. 31 no. 1 (Summer 2006): 165–99; James Hollifield, "The Emerging Migration State," *International Migration Review* vol. 38 no. 3 (Fall 2004): 885–912.

[21] William Roger Brubaker, *Immigration and the Politics of Citizenship in Europe and North America* (Lanham, MD: Rowman & Littlefield, 1989).

combinations, the Cuban government, ordinary Cubans, and Cuban immigrants shaped US Cuban immigration policy. As small a state as Cuba has exercised outsized influence over US policy, while on several occasions Cubans, through their transnational ties, have defied US immigration regulations to the point of convincing Washington to alter policy in their favor. US Cuban immigration, as a result, has only partially been by design, through what Aristide Zolberg defined as the "front gate."[22]

For half a century, Castro influenced US Cuban immigration policy when he allowed Cubans to head for the United States without US entry permission, causing the United States to lose control over its borders. On three occasions he unleashed mass migrations that led US presidents to modify US Cuban immigration policy: to admit more Cubans, independently of congressional-set regulations. His government tolerated, if not outright encouraged, defiance of US immigration regulations when it had least to lose and a considerable amount to gain: during the Cold War, when it was minimally dependent on the United States economically, and when it was faced with the dire economic crisis that the collapse of Soviet aid and trade caused. When the United States and Cuba committed to normalize relations, the risks to Cuba of defying US immigration policy were high.

Typically neglected in policy analyses is the role ordinary people may play, including informally, outside formal channels, and transnationally, across country borders. Indeed, it was not the Cuban government as such, but rather unauthorized Cubans with their force of numbers, that led the United States on different occasions to modify Cuban immigration policy. The large exodus of unauthorized Cubans in 1965 from Camarioca led President Johnson both to authorize the "Freedom Flights" that brought some 270,000 Cubans to the United States and to convince Congress to enact the most significant legislation that privileged Cubans: the Cuban Adjustment Act. The far larger exodus from Mariel in 1980 led President Carter to invent a new basis for admitting the unauthorized Cubans and entitling them to refugee benefits as nonrefugees, and President Reagan to negotiate a new, bilateral migration agreement to address problems that the Mariel migration had generated. In turn, President Clinton responded to the "rafter crisis" in 1994 not only by admitting tens of thousands of unauthorized

---

[22] On the "main gate," see Zolberg, *A Nation by Design*.

Cubans into the United States but also by negotiating a new migration agreement that granted Cubans new, unique immigration entitlements (while allowing for the repatriation of Cubans who were interdicted at sea). The United States would have been unlikely to implement the inclusionary policies had ordinary Cubans not, through their force of numbers, undermined US control of its borders. Then, in 2017 the Obama administration responded to an even larger wave of unauthorized Cuban arrivals by negotiating changes in US Cuban immigration policy with Cuba: this time, however, by retracting without concomitantly extending new immigration entitlements to Cubans.

Ordinary Cubans' influence over Washington immigration policy came not merely from their force of numbers but also from their transnationally embedded ties. Cubans in the diaspora took it on themselves to help family in Cuba come to the United States without, as well as with, authorization. They financed much of the unauthorized immigration, which became exceedingly expensive as Cubans resorted to human smugglers to help them evade US policing of the Florida Straits. Human smugglers with transnational networks became informal immigration enablers, enticed by the money they could make.

In that the United States blocked unauthorized mass migrations from Haiti, it was not large-scale unauthorized immigration per se that led Washington to modify immigration policy. Rather, the different geopolitical contexts in which the two country-based migrations occurred, and US racial biases, led US presidents to respond in an inclusionary manner toward unauthorized Cubans and in an exclusionary manner toward unauthorized Haitians. Also, Haitians were disadvantaged because they never became a comparable domestic political force to Cubans, able to press for entitlements, and because far fewer of them acquired the economic means to pay human smugglers to help their relatives in Haiti evade US regulations to immigrate.

President Obama succeeded in retracting Cuban entitlements when the Cuban as well as US governments had vested interests in reining in unauthorized immigration and when influential Cuban Americans opposed continued privileging of Cuban immigrants. President Obama wanted the change, but new state and societal, domestic and foreign, conditions made it possible.

Thus, analyses that focus empirically and analytically only on official decision-making, on state interests, on formal political institutions, and on formal politics leave undocumented and unexplained important forces that may shape immigration and immigration policy. Ordinary people, including in their transnationally embedded networks, need to be incorporated into analyses in order to fully understand immigration policy, its limits and possibilities.

****

In summary, US Cuban immigration policy is a history of failed policy, in that it never achieved its initial goal of spurring regime change or even President Clinton's more modest goal of making Cuban immigration safe, legal, and orderly, except in the short-term. The Cuban experience suggests important lessons to be learned about policymaking and implementation. While America has benefited from the over one million Cubans who immigrated outside Congress-regulated admission channels, US policymakers would do well to take into account the range of forces, formal and informal, domestic and international, that shape policy outcomes.

WHAT TO DO?

How might US Cuban immigration policy be improved, and how might the Cuban experience be drawn on to improve immigration policy involving other nationals? The Cuban experience suggests that:

1. Both the Executive Branch and Congress should use their respective authority to make immigration policy more equitable. People from no country should be privileged over others, especially after the conditions that may have justified privileging cease to exist. By the same token, people from no country should be singled out for discriminatory treatment, as have Haitians. Differential treatment of different immigrant groups contradicts basic American values of fairness and equity, and highlights how US immigration policy remains racially biased on a country basis despite the official end of national origins-based immigrant admissions.
2. Policies that do not accomplish the purpose for which they were intended should be disbanded. Constituencies with their own vested interests should be kept from perpetuating them.
3. Immigration should only sparingly be used as a foreign policy instrument. The Cuban experience suggests that immigration as a "soft power" strategy is ineffective. The unique immigration and immigrant entitlements that the United States granted Cubans proved good for the beneficiaries, but they failed to bring about the regime change intended.

4. Legislated immigration policies should have end dates in that it is easier to enact than to revoke laws, and no immigrant group should have unique open-ended entitlements embedded in legislation. There is no justification for the continued extension of unique rights of Cubans to welfare and to lawful permanent residency when entering the United States without authorization. The CAA illustrates the difficulty of sunsetting legislation that is enacted without an expiration date. Despite ongoing criticism of the CAA, and efforts of some legislators to sunset it, it has remained in effect for over half a century.
5. Congress should provide unauthorized immigrants who have lived in the United States for a set period of time, and have shown themselves to be law-abiding, with a path to lawful permanent residency and citizenship. The Cuban experience demonstrates how immigrants benefit from legal status, and how the broader society benefits, in turn. Legal status has been shown to benefit immigrants from other countries as well.

***********.

For nearly sixty years, Cubans who were unhappy with conditions in their homeland, whether economic or political, found themselves with an attractive alternative in the United States. If one wished to immigrate, it was good to be Cuban. However, all good things do not necessarily continue indefinitely, and the privileging of Cubans is no exception. Beginning in President Obama's last full week in office, Cuban privileging "as we knew it" abruptly ended, although entitlements that remained continued to privilege Cubans over other immigrants.

Meanwhile, the Haitian experience is a reminder that America will not be great until de facto racial biases in immigration policy end. Haitians deserve better and equitable treatment, both as refugees and immigrants.

The United States is a nation of immigrants. To perfect our democracy all immigrants should be treated equally and with respect. Work remains to be done.

Index

African Americans
  compared to Cuban immigrants and native-born, 59, 67–72
  against Mariel Cubans, backlash of, 120–21
  Miami, Cubans and, 54, 69–72
  Miami protests, riots of, 71, 120–21
  in schooling, Cubans and, 70–71
Amerasian immigrants, 207
anti-immigrant initiatives, under Trump, 288, 291, 330–31, 333, 335
anti-immigrant sentiment
  under Clinton, 218–21, 225, 240
  toward Mariel Cubans, 118–24
  under Reagan, 127–28
  under Trump, 287–90, 315, 330–31, 333
Aristide, Jean-Bertrand, 174, 214–16
  Clinton and, 211–12, 215
  coup against, 1991, sanctions proposed for, 213–14
  coup ousting, 2004, 278
Ashcroft, John, 278–79
Asylum Cooperation Agreements (Safe Third Country Agreements), 308–12
asylum-seekers. *See also* Peruvian Embassy asylum-seekers; refugee and asylee status adjustments
  to Central America, off-shoring exclusion of, 300, 308–13
  Europe off-shoring exclusion of, 312

  under Clinton, 184–85
  under Trump, 296–313, 335, 337
Atlanta federal penitentiary, Mariel Cubans detained in, 116, 119, 167–70

Baby Doc. *See* Duvalier, Jean-Claude
Back from the Future (Eckstein), xv
Balanced Budget Act (1997), 206–7, 270–82
Ball, George, 22, 53
Basulto, José, 228–30
Batista, Fulgencio, 1, 156
Bay of Pigs invasion, 15, 27, 29
  aftermath of, 27–32, 35–36, 45–46
  veterans of, 157–60, 228–29
Benes, Bernardo, 75
Biden, Joe, 291–92, 311, 314–15, 328
Black Caucus, Congressional, 113, 213–14
Blue Fire (Cuban freighter), 83–84, 87
boatpeople, unauthorized
  Clinton migration agreements and, 190–93, 195, 198–202, 209, 215–16, 218–20, 224–25, 325, 339–40
  Cubans in Florida, 187–88, 218–20
  exclusion of, 190–91, 198–99, 209–11, 220, 222–23, 336–37
  Haitian, xi, 212, 215–16, 218, 228
  new immigration status for, 201–3, 318–19
  off-shore detention of, 187–91, 193–94, 199–203, 215, 219–20, 222–26, 231, 281
  repatriation of Cuban, 192–95, 225–28, 245

343

Boland Amendment, 157
El Bombo. *See* Special Cuban Migration Program
border cities, Cubans in Mexican, 301–4
Border Patrol, US, 304, 308
Bosch, Juan, 321–22
Bosch, Orlando, 38, 40–41, 158–59
Brazil, Haitians emigrating from, 282–83
Brothers to the Rescue (BTTR), 227–32
Bundy, McGeorge, 31–32, 36, 39, 64
Bush, George H. W., 102, 147, 153, 300, 320, 323
  Bosch, O., and, 41, 158–59
  Central American immigrants under, 145
  Central American intervention and, 159
  Cuban American National Foundation (Foundation) and, 162–64
  Cuban entitlements extended under, 127–28
  Cuban Exodus Relief Fund (CERF) and, 165–66
  deportations under, 146–47, 170
  Florida and, 175
  Haitians under, xi, 127–28, 145, 170–71, 173–75, 179–80, 211–12
  Immigration Act of 1990, under, 145, 179
  Mariel Cubans, unrest of, under, 170
  Mas Canosa and, 161
  Nicaragua and, 159
  under Reagan, covert efforts and, xviii, 156, 158
  refugees under, 145–46
  Republican Party, Cuban American community, and, 155–56
Bush, George W., 329–30
  Cuba, US relations with, under, 241–43, 246–47, 249
  Cuban American community and, 237–38, 240, 244, 246–47, 262
  Cuban entitlements expanded under, xviii, 240–47, 318–19, 332
  Cuban family reunification entitlement, 244–45
  Cuban Medical Professional Parole Program (CMPPP) under, 243–45, 318–19
  Dominican Republic migration agreement, 327
  González, Elián, and election of, 237–38
  Haitians under, 242, 278–80, 327–28
  immigration reform, 246–47
  irregular Cuban arrivals under, 245–46
  Obama, continued policies of, xviii, 241–42, 252–53
Bush, Jeb, 162–63, 165–66
  émigrés, anti-Castro, and, 41, 158–59
  Republican Party, Miami, and, 155–56, 159, 219–20
Byrd, Robert, 213, 216–17

CAA. *See* Cuban Adjustment Act
CABA. *See* Cuban American Bar Association
CABA v. Christopher, 223–24
CAF. *See* Cuban American Foundation
Cahill, William, 57–58
California, Proposition 187 in, 218–19
Camarioca, Cuba, exodus from, 17, 75–76
  Freedom Flights and, 17–19, 78–79, 94–96, 339–40
  legacy of, 78–80, 94–96, 184
caravans, immigrant, 306–7
Card, David, 120
Carollo, Joe, 12, 227, 236
Carter, Jimmy, 82–85, 193. *See also* Mariel, mass exodus from, 1980
Castro, F., and, 19–41, 75–76, 79, 81, 84–85
Coast Guard under, Mariel Cubans and, 173
Cuba, relations with, under, 19–41, 74–76, 78–80, 106, 180
Cuban Adjustment Act (CAA) and, 74–75, 105–6
Cuban American community and, 93–95, 102
Cuban entitlements limited under, xvii, 23, 42, 74, 336–37
Cuban entitlements resumed under, xvii–xviii, 76, 92–96, 125–26, 336–37
Dialogue under, 19–41, 75, 78
in election, 1980, 102, 124–26, 147–48
Entrant status under, 103–10, 114, 128–29, 134, 149–50, 201, 282, 318–19, 339–40
exile raids under, 19–40
Florida and, 124, 335
Freedom Flotilla, 90
Haitians under, 76, 86, 103–14, 116–17, 124, 127, 170–71, 195–96, 251–80, 321, 332
illegal immigration under, 105–6

inadmissibles, excludables under, 98–99, 116, 148–49
Iranian hostage crisis under, 124
parole under, 99–100, 104–5
Peruvian Embassy asylum-seekers and, 80–83, 87, 91–92, 101–2, 113–14
political prisoners, Cuban, admitted under, 23, 75–77, 106
Reagan and legacy of, 127–31
Refugee Act under, 4–6, 81, 86, 88, 99–101, 105, 108, 111
Refugee Education Assistance Act (REAA) under, 108–9, 116–17, 124–25, 133, 209–10
refugee status under, Cuban, 80–82, 99–103, 139–40
US Interests Section, Havana, under, 148, 237
unique basis for admission under, 103–10, 339–40
Castillo, Leonel, 111–12
Castro, Fidel, 158, 242–43, 323, 331, 339
  anti-government demonstration under, 1994, 186
  asylum-seekers, under Clinton, and, 184–85
  Brothers to the Rescue (BTTR) and, 228–29
  Bush, G. W., and, 242–51
  Carter and, 19–41, 75–76, 79, 81, 84–85
  Clinton and, 184–85, 190–91, 223–25
  Cubans turning against, 77–78
  death of, xiii, 241, 318–19
  departures permitted by, 1994, 183, 186
  departures restricted under, 18–20
  Eisenhower and, xiii–xiv, xvi, xxi, 2–3, 23–25, 32–33, 42, 99
  on emigration, Cuban, 16–17
  Freedom Flights and, 18–19, 23, 76–77
  González, Elián, and, 237
  Guantanamo Bay and, 174
  under Kennedy, J., activities against, xiii–xiv, xvi, xxi, 2–3, 15, 25–36, 39, 42, 45–46
  Mariel Cubans and, 75–76, 79, 82, 84–85, 92–93, 96, 114–16, 121–22, 148
  Mariel mass exodus, prelude to, and, 79–81
  Mariel port closed by, 84–85, 89, 91–92, 96, 115–16, 141, 144, 148
  Marxist-Leninist turn of, 1–2, 8, 12, 77–78
  Nixon Administration and, 40–41
  Obama and, 241
  Peruvian Embassy asylum-seekers and, 80–82, 92–93
  Radio Martí, TV Martí, and, 150, 152–53, 162–63, 185, 190–91, 223–25
  revolutionary takeover by, xiii–xv, 1, 8
  revolutionary takeover by, immigration after, 3, 332–34
  Soviet Union and, 1–4, 12, 75–78
Castro, Raúl, xiii, 242–43, 246, 318–19
  González, Elián, and, 237
  Obama and, 241, 254–55, 286
CDA. See Cuban Democracy Act
Cejas, Paul, 138–39
Central America, 299–300. See also specific countries
  Asylum Cooperation Agreements with, 308–12
  Bush, G. H. W., and, 159
  civil wars in, US aid and, 142–43
  Cuban immigrants and intervention in, 154–59
  Cuban immigrants in, 310–11, 315
  Reagan and, xviii, 142–43, 147, 154–59, 179–80
  after Soviet Union collapse, 180–81
  under Trump, off-shoring US exclusion to, 300, 308–13
Central American immigrants, 142, 297, 300
  under Bush, G. H. W., 145
  caravans of, 306–7
  Nicaraguan, 105–6, 136, 145, 281, 310–11
  Nicaraguan Adjustment and Central American Relief Act (NACARA) for, 207–8, 216–17, 221
  under Reagan, 136, 142–45, 156–58
  Salvadoran, 136, 142–43, 145–47, 207–8, 281, 293–94, 298–300, 310
  Temporary Protected Status (TPS) for, 145, 281, 310
  under Trump, 293–94, 298–300, 310–11, 320–21
Central Intelligence Agency (CIA), 78–79, 220–27
  Bay of Pigs invasion and, 15, 27–32, 36
  Bay of Pigs veterans and, 157–60, 228–29

Central Intelligence Agency (CIA) (cont.)
  BTTR members trained by, 228–29
  under Eisenhower, 24–25, 33
  émigré terrorism and, 37–38, 40–41
  émigrés, anti-Castro, and, xvi, 24–36, 228–29
  under Kennedy, J., xvi, 25–36, 39
  under Reagan, 24–25, 33
CERF. See Cuban Exodus Relief Fund
CFRPP. See Cuban Family Reunification Parole Program
Chase, Gordon, 68
Chiles, Lawton, 187–88, 206–7, 219–20, 270
China, US Embassy in, 291
CHTF. See Cuban-Haitian Task Force
CIA. See Central Intelligence Agency
Clark, Ramsey, 51–53
Claver-Carone, Mauricio, 313–14
CLC. See Cuban Liberty Council
Clinton, Bill, xvii–xviii, 153, 167
  anti-immigrant backlash under, 218–21, 225, 240
  asylum-seekers under, 184–85
  Cold War, end of, and, 180–81, 183–84, 210–11, 218, 239–40, 324–25
  Cuban Adjustment Act (CAA) under, 187, 200, 202–24, 228, 232–33
  Cuban American National Foundation (Foundation) and, 163–64, 227, 231
  Cuban American politicians under, 203
  from Cuban Americans, pressures on, 221–27, 230–32, 239–40
  Cuban government shoot-down under, 227–32
  Cuban immigration under, orderly, 186, 192, 241, 324–25, 341
  Cubans vs. Haitians under, 211–18
  exclusion, of Cuban boatpeople, under, 190–91, 198–99, 209–11, 220, 222–23, 336–37
  exemption on restrictions under, Cuban, 206–10
  Florida and, 187–88, 194, 211, 218–20, 222, 227, 230–32
  Fort Chaffee, Mariel Cuban detention in, and, 98–99, 193–94, 210–11
  González, Elián, fight for, under, 232–40
  Haitians under, xi, 188–89, 211–18, 228, 270–82
  Helms–Burton bill under, 205–6, 228, 231–32
  human smuggling and, 258–59, 307, 325
  as illegal immigrants, Cuban refugees under, 194–95
  immigration pressures, new, under, 184–86
  inadmissibles and, 98–99, 196
  INS under, xi, 189, 197, 199–203, 208–10, 216, 219, 227, 235, 245–46
  irregular ways, Cubans arriving in, under, 191–92, 195, 200–1, 209, 216, 245–46
  Mariel Cubans, example of, and, 210–11, 220–27, 229
  Mas Canosa and, 194, 222–25, 231
  Meissner Memo under, 200–1, 208–10, 216, 227, 235, 245–46
  new immigration statuses under, for Cubans, 201–3, 318–19
  off-shore detention, of boatpeople, under, 187–91, 193–94, 199–203, 215, 219–20, 222–26, 231, 281
  Refugee Act and, 198, 205, 208
  refugee admissions under, new unique bases for, 197–233
  repatriation, of Cuban boatpeople, under, 192–95, 225–28, 245
  Special Guantanamo Entrants under, 202–3, 318–19
  welfare reform, 206–7, 221, 268–82
  wet foot/dry foot policy under, 192–93, 200–1, 209, 227, 245, 270–82
Clinton, Bill, Cuban entitlements under
  Congress and, 203–8
  new and restored, 183–84, 195–203, 207–10, 239–40, 324, 336–37
  retraction of, 183–84, 187–95, 203–7, 239–40, 319–20
  rollback and expansion of, 210–11, 239–40
Clinton, Bill, Cuban migration agreements under, 190, 195–96, 241, 259, 324–25
  boatpeople and, 190–93, 195, 198–202, 209, 215–16, 218–20, 224–25, 325, 339–40
  under Bush, G. W., 244–46
  under Obama, 249–52, 254, 325
CMPPP. See Cuban Medical Professional Parole Program
Coast Guard, US, 11, 173, 294, 318

Cuban boatpeople and, under Clinton, 187–89, 192, 194–95, 200–1, 224–25, 227–28
Haitian interdiction, repatriation and, 172–74, 215, 228, 280
Codina, Armando, 155–56
Cold War, xiii–xiv, xvi, xxi, 111
of Bush, G. W., against Cuba, 241–43, 246–47
Clinton and end of, 180–81, 183–84, 210–11, 218, 239–40, 324–25
Communist countries after, 180–81, 183
Haitian immigration under, xix, 331–32
Mariel Cubans and, 90
under Reagan, 156–58, 180
thawing, 1970s, 72–76
US Cuban immigration policy and, 2–5, 72, 96, 180, 324, 335, 337, 339
Committee of 75, 19–41, 75
Communist countries
after Cold War, 180–81, 183
refugees from, 49–50, 99–100, 111, 122–23, 136
Communist Party, Cuban, 1–2, 33–34, 48, 80, 84, 237
Concilio Cubano, 230
Congress, US, 320
under Clinton, Cuban entitlements and, 203–8
on Cuban Adjustment Act (CAA), repealing, changing, 203–6, 320, 337, 342
immigration policy and authority of, 338, 341
Congressional Black Caucus, 113, 213–14
Constitution, Cuban (1976), 48
constructivists, xxi
Contras, 157–59
Costa Rica, 80–82, 88, 92–93
COVID-19 pandemic, 289, 293–94, 297–98
CRC. *See* Cuban Revolutionary Council
Crockett, George, 138
Crosland, David, 88
CRP. *See* Cuban Refugee Program
Cruz, Celia, 44–45
Cuba, US relations with
under Bush, G. W., 241–43, 246–47, 249
under Carter, 19–41, 74–76, 78–80, 148, 180
under Clinton, 186, 190–91, 223–25

under Clinton, migration agreements, 190–93, 195–96, 198–202, 209, 215–16, 218–20, 224–25, 241, 259, 324–25, 339–40
Clinton migration agreements, under Bush, G. W., 244–46
Clinton migration agreements, under Obama, 249–52, 254, 325
Cuban Democracy Act (CDA), 163–64, 215–16, 222–25
diplomatic relations, severing, 14–15
Mariel Accord, 149–51
under Obama, xiv–xv, xviii–xix, 241, 247–50, 254, 276–77, 313, 339, 342
under Reagan, 147–54, 162, 190–91
after Soviet Union collapse, 183
thawing, 1970s, 72–76
under Trump, 313
Cuba Study Group, 239
Cuban Adjustment Act (CAA), 54–55, 321–22, 326–27, 329–30. *See also* lawful permanent residency
abuse of, 264, 270
under Bush, G. W., 245–47
Carter and, 74–75, 105–6
change, repeal of, politicians on, 105–6, 203–6, 266–67, 270, 273–77, 320, 337, 342
under Clinton, 187, 200, 202–24, 228, 232–33
on Cuban Americans, political impact of, 62–63, 95, 155, 206, 222, 337
Cuban Americans on changing, 270, 273–77
on Cuban immigrants, impact of, 59–63
Díaz-Balart, Mario, and, 264, 266
Dominican immigrants and, 58
Freedom Flights and, 57–58
González, Elián, and, 233, 236–37
Haitians and, 171, 213–14, 217, 278
Hart–Celler Act and, 49–52, 55–56, 135
INS on, 55, 140
IRCA and, 144, 204–5
Johnson Administration arguments for, 50–54, 71, 339–40
New Cubans on, 262
under Obama, 247–83
Reagan and, 128–29, 131–40, 144
Refugee Act and, 205, 208
Rubio on, 265–67, 276

Cuban Adjustment Act (CAA) (cont.)
  sunset proposed for, 203–6, 320, 337, 342
  under Trump, 294, 296
  unique rights embedded in, 55–59
Cuban American Bar Association (CABA), 223–24
Cuban American community, 331
  Biden and, 314–15
  Bush, G. W., and, 237–38, 240, 244, 246–47, 262
  Carter and, 93–95, 102
  on changing the Cuban Adjustment Act (CAA), 270, 273–77
  Clinton pressured by, 221–27, 230–32, 239–40
  of Cuban Adjustment Act (CAA), political impact on, 62–63, 95, 155, 206, 222, 337
  divide in, political change and, 260–61, 337
  divide in, Trump and, 291–92, 337
  of exceptionalism, political impact on, 62–63
  González, Elián, and, 232–40
  New Cubans, 261–63, 268, 285–86, 314–15
  Obama and, 255, 260–63
  Peruvian Embassy asylum-seekers and, 92
  under Reagan, political power of, xiv, 127–28, 151, 154–56, 159–62, 164–66, 180
  Republican Party and, 154–56, 159, 180, 261–68, 270–78, 335
  Republican Party and, under Clinton, 203
  transformation of, 261–63
  Trump and, 291–92, 313–15, 337
  voter registration, 155
  on wet foot/dry foot policy, 260–62
Cuban American Foundation (CAF), 161, 164–67
Cuban American National Foundation (Foundation), 155–56, 239, 277–78
  Bush, G. H. W., and, 162–64
  Bush, Jeb, and, 162–63
  Clinton and, 163–64, 227, 231
  fight for Elián González, 233, 235, 238–39
  lobbying of, 161–66
  Mas Canosa and, 44–45, 159–61, 164–65, 167, 222–23, 244, 265–66
  PAC of, 161–63, 207–21, 230, 244, 265–66
  under Reagan, 158–62, 164–66
  splintering of, 244
Cuban American politicians, 337
  on changing the Cuban Adjustment Act (CAA), 264, 266–67, 270, 273–77
  under Clinton, 203
  Cuban immigrants criticized by, 263–68, 270–74, 286
  under Obama, on retracting entitlements, 274–78
  under Trump, 291–314
Cuban Americans, interviews with, xxii
Cuban Democracy Act (CDA), 163–64, 215–16, 222–25
Cuban Exodus Relief Fund (CERF), 164–67
Cuban Family Reunification Parole Program (CFRPP), 244–45, 251–81, 290, 292–93, 332
Cuban Immigrant Work Opportunity Act (2015), 270–71, 273–74
Cuban Liberty and Democratic Solidarity Act. *See* Helms–Burton bill
Cuban Liberty Council (CLC), 238–39, 277–78
Cuban Medical Professional Parole Program (CMPPP), 275
  under Bush, G. W., 243–45, 318–19
  under Obama, 248–51, 274–75, 290–314
Cuban Missile Crisis, 12–15, 30–32
Cuban Refugee Adjustment Act. *See* Cuban Adjustment Act
Cuban Refugee Emergency Center, 44, 47
Cuban Refugee Program (CRP), 45–49, 107, 109, 117–18, 334
  benefits, 64–65, 69, 71
  cutting, 46–47, 132, 206, 335
  impact on Cuban immigrants, 60–70, 261–62
Cuban Revolutionary Council (CRC), 33–35
Cuban/Haitian Adjustment Act, 135–39, 149
Cuban-Haitian Entrant Act, proposed (1980), 105–6
Cuban-Haitian Task Force (CHTF), 97, 104, 107–8
Cuban/Haitian Temporary Resident Status Act, proposed (1981), 129–31

Curbelo, Carlos, 270, 273–76, 291–314

"A Day without Immigrants" Demonstrations (2006), xi–xii
Dellums, Ronald, 214
Department of Homeland Security (DHS), 244–45, 251, 284, 288
departures, Cuban government on
  permitting, 1994, 183, 186
  restricting, 18–20
deportations
  under Bush, G. H. W., 146–47, 170
  from Mexico, Cuban, 305–6
  under Obama, of Cubans, xii, 251–52, 283–85
  under Obama, of Haitians, xii 283–85
  under Reagan, 146
  under Trump, 288, 295, 306
detentions, 209
  in Guantanamo Bay, Cubans, 187–91, 193–94, 199–203, 215, 219–20, 222–26, 231, 281
  in Guantanamo Bay, Haitian, 174–75, 187–88, 215, 228
  in Guantanamo Bay, Muslim, 246
  of Haitians, in United States, 175–76, 180, 278–80, 283–84, 321, 331–32
  of Mariel Cubans, 97–99, 116, 118–19, 167–70, 193–94, 210–11, 251
  in Panama, of Cubans, 188–89, 193, 226
  under Reagan, 146
  under Trump, 288, 294–95
  unrest among Mariel Cubans, 118–19, 168–70
DHS. *See* Department of Homeland Security
the Dialogue, 19–41, 75, 78
Diaz, Manny, 217–18
Díaz-Balart, Lincoln, 155–56, 206–8, 230, 270–82
  Cuban Adjustment Act (CAA), sunset for, and, 203
  González, Elián, and, 234
Díaz-Balart, Mario, 264, 266, 268, 270, 275, 291–314
Díaz-Canel, Miguel, 293
doctors, Cuban immigrant, 59–60
Dominican Republic

Bush, G. W., migration agreement with, 327
Johnson, L., and, 36–37, 58, 321–22
military intervention in, 58, 321–22
Dominican Republic, immigrants from, 323
  Cuban immigration compared with, xix, 317, 320–21, 323–24, 328
  immigration rates for, xix, 317, 320–21
  under Johnson, L., 58, 321–22
  LPR for, 321, 323–27, 330
  refugee and asylee status adjustments for, 330
dry foot policy, 245, 259–62
  under Clinton, 200–1, 209, 227
  Obama ending, 250–51, 256, 275–76
Duvalier, Francois (Papa Doc), 110
Duvalier, Jean-Claude (Baby Doc), 110, 172–73

East Germany, Communist government ending in, 182
Eastern European immigrants, 208
Eastern Hemisphere, immigration capped for, 5
Eckstein, Susan Eva, xv
Ecuador, 259
education. *See* schooling
Eglin Air Force Base, Mariel Cubans detained at, 118
Eidenberg, Eugene, 88, 97
Eisenhower, Dwight, 48–49
  Castro, F., and, xiii–xiv, xvi, xxi, 2–3, 23–25, 32–33, 42, 99
  CIA under, 24–25, 33
  for Cuban immigrants, special entitlements under, xiii–xiv, xvi, xx–xxi, 4–5, 8–13, 42–44, 331
  Cuban Refugee Emergency Center under, 44
  émigrés, anti-Castro, under, xvi, 2–3, 23–25, 32–33, 38–39, 42
  Hungarian refugees under, 49–50, 136
  parole under, 4–5, 13, 191–92
  path dependency after, 336, 338
  soft power and Cubans under, xx–xxi, 2, 42
  unaccompanied minors, program for, under, 11–13
Eizenstat, Stuart, 113–14
El Salvador
  asylum-seekers, 309–10

El Salvador (cont.)
  immigrants from, 136, 142–43, 145–47, 207–8, 281, 293–94, 298–300, 310
  military of, United States and, 157–58
  off-shoring US exclusion to, 308–12
election, 1980 (US), 102, 124–26, 147–48, 238
election, 2000 (US), 237–38, 240
embargo
  Clinton and, 190–91, 223–25, 231–32
  Cuban Democracy Act (CDA) on, 163–64
  New Cuba PAC on, 314
  personal, 190–91, 223–25, 262, 264–65, 267–68, 273–74, 285–86
embassies. *See* China, US Embassy in; Havana, Cuba, US Embassy in
Emergency Refugee and Migration Assistance Fund, 107, 115
émigrés, anti-Castro, 32–37, 228–30
  Bay of Pigs invasion, 15, 27–32, 35–36, 45–46
  Bay of Pigs veterans, 157–60, 228–29
  Bush, Jeb, and, 41, 158–59
  CIA and, xvi, 24–38, 40, 228–29
  Clinton and, 194, 227
  Cuban government shoot-down provoked by, 227–32
  Dialogue and, 75
  under Eisenhower, xvi, 2–3, 23–25, 32–33, 38–39, 42
  exile raids, 19–37, 41–42
  under Kennedy, J., xvi, 2–3, 15, 25–36, 38–40, 42, 45–46
  Mariel Cubans and, 93–94
  New Cubans, versus exiles, 262–63
  under Nixon, 36–37, 40–41
  under Reagan, xviii, 24–25, 33, 126–28, 147, 154–62
  terrorist attacks by, 19–37, 39, 41–42, 75, 158–60, 164, 246
Engstrom, David, 94–96
entitlements, Cuban, abuse of, 264–70, 286
Entrants
  under Carter, 103–10, 114, 128–29, 134, 149–50, 201, 282, 318–19, 339–40
  Cuban/Haitian Adjustment Act for, 135–39, 149
  Cuban-Haitian Entrant Act, proposed, 1980, 105–6

  Fascell–Stone Amendment for, 108–10, 116–17, 124, 133, 160
  Haitian, 103–6, 108–9, 114, 117–18, 128–29, 134–39, 150, 170–71, 217, 282, 323
  IRCA and, 144, 217, 323
  under Reagan, 117, 127–35, 139–41
  under Reagan, delinking Cuban and Haitian, 139–41
  Special Guantanamo Entrants, under Clinton, 202–3, 318–19
entrants without inspection (EWIs), 207–8
Estefan, Gloria, 233–34
Europe, asylum-seekers and, 312
European immigration, declining, 6–7, 332–33
EWIs. *See* entrants without inspection
exceptionalism, Cuban immigration
  on Cuban Americans, political impact of, 62–63
  immediate impact of, 59–72
  impact on African Americans, 59, 67–72
  impact on native-born, 63–67
  making of, 1959-1979 1–3, 8–16
  Miami Cuban community and, 60–63, 73, 95, 261–62
excludables. *See* inadmissibles
exile raids, 19–37, 41–42
exiles, Cuban émigrés as, 23–24
exit passes, 305–6

family visits, cross-border, Trump restricting, 295–96
Fascell, Dante, 108, 160, 162
Fascell–Stone Amendment, 108–10, 116–17, 124, 133, 160
Federal Emergency Management Agency (FEMA), 97, 115–16
Florida, xxii, 154–56, 159, 331. *See also* Miami, Florida
  boatpeople and, 187–88, 218–20
  Bush, G. H. W., and, 175
  Bush, G. W., and, 237–38, 244
  CABA v. Christopher case in, 223–24
  Carter and, 124, 335
  Clinton and, 187–88, 194, 211, 218–20, 222, 227, 230–32
  Cuban American politicians, 263–68, 270–74, 291–314

Cuban community in, immigrant exceptionalism and, 60–63, 73, 95, 261–62
on Cuban welfare rights, politicians of, 206–7
election, 2000, and, 237–38
financing, of immigrants, in, 107–9, 133, 335
Fort McCoy, Mariel Cuban riots at, 118–19
González, Elián, in, 232–39
Krome North, 176, 209
Reagan funding Entrant entitlements in, 133
Ford, Gerald, xvii, 7, 23, 42, 62–63, 74–75
Fort Allen, Puerto Rico, 98
Fort Chaffee, Arkansas, Mariel Cuban detention in, 97–99, 116, 118, 193–94, 210–11
Fort McCoy, Florida, Mariel Cuban riots at, 118–19
Foundation. *See* Cuban American National Foundation
Frank, Barney, 213–14
FRD. *See* Frente Revolucionario Democrático
Free Cuba PAC. *See* Cuban American National Foundation
Freedom Flights, 23, 48, 76–77
under Johnson, L., 17–21, 46–47, 49, 57–58, 64–65, 67, 70–71, 78–79, 90–91, 94–96, 321–22, 339–40
Nixon terminating, 17–21, 23, 46–47, 72
Freedom Flotilla, 90
Freedom Tower (Miami), 44–45
Frente Revolucionario Democrático (FRD), 32–33, 35

Gang of Eight, 266
García, Andy, 233–34
García, Joe, 266–67, 271–72
Gardner, John, 52
Ghougassian, Joe, 134, 153–54
globalization, of Cuban immigration privilege. *See* Cuban Medical Professional Parole Program
González, Elián
Cuban American community and, 232–40
Cuban government and, 236–37
election, 2000, and, 237–38
raid retrieving, 235–36, 239
González, Lázaro, 233–36
González Quintana, Juan Miguel, 233–37
Gore, Al, 237–38
Gosar, Paul, 273–76
Graham, Bob, 218–20, 230
Cuban Democracy Act (CDA) sponsored by, 163
on Guantanamo, detention in, 199, 219, 225–26
Gross, Alan, 249
Guantanamo Bay, Cuba, 174, 188
Clinton and Cuban detention in, 187–89, 193–94, 199–203, 215, 219–20, 222–26, 231, 281
Haitians detained in, 174–75, 187–88, 215, 228
Muslim terrorists, alleged, detained in, 246
Special Guantanamo Entrants, under Clinton, 202–3
Guatemala, 24–25, 142
immigrants from, 142–43, 311
off-shoring US exclusion to, 308–12
Guevara, Ernesto (Che), 157

Haitian Adjustment Equity Act, 213–14
Haitian Family Reunification Parole Program (HFRPP), 281–82, 292–93, 332
Haitian Program, 109–12, 251–80, 323–24
Haitian Refugee Center, 171–77
Haitian Refugee Center v. Civiletti, 112–13
Haitian Refugee Immigration Fairness Act (HRIFA), 217, 221, 325, 327–28
Haitians
from Brazil, emigration of, 282–83
under Bush, G. H. W., xi, 127–28, 145, 170–71, 173–75, 179–80, 211–12
under Bush, G. W., 242, 278–80, 327–28
under Carter, 76, 86, 103–14, 116–17, 127, 170–71, 251–80
under Carter, Cuban entitlements extended to, 110, 124, 128–31, 135–39, 209–10, 321, 332
under Clinton, xi, 188–89, 211–18, 228, 270–82
Cold War and, xix, 331–32
Cuban Adjustment Act (CAA) and, 171, 213–14, 217, 278

Haitians (cont.)
  Cuban/Haitian Adjustment Act, 135–39, 149
  Cuban-Haitian Task Force (CHTF), 97, 104, 107–8
  Cubans compared with, 317, 320–21, 328, 330, 333–34, 337, 340
  detention of, 174–76, 180, 187–88, 215, 228, 278–80, 283–84, 321, 331–32
  discrimination against, xix, 110–14, 137–39, 170–71, 176–79, 212–18, 279–80, 317, 321, 332, 337, 341–42
  earthquake and, 242, 280–81, 298–99, 328
  Entrants, 103–6, 108–9, 114, 117–18, 128–29, 134–39, 150, 170–71, 217, 282, 323
  exclusionary policies for, 170–80
  fair judicial treatment denied to, 177–79
  Haitian Program, 109–12, 251–80, 323–24
  Hurricane Matthew and, 284
  INS and, 109–12, 136–38, 177–79, 279–80
  interdiction and repatriation of, 172–75
  IRCA and, 144, 217, 323–24, 332
  legal advocacy for, 111–13
  LPR and, 217, 251–82, 317, 321, 323–25, 327–28, 330, 332
  Mariel Cubans and, 103–6, 108–9, 114, 124, 128–31
  Miami and, 134–35, 138–39
  under Obama, 242, 255–56, 278, 280–84, 298–99, 327–28
  under Obama, deporting, xii, 283–85
  under Obama, temporary inclusionary policies for, 280–85, 292–93, 321, 328, 332
  path-dependent Cuban privileging and, 180, 337
  Peruvian embassy asylum-seekers and, 113–14
  political advocacy for, 112–14, 213–14
  under Reagan, 125, 127–29, 134–42, 144, 170–73, 175–80, 192–93, 323–24
  under Reagan, Temporary Resident status proposed for, 129–31, 136
  Refugee Act and, 111
  refugee and asylee status adjustments for, 326–30
  Temporary Protected Status (TPS) and, 179, 280–84, 298–99, 328, 332
  under Trump, 292–93, 298–99, 310, 328
Hart–Celler Act (1965), 5–6, 15–39
  Cuban Adjustment Act (CAA) and, 49–52, 55–56, 135
  Cubans circumventing requirements under, 17–19, 22, 55
  Mariel Cubans and, 99
  national origins policy ended by, xvi–xvii, xix, 5–7, 17–18, 20
Havana, Cuba, US Embassy in
  shuttering of, 53
  under Trump, visa-processing halted by, 290–96
Havana, Cuba, US Interests Section in, 79, 106, 148, 150–51, 237
Hawkins, Paula, 162
Hays, Dennis, 194
Health, Education, and Welfare, Department of (HEW), 51–54
Helms–Burton bill (Cuban Liberty and Democratic Solidarity Act) (1996), 205–6, 228, 231–32
Hernández, Francisco José (Pepe), 158
HEW. *See* Health, Education, and Welfare, Department of
HFRPP. *See* Haitian Family Reunification Parole Program
hijackings, 77, 79, 185–86, 252
homeland visit restrictions. *See* travel restrictions
Honduras, 308–12
Horowitz, Mike, 171–77
HRIFA. *See* Haitian Refugee Immigration Fairness Act
human smuggling, 312, 340
  under Clinton, 258–59, 307, 325
  under Obama, 252, 258–60, 307
Hungarian refugees, 49–50, 136
Hunton, Harold, 63–64
Hurricane Matthew, 284

ICE. *See* Immigration and Customs Enforcement
ICFRA. *See* Immigration Control and Financial Responsibility Act
IIRIRA. *See* Illegal Immigration Reform and Immigrant Responsibility Act
illegal immigrants
  under Bush, G. W., 246–47

under Carter, 105–6
under Clinton, 194–95, 218–21, 240
"A Day without Immigrants" demonstrations of, xi–xii
legislated restrictions on, Cubans exempted from, 208–10
Mexican, Central American, 105–6, 127, 142–43
under Obama, increasing, 240, 254–60, 337
under Reagan, 127, 131, 139, 141–46, 288–89
resentment against, 122–23
Illegal Immigration Reform and Immigrant Responsibility Act (IIRIRA) (1996), 7, 205–6, 221, 232, 258–59
under Bush, G. W., Haitians and, 278–79
Cubans exempted from, 208, 210, 235
imagined refugees. *See* refugees, imagined
The Immigrant Divide (Eckstein), xv
immigrants, unauthorized. *See* illegal immigrants
Immigration Act of 1990, 7, 145, 179, 201–2
Immigration and Customs Enforcement (ICE), 294–95
Immigration and Nationality Act (INA) (1952)
amendments to, 1976, 7, 23, 55–56, 58–59, 99, 130, 135, 323, 331
under Johnson, L., amending, 5–6, 49–50
parole under, 4–6, 13, 22
Immigration and Naturalization Service (INS)
under Castillo, Haitians and, 111–12
under Clinton, xi, 189, 197, 199–203, 208–10, 216, 219, 227, 235, 245–46
on Cuban Adjustment Act (CAA), 55, 140
González, Elián, and, 233, 235
Haitians and, 109–12, 136–38, 177–79, 279–80
under Kennedy, J., Cubans and, 11, 15
on Land Mariel Type Influx, 300
Mariel Cubans and, 88–89, 98–99, 115–16, 168
under Reagan, 136–41, 143–45, 168–70
Immigration Control and Financial Responsibility Act (ICFRA), 205
immigration policies, US, xvi, xxi, 3–7, 341–42

Cold War and Cuban, 2–5, 72, 96, 180, 324, 335, 337, 339
Congressional authority and, 338, 341
immigration rates, comparative, xix, 317, 320–21
immigration reform
under Bush, G. W., 246–47
Hart–Celler Act, xvi–xvii, xix, 5–7, 15–39, 49–52, 55–56, 99, 135
under Obama, Gang of Eight on, 266
Immigration Reform and Control Act (IRCA) (1986), 7, 143–44, 146, 218–19, 246–47
Cuban Adjustment Act (CAA) and, 144, 204–5
Dominicans and, 323–24
Entrants and, 144, 217, 323
Haitians and, 144, 217, 323–24, 332
Immigration Reform and Control Act, proposed (1983), 131, 135–37, 139–40. *See also* Omnibus Immigration Control Act, proposed
INA. *See* Immigration and Nationality Act
inadmissibles
under Carter, 98–99, 116, 148–49
under Clinton, 98–99, 196
under Obama, 251–52
under Reagan, 116, 147–50, 152–53, 162–63, 167–70
rebellions by, 168–70
in-country processing, 198–233
Indochinese refugees, 97, 99–100, 136, 145
inequitable treatment, of immigrant groups, 331–33
INS. *See* Immigration and Naturalization Service
Iran-Contra affair, 157–58
Iranian hostage crisis, 124
IRCA. *See* Immigration Reform and Control Act
irregular migration, 307
irregular ways, Cubans arriving in, 259
under Bush, G. W., 245–46
under Clinton, 191–92, 195, 200–1, 209, 216, 245–46
under Obama, 248–51

Johnson, Jeh, 251, 284
Johnson, Lyndon, xx–xxi, 8

Johnson, Lyndon (cont.)
  African Americans and Cuban exceptionalism under, 68–71
  Camarioca exodus under, 17–19, 75–76, 78–79, 94–96, 184, 339–40
  Cuban Adjustment Act (CAA) under, 49–60, 71, 135, 339–40
  Cuban immigration financed under, 11, 17–21
  Cuban Refugee Program (CRP) under, 46–47, 59–60
  Dominican Republic and, 36–37, 58, 321–22
  émigré terrorism under, 40, 42
  entitlements, Cuban, expanded under, xvi–xvii, 16–17, 22, 42–44, 46–47, 49–59, 78–79, 336
  exile raids under, 38–40
  Freedom Flights under, 17–21, 46–47, 49, 57–58, 64–65, 67, 70–71, 78–79, 90–91, 94–96, 321–22, 339–40
  Hart–Celler Act under, xvi–xvii, xix, 5–7, 15–39, 49–52, 55–56, 99, 135
  Liberty Island speech of, 70
  LPR and, 49–55, 336
  native-born under, Cuban exceptionalism and, 63–67
  parole under, 21–22, 49, 51, 53–57
  status adjustment proposed under, 15–39
  third countries, Cubans in, under, 21–22
Joint Communique on Migration, 190–93, 196–201, 209, 216
Joint Declaration, Mexico and United States, 307
Joint Statement with the Republic of Cuba on Normalization of Migration, 192–93, 198–99, 215–16, 224–25

Kami, Hideaki, 96
Kennedy, Edward, 102, 108
Kennedy, John, 15
  Bay of Pigs invasion under, 15, 27–32, 35–36, 45–46
  Castro, F., regime, activities against, under, xiii–xiv, xvi, xxi, 2–3, 15, 25–36, 39, 42, 45–46
  Cuban immigration financed under, 11
  Cuban Missile Crisis, 12–15, 30–32
  émigrés, anti-Castro, under, xvi, 2–3, 15, 25–36, 38–40, 42, 45–46

  exile raids under, 38–40, 42
  INS under, Cubans and, 11, 15
  LPR and, 48–49, 336
  Migration and Refugee Assistance Act under, 3–4
  parole under, 13–14, 49
  soft power and Cubans under, xx–xxi, 42
  special entitlements, Cuban, under, xiii–xiv, xx–xxi, 8, 10–15, 42–46, 336
  unaccompanied minors, program for, under, 11–13, 19
  visas, for Cubans, under, 10–14
King, James Lawrence, 112–13, 178
Kissinger, Henry, 36–37, 40–41
Kopetski, Mike, 204
Kozak, Michael, 152–53
Krome North Processing Center, Florida, 176, 209

Land Mariel Type Influx, warning of, 300–1
Lautenberg, Frank, 151–52
lawful permanent residency (LPR), 21, 319, 335, 342
  to authentic refugees, limiting, 264–65
  under Bush, G. W., 245–46, 325, 329–30
  under Clinton, Meissner Memo and, 208–9
  for Cubans, Haitians, Dominicans compared with, 321, 323–27, 330
  for Dominicans, 321, 323–27, 330
  for Haitians, 217, 251–82, 317, 321, 323–25, 327–28, 330, 332
  Hart–Celler Act and, 49–52, 55
  imagined refugees, Cubans as, and, 329–30
  under Johnson, L., 49–55, 336
  under Kennedy, J., 48–49, 336
  Nicaraguan Adjustment and Central American Relief Act (NACARA) on, 207–8
  parole and, 51, 53–55, 187, 318
  path dependency and, 336–37
  Temporary Resident status, proposed, and, 130
  under Trump, 297
Leshaw, Gary, 168–69
López Obrador, Andrés Manuel, 301–2, 307, 311–12
lottery, immigration, 196–97, 325, 332–33

LPR. *See* lawful permanent residency

Maduro, Nicolas, 299
Mariel, mass exodus from, 1980, 75–76, 82–87
  Carter Administration response to, 85–96
  prelude to, 76–82
  Mariel Accord, 149–51
Mariel Cubans, 125–27, 175. *See also* Entrants
  backlash against, 118–25
  Castro, F., and, 75–76, 79–82, 84–85, 92–93, 96, 114–16, 121–22, 141, 148
  Castro, F., closing Mariel port, 84–85, 89, 91–92, 96, 115–16, 141, 144, 148
  Clinton and example of, 210–11, 220–27, 229
  Coast Guard and, 173
  Cold War and, 90
  Cuban/Haitian Adjustment Act for, 135–39
  in detention facilities, unrest among, 118–19, 168–70
  detention of, 97–99, 116, 118–19, 167–70, 193–94, 210–11, 251
  election, 1980, and, 102, 124–26, 147–48
  émigrés, anti-Castro, and, 93–94
  entitlements for, financing, 106–10
  fiscal costs of admitting, 114–18
  Haitians and, 103–6, 108–9, 114, 124, 128–31
  Hart–Celler Act and, 99
  inadmissible, excludable, 98–99, 116, 147–50, 152–53, 162–63, 167–70, 251–52
  INS and, 88–89, 98–99, 115–16, 168
  Land Mariel Type Influx, warning of, 300–1
  Miami and, 92–93, 119–21
  political costs of admitting, 114–15, 123–25
  problems processing, 96–99
  under Reagan, Temporary Resident status proposed for, 129–31, 136
  Reagan and, 127–36, 147–49, 323, 339–40
  Refugee Act and, 86, 88, 99–101, 105, 108, 116–17, 129
  refugee status for, contested, 101–3, 108, 134–35, 139–40

  refugee status for, proposed by Reagan, xviii, 102, 134–35, 139–40, 144, 179–80, 318–19, 335
  social costs of admitting, 114–15, 118–23
  unique basis for admitting, 103–10
  unique entitlements for, legacy of, 209–10
Marxist-Leninist turn, Cuban, 1–2, 8, 12, 77–78
Mas Canosa, Jorge, 160, 169, 230
  Bush, G. H. W., and, 161
  Clinton and, 194, 222–25, 231
  Cuban American National Foundation (Foundation) and, 44–45, 159–61, 164–65, 167, 222–23, 244, 265–66
  Radio Martí, TV Martí, and, 162, 185, 223–25
Mas Santos, Jorge, 227, 238–39, 277–78
Mazzoli, Romano, 131, 204–5
McCarran–Walter Act. *See* Immigration and Nationality Act
McNamara, Robert, 25–26, 30–31
Meissner, Doris, 103, 189, 199
Meissner Memo, 200–1, 208–10, 216, 227, 235, 245–46
Memorandum of Understanding (MOU), 18–19
Menéndez, Robert, 155, 203, 234, 264, 266
  Clinton criticized by, 225
  on entitlements, Obama retracting, 276–77
  in Gang of Eight, 266
  González, Elián, fight for, and, 234
  under Trump, 291–314
metering, for asylum-seekers, 301–2, 311
Mexican immigrants, 105–6, 127, 142, 255–56, 287–88, 320–21
Mexico, 143, 301–5
  border cities, 301–4
  Cuban deportation from, 305–6
  Cuban immigrants in, 53, 248–49, 301–6, 312–13, 315
  exit passes stopped by, 305–6
  human smuggling and, 307
  Joint Declaration of United States and, 307
  López Obrador, Andrés Manuel, 301–2, 307, 311–12
  metering in, 301–2, 311

Mexico (cont.)
  Migrant Protection Protocols (MPP), 302, 304–5, 311
  under Obama, 248–49
  under Trump, 282–83, 287–88, 300–8, 311–13
Miami, Florida, 48, 223–24, 238
  African Americans in, 54, 69–72, 120–21
  Cuban Americans in, 60–63, 73, 92, 95, 261–62
  Freedom Tower, 44–45
  Haitians and, 134–35, 138–39
  Mariel Cubans and, 92–93, 119–21
  native-born versus Cuban immigrants, 63–67
  Republicans in, 155–56, 159, 219–20
  schooling in, Cuban immigrants and, 67, 70–71
  terrorism and, 160
Miami-Dade County Commission, 267, 291–92
Migrant Protection Protocols (MPP), 302, 304–5, 311
Migration and Refugee Assistance Act (1962), 3–4
MOU. *See* Memorandum of Understanding
MPP. *See* Migrant Protection Protocols
Mucarsel-Powell, Debbie, 291–92
Mulvaney, Mick, 315
Muslim ban, of Trump, 287–88

NAACP. *See* National Association for the Advancement of Colored People
NACARA. *See* Nicaraguan Adjustment and Central American Relief Act
NAFTA. *See* North American Free Trade Agreement
National Association for the Advancement of Colored People (NAACP), 69–70
National Endowment for Democracy (NED), 160
National Guard, Mexican, 307
national origins policy, ending, xvi–xvii, xix, 5–7, 17–18, 20
native-born, Cuban exceptionalism and. *See* exceptionalism, Cuban immigration
nativism. *See* anti-immigrant sentiment
NED. *See* National Endowment for Democracy
Nelson, Alan, 136–38, 140–41
New Cuba PAC, 314

New Cubans, 261–63, 268, 285–86, 314–15
New Jersey Cuban community, 151, 155, 234, 266
Nicaragua, 299–300
  immigrants from, 105–6, 136, 145, 281, 310–11
  US involvement in, 157–59
Nicaraguan Adjustment and Central American Relief Act (NACARA) (1997), 207–8, 216–17, 221
Nixon, Richard, 23–24, 206
  Cold War thaw under, 72–75
  Cuban privilege limited under, xvii, 23, 42, 74, 319–20
  émigrés, anti-Castro, under, 36–37, 40–41
  Freedom Flights terminated by, 17–21, 23, 46–47, 72
non-*refoulement*, principle of, 4, 9, 96–97, 194–95
North American Free Trade Agreement (NAFTA), 301–2
Northern Triangle countries. *See* Central America
Nuevo Laredo, Mexico, 301–3
Nye, Joseph, Jr., xx–xxi

Oakdale, Louisiana, federal prison, 98–99, 116, 119, 167–69
Obama, Barack, xix, 314
  Bush, G. W. policies continued under, xviii, 241–42, 252–53
  Cuban Adjustment Act (CAA) under, 247–83
  Cuban American community and, 255, 260–63
  Cuban immigrant entitlements continued, 247–49, 252–53, 285
  Cuban immigrant entitlements retracted, xiii–xv, xviii, 240–42, 248–56, 259–61, 274–78, 281, 285, 290–314, 319–20, 339–40, 342
  deportations under, xii, 251–52, 283–85
  Haitians under, xii, 242, 255–56, 278, 280–85, 292–93, 298–99, 321, 327–28, 332
  human smuggling under, 252, 258–60, 307
  illegal immigration surge under, 240, 254–60, 337

immigration reform under, Gang of Eight on, 266
inadmissibles under, 251–52
irregular ways, Cubans arrived in, under, 248–51
Mexican immigrants and, 255–56
Mexico and, 248–49
parole under, 251–56, 275, 281–83, 292–93, 297, 329–30, 332
refugee and asylee status adjustments under, 329–30
remittance-sending restrictions removed under, 257–58
Republicans under, Cuban Americans and, 262–63, 274–78
Trump response, 286, 290–314
Obama, Barack, Cuba foreign policy of, xiv–xv, xviii–xix, 254–55, 286, 313
bilateral migration meetings in, 247–49
bilateral trust-building in, 249–50
Clinton migration agreements and, 249–52, 254, 325
full diplomatic relations, normalization in, 241, 247–50, 254, 276–77, 339
repatriation, deportation agreements, Cuban, in, 251–52
travel restrictions ended under, 257, 262–63, 265–66, 268, 285–86, 295–96
Omnibus Immigration Control Act, proposed (1982), 129–31, 143
Operation Mongoose, 31–32, 39
Operation Peter Pan, 11–13, 19, 138–39

Palmieri, Victor, 91, 94, 97, 104–5, 114
Panama
Cubans detained in, 188–89, 193, 226
tourist visas in, 299–300
Papa Doc. See Duvalier, Francois
parole, 5–6
under Bush, G. W., 244–45, 318–19
under Carter, 99–100, 104–5
under Clinton, 187, 189, 198–201, 209–10
under Eisenhower, 4–5, 13, 191–92
humanitarian, for Haitians, 282–83
under INA, 4–6, 13, 22
under Johnson, L., 21–22, 49, 51, 53–57
under Kennedy, J., 13–14, 49
LPR and, 51, 53–55, 187, 318
under Obama, 251–56, 275, 281–83, 292–93, 297, 329–30, 332

under Reagan, Mariel Cubans, Haitians, and, 129
Refugee Act and, 5, 100, 129
path-dependent, Cuban privileging as, xx, 42, 72, 180, 335–38
after Eisenhower, 336, 338
Haitian disprivileging and, 180, 337
Penelas, Alex, 234, 236, 238
Pepper, Claude, 70, 155
personal embargo. See embargo
Personal Responsibility and Work Opportunity Reconciliation Act (PRWORA), 206–7, 221, 270–82
Peruvian Embassy asylum-seekers
Carter Administration and, 80–83, 87, 91–92, 101–2, 113–14
Castro, F., government and, 80–82, 92–93
Cuban American response to, 92
Haitians and, 113–14
political prisoners, Cuban, 19–20, 23, 75–77, 106
Pompeo, Mike, 311–12
Posada Carriles, Luis, 40–41, 158, 246
Powell, Jody, 90–91
preference system, 5–6
Private Sector Initiative (PSI), 164–66
Proposition 187 (California), 218–19
PRWORA. See Personal Responsibility and Work Opportunity Reconciliation Act
PSI. See Private Sector Initiative
Puerto Rico, 98

race. See also national origins policy, ending
Cuban immigration and, 20, 217, 245, 332–33
Haitian immigration and (See Haitians)
Trump immigrant crackdown, 288, 292–93, 298–99
Radio Martí. See also TV Martí
Castro, F., and, 150, 152–53, 162–63, 185, 190–91, 223–25
Mas Canosa and, 162, 185, 223–25
scandals, financial problems, 163
rafters. See boatpeople, unauthorized
REAA. See Refugee Education Assistance Act
Reagan, Ronald, 97, 122–23, 320
anti-immigrant sentiment under, 127–28
benefit cuts under, 130–33, 146
Carter legacy and, 127–31

Reagan, Ronald (cont.)
  Central America and, xviii, 142–43, 147, 154–59, 179–80
  Central American immigrants under, 136, 142–45, 156–58
  Cold War under, 156–58, 180
  Cuba, US relations with, under, 147–54, 162, 190–91
  Cuban Adjustment Act (CAA) and, 128–29, 131–40, 144
  Cuban American National Foundation (Foundation) under, 158–62, 164–66
  Cuban American political power under, xiv, 127–28, 151, 154–56, 159–62, 164–66, 180
  Cuban entitlements under, xiv, 126–28, 132–35, 147, 149–50, 164–66, 179–80
  Cuban immigrant entitlements retracted by, 150–51
  Cuban immigration rights reinstated under, 151–54
  Cuban/Haitian Adjustment Act proposed under, 135–39, 149
  detentions and deportations under, 146
  in election, 1980, 102, 124, 147–48, 238
  émigrés, anti-Castro, under, xviii, 24–25, 33, 126–28, 147, 154–62
  Entrants under, 117, 127–41
  Florida Entrant entitlement funding under, 133
  foreign policy of, Cuban immigrants in, 156–58
  Haitians under, 125, 127–29, 134–42, 144, 170–73, 175–80, 192–93, 211, 323–24
  Haitians under, Temporary Resident status proposed for, 129–31, 136
  on illegal immigrants, war of, 139, 141–46, 288–89
  illegal immigrants and, 127, 131, 142–44
  immigration compromise of, 143–46
  inadmissibles, excludables under, 116, 147–50, 152–53, 162–63, 167–70
  in-country processing under, 198
  INS under, 136–41, 143–45, 168–70
  IRCA under, 7, 143–46, 204–5, 217–19, 246–47, 323–24, 332
  Mariel Accord, 149–51
  for Mariel Cubans, refugee status proposed by, xviii, 102, 134–35, 139–40, 144, 179–80, 318–19, 335

  Mariel Cubans and, 127–36, 147–49, 323, 339–40
  Mexican, Central American immigrants blocked by, 142–43
  new Cuban immigrants shut out by, 147–49
  new unique immigration entitlements under, 149–50
  PSI under, 164–66
  REAA under, 130–31, 133
  Refugee Act under, 129, 132–34
  for refugees, cutbacks under, 132, 146
  as Republican base, Cubans, and, 154–56, 180, 335
  Temporary Resident status proposed under, 129–31, 136
Reaganomics, 130–35, 146
refoulement. See non-refoulement, principle of
Refugee Act (1980), 326–29, 334–35
  under Bush, G. H. W., 146
  under Carter, 4–6, 81, 86, 88, 99–101, 105, 108, 111
  under Clinton, 198, 205, 208
  Haitians and, 111
  Indochinese refugees and, 99–100
  Mariel Cubans and, 86, 88, 99–101, 105, 108, 116–17, 129
  under Obama, 290
  parole and, 5, 100, 129
  under Reagan, 129, 132–34
  under Trump, 290, 293
  for victims of Communism, 99–100
refugee and asylee status adjustments, 326–30
refugee doctors, Cuban, 59–60
Refugee Education Assistance Act (REAA) (1980), 124–25, 133, 202–3, 209–10
  Fascell–Stone Amendment to, 108–10, 116–17, 124, 133, 160
  Haitians and, under Obama, 282
  under Reagan, 130–31, 133
refugee policy, US, history of, 3–7
refugee policy, United Nations. *See* United Nations Convention Relating to the Status of Refugees
refugee status, xxi, 67, 102
  under Carter, Cuban, 80–82, 99–103, 139–40
  under Clinton, new unique bases for, 197–233

Index

under Clinton, reclassification as illegal immigrants, 194–95
for Mariel Cubans, contested, 101–3, 108, 134–35, 139–40
for Mariel Cubans, under Reagan, xviii, 102, 134–35, 139–40, 144, 179–80, 318–19, 335
social construction of, 333–35
refugee tourism, 9–10
refugees
authentic, Cuban American politicians on, 263–68, 272–74
under Bush, G. H. W., 145–46
from Communist countries, 49–50, 99–100, 111, 122–23, 136
Hungarian, under Eisenhower, 49–50, 136
Indochinese, 97, 99–100, 136, 145
under Reagan, 132, 146
under Trump, 293–94
refugees, imagined
Cubans as, 43–48, 72, 329–30, 334–35
Haitians as, 330
Regalado, Tomas, 277
Remain in Mexico. *See* Migrant Protection Protocols
remittance-sending restrictions, removed by Obama, 257–58
Reno, Janet, 196–97, 210–11, 231
Cuban boatpeople and, 187–89, 195, 218–20
González, Elián, controversy, 235–36
repatriation
under Bush, G. H. W., Haitian, xi, 173–74, 212
under Bush, G. W., Cuban, 245
under Clinton, Cuban, 192–95, 225–28, 232–33, 245
under Clinton, Haitian, xi, 188–89, 212, 215–16, 218
Obama agreements on Cuban, 251–52
under Trump, Cuban, 294
Republican Party
on Cuban Adjustment Act (CAA), 203, 205–6
Cuban American community and, 154–56, 159, 180, 261–68, 270–78, 335
Cuban American politicians of, 263–68, 270–74

Cuban Americans as base in, under Reagan, 154–56, 180, 335
Cuban Americans under Obama, 262–63, 274–78
in Miami, 155–56, 159, 219–20
return-visits to Cuba by Cuban Americans, 78
Rhodes, Ben, 256
Rice, Condoleezza, 242–51
Rivera, David, 264–65
Robinson, Randall, 213
Rodino, Peter, 135–36, 138–39
Rodríguez, Carlos Rafael, 79
Rodríguez, Félix, 157–58
Román, Agustín, 169
Romney, Mitt, 263
Roque, Pablo, 230
Ros-Lehtinen, Ileana, 155, 203, 206–7, 270–71, 291–314
on entitlements, Obama retracting, 273–76
González, Elián, and, 234
Rubio, Marco, 44–45, 264
on Cuban Adjustment Act (CAA), 265–67, 276
entitlements, Cuban, criticized by, 265–66, 271–74, 313
on entitlements retracted by Obama, 274–76
in Gang of Eight, 266
Trump and, 291–314
Rusk, Dean, 26, 50–51

Safe Third Country Agreements. *See* Asylum Cooperation Agreements
Saladrigas, Carlos, 239
Salazar, María Elvina, 291–314
Salinas, Carlos, 190
Salvadoran immigrants. *See* El Salvador
Salvadoran military. *See* El Salvador
Samet, Seymour, 69–71
Sandinistas, 157–59, 207–8
Schlesinger, Arthur, 26–27, 31–32
schooling, 67, 70–71
SCLC. *See* Southern Christian Leadership Conference
SCMP. *See* Special Cuban Migration Program
Scott, James C., 96
screening, of departures, by Cuba, 18

September 11, 2001, attacks. *See* terrorism, war on
Sessions, Jeff, 298
Sheehan, John, 200
Skoug, Kenneth, 152–53
Smith, Wayne, 79, 83–84, 166
soft power, xx–xxi, 2, 42, 341
Somoza, Anastasio, 157
sonic attacks, on US embassies, 291–96
sources, xxii–xxiii
Southern Christian Leadership Conference (SCLC), 68–69, 71
Soviet Union, 39, 337
  Castro, F., and, 1–4, 12, 75–78
  fall of, 180–81, 183–84, 190–91, 257, 324, 339
Spain, Cuban independence from, 174, 188, 230
Spain, Cubans in, 23, 76–77, 133–34, 242–43
Special Cuban Migration Program (SCMP) (El Bombo), 196–97
Special Guantanamo Entrants, 202–3, 318–19
state policy, limits to, 338–41
Stone, Richard, 108

Talladega, Alabama, Mariel Cubans rebelling in, 170
Tarnoff, Peter, 193
temporary entry rights, Cuban Adjustment Act (CAA) and, 54–55
Temporary Protected Status (TPS)
  for Central Americans, 145, 281, 310
  for Cubans, 201–2, 281
  for Haitians, 179, 280–84, 298–99, 328, 332
temporary residency rights, under Eisenhower, 48–49
Temporary Resident status, proposed, 129–31, 136
terrorism, émigrés, anti-Castro, and, 75, 164
  Bosch, O., 38, 40–41, 158–59
  under Carter, 19–40
  CIA and, 37–38, 40–41
  under Eisenhower, 38–39
  under Johnson, L., 40, 42
  under Kennedy, J., 38–40, 42
  Miami and, 160
  under Nixon, 40–41
  Posada Carriles, 40–41, 158, 246
terrorism, war on, 241–51
third countries, Cubans in, 23, 76–77, 80, 133–34, 242–43, 334. *See also* Asylum Cooperation Agreements
  under Johnson, L., 21–22
  reinstatement of immigration rights, 151–52
  under Trump, 290–96
Torres, Esteban, 93
Torricelli, Robert, 163, 215–16
TPS. *See* Temporary Protected Status
travel restrictions
  under Obama, lifted, 257, 262–63, 265–66, 268, 285–86, 295–96
  under Trump, reinstated, 295–96
Trujillo Molina, Rafael Leonidas, 321–22
Trump, Donald, 315, 319, 325–26
  anti-immigrant initiatives of, Cubans and, xv, 288, 291, 330–31, 333, 335
  anti-immigrant sentiment and, 287–90, 315, 330–31, 333
  Asylum Cooperation Agreements under, 308–12
  asylum-seekers under, 296–313, 335, 337
  Central America, off-shoring US exclusion to, under, 300, 308–13
  Central American immigrants under, 293–94, 298–300, 310–11, 320–21
  Cuban American community and, 291–92, 313–15, 337
  Cuban American politicians under, 291–314
  Cuban economy and, xviii–xix, 286, 299
  Cuban immigrants under, xv–xvi, xviii–xix, 286, 313–15, 327–28
  detentions and deportations under, 288, 294–95, 306
  Dominican immigrants under, 330
  entitlements, Cuban, continued by, 290–94
  entitlements, Cuban, restricted by, 290–94, 313, 315, 319–20
  family visits, cross-border, restricted under, 295–96
  Haitians under, 292–93, 298–99, 310, 328
  on Mexico, US border with, 282–83, 287–88, 307–8
  to Mexico, immigrant control outsourced under, 305–8, 312–13

Mexico and asylum-seekers under, 300–8, 311
Muslim ban of, 287–88
Obama, entitlements retracted by, and, 286, 290–314
on Obama, 287–88
race and immigrant crackdown of, 288, 292–93
Refugee Act and, 290, 293
refugee and asylee status adjustments under, 329–30
against refugees, turn of, 293–94
repatriation, Cuban, under, 294
United States–Cuba Democracy PAC under, 265–66
war on immigrants, 287–90, 298, 330–31, 333, 335, 337
TV Martí, 162–66, 223–25
2506 Brigade, 157

US border. *See* Mexico
US Citizenship and Immigration Services Agency (USCIS), 244–45, 292–93
US Interests Section, Havana. *See* Havana, Cuba, US Interests Section in
US–Cuba Democracy PAC, 244, 255, 265–67, 313–14
unaccompanied minors, Cuban, program for, 11–13, 19
Union City, New Jersey, Cuban community in, 266
United Nations Convention Relating to the Status of Refugees, 4, 194–95, 309
United States-Mexico-Canadian Agreement (USMCA), 301–2
USCIS. *See* US Citizenship and Immigration Services Agency
USMCA. *See* United States-Mexico-Canadian Agreement

Venezuela, 299, 314–15
visa waivers, 10, 12–13, 296

visas
under Eisenhower, for Cubans, 8–10
humanitarian, Mexican exit passes, 305–6
under Kennedy, J., for Cubans, 10–14
Mariel Cubans and, 106, 148
in Nicaragua, Panama, tourist, 299–300
under Trump, 290–92, 295–96
US Interests Section halting, 106, 148, 150–51
voluntary agencies (VOLAGS), 98, 114–16
voter registration, Cuban American, 155

Walsh, Bryan, 12–13, 138–39
war on terrorism, 241–51
Watson, Jack, 88, 113–14
Watts neighborhood, Los Angeles, California, 68–69, 71
welfare chiselers, 270–74
welfare reform, under Clinton, 207, 221, 268–74. *See also* Personal Responsibility and Work Opportunity Reconciliation Act
Cuban exemptions from, 206–7, 270–82
Haitians and, 270–82
Wenski, Thomas, 138–41
Western Hemisphere, immigration capped for, 5–6
wet foot policy
under Clinton, 192–93, 200–1, 209, 227, 245, 270–82
Cuban Americans on, 260–62
Whitaker, Hugh, 53
Winston, Ellen, 51–54, 71
World Trade Center attack, 2001. *See* terrorism, war on
World War II, 3–4

Zolberg, Aristide, 339

For EU product safety concerns, contact us at Calle de José Abascal, 56–1°,
28003 Madrid, Spain or eugpsr@cambridge.org.

www.ingramcontent.com/pod-product-compliance
Lightning Source LLC
LaVergne TN
LVHW040748250326
834688LV00034B/498